Ambiguous Bodies

Ambiguous Bodies

READING THE GROTESQUE
IN JAPANESE SETSUWA TALES

Michelle Osterfeld Li

STANFORD UNIVERSITY PRESS
STANFORD, CALIFORNIA

Stanford University Press
Stanford, California

© 2009 by the Board of Trustees of the Leland Stanford Junior University.
All rights reserved.

Printed in the United States of America on acid-free, archival-quality paper

Library of Congress Cataloging-in-Publication Data

Li, Michelle Ilene Osterfeld, 1962-
  Ambiguous bodies : reading the grotesque in Japanese setsuwa tales / Michelle Osterfeld
Li.
      p. cm.
  Includes bibliographical references and index.
  ISBN 978-0-8047-5975-5 (cloth : alk. paper)
  1. Folk literature, Japanese--History and criticism. 2. Tales--Japan--History and criticism.
  3. Japanese literature--To 1600--History and criticism. 4. Grotesque in literature. I. Title.
GR340.L5 2009
398.20952--dc22

                          2008043097

Typeset by Bruce Lundquist in 11/14 Adobe Garamond

To Jiayi
And to Our Children: Dayna, Jillian, and Walter

Contents

Acknowledgments

My studies of grotesque representations in *setsuwa* and my writing of this book occurred in many places: Princeton, New Jersey; Kobe and Osaka, Japan; New Canaan, Norwalk, and New Haven, Connecticut; Stanford and Palo Alto, California. Sometimes I went somewhere specifically for the book and other times I moved because of how my academic and personal lives meshed. No matter where I was, I benefited greatly from the guidance and suggestions of brilliant scholars in East Asian studies. I am grateful for how they helped me grow intellectually.

I thank Richard Okada for his support, friendship, and practical help during the past sixteen years, beginning from when I started as a graduate student at Princeton. I also greatly appreciate Jacqueline Stone for her encouragement and all she taught me about Japanese religions. Studying medieval Japanese history and Japanese Buddhism with Martin Collcutt was also wonderful, as is just knowing him. Along with Christine Marran, with whom I did not get the opportunity to study, these professors read and responded to the earliest version of this book, the dissertation. My knowledge of Chinese religions owes much to Stephen Teiser. In addition, I am grateful to have studied with Aileen Gatten, who came to Princeton as a visiting professor one year. She helped me strengthen my reading skills in classical Japanese and introduced me to the late Marian Ury, with whom I would have liked to talk about setsuwa more. Imai Masaharu, of the University of Tsukuba, also taught me at Princeton. I greatly appreciate how he guided me during an independent reading course on *Konjaku*, added to my knowledge of Japanese Buddhism, and connected me with a prominent setsuwa scholar in Japan. That professor, Ikegami Jun'ichi of Kobe University, helped me with dissertation research in the summer of 1995. He encouraged me to come to Japan and work with him despite the hardship he was still facing after the Great Hanshin Earthquake of January 17, 1995.

Edward Kamens enabled me to spend a year at Yale University as an exchange research student. I benefited from having library privileges at Yale for three years while my husband, Jiayi, pursued a fellowship in gastroenterology there and by working for a short time as an assistant in instruction in the Department of East Asian Languages and Literatures.

Margaret Childs contributed to this book by responding to two conference papers, once informally and once formally. I especially appreciated the time, when acting as a discussant for a panel on the configuration of belief in Heian and medieval Japan, she not only helped me improve my paper, but also read it for me because I was too far along in my third pregnancy to travel. Other panel discussants who helped me develop my thinking on setsuwa and the grotesque during conferences are Linda Chance, Susan Klein, Kathryn W. Sparling, and Meera Viswanathan (my former teacher at Brown University when I was an undergraduate). My friendship with Thomas Howell Jr. began through conferences and grew initially from our shared interest in setsuwa. I have consulted him on a number of issues over the years.

While in graduate school at Princeton, I was lucky to have had truly distinguished classmates and friends to inspire me: Brian Ruppert, Terry Kawashima (who was an exchange scholar from Harvard at the time), Jonathan Todd Brown, Reiko Sono, Melissa McCormick, and others. Brian Ruppert and Keiko Tanaka generously allowed me, my mother, and my then three-year-old daughter, Dayna, to live with them for a month in Osaka while I was doing research in Kobe. (There was no housing in Kobe at the time because of the then recent earthquake.) At Princeton, I was happy to have friends who were also juggling academic pursuits or other work and parenthood: Margrét Jónsdóttir, Sandy Rosenstock, and Donna Welton. It made a difference not to be alone as a mother and a scholar.

Next, I wish to express my appreciation to Professor Asai Kiyoshi of Ochanomizu University, with whom I studied modern Japanese literature for close to four years, for his encouragement of this project when I visited him in Tokyo in 1996. (I was worried that he would be angry with me for switching to premodern literature.)

Of course, I could not have earned a PhD and written the dissertation without financial support. The Department of East Asian Studies of Princeton University awarded me six years of funding through Foreign Language and Area Studies Fellowships, department funds, and the J. Levy Prize Fellowship in East Asian Studies. A Mellon fellowship supported my dissertation research in Japan. The Dean's Fund for Scholarly Travel and departmental support at Princeton enabled me to give papers at several conferences. Additionally, and for work on the book version, I sincerely appreciate the Freeman Spogli Institute for International Studies of Stanford University for granting me a postdoctoral fellowship in Japanese Studies from 2001 to 2003.

At Stanford, I would like to thank the Department of Asian Languages, especially Yoshiko Matsumoto, James Reichert, Chao Fen Sun, and John Wallace for contributing to my experience as a scholar and teacher during my postdoctoral fellowship. I would have liked to discuss medieval Japanese history with the late Jeffrey Mass, who I heard was on the selection committee when I was chosen. I arrived in California the year the Stanford Center for Buddhist Studies held the colloquium "Asian Gods and Demons." I thank the leader of that series, Bernard Faure, for inviting me to participate in the conference and a class on the same subject. I am indebted to the kind Carl Bielefeldt and the Center for Buddhist Studies, with the help of Wendy Abraham and, more recently, Irene Lin, for keeping me connected to Stanford as a visiting scholar after the postdoc so that I could easily continue my research and writing. Adrienne Hurley, who was also a Stanford postdoc, has been a warm friend and a great inspiration. Always cheerful and energetic, Miri Nakamura kindly read early versions of the introduction to this book, parts of which are now in Chapter 1. I am lucky to be able to share my interest in Japanese demons and other creatures with Michael Foster. He was also very supportive, addressing many of my questions and concerns.

In addition, I want to express gratitude to the faculty of the Department of Foreign Languages of San José State University, particularly to Dominique van Hooff and Seiichirō Inaba as well as to my former students, for teaching experiences that, stimulating and pleasant, added balance to my life while I was writing. I can always rely on Tazumi Otsuka-Scearce, who was initially a colleague there. Among other things, she kindly edited letters and e-mails that I wrote in Japanese.

I would like to thank former acquisition editor in Asian Studies, Muriel Bell, at Stanford University Press for her interest in and support of this book. The two not so anonymous readers, Janet Walker and Charo B. D'Etcheverry, provided me with insightful observations and suggestions that helped me improve the manuscript. Another scholar I wish to thank for helping me turn my work into a book is Keller Kimbrough. He had been, in fact, the chair and organizer of the previously mentioned panel on the configuration of belief in Heian and medieval Japan. Since I had to miss that conference, I was unable to benefit from his expertise and warm personality then. However, after reading the manuscript of this book when it was already in the production phase, Keller took the time to provide me with an invaluable list of suggestions and corrections for every chapter.

I am also deeply grateful to the production editor, Emily Smith, for her friendliness and hard work. Special appreciation goes to Richard Gunde, the copy editor. The book benefited greatly from his sharp eye and mind. Nor would the book have been possible without the rest of the team: sponsoring editor, Stacy Wagner; marketing manager, David Jackson; and art director, Rob Ehle. I also thank editor-in-chief Alan Harvey, editorial assistants Jessica Walsh and Joa Suorez, and former editorial assistant Kirsten Oster as well other people who worked on my book at Stanford University Press. The beautiful cover design by Leslie Fitch delights me. For permission to use the image from *Jigoku zōshi* (*Scroll of Hells*), I am indebted to Director Ken'ichi Yuyama and Ms. Kimiyo Kagitani of the Nara National Museum.

This book would not have been possible if I had not had certain experiences leading up to its writing. The friendship and support of Jane Marie Law of Cornell University was extremely important. In addition, she and Karen Brazell guided me through my first project on setsuwa (a master's thesis).

For my love of Japanese culture or, at least the beginning of it, thanks must be given to the Rotary Club of Farmingdale, Long Island, for sending me to Japan for a year as an exchange student when I was sixteen and the Rotary Club of Sakata City, Yamagata Prefecture, for hosting me. I will always have a warm place in my heart for the Okabe, Fushiki, and Itō families, who took me into their homes; for my teachers at Tenshin High School, especially Matsuzawa Shinji, and elsewhere, as well as friends in Sakata. Those people changed my life with their gentleness and by taking an interest in a young me.

It would have been impossible to succeed without the support of my mother, Rhoda Osterfeld. She has always been a wonderful role model as an avid reader and teacher. Moreover, she came to Japan with me to help care for Dayna so that I could work on the early research and assisted me countless other times. I also appreciate the assistance of my mother-in-law, Fuqing Shen, who took time off from her own life to help me with childcare (this time, for Jillian). Additionally, I greatly appreciate Hui Chen for the years of babysitting Walter before he started preschool. I was encouraged by the emotional support of my sister and brother, Diana and Adam Osterfeld, and my sister in-law, Janice Hogan. When I was writing the dissertation, my friendship with Mary Rutkowski was a precious gift.

Ambiguous Bodies is also for my nephews, Ellis and Jesse (when they grow up).

I could never have completed this book without the help of my husband, Jiayi Li. When, especially toward the end, the goal to finish it took over my life, it almost did his life, too. At critical times, he did almost all of the cooking, straightened up the house, and drove our children to their many lessons whenever he could, even after working a full day as a doctor. His love makes everything possible.

My three children, Dayna, Jillian, and Walter, cannot remember a time when I was not working on this book in some form. As I was writing and rewriting and adding research, Dayna grew up and became a high school student; Jillian, who was born while I was writing the dissertation, is now almost finished with elementary school; Walter, the four-month-old I brought to Stanford, is suddenly a second grader. Although I tried to strike a balance between parenting and academics, the hardest part of the book was the time it took away from them. I want to thank my children for the happiness they bring into my life (not to mention all the other things).

Finally, may this book honor the memory of my father, Walter Osterfeld (1926–68). Although our lives overlapped for only six short years, my father shared with me the joy of traveling abroad and learning about other cultures. I wish I could show him this book.

Ambiguous Bodies

Introduction

Grotesque representations inform many *setsuwa*: short Japanese tales that depict extraordinary events, illustrate basic Buddhist principles or, less frequently, other Asian religious and philosophical teachings, and transmit cultural and historical knowledge. These narratives were compiled from roughly the ninth through mid-fourteenth centuries in collections such as *Konjaku monogatari shū* (*Tales of Times Now Past*, ca. 1120).[1] Among the many types of setsuwa abound stories marked by bizarre events and creatures, frequently subverting or simultaneously subverting and sustaining authority. A fox impersonating a grandmother murders a baby; animal spirits and demons appear as beautiful women; bird spirits kill men trying to fell a zelkova tree; an acolyte transforms into a woman so that she can be impregnated by a monk and give birth to gold; a senior official magically steals the penises of visitors allured by his seductive wife, but later returns them. While most setsuwa purport to be about real people and events, the peculiar realities they often portray belie this assertion.

No single interpretative strategy is appropriate for making sense of all the strange or fantastic phenomena and extraordinary beings in setsuwa.

Because of the large number of such tales and the diversity in how they function, addressing every occurrence and creature, even by accounting for many indirectly through generalizations, is impossible. This study considers similarities in the roles of creatures such as animated detached body parts, flesh-eating demons, demonic women, and animal spirits without downplaying the diversity of such representations. Are there ways to connect seemingly dissimilar unreal events and creatures in tales to each other? Reading the grotesque in setsuwa enriches our interpretations of individual tales and deepens our understanding of the strange and extraordinary in the ancient, classical, and early medieval periods. The most relevant portion of ancient Japan in this study is the Nara period (710–84), although some setsuwa concern events from an even earlier time. *Classical* refers mainly to the Heian period (794–1185). *Medieval* is used in the traditional sense to mean from the Kamakura period (1185–1333) to the start of the Edo or Tokugawa period (1600–1868), beginning roughly when the warrior government replaced the government of the Heian court after the Genpei War.

Identifying and comprehending the grotesque in setsuwa makes further sense when we consider that, in the words of theorist Wolfgang Kayser, "the phenomenon is older than the name we assign to it, and . . . a complete history of the grotesque would have to deal with Chinese, Etruscan, Aztec, and Old Germanic art as well as with Greek (Aristophanes!) and other literatures."[2] These other literatures are equally important. Although no theoretical concept corresponding to the grotesque emerged in Japan, Japanese representations of the strange and extraordinary became increasingly formulaic with time. We can identify patterns of bizarre and heterogeneous elements in Japanese literature similar to representations identified as grotesque in other cultures. This book develops and refines critical thinking on the grotesque by including an aspect of its unwritten history, certain setsuwa, in the category.[3]

The grotesque in setsuwa can be generally defined at this early point in the study while concrete examples will support and further flesh out this working definition throughout the book. A mode of representation, it centers on exaggerated or fantastic depictions of the body or bodily realities such as eating, drinking, smelling, evacuating, copulating, and giving birth. The bodies include transformations and extensions into other natural and supernatural forms—human, animal, plant, vegetable, or monster. Such representations typically undermine hierarchies and dominant ideologies. They invite multiple interpretations and tend to create confusion or uncertainty. The phrase *ambiguous bodies* in the title of this study refers to how these bodies often transform or extend beyond the ordinary as well as to their multivalent and disruptive nature. Grotesque representations also have ludicrous, comic, or fearful elements, which can appear in combinations and inform one another.

The grotesque in setsuwa is thus defined not only by what it describes but also by how it functions. Shifts in emphasis from the physically high and spiritually elevated toward the physically low and earthbound are used to reduce people in status and dignity and to challenge official discourses. These downward movements are often enacted on the body but are not always overtly sexual. They may be otherwise connected to the gratification of the senses, as in two stories discussed in Chapter 6 concerning the desire for the beauty and fragrances of flowering trees.

The emphasis on degradation does not inevitably lead to the uncontested triumph of weaker figures or ideas. Most often, grotesque representations give setsuwa the potential to simultaneously subvert and support the official aristocratic and ecclesiastical discourses of the times. As Geoffrey Galt Harpham writes, "we apprehend the grotesque in the presence of an entity—an image, object, or experience—simultaneously justifying multiple and mutually exclusive interpretations which commonly stand in a relation of high to low, human to subhuman, divine to human, normative to abnormal, with the unifying principle sensed but occluded and imperfectly perceived."[4] Subversive elements in setsuwa can help to sustain people in power when appropriated by the very authority they undermine. Aristocrats and members of the imperial family co-opt demons who debase them in order to affirm their own superiority. Similarly, setsuwa depicting the vulnerability of Buddhists to such things as animal spirits or uncontrollable sexual desire probably helped to prevent religious figures from being overly esteemed, but they also suggest that Buddhists excelled at embracing criticisms to strengthen their positions in society. Depending on the tale, priests or monks affiliated with institutions may have used setsuwa to discredit *hijiri*, independent mountain ascetics whose increasing popularity threatened them, while *hijiri* disassociated themselves from Buddhists with prestigious affiliations but questionable moral standards.

Another characteristic of the grotesque is that, at some stage in its development, it is always a communal project. That many people with different agendas participated in creating, telling, recording, and writing setsuwa over time amounting to as much as centuries contributes to the multivalence of grotesque representations. Compilers add to the meanings of setsuwa with comments or by their positioning of stories in collections. The appropriation of certain types of representations by different people produced similar results. The flesh-eating demon is ancient, but it accumulates added meanings with new audiences and stories. Some people, especially those invested in a particular message, were likely to embrace one meaning and suppress others, but they would not have been the only type of audience. The grotesque is potentially liminal in its ability to carry readers or listeners to a place "between two worlds" or between two or more perspectives.[5] It crosses physical and conceptual boundaries, thereby leading audiences into formerly unexplored intellectual and imaginative territory.

Because theories of the grotesque emerged first in Europe with Western art and literature as their objects of study, considering how grotesque elements function in other realms requires flexibility. Knowledge and continued exploration of the relevant cultural and historical contexts need to shape our sense of the material studied. I build on various theories of the grotesque discussed in Chapter 1, "*Setsuwa* and the Grotesque," but draw mostly from Mikhail Bakhtin in *Rabelais and His World*. His theoretical framework informs this study whereas I tend to borrow only isolated concepts from other theorists. At the same time, an understanding of the grotesque in setsuwa must necessarily deviate from Bakhtin, who develops his theory mainly from his analysis of the sixteenth-century series of novels *Gargantua and Pantagruel* by François Rabelais (ca. 1494–1553), his knowledge of medieval Europe and the French Renaissance, and his research on the development of popular culture, especially "the folk culture of humor."[6] While *Rabelais and His World* has wider implications for diverse studies, it is also an interpretation of particular books. Given the vast differences between *Gargantua and Pantagruel* and setsuwa collections as well as between their respective historic and cultural backgrounds, Bakhtin could not possibly offer an intact model of interpretation for setsuwa. His ideas serve instead as starting points for developing a theory of the grotesque relevant to ancient, classical, and early medieval Japan.

Rather than impose a strict model of interpretation on the tales, I allow the tales themselves to shape the theory of the grotesque in setsuwa as much as possible. This study is grounded in scholarship on individual tales and setsuwa collections, Japanese spirits and ghosts, and the religion, history, and literature of the Nara, Heian, and Kamakura periods.

The grotesque in setsuwa has precedents in early Japan, China, and India in contrast to the precedents Western grotesque representations have in ancient Greece and Rome. Japanese grotesque representations often seem connected to specific figures in myths and legends predating them, as suggested in my discussion in Chapter 4 of the one-eyed demon in *Izumo no kuni fudoki* (*The Topography of Izumo Province*, ca. 733) and elsewhere in my analyses of tales.[7] The hags (*shikome*) who pursue Izanagi in the land of Yomi in the early histories *Kojiki* (*Records of Ancient Matters*, ca. 712) and *Nihon shoki* (*Chronicles of Japan*, ca. 720) are among such figures, as is the raging god Susano-o. When Susano-o throws a skinned colt through a hole in the roof of the heavenly weaving maiden's workplace, she hits her genitals against the shuttle and dies from the injury. There is also Toyotama-hime, whose husband shames her by glimpsing her true form of *wani* (crocodile or sea-monster) when spying on her during childbirth.[8] Many mythical events, such as marriages of humans to animals or deities, also reverberate in setsuwa with new meanings emerging in the non- and semi-mythical contexts.

Indian and Chinese textual traditions helped to shape the grotesque in setsuwa as well. The appropriation of certain grotesque representations, types of descriptions, and motifs was part of the larger process of incorporating Indian and Chinese short narrative traditions into Japanese culture. We see this trend most obviously in stories that come more or less directly from Chinese sources. Many are translations or freer renderings of sections of Indian sutras, particularly *avadāna* sutras or collections of tales concerned with the previous lives of the Buddha "innumerable ages ago" and other manifestations of karma. Compilers also appropriated narratives from collections of stories extracted from sutras and supplemented with Chinese tales as well as from hagiographies, travel accounts, miscellaneous Buddhist collections, historical and philosophical works, and collections of tales of the strange.[9] The relationship of a setsuwa set in Heian Japan to Chinese short narrative traditions can be subtle. It may be apparent in certain ideologies and concepts not only from Buddhism, but also from Confucianism, Daoism, and other systems of beliefs and practices, including in a particular focus such as on the divine intervention of the Bodhisattva Avalokiteśvara (Kannon) or the importance of filial piety.

Chinese tales of the strange, called *zhiguai*, exhibit degrees of bizarreness. The most extreme elements are similar to or the same as representations of the grotesque in setsuwa. (Some zhiguai are included in setsuwa collections with little modification.) Such tales appear in large numbers from the Han dynasty to the end of the Sui (roughly 206 B.C.E.–618 C.E.) and continue with Tang zhiguai, a subdivision of the genre *chuanqi* or Tang dynasty (618–907) tales of the extraordinary. (*Chuanqi* are usually longer and more literary than the brief accounts of anomalies preceding them.) In Buddhist miracle tales, considered a subgenre of zhiguai, anomalous or miraculous events and the explanations or resolutions of them illustrate Buddhist teachings.[10] The oldest extant setsuwa collection, *Nihon ryōiki* (*Miraculous Stories of Japan*, ca. 823), is clearly a descendant of Tang dynasty tales of the strange: its accounts of bizarre events are explained mainly in terms of karma, transmigration, and other Buddhist beliefs.[11] Moreover, its compiler, Monk Kyōkai, mentions two Chinese collections of miracle tales that inspired him: *Mingbaoji* (*Records of Miraculous Retribution*, ca. 650–55) and *Jingang bore jing lingyanji* (*Records of Miracles Concerning the Diamond Wisdom Sutra*, ca. 718).[12] William LaFleur's understanding in *The Karma of Words* of the *ryōiki* of *Nihon ryōiki* as *anomaly* rather than *miracle* further suggests the zhiguai.[13] Perhaps the strongest link of setsuwa to zhiguai is the juxtaposition of the ordinary and the extraordinary in both.[14]

In the past, a narrative coming directly from a Chinese or an Indian collection seemed obviously foreign even if deeply embedded in Japanese culture. The story of Broad-of-Brow discussed in Chapter 2 has Chinese origins, but it is included in numerous Japanese books. It has a larger role in Japanese culture than many tales deemed indigenous. In *Uncovering Heian Japan*, Thomas LaMarre emphasizes that premodern Japanese people did not have the same sense of physical or artistic and intellectual borders as modern Japanese.[15] With multicultural connections, setsuwa can contribute to our rethinking of the concepts of indigenous and foreign in earlier times. Many scholars have simply assumed that geographical distinctions, such as the division of *Konjaku* into tales of India, China, and Japan, and the awareness of events occurring in other lands resemble modern concepts of borders and nations, but how could they have?

Setsuwa studies pioneer Haga Yaichi (1867–1927), in his introduction to the three volume *Kōshō Konjaku monogatari shū* (*Konjaku monogatari shū and Its Literary Parallels*, 1913–21), a seminal work discussed in Chapter 1, saw foreign elements as dominating even the "Tales of Japan" section of *Konjaku*. His examples are snakes violating women, marriages between humans and animals, demons, *tengu*, and mountains for disposing of the elderly.[16] Yet, we can look at the same representations as part of a larger, multicultural tradition. Chinese tales might provide types of representations and plot elements for stories set in Japan, but the storyteller/writer re-creates them in a new context. In Chapter 6, I mention a tale about a virgin-eating serpent from a collection of tales of the strange called *Soushenji* (*In Search of the Supernatural*, ca. 335–49) in relation to a *Konjaku* tale in which monkey gods have similar appetites.[17] While the idea of a deity consuming maidens appears in China before Japan, the two narratives have many differences. In addition to the cultural contexts being dissimilar, the slayer of the evil deity is a woman in the Chinese story and man in the Japanese. The second tale cannot be described as purely Japanese, but neither is it Chinese. Additionally, many Chinese and Indian representations probably reinforced concepts previously entertained in Japan. General ideas such as marriages between animals and humans can be found in many cultures.

Often exhibiting a multicultural blend of elements, the grotesque in setsuwa can further our understanding of the psychological and spiritual realities of Japanese people from ancient through early medieval times. However, we must avoid naively viewing the characters and events mimetically. Representations of people from different socioeconomic classes are shaped by the biases of the people who created them and may not coincide with how represented people saw themselves or even with the majority of the audience. The numerous stock characters, such as greedy provincial governors and licentious priests, should encourage us to consider the motivations and prejudices behind these depictions. Fiction writer Akutagawa Ryūnosuke (1892–1927) felt that, whenever he opened *Konjaku*, "the cries and laughter of people from those times" would rise from the pages. He believed that "the author of *Konjaku monogatari* depicts reality without modifying it at all. The same can be said of how he depicts human psychology."[18] Yet, Akutagawa's own stories reveal his interest in the fantastic and ambiguous elements of *Konjaku* as well as his sense of the reality of fiction. The clear and direct voices in *Konjaku* rarely belong to the people represented, having been imagined for them. The creators and compilers of tales had their own ideological and political reasons for choosing certain details. Even if they seem to appropriate the words of others, those voices and visions are necessarily filtered through their own.

Consequently, I do not rely solely on the representations of people when exploring the psychological and spiritual realms in setsuwa. Information on the emotions and beliefs of various individuals or groups is often buried in the narratives. We gain insight into these realms by considering the significance of the details of tales and by putting tales into dialogue with each other and other texts. It is important not only to contemplate the links of setsuwa with other texts, but also to use information to speculate beyond the narratives. Only then do certain voices call out from the tales—voices that compilers and perhaps some storytellers failed to hear or heard and attempted to suppress.

Historical situations also come into play when studying the grotesque in setsuwa. The late Heian period was marked by political and social tumult that ultimately led to the Genpei wars—the battles of 1180–85 between the Taira and Minamoto *uji* (lineage groups or "clans")—and to the establishment of the warrior government.[19] Before then, the hegemony of the Fujiwara regent's house had been destroyed in the third decade of the eleventh century when Emperors Go-Sanjō and Shirakawa acted to secure the independence of the imperial house so that it could compete for power and wealth.[20] The influence of an abdicated emperor—most likely Shirakawa, since he died in 1129—would have been quite strong around the time of the creation of *Konjaku*. The militarization of religious institutions with their armies of monks and hired soldiers and the increasing strength of warriors in both the capital and the provinces also added to the instability of the times, as did pirates and bandits, who made travel difficult.[21] Furthermore, the people endured fires and natural disasters such as terrible storms, famines, epidemics, drought, and the eruption of a volcano (Mt. Asama in 1108).[22] Sometimes setsuwa are considered nostalgic, but they hardly idealize life in earlier times. Grotesque tales undermine the values and lifestyle of aristocrats. Political tensions are shown to have always existed, so that every influential person was vulnerable. Individual tales voice the aspirations and concerns of people living when the tales are set as well as those of later storytellers and commentators. Any study of setsuwa requires looking at multiple histories.

This study considers in varying degrees of depth, from brief mention to detailed analysis, slightly over one hundred tales from sixteen setsuwa collections. The collections are listed here with the English translation of the title and known or approximate date of compilation in parentheses: *Nihon ryōiki* (*Miraculous Stories of Japan*, ca. 823); *Sanbōe* (*The Three Jewels*, 984); *Nihon ōjō gokurakuki* (*A Record of Japanese Born in the Pure Land*, ca. 985–6); *Dainihonkoku hokekyōkenki* (abbreviated as *Hokkegenki*, *Miraculous Tales of the Lotus Sutra*, 1040–44); *Shūi ōjōden* (*Gleanings of Biographies of People Born in the Pure Land*, ca. 1111); *Gōdanshō* (*The Ōe Conversations*, ca. 1111); *Konjaku monogatari shū* (*Tales of Times Now Past*, ca. 1120); *Goshūi ōjōden* (*More Gleanings of Biographies of People Born in the Pure Land*, ca. 1138);

Kohon setsuwa shū (*Old Book of a Setsuwa Collection*, ca. 1180); *Uji shūi mono-gatari* (*A Collection of Tales from Uji*, ca. 1190–1242); *Kankyo no tomo* (*A Companion in Solitude*, ca. 1222); *Jikkinshō* (*Selected Anecdotes to Illustrate Ten Maxims*, 1252); *Kokon chomonjū* (*Notable Tales Old and New*, ca. 1254); *Senjūshō* (*Collection of Selected Excerpts*, ca. 1250–87 or 1315); *Shichiku kuden* (*Secret Teachings about Strings and Winds*, 1327); and *Shasekishū* (*Sand and Pebbles*, 1279–83).[23]

Most stories in this study come from *Konjaku*, either exclusively or from it and at least one other collection. Many of these are from Book 27 of *Konjaku*, especially in the two chapters on demons, since that section lends itself to being studied in terms of the grotesque with its particular use of haunting spirits. Similarly, some of the tales are taken from the second section of *Kokon chomonjū* Book 17. Entitled "Henge" ("metamorphoses" or "metamorphosed things"), it also focuses on spirits and spirit-creatures including shape shifters. After *Konjaku*, the *Nihon ryōiki, Hokkegenki, Gōdanshō, Uji shūi*, and *Kokon chomonjū* are most important to my study in terms of the number of tales studied or depth of analysis. Strictly speaking, setsuwa are stories in the collections mentioned or others like them, called *setsuwa shū*. However, brief stories and anecdotes in other literature, such as the previously mentioned topography, are often considered setsuwa. I refer to setsuwa-like stories recorded in other types of work as well, including *uta monogatari* (poem-centered stories) and *rekishi* and *gunki monogatari* (historic and martial tales, respectively).

With the exception of *Konjaku*, I did not begin my research with the goal of drawing more from one collection than another. Rather, my interests in specific topics led me to certain stories, so that some collections became more important to this book than others. Yet, the grotesque sensibility in these collections is not necessarily stronger or more frequent than in others. The key factors in determining my selection were how well the grotesque could be shown to function within individual tales and what seemed the interest value of particular stories and the issues they raise. I chose not to focus on a single book of *Konjaku* or another collection in part to avoid giving the impression that the grotesque in setsuwa is confined to certain sections of particular collections. The grotesque can be found throughout the genre in different degrees, sometimes quite subtle. Insofar as tales depict the anomalous or strange (as most do), they usually show at least traces of grotesque thought. The focus on tales with strong grotesque elements promised to bring deeper knowledge of specific tales and certain aspects of the genre.

Broader studies that attempt to deal with setsuwa in general inevitably gloss over the unique or rare qualities of particular tales.

The types of stories I analyze do not dominate setsuwa collections in number, but they stand out because of the intriguing and often unique nature of what they describe. The quantity of any one type of tale would not necessarily have correlated with its impact on people. If a certain representation or motif was too familiar, it may have even lost some of its effect whereas unusual representations and plots may have left a deeper impression. Unfortunately, with almost no data on the audiences of setsuwa (an issue addressed further in Chapter 1), we usually cannot know what impression grotesque tales (or any) had on their early audiences.

The commentaries frequently added to tales can give insight into the readings of compilers, but they are often misleading. Many seem to be tacked-on stock phrases. In "Monogatari to hyōgo no fuseigo" ("Discordance between the Story and the Commentary"), Mori Masato demonstrates how the final remarks of the *Konjaku* compiler often jar with the story portion of tales.[24] Final comments frequently ignore or downplay significant aspects. For example, a tale discussed in Chapter 5 describes a pregnant woman planning to abandon her infant in the mountains after secretly giving birth there. She changes her mind because an old woman helps her through the birth, but the old woman later appears to be a demon hungry for the newborn. Although the tale is rich in meaning (as will be discussed), the commentator offers only a banal warning against traveling alone to isolated places.[25] With responses that tend to be emotionally disengaged, commentators leave larger questions for audiences. They miss, ignore, or actively manipulate powerful nuances and messages of tales.

The six chapters of this book demonstrate how theories of the grotesque, combined with careful consideration of the cultural, historical, and social contexts of tales, can enrich our understanding of setsuwa. As discussed in Chapter 1, the concepts of setsuwa and the grotesque developed separately, but many aspects of grotesque theory, particularly the arguments of Bakhtin, are relevant to setsuwa. The basic knowledge of setsuwa collections, of their purposes and audiences, and even of the establishment of setsuwa as a literary genre has huge gaps, forcing us to piece together mere scraps of information. In contrast, ideas about the grotesque (whether complete theories or single thoughts) can be overwhelming in their number and diversity. Yet, knowledge of the histories of both concepts provides a foundation for reading the grotesque in setsuwa.

As demonstrated in Chapters 2–6, closely examining the details of individual tales and putting the tales into dialogue with other relevant texts are necessary strategies for understanding how representations function. In Chapter 2, tales centered on body parts that either act independently from the body or are otherwise fantastic in a severed state illustrate social and political struggles between men. Here and in other chapters, vulnerability equalizes people. The grotesque representations of copulation, conception, pregnancy, and birth in Chapter 3 function to debase authority. While central in these acts of undermining, the female body proves limited as a site of resistance.

Oni (demons) are the most prominent monsters in tales of the grotesque. They respond to the fears and aspirations of premodern Japanese, as the exploration of their roles in Chapters 4 and 5 demonstrates. In Chapter 4, tales depicting gender-less demons or those incarnated as men both affirm and undermine powerful men. They challenge certain assumptions and claims to authority and control, but the opportunity to confront a demon is often reserved for the politically powerful. While the tensions in Chapters 3 and 4 are frequently acted out on the bodies of women, the ideas of women sharing things in common with demons and of female demons, discussed in Chapter 5, also come into play. In genres other than setsuwa, women are juxtaposed with demons in potentially positive ways. In setsuwa, there is ambiguity in what superficially appears to be only negative. The associations of women and demons are not mainly attacks on women, as they tend to direct audiences back to men. So-called female demons are often other than female and even gender-less despite their impersonations. Or, they direct attention to issues that affect many women, not just those with political importance. Lastly, the animal spirits addressed in Chapter 6 blur the lines between the realms of animal, spirit, and human; the subsequent gray areas are fertile for revealing the fragility of people, especially in their attempts to conquer fears and illusions.

Before moving to the first chapter, I need to say a word about my choice of translating tales in the historical present, the tense that most closely approximates the Japanese use of the auxiliary verbal suffix *keri*. The use of *keri* coincides with the effort in most of the narratives to create an experience of the past in the present, as suggested by the opening phrase of many setsuwa and standard in *Konjaku*: "ima wa mukashi."[26] Previous translators use the past tense in English for both *keri* and *ki* in setsuwa. (They may also simultaneously indicate other meanings, such as recollection for *ki* or hearsay for *keri* when the narratives support such interpretations.) Using the past tense conforms to the convention of how most tales are written or translated and told in English. We are perhaps most comfortable hearing or reading tales that conform to our expectations, but translating from Japanese is an opportunity to reach beyond them.

As H. Richard Okada discusses, linguists interpret the suffixes *keri* and *ki* in other ways. He writes, "To my mind, *keri* and *ki* are 'narrative' or 'recitative' markers that also suggest an in-group situation."[27] He suggests that *keri* refers to a past that is alive in the imagination, resembling the "present of past things" in memory.[28] The past exists in the minds of the storytellers and their audiences as a story is told or in the minds of authors and readers as it is being written or read. It is real and immediate for the moment. According to this view, a sentence such as "Ima wa mukashi kyō yori Mino Owari no hodo ni kudaramu to suru gerō arikeri"[29] could be read "Now it is the past; the situation is that there was a person of low birth who decided to travel from the capital to the Mino-Owari vicinity." Of course, it would be awkward to translate an entire tale in this manner since the weak subject clause would have to be repeated numerous times.

The historical present tense in English gives audiences the impression of being close to the events and the people in the story. Details about place and time and the fact that the audience is hearing or reading a story rather than living it reveal that a tale is not about the perceptual present despite the use of the present tense but about a presence of things past in the imagination. The historical present is dynamic and vivid. It conveys a sense of the past being alive while also allowing us to avoid awkward shifts in verb tense.

Of course, no tense in English is perfect for conveying how *keri* functions in classical Japanese. A problem I encountered with my choice was an inability to distinguish between the tenseless variant Chinese (*hentai kanbun* or *kanbun*) of the stories in *Nihon ryōiki* and other texts and those written with *keri* as a common suffix.[30] Both seem best translated in the historical present to indicate an implied past conveyed without the use of the past tense, but the subtle differences between the two forms of discourse are lost in English.

Finally, construction of a past in the present in setsuwa necessarily differs from the memory of the individual. Its highly structured form does not assimilate memory. There is rarely a single and sustained present "I"/"eye" who experienced the past personally and is reflecting on it. Setsuwa might be seen as an effort at creating a historical and religious collective memory, except that the stories distort and create fact. Can people remember or relive things that they never experienced or that never even occurred? The answer can be yes when the subject is a society over many generations. Tales set in the past are a reaffirmation, a re-creation, or a "re-presentation"[31] of a time no longer accessible through direct perception but that can be communally imagined or "remembered."

I have introduced the main ideas of this study and mapped out the book in hope of making the journey through it easier. It may also help my readers to note that I use the Hepburn system for all Japanese and pinyin for Chinese. Japanese names appear in the traditional order (last name first) in the text and Notes when the work discussed is in Japanese. I follow the lead of most standard Japanese dictionaries when including the "no" in names from the Heian period and earlier.

CHAPTER I

Setsuwa and the Grotesque

The concepts of both *setsuwa* and *grotesque* have complicated histories. In each case, scholars have attempted to define the term while acknowledging its resistance to definition, or they have simply grappled with a particular sense of it. Of the two, setsuwa has clearer parameters. There is a consensus on what narratives fall into the category, and the historical period of setsuwa production is broad but limited. More open-ended, *grotesque* has been used to describe diverse works: a form of ancient Roman ornamentation, sixteenth-century paintings depicting demons and skeletons, caricature and comic plays, *Tales of the Grotesque and Arabesque* (1840) by Edgar Allan Poe, and *Death in Venice* (1912) by Thomas Mann are among numerous examples. In this chapter, I lay the groundwork for reading the grotesque in setsuwa by first considering the emergence and development of each term separately in two sections. *Konjaku* figures prominently in the section on setsuwa because the modern understanding of the concept begins with a focus on that collection. Lastly, I situate Bakhtin in this study in several short sections each of which addresses an element of his theory.

THE CONCEPT OF SETSUWA AND KONJAKU

The use of the term *setsuwa* to refer to specific classical and early medieval tale collections was new in modern Japan, but the word itself was not. According to Takahashi Tōru and Komine Kazuaki in different articles, *setsuwa* appears first in the extant literature in *Juketsu shū* (*Collection of Orally Transmitted Teachings*, ca. 853) by Tendai priest Enchin (814–91). This work supposedly records oral teachings of Priest Liangxu heard by Enchin while studying Buddhism in China. In one passage, *setsuwa* refers to a parable "a Chinese person," namely Priest Liangxu, told during a certain public lecture or sermon.[1] In the Song dynasty (960–1279), *shuohua* (the Chinese for the characters *setsuwa*) in the nominal form refers more generally to the art of oral storytelling, including religious stories, but more often other types. Whether it had the same or similar meaning during the Tang dynasty (618–907) is debated in Chinese studies. If any sense of *shuohua* as oral entertainment existed in China when Enchin visited, he could have had that understanding of the term as well.[2]

In several writings by Sōtō Zen founder Dōgen (1200–53), the word means small talk or chitchat prohibited during Buddhist practice. The several other extant examples Komine cites all appear in texts written by Buddhists in relation to either preaching on one hand or to idle talk on the other. As Komine observes, both concepts of setsuwa, of parable and of small talk or gossip that presumably develops into entertaining stories, come into play in the narratives now called setsuwa.[3] It is tempting to conclude that these stories were so named because of these early uses of the term, but the gap in time is over six hundred years. In addition, there is no premodern reference to those stories as setsuwa or any other record of a connection. Although one collection is entitled *Kohon setsuwa shū* (*Tales of an Old Book*, ca. 1130), it was so named upon its discovery in 1943.[4] As I will discuss, setsuwa has a different meaning in the Taishō period (1912–26). Moreover, few scholars would argue that all setsuwa can be understood in terms of these two definitions. The Buddhist sense is weak in some, as is the connection to light conversation in others.

Takahashi also mentions some uses of the word *setsuwa* by Edo-period (1600–1868) writers Ueda Akinari (1734–1809) and Kyokutei Bakin (1767–1848). In *Ugetsu monogatari* (*Tales of Moonlight and Rain*, 1776) by Akinari and *Nansō Satomi hakkenden* (*The Eight Dog Chronicles*, 1814–42) by

Bakin, phonetic symbols (*furigana*) indicate that *setsuwa* and *wasetsu* (*setsuwa* with the Chinese characters reversed) are read *monogatari*.[5] *Monogatari* (a story or long tale) is arguably an even broader term than *setsuwa*, but included in its meaning in these works is the idea of an oral account of something. For example, in "Buppōsō" (*Bird of Paradise*) by Akinari, a ghost of a nobleman is unhappy because a long time has passed since he heard the monogatari (written with the characters for *setsuwa*) of Satomura Jōha (1524–1602), a deceased renowned linked-verse master and Buddhist priest. The nobleman summons Jōha and asks him to talk about "classical matters." The talk itself is not depicted, but it seems to have been about a literary tradition. The nobleman then goes on to ask specific questions about a poem by Kūkai (774–835), the founder of Shingon Buddhism. Here, *monogatari* (again written *setsuwa*) apparently refers to a short lecture. The link between setsuwa and monogatari established by this reading of the characters for *setsuwa* possibly influenced the first setsuwa scholars. It would have suggested overlap between monogatari and setsuwa.

Yet, the scholars who launched setsuwa research did not mention earlier uses of the word. Predating the term, a concept of setsuwa began to develop along modern lines soon after the establishment, in the late 1880s and early 1890s, of the institution of national literature (*kokubungaku*), when many texts were still being added to the canon. Since *Konjaku* is the key collection in the creation of the genre setsuwa, we should review some basic information about it before considering the emergence of the term in the Taishō period.

While *Nihon ryōiki* dates around the early ninth century, the practice of compiling short tales reaches its peak in Japan during the late Heian and early Kamakura periods, and then quickly declines in the Muromachi period (1392–1573). Compiled during the flourishing of setsuwa, *Konjaku*, the largest collection of tales, in its present form contains one thousand forty tales (about thirteen of which are fragments and many with lacunae) and nineteen titles missing stories. The work consists of "Tales of India" (*Tenjiku*, Books 1–5), "Tales of China" (*Shindan*, Books 6–10), and "Tales of Japan" (*Honchō*, Books 11–31). Books 8, 18, and 21 are either missing or never existed and, as indicated by skips in the numbering of tales, Books 7 and 23 appear to have lost twenty tales in total, eight and twelve respectively.[6] The total, then, would have been 1,079 tales, not counting the missing Books. Each section begins with overtly Buddhist tales. Most in the Indian section are Buddhist, excepting a handful in Book 5, as Buddhist scriptures in Chinese translation played a key role in their transmission. The Chinese and

Japanese sections are divided into Buddhist and secular tales, but this division is not always sharp. For example, tales in Book 26 refer to the workings of karma despite their positioning in the so-called secular Japanese section. The structural similarities of *Konjaku* tales include the framing device of "now it is the past" (*ima wa mukashi*) at the opening and "and so the story is told and passed down" (*to namu katari tsutaetaru to ya*) at the end.

Almost all fundamental questions about *Konjaku*, such as its date of compilation and compiler, have no definite answers.[7] Scholars frequently give 1120 as its probable compilation date in part because the latest known source in the collection was transmitted to Japan around then.[8] Of course, a scholar's choice of date affects his or her stance on the identity of the compiler and vice versa.

The most popular compiler theory from the Meiji period (1868–1912) through World War II (1939–45) names Minamoto no Takakuni (1004–77), a high-ranking Heian aristocrat, as sole compiler. The theory ironically stemmed from a setsuwa-like account of how a certain *Uji dainagon monogatari* (*Tales of the Uji Major Counselor*) was created. (That collection is now non-extant.) According to the preface of the 1659 edition of *Uji shūi*, an eccentric Uji Major Counselor (Takakuni) collects tales while on a retreat to Nansen-bō, a place near the famous temple Byōdōin in Uji. He calls to people passing by and, regardless of their social rank, has them stop and tell him stories, which he records while in a reclining position. Edo period bibliographers and a bookseller created a connection between Takakuni and *Konjaku* by viewing the title *Uji dainagon monogatari* as a reference to *Konjaku*.[9] The *Uji shūi* passage also contributed to the now obviously false sense that compilers collected and recorded setsuwa casually and often on the spot as people told them.

As early as 1903, scholars found evidence that Takakuni died before *Konjaku* could have been completed. Alternative theories centered on either single or multiple compilers. At the height of the debates, many scholars singled out a certain court noble or temple abbot while others argued against the involvement of an aristocrat.[10] The idea of a committee of compilers appeared in the 1950s and remains popular. Scholars embracing it usually argue that Buddhist monks created *Konjaku* under the supervision of a superior.[11] Some theories include people outside the Buddhist clergy to better account for the recording of both secular and religious tales. Kunisaki Fumimaro writing in the early 1960s argued that Retired Emperor Shirakawa (1053–1129, r. 1072–86) oversaw a compilation committee comprised of his retainers and Buddhist monks. He later retracted this idea to assert that the aristocrat Minamoto no Toshiyori (1055–1129) is the compiler, but his first theory remained influential.[12] Maeda Masayuki built on it over twenty-five years later in "Konjaku monogatari shū no 'kokka' zō" ("Representation of the State in *Konjaku monogatari shū*"), discussed in Chapter 6 of this book.[13] Similarly, H. Richard Okada considered the possible connection of an emperor to *Konjaku*, writing that the collection "has been characterized as one produced in response to an imperial command."[14]

The role of multiple compilers is likely, given the size of *Konjaku*. The compilers must have been working under a figure with authority, such as a high-ranking priest, a court noble, or even an emperor, because such projects were costly and time-consuming. The prevalence of Buddhist concerns and details (two-thirds of the tales are considered overtly Buddhist) suggests that the people on the committee were either monks or laymen interested in basic Buddhist ideology.[15]

Konjaku gives us the best sampling of setsuwa-type tales because, in addition to being huge, it overlaps with numerous other collections. For example, it includes roughly seventy-five of the one hundred and sixteen tales of *Nihon ryōiki* and ninety-seven of the one hundred and twenty-nine tales of the *Hokkegenki*. Nearly identical versions of tales often appear in two or more collections, as demonstrated in research on the indirect correspondence between *Konjaku*, *Uji shūi*, *Kohon setsuwa shū*, and *Kojidan* (*Record of Ancient Events*, ca. 1212–15). Connections between *Konjaku* and other texts extend beyond setsuwa, literature, and Japan.[16]

The expansive nature of this collection attracted the attention of a key figure in the Meiji national literature movement. As mentioned in the Introduction, Haga Yaichi helped pave the way for *Konjaku* studies and the field of setsuwa research by editing and annotating *Kōshō Konjaku monogatari shū* (*Konjaku monogatari shū and Its Literary Parallels*). Published in 1913, the first volume consists of his introduction to the entire work followed by "Tales of India" and "Tales of China." "Buddhist Tales of Japan" came out as the second volume in 1914. The so-called secular tales of Japan appeared only much later, in 1921. In addition to editing *Konjaku*, Haga researched the "variants and possible sources of each story."[17] Whenever possible, he placed one or more related short narratives from other texts after each *Konjaku* tale.

In the introduction, Haga writes: "As the oldest and largest setsuwa collection in the national language, *Konjaku monogatari shū* ought easily be considered a treasure of world literature."[18] The word *setsuwa* appears many times throughout the essay in such combinations as *kōshi* (Confucian) *setsuwa*, *Indo* (Indian) *setsuwa*, *sekai* (world) *setsuwa*, *buppō* (Buddhist truth) *setsuwa*, *Nihon* (Japanese) *setsuwa*, and *minkan* (folk) *setsuwa*. Although Haga never defines *setsuwa*, he is obviously not referring to a uniquely Japanese form or to stories only in Japanese or Buddhist collections, but, in a general sense, to traditional stories passed down from one generation to another or through many generations. This transmission can be oral or written. He refers to the stories in the Indian section as translations.[19]

Had someone introduced the term *setsuwa* in its modern sense before the publishing of *Kōshō Konjaku*, surely Haga would have mentioned it. Instead, *setsuwa* begins to appear in the scholarship without definition or explanation as if it were already accepted terminology.[20] After Haga, it can be found again in *Konjaku monogatari shū no shin kenkyū* (*New Research on Konjaku monogatari shū*) by Sakai Kōhei and *Kamakura jidai bungaku shin-ron* (*A New Discussion of Kamakura Period Literature*) by Nomura Hachirō. The former was first published in 1923 but based on a graduation thesis completed in 1915 while the latter was first published in 1922. Both scholars employ the term without explanation and without conveying a sense of it as a modification of an old term or as newly introduced. However, at one point in his research, Sakai treats it as more than a convenient name for a variety of self-contained short narratives.[21]

According to Sakai, "Buddhist belief (interest)" led the compiler to select both Buddhist and secular entries. The inclusion of secular tales does not strike him as odd, as it will many later scholars, because he sees all experience as falling within the Buddhist worldview. The compiler makes sense of events in Buddhist terms whether or not they are overtly connected to Buddhist teachings. Sakai reasons that "someone who was gathering all the general knowledge available at that time transmitted through Buddhism would naturally attempt to collect related setsuwa from various times and places."[22] An "interest in history" and "an interest in setsuwa" are evident in both Buddhist and secular entries. The interest in setsuwa is a synthesis of three elements: setsuwa "as teaching," "as knowledge," and "as pleasure." In contrast, "an interest in history" breaks down into history "as change," "as knowledge," and "as criticism." In other words, according to Sakai, both setsuwa and history demonstrate an interest in knowledge, but setsuwa are also meant to instruct and entertain.[23]

Sakai ultimately lays out a four-branch genealogical scheme for Japanese literature: Buddhist, *kanbun* (modified Chinese style), idiosyncratic/

indigenous, and Shinto literatures, with some overlap between branches.[24] Although this scheme as a whole did not influence later scholars, it provides additional insight into Sakai's sense of setsuwa, traces of which persist today in the writing of others. The branch he calls idiosyncratic/indigenous literature "centers on ideas, sentiments, and interests that can be seen as idiosyncratic to the Japanese people, as having a unique literary form, or as containing the embryos of other works, such as in the literary trends of the eighth-century histories *Kojiki* and *Nihon shoki*."[25] Both idiosyncratic/indigenous literature and Shinto literature develop from idiosyncratic/indigenous thought, which he contrasts with foreign ideas.

Sakai's inclusion of this branch echoes the goal, pursued vigorously by Meiji scholars, of forming a national identity and literature. In *Uncovering Heian Japan*, LaMarre discusses how modern Japanese scholars erroneously searched for "territorial consolidation, linguistic purification, and ethnic or racial unification" in Nara and Heian Japan to construct a modern Japanese nation and how this has obscured our knowledge of classical history and culture.[26]

Sakai associates setsuwa with the idiosyncratic/indigenous branch. The two sources of all "idiosyncratic literature" are *kayō* (song) and setsuwa. Following *Kojiki* and *Nihon shoki*, Japanese literature splits into the poetic monogatari line (*uta monogatari kei*) and the narrative monogatari line (*setsuwa bungaku kei*). Works associated with the *setsuwa bungaku kei*—such as *Taketori monogatari* (*Tale of the Bamboo Cutter*, ca. 903–33), *Utsuho (or Utsubo) monogatari* (*The Tale of the Hollow Tree*, ca. 982), *Sumiyoshi monogatari* (*Tale of Sumiyoshi*, ca. 1186), *Hamamatsu chūnagon monogatari* (*Tale of the Middle Counselor Hamamatsu*, ca. 1053), and the lost *Uji dainagon monogatari*—reveal aspects of the lives of ordinary people. He sees this branch as originating in oral folklore and legends.[27]

Narratives linked to idiosyncratic/indigenous oral traditions exist in other cultures as well, but here Sakai is referring to Japanese oral traditions. He combines *setsuwa* with "-esque" (*setsuwa-teki*) and "lineage of literature" (*bungaku keitō*) to indicate what he perceives as a dominant characteristic of certain literary works. His description of this characteristic is vague, but true setsuwa in his view seem to be precedents of the narratives that now go by that name: perished oral stories treated as ancestors with only the descendants, texts of the lineage, affirming their previous existence. Sakai apparently sees indigenous elements in both the Buddhist and so-called secular sections of "Tales of Japan."

He ultimately categorizes *Konjaku* as Buddhist literature, but it is setsuwa-esque Buddhist literature.[28] His view that Buddhist interest or belief motivated the compiler leads him to stress the connection of *Konjaku* to Buddhist tradition. Yet, he does so while acknowledging the central position of the collection in the development of the setsuwa-branch. *Konjaku* is not predominately a setsuwa collection but Buddhist literature with characteristics of setsuwa.

The seeds of a genre as well as what becomes in setsuwa studies a preoccupation with distinguishing between the native and the foreign are apparent in Sakai's book. We are left to wonder when exactly the emphasis switched, so that scholars began to perceive *Konjaku* as a setsuwa collection either Buddhist or two-thirds Buddhist rather than as a setsuwa-esque Buddhist collection. Once that shift took place, the numerous collections overlapping in tales with *Konjaku* would have naturally fallen under the same category, effectively forming a genre. Since most setsuwa collections have a connection to Buddhism, the definition of setsuwa necessarily changed as well. However, a gap formed between the sense of setsuwa as a predominately indigenous narrative of any country and the then emerging view of it as a specific type of tale or collection usually situated within Buddhist tradition.

Adding to the confusion about the nature of setsuwa was the hazy relationship of setsuwa and monogatari, foreshadowed by the previously discussed Edo period reading of *setsuwa* as *monogatari*. Several setsuwa collections were monogatari before they were setsuwa, as suggested by their titles. *Konjaku* was first "historical literature" (*rekishi bungaku* or *rekishitai no bungaku*, literature in the style of history). The history that scholars using those terms often seem to have in mind is of the Heian people, not of Buddhism in three lands. Among the first modern literary histories, *Nihon bungakushi* (*History of Japanese Literature*, 1890) by Mikami Sanji and Takatsu Kuwasaburō includes *Konjaku* in the chapter "Rekishitai no bun" ("Writings in the Style of History"). Also referred to as *Uji dainagon monogatari*, it is grouped with two books focused on the hegemonic Fujiwara house: *Eiga monogatari* (*A Tale of Flowering Fortunes*, ca. 1092) and *Ōkagami* (*The Great Mirror*, ca. 1119).[29] However, the treatment of *Konjaku* suggests that Mikami and Takatsu sensed fundamental differences between *Konjaku* and these other texts. Although they conclude the chapter by stating that "the three texts exemplify historical literature of the Heian era,"[30] only *Eiga* and *Ōkagami* appear as examples of historical literature when the chapter opens.[31]

As Imanari Genshō has argued, a new genre can be perceived in a portion of an already existing genre and extracted from it. The setsuwa collections initially placed with (*rekishi*) monogatari must have eventually stood out as different from the other narratives while sharing characteristics with each other, thereby allowing for a new genre.[32] According to Mikami and Takatsu, the entertainment value of historical literature (its monogatari aspect) distinguishes it from history, as does the use of language. They argue that, while inferior in style to *Genji monogatari* (*The Tale of Genji*, ca. 1011) and *Makura no sōshi* (*The Pillow Book of Sei Shōnagon*, ca. 996), *Eiga*, *Ōkagami*, and *Konjaku* all exhibit a degree of elegance or literary flourish and a style quite different from "dry" history written in *kanbun*.[33] Still in their view, these works should be discussed as literature because of these differences. Moreover, while the genre of setsuwa is yet to be created, Mikami and Takatsu mention two other collections in relation to *Konjaku* that will be classified as setsuwa eventually: *Uji shūi* and *Kokon chomonjū*. They view the first as a supplement to *Konjaku* written in an old-fashioned style and the second as merely a Kamakura-period work modeled after *Konjaku*. Here the field of setsuwa begins to emerge in the connections perceived between these three texts. Significantly, Mikami and Takatsu do not link these other two collections to historical literature. They must have had some awareness of similarities in *Konjaku*, *Uji shūi*, and *Kokon chomonjū* unrelated to their notion of it.

In *Kokubungakushi jikkō* (*Ten Lectures on the History of Japanese Literature*, first published in 1899), Haga argues against classifying *Konjaku* with *Eiga* and *Ōkagami* because it is a collection of miscellaneous stories, including tales of ghosts and the strange, whereas the others are not. In reference to *Konjaku* tales, he writes:

> Within these stories, there are both truths and falsehoods; all kinds of things are mixed. Through this text, we can know the superstitions and customs of people of the period. Moreover, we know from it that much of what is written in *The Tale of Genji* about the relations of men and women and so forth were real. This text descends from the lineage of *Nihon ryōiki*, written in kanbun at the beginning of the Heian period. . . . By its third phase, monogatari gradually changed. Concerning even the writing itself, women no longer wrote and authorship switched to men. Consequently, the concerns and subject matters addressed also changed considerably. The style and wording grew stronger to some degree. The result was what became Kamakura period literature.[34]

The emphasis here is on the significance of *Konjaku* to Japanese cultural history and to how, as a *monogatari*, it exemplifies Japanese literature in transition.

Written after *Kokubungaku jikkō*, the previously discussed *Kōshō Konjaku* exhibits a very different approach to the collection. In its introduction, Haga values *Konjaku* for giving Japan a place in the world arena with its Indian, Chinese, and Japanese sections (although Haga continues to find the Japanese most interesting). He emphasizes seeing the tales as transmitted (written) texts coming from China and India via China, or, when set in Japan, as heavily influenced by the texts of those cultures. Derived from foreign traditions, Japanese Buddhist tales are valued for what they reveal of "how Buddhist tales swayed the spirit of the country."[35] Haga seems comfortable with the idea of a Japan with multicultural origins and with certain superstitions described in *Konjaku* as being both foreign and Japanese. However, this view of *Konjaku* was not popular. Shortly after Haga expressed it, Akutagawa praised *Konjaku* for beautifully revealing the raw side of Heian culture and its people. Similarly, what captured the interest of Meiji and Taishō period scholars, particularly those promoting public education, was the insight *Konjaku* provides into beliefs, customs, perceptions, and experiences of the Heian Japanese. They played down or ignored the Indian and Chinese features.

Studies of folklore contributed to the minimizing of foreign connections in *Konjaku* with their interests in the local and the oral. The first modern journal on folklore, *Kyōdo kenkyū* (*Local Studies*), appeared the same year— 1913—as volume one of *Kōshō Konjaku*. The then emerging folklorist Yanagita Kunio (1875–1962) wrote for this journal and edited it after the second volume. This development encouraged an interest in the folkloric elements of *Konjaku* and similar collections, but Yanagita's use of the term *setsuwa* contributed to an imprecision never fully resolved. According to Honda Giken, he initially rejects the understanding of it first promoted by Haga, which takes into account the appropriation and impact of Chinese texts and the influence of the Indian and Chinese cultures, especially Buddhist, on Japan. Although Yanagita sometimes employs the term in a specific sense— for example, in reference to Grimm's fairytales (*Märchen*)— he tends to use *setsuwa* generically to mean oral narrative transformed into written literature.[36] In contrasting the newness of the tales of his own first collection, *Tōno monogatari* (*The Legends of Tōno*, 1910), to the old character of *Konjaku* tales, he draws a parallel between the works.[37] Yet, later, he appears to see the setsuwa of classical and medieval collections as separate from Japanese folk literature. He even writes "the histories of how folk literature developed and the origins of setsuwa are different."[38]

With most setsuwa, "folk" can be understood only in a very general sense of "a traditional story handed down, in either written or oral form," and not with the connotations it usually has of originating in the lives of commoners or of including only tales with an oral genesis.[39] Any use of folk with the latter connotations is relevant to a relatively small number of setsuwa or to elements within the tales. However, the large picture of setsuwa is skewed because, while setsuwa scholars have generally seen the folk as only one dimension of the genre, many were inspired more by this dimension than others or have had ideological reasons for writing about it.

The insistence on how the essence of setsuwa is connected to indigenous, oral culture stems partially from the belief in the late Meiji and early Taishō periods that, as Haruo Shirane writes, "the spirit of the people could be found in a commoner culture, often prior to writing."[40] The idea of the folk as an underlying phenomenon of ethnic nationalism (as "a sense of the nation bound by blood and kinship ties"[41]) had previously emerged in Germany. Although Haga wrote *Kokubungaku jikkō* before studying philology in Berlin from 1900 to 1902, Japanese scholars had already begun to design a Japanese national literature relying heavily on German philological methods.[42] Overt influences from German literary theory, including terminology, mark Sakai's work. Sakai ignores that Haga changes his mind (at least temporarily) about *Konjaku* after examining its textual connections. Consequently, Sakai faces the problem of excavating portions of a Japanese past and identity from a text seeped in Indian and Chinese culture. The effort to solve this dilemma apparently shapes his notion of setsuwa as a characteristic of the tales separate from foreign elements, particularly Buddhist. Here, he draws from the popular view emphasizing the indigenous aspects of *Konjaku*. Politically motivated, this choice was the only means of bringing the collection and the new genre into the canon of Japanese literature, albeit in a marginal position. The foreign elements of *Konjaku* would not have won it a place in the canon.

Konjaku could be used to fill in certain gaps in the creation of a national literature. If literature was to have greater relevance to the question of what it means to be Japanese, then narratives about all kinds of people, not just the elite, had to be included. At the linguistic level, the original orthographic style of *Konjaku* bridges the gap between classical and later styles of writing. Called *kana-majiribun* (mixed-kanji/kana style), it combines the angular symbols of the Japanese syllabary *katakana* and Chinese characters (*kanji*) in Japanese syntax. The *Konjaku* style is sometimes viewed as a form of the imperial decree style (*senmyōgaki*) partly because the *katakana* is written smaller than the Chinese characters. Yet, it is also a precursor of *wakan konkōbun*, the style mixing Japanese symbols (strictly speaking, the curved syllabic symbols called *hiragana*) and Chinese characters in a literary form of Japanese (*wabun*). *Wakan konkōbun* would come into the fore during the Kamakura period.[43] Moreover, both the language and content of *Konjaku* were considered masculine. Since most Heian literature was written by women or by men in the feminine orthographic style, *hiragana*, *Konjaku* could be seen as helping to complete the picture in this way, too.

According to Shirane, "one of the key distinctions between canonized texts and noncanonical texts is that canonized texts are the objects of extensive commentary and exegesis or are used widely in school textbooks, whereas noncanonical texts, no matter how popular, are not."[44] Inclusion of certain collections in Meiji period textbooks suggests that such works were becoming canonical texts. In the Meiji period alone, roughly half of the textbooks for middle school students have entries from *Konjaku*. Selections from other collections, especially *Uji shūi* and *Kokon chomonjū*, are less common.[45]

In the widely used *Middle School Japanese Reader* (*Chūtō kokubun tokuhon*, Meiji shoin, 1896), editor Ochiai Naobumi indicates that selections of literary texts were chosen as models for writing Japanese. At the same time, the choice of *Konjaku* tales promotes the sense that the value of the collection lies in what it reveals about Heian Japan. Three tales are included. Taken from Book 24 in the so-called secular section of "Tales of Japan," they focus on masters of various arts and learning in Japan: skilled painters and artisans, musicians, and a poet of Chinese-style Japanese poetry. There are Buddhist elements in two tales, but the stories are not about Buddhism per se.[46] Similarly, in the first full-length history of Japanese literature in English (1899), W. G. Aston writes: "Most of the stories so collected are obviously fictitious; but, true or false, they have a special interest, inasmuch as they present a fuller and livelier picture of the lives and ideas of the middle and lower classes than most other works of this period."[47] Referring to Heian Japan, his comments are based on a similar characterization of *Konjaku* made by Mikami and Takatsu.

As more collections were classified as setsuwa, this narrow sense of *Konjaku* along with its instrumental role in the creation of the genre contributed to the uncertainty in the field about what setsuwa actually means. The question "what is setsuwa?" (*setsuwa to wa nani ka*) recurs in the scholarship on the genre, appearing among other places as the title of a relatively recent collection of essays by leading setsuwa scholars.[48] The term now most commonly refers to short prose narratives compiled in specific classical and medieval Japanese collections and the collections themselves. *Setsuwa bungaku* (literature) is sometimes used to differentiate the stories or collections associated with the genre or the genre itself from the general use of the word for a traditional story.

One cannot provide a concise and narrow definition of setsuwa as a single entity without glossing over or ignoring important differences between stories and collections or denying the existence of many unanswered questions regarding them. The lengthy definitions of setsuwa given by modern and contemporary scholars often need to be gleaned from several pages or entire articles, thereby attesting to the complexity of the term. Since so much knowledge of setsuwa is necessarily speculative, there can be no definitive answer to "what is setsuwa?" What we know best is how scholars have perceived the tales and collections.

The following summary is based on general perceptions that emerged in the field of Japanese literature predominately in Japan. However, scholars writing in English have typically built on the work of Japanese scholars to define setsuwa.

Usually written with straightforward, unadorned language, setsuwa range from a few lines or passages to several pages. They share a clearly identifiable form with some variation. After stating or implying that the story occurs in the near or distant past, the narrator introduces a protagonist who supposedly lived. Something happens to him or her. This event is usually marked by a progression from the ordinary to the unusual or extraordinary. We lack records of how early audiences reacted to setsuwa, but there seems to have been interplay between what they did and did not expect; in the words of Marian Ury in *Tales of Times Now Past*, the best setsuwa are both "typical and astonishing."[49] Setsuwa often end with observations or a moral by a commentator apart from the narrative. The observations may include a brief statement about the reactions of witnesses or people who heard about the event, typically a sense of strangeness or awe, whereas the morals may take the form of a warning or practical advice. The final passage frequently states that the story was told and passed down and may even indicate the first person to transmit it. Some scholars have touted different aspects of this form as central to the general definition of setsuwa, especially the framing mechanism (the opening and closing). Most recognize setsuwa as having all or most of these structural parts.

In addition, many scholars view setsuwa as exhibiting a unique sense of earlier times. The past is mingled or re-created in the present, as suggested by the opening phrase of *Konjaku* tales: "now it is the past" (*ima wa mukashi*). Another defining feature of setsuwa is a presumed connection of stories to real events as stated or implied. The reliance of the narratives on hearsay, whether real or constructed, allows for ambiguity concerning truth. Stories allude to the possibility of discrepancies in how people experience and interpret events—to the subjective nature of perception.

As the inclusion of the word *bungaku* (literature) in the phrase *setsuwa bungaku* implies, setsuwa are considered more than mechanical recordings of facts. The tales transform events and experiences. Along with *nikki* (a type of memoir) and *rekishi monogatari* (historical stories), they combine fictive and non-fictive elements while claiming to concern real people and true events. Yet, setsuwa are not part of a larger story pieced together, and their protagonists frequently lack historical importance. While meant to be entertaining, they are not literature in the same sense as *Genji* or other so-called *tsukuri monogatari* (invented stories). The insistence in setsuwa on the factual nature of both the real and imagined enables scholars to distinguish them from *tsukuri monogatari*, which are seen as emphasizing fictive elements although they can include historical facts.

Scholars have traditionally seen a universal dimension in setsuwa, although less so in recent years. The tales are valued not only for what they tell us about the lives of people outside elite circles but also for revealing facets of human nature. Communal sensibilities are seen as informing them, although the compilers are all either men or, because there are no known women compilers, assumed to be.

Individual narratives either have precedents or serve as such. Following Haga, scholars connect particular setsuwa to what they consider either source tales or different versions, ranging from the loosely related to the nearly identical. These appear in Chinese as well as in Japanese collections and in various literary genres as well as in histories and sutras. In *Konjaku*, most narratives are apparently copied from other, known, texts, although less obviously so with the stories of the so-called secular section of "Tales of

Japan."[50] There is also speculation about indirect connections between extant texts and lost collections.[51] Nearly identical tales in different collections, such as *Konjaku* and *Uji shūi*, are believed to be from the same lost work, often *Uji dainagon*. Broader forms of research along these lines consider the links between entire tale collections or between a given setsuwa collection and other books. Despite an abundance of studies tracing various textual connections, scholars tend to take claims of oral origins within stories at face value. They speculate that many tales were initially told aloud and perhaps repeated for a while in Japan (or India or China) before being recorded.

Even scholars who question the theory of oral origins of setsuwa see them as connected to oral tradition in other ways. The belief that setsuwa were recited or read aloud may explain why stories relatively simple in syntax, diction, and religious meaning are recorded in orthographic styles intelligible to educated Buddhist practitioners and aristocratic men but few others. Collections are written in *kanbun* (Chinese characters), *kana-majiribun* (usually *kanji* with *katakana*), and *hiragana*. Most aristocratic women would have been able to read only in the last style comfortably (the least used by compilers) and commoners were usually illiterate. Yet, setsuwa would have been easily understood when read aloud or recited.

Speculations about the oral use of setsuwa concentrate on the belief that Buddhists commonly employed them in preaching. Scholars debate about the relationship of certain collections to popular sermons, and consider other collections as exclusively or mostly secular. However, the connection of *Nihon ryōiki, Hyakuza hōdan kikigakishō* (*Summary Notes of One Hundred Lectures on Dharma*, ca. 1110), *Uchigiki shū* (*Collection of Things Heard*, ca. 1111–34), and some other setsuwa collections to sermonizing is either probable or clear.[52] Since sermons were initially aimed at aristocrats, who could be patrons, some scholars have argued that aristocrats were the primary audience of setsuwa. Yet, itinerant monks are known to have preached and performed with music, dance, and stories from the beginning of the tenth century or earlier. If their sermons included setsuwa, then commoners would have also heard them.[53] The argument that commoners were among the audiences of Heian and early Kamakura period setsuwa has no historical data to support it, but the lack of evidence does not disprove it, either.

On the rare occasions when a Heian text mentions that someone heard a setsuwa, the listener is an aristocrat. One well-known reference comes from *Chūyūki* (*The Diary of the Fujiwara Minister of the Right*, 1095–1129). Author Fujiwara no Munetada (1062–1141) records two stories that monk Keizen from the temple Miidera told him about people born in the Pure Land after death (*ōjōden*).[54] Another example comes from *Chūgaishō* (*Selections of Major Secretary Nakahara*, 1137–54). This book supposedly consists of things said by Fujiwara no Tadazane (1078–1162) recorded by his retainer Nakahara no Moromoto (1109–75). Along with *Gōdanshō*, also considered the conversation of one person recorded by another (Fujiwara no Sanekane, 1085–1112, writing down the speech of Ōe no Masafusa, 1041–1111), the *Chūgaishō* contains many entries resembling or identical to setsuwa and is sometimes considered a setsuwa collection. In an entry from the year 1150, Tadazane tells how he decided to give up falconry. Two experiences led to this change. When he was still an adolescent, a pheasant attempting to escape from its predator landed on his bamboo hat, moving him with pity. Still he did not give up hunting with hawks until years later, when he heard a lady-in-waiting read a tale about a falconer transformed into a pheasant and pursued by a hawk.[55] Tadazane notes that the story comes from *Uji Dainagon monogatari*. While that collection is non-extant, we nonetheless have a rare mention of a *setsuwa* collection in another Heian text. *Chūgaishō* does not record the tale about the transformed falconer, but the story was probably the same as or similar to "How a Falconer on the West Side of the Capital Takes Vows Because of a Dream" in *Konjaku*. In other words, its mention indirectly links *Konjaku* to an account of a lady-in-waiting reading a tale aloud.[56]

The description of the encounter of Munetada with Keizen confirms the belief that Buddhist monks told such tales orally to other people, here informally, whereas the experience of Tadazane indicates that people other than preachers told setsuwa aloud. We know that aristocratic women read other stories (monogatari) to each other for entertainment, so possibly setsuwa were among their selections. Since the people mentioned here are aristocrats and a monk associating with the elite, the accounts fail to suggest that setsuwa had an influence on commoners.

The stories demonstrate that setsuwa were shared outside the context of sermons, but not to what extent. Since no one expresses surprise at the telling of setsuwa in either account, the behavior was probably ordinary. Still, we lack the large number of examples that would enable us to determine in general what kinds of tales were told aloud, to whom, why, and in what settings. Nor can we tell if people ever read the collections through. Once again, the lack of evidence prevents us from determining much about the early audiences and reception of setsuwa. Such gaps in our knowledge greatly affect all areas of setsuwa studies. In developing a theory of the grotesque in setsuwa, we have no descriptions of the responses of readers or listeners to grotesque representations within tales, so we are limited in our discussions of the emotions any representation might have evoked from them. When we contemplate how representations may have affected Heian people, our ideas must be based on details within the tales or indirectly from things in other texts. Before moving in that direction, we need to consider how the grotesque has been approached in the past.

THEORIES OF THE GROTESQUE

The phenomenon of the grotesque may date back to before ancient times. According to Geoffrey Galt Harpham in *On the Grotesque: Strategies of Contradiction in Art and Literature*, it existed in prehistoric cave art and religious rituals performed in caves. It can be traced to the tension between life-giving and destructive forces in the human psyche (the fatality/fertility complex) as exemplified by Osiris, the Egyptian god. Murdered by his brother, Osiris is resurrected by his wife to impregnate her. He then becomes god of both vegetation and the underworld, associated with life, fertility, and death.[57] Of course, theories about the earliest forms of the grotesque or its origins are necessarily speculative. Harpham writes, "as the grotesque is as much a mental event as a formal property, its history is impossible to narrate."[58]

In contrast, the development of grotesque theory can and has been studied. It spans six centuries, involves many countries, and is not linear. Histories of grotesque theory are included in such books as *The Grotesque in English Literature* by Arthur Clayborough, *The Grotesque* by Philip Thomson, *The Grotesque: A Study in Meanings* by Frances K. Barasch, *Staging the Savage God: The Grotesque in Performance* by Ralf Remshardt, and the previously mentioned book by Harpham.[59] Some accounts are several or more chapters long yet still seemingly far from complete as each study contains some information not mentioned in others. The huge amount of relevant material prevents me from including a comprehensive history of grotesque theory here, but the summary below will introduce key thinkers and concepts.

In *Lives of the Painters, Sculptors and Architects*, Italian painter, architect, and biographer Giorgio Vasari (1511–74) mentions a late fifteenth-century discovery and excavation pinpointed by recent scholars as the start of grotesque theory or at least of the word: that of certain frescos in the Golden

Palace (Domus Aurea) of Nero.[60] Created by a painter/decorator named Fabullus (or Famulus), they depict creatures of mixed human, animal, and plant parts. Some show mythological figures such as satyrs and cupids. While such forms were new and exciting to sixteenth-century artists, they had been popular in Rome around 100 B.C.E. Still, according to Vasari, Giovanni da Udine (1487–1564) and his teacher Raphael (Raffaello Sanzio, 1483–1520) visited the underground site and were amazed "at the freshness, beauty, and excellence" of the designs, "which were called grotesques from their having been discovered in the underground grottos."[61]

Since the Golden Palace was never supposed to be underground, the word *grotesque*, or more precisely *grottesche*, is a telling mistake with symbolic implications. Defining it as "of or pertaining to underground caves," Harpham points to its connection to the Latin word for *crypt* and the Greek word for *vault*.[62] The ideas "of the underground, of burial, and of secrecy" eventually pertain to many grotesques.[63] The cave is associated with the womb as well: a hollow space with the potential of protecting or producing life, and conveying the sense of birth or rebirth. Yet, the cave-like womb could become a site or cause of death; infants and women could die during birth, a feared outcome before effective obstetrics. The cave is further associated with excrement, the underworld, and hell among other things.[64]

However, in the beginning, the grotesque did not have dark and terrible characteristics. The charming style of the frescos was rejected for other reasons. Even in ancient Rome, some intellectuals loathed decorative art with representations contradicting nature. In opening "The Art of Poetry," Horace (65–8 B.C.E.) writes:

> If a painter chose to join a human head to the neck of a horse, and to spread feathers of many a hue over limbs picked up now here now there, so that what at the top is a lovely woman ends below in a black and ugly fish, could you, my friends, if favoured with a private view, refrain from laughing? . . . Quite like such pictures would be a book, whose idle fancies shall be shaped like a sick man's dreams, so that neither head nor foot can be assigned to a single shape.[65]

He goes on to suggest that the license of artists and poets should have some limits. Other intellectuals, too, could not tolerate hybrid beings or things otherwise defying physical properties of the real world, such as delicate stalks and tendrils supporting statues. Jarred by the juxtaposition of the realistic with the fantastic, Vitruvius (ca. 80/70–25 B.C.E.) objects to the portrayal of things drawing from nature but not observable in it. The grotesque is pitted against the classical art style, which adheres to concepts of restraint, rational order, proportion, and perfected forms. Meanwhile, the public apparently likes the strange creatures, as Vitruvius laments: "Yet when people view these falsehoods, they approve rather than condemn."[66]

Appropriated by artists, the grotesque style grew popular in the decorative arts throughout sixteenth-century Europe. It was used in cathedrals, mansions, and palaces. Vasari extends the meaning of grotesque to include sculpture when describing the sculptural and architectural style of Michelangelo (1475–1564) in the Medici Tombs.[67] He writes that Michelangelo "departed not a little from the work regulated by measure, order, and rule, which other men did according to a common use and after Vitruvius and the antiquities, to which he would not conform."[68] Michelangelo's break away from convention gave other artists the courage to follow, so that, according to Vasari, "new fantasies have since been seen which have more of the grotesque than of reason or rule in their ornamentation."[69] Grotesque is then associated positively with artistic freedom. Breaking away from classical thought can produce interesting or beautiful results. Viewed negatively, it is considered wild, irrational, or even licentious.

Also evoking a mixed response were early grotesque representations not associated with the ornamentation of the Golden Palace, such as demons populating Christian decorative art beginning in the twelfth century. A future saint, Bernard of Clairvaux (1090–1153), questions the wisdom of using hybrid beasts to decorate cloisters in a letter to another abbot because "indeed there are so many things, and everywhere such an extraordinary variety of hybrid forms, that it is more diverting to read in the marble than in the texts before you."[70] In a study of the bizarre shapes and demons in the margins of medieval illuminated manuscripts and architecture, Michael Camille observes that the "metaphor of 'reading' in images rather than in books . . . suggests investing marginal imagery with the time and space of meaning."[71] While he focuses on literal margins on paper and the edges of stone edifices, the grotesque acts similarly when margins and borders are abstract. According to his study, figures in the margins "gloss, parody, modernize and problematize the text's authority while never totally undermining it."[72] Even blasphemous representations often affirm the authority of the Christian teaching they border or "reinstate the very models they oppose."[73]

Grotesques derived from Roman ornament are similarly positioned in relation to Christian teachings and beliefs. The decorations of the Vatican

Loggias created by Raphael and Giovanni da Udine (inspired by the frescos of the Golden Palace) are an example. On the walls and vaults of these passageways, grotesque pagan designs fantastically combining plants, animals, and humans surround biblical scenes. The ambivalence toward such representations is apparent in the desire to allow them on the one hand and to limit them to designated, subordinate spaces on the other. However, as Harpham notes, they also compete for attention with the centrally placed Christian objects, blurring the distinction between the center and the margins by attracting and distracting the viewer.[74]

New meanings and uses of *grotesque* began to emerge even in the sixteenth century, but when and why the additions occurred is often unclear. Some seem unconnected to art, such as Rabelais's use of the word as one of numerous possible adjectives for modifying *couillon* (bollock or testicles).[75] Yet, others demonstrate the connection of the word to art, sometimes also extending the definition. After observing a painter creating various strange grotesques, Michel de Montaigne (1533–92) writes of his essays: "And what are these things of mine, in truth, but grotesque and monstrous bodies, pieced together of divers members, without definite shape, having no order, sequence, or proportion other than accidental?"[76] In France by the early seventeenth century, *grotesque* commonly referred to literature, people, and other things. The word there had a variety of meanings, including *absurd, bizarre, fantastic,* and *extravagant.*[77]

From around the mid-seventeenth century, literary critics frequently appropriated art in their discussions of literature or otherwise compared writing to art. According to Barasch, dramatist John Dennis (1657–1734) was one of the first critics to connect the burlesque and grotesque; in his dedication to *Poems in Burlesque,* he sees the former in poetry as analogous to the latter in art. Both burlesque and grotesque here mean "works composed of incongruous parts and irreconcilable tones."[78]

Another early connection of the grotesque to the burlesque appears in the view of popular commedia plays (*commedia dell'arte*) as grotesque. Usually performed outdoors by traveling troupes, these plays relied on stock characters and situations and frequently functioned as satire. Copper engravings and sketches of characters from these plays along with demonic figures and deformed people in other contexts by Jacques Callot (1592–1635) were labeled grotesques and sold inexpensively throughout Europe.[79] Such developments also shaped the meaning of the word.

Contributing to a negative sense of the grotesque is the view critics such as Nicolas Boileau-Despréaux (1636–1711) had of commedia plays, along with most burlesque poetry, as vulgar forms of art.[80] In "A Parallel of Painting and Poetry," John Dryden (1631–1700) compares the plays to grotesque painting and judges them as inferior to naturalistic forms of comedy. To him, the main value of this comedy or farce is to keep the peasants content. Laughter distinguishes people from animals in his view, but just barely. He writes in reference to the plays: "if a straw can tickle a man, 'tis an instrument of happiness."[81]

The dominance of neoclassicism and rationalist thought prevented many eighteenth-century theorists from esteeming the grotesque or even from giving it anything but a low assessment. Following Immanuel Kant (1724–1804) in *Critique of Judgment*, Edmund Burke (1729–97) and others pursued ideas of the beautiful and sublime at this time. The beautiful is aesthetically pleasing or satisfying whereas the sublime conveys a compelling sense of transcendent magnificence along with a power that can destroy. (Mountains and oceans are sublime.) The issue then becomes whether caricature, the grotesque, or any work of art or literature rooted in the mundane and physical can be meaningful. Acknowledging the significance of the ugly or incongruous in art is to throw into question classical and neoclassical ideals of art aspiring to imitate a perfect universe. New literature, such as novels by Henry Fielding (1707–54), also challenged rationalist and neoclassical values. (Fielding's characters often have an exaggerated ugly appearance mirroring a moral lack.)

However, the comic grotesque had its scholarly defenders in the eighteenth century. In Germany, the popular Harlequin figure outraged the neoclassical sensibility. A servant who never serves properly and acrobatic clown, Harlequin is often an instrument of parody and satire. In "Harlequin, or the Defense of the Grotesque-Comic," Justus Möser (1720–94) has Harlequin argue in favor of himself. Harlequin reasons that he is not obliged to adhere to the aesthetics of the beautiful and sublime because his world of commedia dell'arte has its own order. Through Harlequin, Möser also points out that the literature and art of the ancient Greeks and Romans had its own hybrids.[82] Another person who took the comic seriously is Karl Friedrich Flögel (1729–88). In "History of the Comic Grotesque," Flögel defines the grotesque in terms of deviation from the usual aesthetic forms, a lack of order, and, in some cases (French mystery plays), a mix of folk and scriptural elements.[83] Lusty and crude, it allows people who must work hard and obey masters "to let off steam."[84]

With *The Castle of Otranto* by Horace Walpole (1717–97) as their debut in 1764, gothic novels brought new meaning to the fearsome and grotesque. The gothic novel is a subject in itself, but it harks back to the medieval grotesque in its use of Gothic architecture and the relationship of evil and disorder among other things. In *Fantasy: The Literature of Subversion*, Rosemary Jackson says of the gothic novel at its onset: "Confined to the margins of Enlightenment culture, these 'fortresses of unreason' were both created *by* the dominant classical order and constituted a hidden pressure *against* it."[85] The gothic resembles earlier forms of the grotesque in its marginal status and its relationship to prevailing cultural views. However, Bakhtin describes the gothic as a variety of the new or Romantic grotesque, distinguishable from the medieval grotesque by the tone of laughter marking it. Laughter ultimately defeats monsters in the medieval grotesque, but not in the Romantic, where, lacking regenerative power, it is "cut down to cold humor, irony, sarcasm."[86]

Grotesque theory and romanticism became intertwined in the eighteenth century with an emphasis on emotion, including terror and awe inspired by the sublime. When theorists saw the grotesque as potentially possessing qualities of the sublime, its status rose. Both the grotesque and romanticism provided a means of breaking away from the earlier conventions of neoclassicism, a move many people now embraced. In *Dialogue on Poetry*, key figure of the Romantic school Friedrich Schlegel (1772–1829) links the arabesque in literature to myth. Arabesque is nearly synonymous with "grotesque" in Germany at this time, especially when used figuratively.[87] Both refer to mixtures marked by heterogeneous and fantastic elements and to orderly structured confusion. Through a fictional conversation of a circle of friends, Schlegel names the qualities of the wit of romantic poetry as exemplified by Cervantes and Shakespeare: "artfully ordered confusion," "symmetry of contradictions," and "perennial alternation of enthusiasm and irony."[88] The wit is an indirect mythology having the same organization as the arabesque (grotesque), and "the arabesque is the oldest and most original form of the human imagination."[89] Later, Kayser identifies in this work by Schlegel "the essential ingredients of the grotesque" without "the abysmal quality, the insecurity, the terror inspired by the disintegration of the world."[90] That is, the grotesque in the Romantic period mirrors the glorified elements of the imagination.

A then contemporary writer whom Schlegel defends along the lines of the grotesque is Jean Paul Friedrich Richter (Jean Paul, 1763–1825).[91] A mix of gruesome, frightening elements with deep sentiment and odd humor often come into play in the stylistically digressive novels of this author. As many scholars have pointed out, Jean Paul himself contributed to grotesque thought not only through his novels but also with a theory of dark humor in *Primer of Aesthetics*. Discussed by both Kayser and Bakhtin, Jean Paul writes on a dark, painful humor that knows evil. Although he never uses the word *grotesque*, his view of laughter as a destroyer (the devil is potentially the greatest humorist) helped shape understandings of the grotesque, particularly that of Kayser in the twentieth century. (Bakhtin, in contrast, sees the grotesque and carnivalesque in places where John Paul observes derisive humor: in carnivals as well as in Rabelais and Shakespeare.) Whereas Kayser sees satanic humor as that "which destroys us and estranges without lending us wings for a flight into heaven,"[92] Jean Paul reasons that dark humor is not entirely negative because the destruction of reality allows for transcendence.

In "On the Essence of Laughter," Charles Baudelaire (1821–67) also views laughter as fundamentally diabolical, stemming from our sense of our own superiority in relation to other, relatively weakened people. However, in contrast to this ordinary or "significative comic," the grotesque or "absolute comic" is rooted in our sense of superiority over nature. The grotesque is a more profound form of humor in part because it is "closer to the innocent life and to absolute joy."[93] It harks back to childhood and the primordial, and its laughter is immediate.

The views of Richter and Baudelaire, and even of Kayser (who does not express faith in a higher power), are rooted in Christian thought and particularly in the concept of fallen humanity. Drawing from a second essay by Baudelaire, Harpham associates Baudelaire's recognition of "satanism and prodigious humor, the Fall and regeneration in the same forms" (in this case, the grotesque in the work of William Hogarth, 1697–1764, and other artists) with the Christian appropriation of mythical figures as demons.[94] Harpham asserts: If, as in Dante, "hell contains myth, then damnation must always be tinctured with regeneration."[95]

In the nineteenth century, the grotesque won over numerous writers and scholars. A new literature, including the stories of E. T. A. Hoffman (1776–1822) and the poems of Robert Browning (1812–89), emerged that incorporated both comic and frightening elements while introducing into stories and poems a self-conscious (yet frequently nightmarish) awareness of the paradoxical and ambiguous nature of life. An early treatment of the grotesque exclusively in literature is "Wordsworth, Tennyson, and Browning; or Pure, Ornate, and Grotesque Art in Poetry" (1864) by Walter Bagehot (1826–77). While Bagehot does not applaud the grotesque, he observes that it represents objects in unfavorable circumstances and struggling with incongruities whereas pure and ornate art depicts things in a favorable light.[96] Around the same time, the culture of the medieval past along with folklore and ballads rediscovered by the Grimm brothers and Hans Christian Anderson sparked the imaginations of writers and artists and provided supernatural elements. Myth was another source of inspiration for the modern grotesque, and many theorists recognized its connection to grotesques of the past. Additionally, more philosophers included ideas of the grotesque in their reflections on aesthetics, although their assessments were not entirely positive.

Contemplation of the grotesque was often part of a larger spiritual quest. Georg Wilhelm Friedrich Hegel (1770–1831) and other philosophers attributed the grotesque in art to the conflict between our sense of the infinite and our experience of our bodily limitations. The emphasis remains on the infinite. Hegel's view of art as a revelation of the spirit and his feelings for the Absolute and Divine led him to understanding the grotesque as an unsuccessful attempt at expressing the spiritual in concrete form.[97]

Along different lines, Victor Hugo (1802–85) justified the ugly and incongruous in art and literature by asserting that they have the primary function of heightening our appreciation of beauty and perfection. In the preface to his drama *Cromwell*, Hugo not only contributes to the trend to value grotesque humor, he renders it a goal. He sees his age as a time when art focused on beauty and the sublime has become wearying. The grotesque provides a different means of reaching an elevated state of understanding. "Sublime upon sublime scarcely presents a contrast, and we need a little rest from everything, even the beautiful. On the other hand, the grotesque seems to be a halting-place, a mean term, a starting-point whence one rises toward the beautiful with a fresher and keener perception. The salamander gives relief to the water-sprite; the gnome heightens the charm of the sylph."[98] The comic-drama, whose master is Shakespeare, seems ideal for expressing the grotesque. Hugo acknowledges the existence of the grotesque in ancient times in figures such as the harpies and cyclopes, but believes it strongest as a modern, Christian sensibility. In his view, which resembles that of Hegel and others, the belief in the duality of human nature—the perishable, mortal body versus the ethereal, immortal soul—gives rise to an enhanced grotesque. Hugo emphasizes that ugliness is a creation of God, not a distortion of nature.

Another writer who shaped the reception and understanding of the grotesque is John Ruskin (1819–1900). In the "Grotesque Renaissance" chapter of his seminal work on Venetian art and architecture, *The Stones of Venice*, Ruskin creates a complex system of standards for the grotesque in which artists and writers are one of four types judged in terms of their morality. Some grotesques are false/ignoble whereas others are true/noble, but each reflects the character of its creator. Grotesques are rooted in how their creators either indulge or repress the instinct of playfulness. For example, men of the highest spirituality play wisely (with a love for God, truth, and humanity) and with restraint. Only such people—and here Dante (1265–1321), author of the *Divine Comedy*, is supreme—can produce a grotesque revealing higher truths about humankind. At the other extreme are men who do not play at all and consequently express themselves only through the "bitterness of mockery."[99] Although Ruskin describes the framework in great depth, I will not address it further here because its details are not what made a great impact on future theories. More generally, Ruskin introduces a connection between grotesque representations and the internal landscape of writers and artists. The need for play and its expression are psychological, and the dispositions of artists shape their art.

The main contribution of Ruskin is his view "that the grotesque is, in almost all cases, composed of two elements, one ludicrous, the other fearful; that, as one or other of these elements prevails, the grotesque falls into two branches, sportive grotesque and terrible grotesque."[100] Yet, the grotesque is rarely one or the other. He continues: "there are hardly any examples which do not in some degree combine both elements; there are few grotesques so utterly playful as to be overcast with no shade of fearfulness, and few so fearful as absolutely to exclude all ideas of jest."[101] Many later scholars appropriated this understanding of the grotesque. Any effort to build on both Kayser and Bakhtin (as I do in this study) evokes this aspect of Ruskin's theory.

Not all nineteenth-century writers on the grotesque understood the phenomenon in terms of a spiritual quest or its lack. In *A History of Caricature and Grotesque in Literature and Art*, Thomas Wright (1810–77) mainly describes works he sees as exemplifying caricature or the grotesque. In contrast to Ruskin, he is more interested in how the grotesque relates to social issues rather than to the spiritual or moral realms. A subtle link between the grotesque and caricature had been made even a while before Wright, but went undeveloped. In *Conversations with the Parson of ****, Christoph Martin Wieland (1733–1813) divides caricature into three types depending on how figures are created: through natural distortions, by exaggerating features, or by rendering features "fantastic or grotesque, where the painter is not concerned with reality and verisimilitude."[102] However, even in Wieland's time, many people did not think that the grotesque was divorced from reality. Nor is the grotesque always related to the fantastic or unreal in Wright. It can pertain to the comically ugly as well.

Barasch distinguishes between caricature and the grotesque in Wright by asserting that "the first word always incorporates the sense of ridicule; the second consistently refers to the fantastic or excessively ugly and comic."[103] However, since the grotesque can function similarly to caricature, the difference between the terms is not always clear. Heinrich Schneegans (1863–1914) added some precision to the terms. Focusing on Rabelais, he distinguishes grotesque-satire from simple caricature through the connection of each to reality and the act of protest. Grotesque-satire is more serious and meaningful. Exaggeration in both caricature and the grotesque is rooted in reality rather than in fantasy, but the grotesque takes the exaggeration beyond the possible. As an example, Schneegans discusses several caricatures of Napoleon III. The exaggerations of the emperor's nose achieve grotesque status when transformed into a crow's beak or pig's snout.[104] In this way, Schneegans locates the roots of the imaginative aspect of the grotesque in reality (here, a nose) as does Bakhtin later on.

While there are other nineteenth-century writers on the grotesque, those mentioned above are arguably the most influential. Because of space constraints, I will now jump ahead to the twentieth century, starting with Kayser.[105] His *Grotesque in Art and Literature* centers on terrifying elements and the sense of alienation in numerous works from mostly the Romantic and modern periods. Kayser ultimately posits the grotesque as "the estranged world," "a play with the absurd," and "an attempt to invoke and subdue the demonic aspects of the world."[106] He builds on Wieland, quoting him as saying that the artist of the grotesque "gives rein to an unchecked fancy (like the so-called Hell Brueghel) with the sole intention of provoking laughter, disgust, and surprise about the daring of his monstrous creations by the unnatural and absurd products of his imagination."[107] Hell Brueghel is the pseudonym given to Pieter Brueghel the Younger (1564?–1638) because of his depictions of fires and demonic figures. He is known mostly as a copyist while his father is more famous for originals. We can see this mixture of the absurd and the frightening in *The Triumph of Death* by Pieter Brueghel the Elder (1525/30–69) in which animated skeletons ride horses, ring bells, and gather corpses.[108]

According to Kayser, the laughter described by Wieland as part of the reaction to the grotesque expresses desperate relief and is an involuntary response to the demonic, cosmic, and impersonal forces in the world. In this way, the grotesque in Kayser's view has a psychological dimension for the creator and the audience (just as it did for Wieland, who was ahead of his time). Kayser mentions a ghostly "It" (Es)—an unnamed force showing us that our world is unreliable and causing a fear of life rather than of death—but states that we cannot know its source.[109] Both Bakhtin and Clayborough associate Kayser's theory with the concept of id: the irrational part of the brain and source of the libido in Freudian theory.[110] Clayborough himself takes a Jungian approach to grotesque aspects of Swift, Coleridge, and Dickens in the second part of his book.

Indeed, the attempt to incorporate psychological theories in the study of the grotesque became common in the twentieth century. Rather than adopting complete frameworks of analysis, many scholars have blended ideas from psychology with other concepts. Harpham introduces Freudian and Jungian ideas into his discussion several times, most notably in relating the grotesque to myth. Bernard McElroy focuses on the grotesque as a force of humiliation in Kafka, Joyce, and other modern novelists while also touching on the Freudian sense of the uncanny. A complex concept that cannot be succinctly explained, the uncanny involves "an eerie, unsettled feeling" caused by a return into our consciousness of "repressed infantile anxieties, and surmounted modes of primitive thought."[111] Mary Russo distinguishes between the uncanny grotesque and the carnivalesque grotesque in *The Female Grotesque: Risk, Excess, and Modernity*, a study that considers the stunt flying of Amelia Earhart and a variety of other cultural, literary, and visual texts. Other concepts, such as transgression, are also crucial to her work.[112]

The tradition of reflecting on the grotesque philosophically continues despite the rise of interest in the psychological components. Harpham provides "formulae or 'master codes' for the entire range of the grotesque."[113] They include the ideas of the grotesque falling between categories or occupying multiple clear-cut categories, acting as a dynamic of the low ascending and the high descending, having a connection to myth, disrupting decorum, and functioning in the discovery of hidden meaning. Yet, he asserts that "really to understand the grotesque is to cease to regard it as grotesque."[114] Harpham builds on Montaigne, who, believing that nothing is a monster to God, observed in nature "a hidden order of apparently disorderly things."[115] A related idea can be found in the last line of "This Lime-Tree Bower My Prison" by Samuel Coleridge, which Harpham quotes: "No sound is dissonant which tells of life."[116] Such views weaken our sense of the grotesque.

At least two other studies should be mentioned here. *The Politics and Poetics of Transgression* by Peter Stallybrass and Allon White incorporates Bakhtinian thought on the grotesque and carnivalesque in a study of hierarchies in early modern and modern Europe. It includes a chapter examining the grotesque in Augustan poetry as the resurfacing of elements of popular culture that the elite sought to reject and repress.[117] *Salome and Judas in the Cave of Sex* by Kuryluk, previously cited in an endnote in regard to the relevance of cave imagery to the grotesque, deals with tension between high and low cultures while focusing on the art of Aubrey Beardsley (1872–98). It also broadens the concept of subcultures in opposition to a dominant culture by adding more sources of resistance, including the feminine in a world controlled by men and childhood in an adult-dominated world.[118] Although these and other recent studies of the grotesque usually focus on modern and postmodern contexts in Western culture, they include some ideas relevant to the grotesque in other times and places.

Some aspects of grotesque theory have no bearing on the premodern Japanese context. It makes little sense to analyze the grotesque in setsuwa in terms of a Christian sense of the absolute or the belief in a fall from grace. Evil things are not necessarily ugly or deformed in setsuwa; rather, they often appear in beautiful forms. Nor are humans considered better than nature in most Japanese contexts, so that humor cannot derive from a feeling of superiority to it. The exceptions are certain animal spirits discussed in Chapter 6. Yet, other facets of the grotesque theory do fit. Grotesque representations in setsuwa often function as designs in the margins or as creatures in subordinate spaces, glossing or otherwise commenting on centrally positioned teachings or ideologies, thereby undermining and sustaining them. The tales address gaps between bodily experiences and spiritual aspirations, albeit in a Buddhist context. Few beasts are composed of heterogeneous parts from animals or plants in setsuwa, but we see mixtures of elements in the transformations of one being into another or in objects functioning unusually. In a tale analyzed in Chapter 3, a radish containing semen after a man masturbated with it acts as an extension of the human body by impregnating a girl who eats the vegetable. While the tale explores the idea of oral impregnation, it also suggests a continuum between human and plant vitality. Characters often resemble caricatures as they are minimally described, often with one or two exaggerated features. The grotesque in setsuwa reveals the weaknesses of people as well. Little is pure or ornate. Moreover, a terrible grotesque and a sportive grotesque are apparent, and they often inform each other. As I discuss in Chapter 4, the demon or *oni* can be amusing or fearsome, or a combination of both. Finally, the question of how the grotesque intersects with reality arises often during the many centuries of grotesque theory, and grotesque representations add to the already complicated relationship of fact and fiction in setsuwa.

Although Bakhtin draws from earlier theories of the grotesque, he presents his own as a corrective, intended to supersede the interpretations of Rabelais, the carnival tradition, and grotesque imagery by the Romantics and later scholars. Despite Kayser's effort to present the grotesque as having transhistorical and transcultural elements, Bakhtin asserts that, strictly speaking, Kayser's theory applies only to modernist forms.[119] Not only does the grotesque in the medieval context fail to instill a fear of life in people, but also life and death are not even opposed to each other. Laughter acquires in the modern world a derisive, cynical, and even satanic tone. The grotesque also takes on a private character from around the eighteenth century. As its focus shifts from the group to the isolated individual, the carnival spirit is "transposed into a subjective, idealistic philosophy."[120] Although Bakhtin is idealistic himself (especially in his concept of carnival), he grounds what he calls "grotesque realism" in the body.

SITUATING BAKHTIN: THE BODY

The "material bodily principle" in Bakhtin can be understood in terms of "the human body with its food, drink, defecation, and sexual life" playing a predominant role.[121] Proof of its functioning and force in setsuwa can be found in how often scholars studying constructions of the body or related topics in ancient, classical, and medieval Japan cite setsuwa and in how issues involving the body and particularly its lower half frequently arise in research on setsuwa. "Black Hair and Red Trousers: Gendering the Flesh in Medieval Japan," and its Japanese version, "Nikutai to yokubō no keiro: *Konjaku monogatari shū* ni miru onna to otoko," exemplify both these tendencies. In these articles, Hitomi Tonomura addresses how constructions of sexuality are gendered in *Konjaku* and medieval Japan. However, since *Konjaku* also has numerous unremarkable or beautifully portrayed bodies similar to the majority in the most esteemed Heian literature, such as *Genji*, Tonomura actually chooses a specific type of body to consider. Although she does not refer to Bakhtin, the strange or exaggerated body with a focus on the lower half is central to her articles. Many tales she selected to illustrate the gendering of sexuality in general are best understood when considered in terms of the grotesque. While they reveal certain attitudes toward women, their focus is nonetheless on the anomalous.[122]

Numerous bodies in setsuwa are capable of transforming or performing extraordinary feats. They are delineated in concrete terms as wholes or in pieces and are very much part of the physical world. Relatively blunt language is used for the genitals and sex.[123] Grotesque representations of the body in setsuwa can be understood along Bakhtinian lines:

> The grotesque body is not separated from the rest of the world. It is not a closed, completed unit; it is unfinished, outgrows itself, transgresses its own limits. The stress is laid on those parts of the body that are open to the outside world, that is, the parts through which the world enters the body or emerges from it, or through which the body itself goes out to meet the world. This means that the emphasis is on the apertures or the convexities, or on various ramifications and offshoots: the open mouth, the genital organs, the breasts, the phallus, the potbelly, the nose.[124]

The grotesque body bleeds, decays, is penetrated or is absorbed by another body or force, or is consumed. It is open in its vulnerability: forces other than time can act upon it and change it in ways different from aging and death. Noses can grow and shrink; women can be maternal, then demons or demonic, and then motherly again; animals can be humans or monsters and later animals. The relationship of the grotesque body in setsuwa to the world is marked by a blending of boundaries: men can eat women and vice versa; birds can be murderers; foxes can be wives. There are gray areas between humans and animals as well as between spirits and humans. Since the boundaries between realms are already indistinct, the idea of transgression on the part of animals and spirits can be vague. The term "supernatural" in reference to incarnated spirits can be misleading because demons and animal spirits act in accordance with natural forces such as karma.

Bakhtin contrasts the grotesque body with classical concepts of the body in "the literary and artistic canon of antiquity"[125] and in modern canons beginning with the Renaissance. The body in Western classic canons is complete and separate from other bodies; the emphasis is on its self-sufficiency and individuality. It lacks apertures and convexities and is usually in the prime of life whereas the grotesque body is closer to the womb or the grave. The classical body never reveals inner processes that involve absorbing or ejecting, and we rarely see its death.

In classical and early medieval Japanese literature, a body less open to outside forces or relatively "closed" and the grotesque body can be seen as opposite ends of the same spectrum with many kinds of representations falling between them. Grotesque tales usually delineate various forms of desire through depictions of unrefined, humorous, and sometimes violent behaviors. Blunt language is often used. In contrast, poetry, diaries such as *Izumi Shikibu nikki* (*The Diary of Izumi Shikibu*, ca. 1008), *Genji* and other works occupying a central position canonically tend to portray sexual accessibility and activity through suggestion.[126] Some setsuwa share the same approach to the physical. Such works usually channel the appetites and passions of the body into something else: the dew or other imagery suggestive of sexual responses. Scenes involving courtly passion focus on the yearning of lovers before and after their meetings, so that, unmentioned, sexual behavior and genitalia are secondary to courtship. The body is manifested in extensions of it—in descriptions of hair and clothing among other things. Its physical and erotic nature is frequently located outside it, in poetic exchanges, genealogical connections (tying it to an elite ancestral body), and language alluding to but not graphically describing intimacy. Such bodies are valued in terms of their adherence to certain standards of beauty and are delineated hardly at all in terms of physical processes.

Moreover, the physical realities and unpleasantness of illness and death are often ignored or denied. In "Death and Salvation in *Genji Monogatari*," Aileen Gatten observes how Fujitsubo, Murasaki, and Ōigimi remain beautiful even after they approach death and die and addresses the relationship of death scenes in *Genji* to setsuwa about people born in the Pure Land.[127] Such tales, *ōjōden*, tell us instead of the beauty of the terminally ill and recently dead, and also of wondrous signs indicating that the deceased reached the Pure Land: celestial music, lovely fragrances, golden or bright light, and purple or five-colored clouds around the body. Beauty in death emphasizes the eminent spirituality of the deceased. Some corpses remain lifelike and odorless while others vanish, the ultimate negation of corporeality.[128]

The valuing of sexual play distinguishes the relatively closed body in classical and early medieval works from its Western counterpart. In contrast to what we find in European literature as understood by Bakhtin, even relatively closed bodies are usually assumed sexually active and accessible. Yet, since the sexual activity must be inferred, the bodies cannot be called open in the Bakhtinian sense of freely interacting with other bodies and the environment. On the other hand, even a relatively closed body resistant to outside influences can be used to undermine other people and ideals. The Moon Princess Kaguyahime in *Taketori monogatari* and the woman in the related *Konjaku* tale are closed in that their suitors have no access to them. Yet, male desire is used in the stories to mock the suitors, turning, in the words of Richard Okada, "historicopolitical success into fictional amorous failure and ridicule."[129] The focus on the lower half of the body is not overt, as it would be with a representation closer to the grotesque end of the spectrum, but the use of sexual desire and determination to undermine powerful men subtly links these stories to those with glaringly grotesque representations.

SITUATING BAKHTIN, II:
TRANSPOSING THE CARNIVALESQUE

Bakhtin's concept of the grotesque is interwoven with his understanding of the medieval carnival as "a completely different, nonofficial, extraecclesiastical and extrapolitical aspect of the world, of man, and of human relations."[130] Medieval European carnivals such as the Feast of Fools and the Feast of the Ass have a basis in historical reality, although some scholars question the accuracy of Bakhtin's interpretation of them. According to Bakhtin, during certain times of the year, nearly everyone in society regardless of class or gender could participate in activities where all hierarchical precedence is suspended, allowing for communication to be "frank and free," unburdened by the norms of etiquette and decency.[131] An ambiguous laughter shared by and directed at all marks the carnival; the atmosphere is gay and triumphant but also mocking and deriding. The carnival is a pure expression of the tradition of folk humor, which Rabelais inherits and supposedly brings to fulfillment.[132]

Although most documented festivities of the Nara and Heian periods were enjoyed exclusively by aristocrats, many apparently have folk origins.[133] During the ancient *utagaki* (song-fence) festivals, young people may have freely sung, danced, and engaged in sex. Additionally, Kawaguchi Hisao has described the popular Buddhist services of China and Japan as carnivals (written with the *katakana kānibaru*), referring to the entertainment for aristocrats such as storytelling, plays, and musical performances.[134] Still, the documentation is scarce. Without any way of knowing the extent to which festivals allowed for a breakdown in existing hierarchies and dominant ideologies, if at all, or when commoners were involved, we had best focus on the metaphorical implications of the carnival.

The carnivalesque pertains to a communal space in literature and art allowing for social subversions. In a carnivalesque way, many setsuwa offer "temporary liberation from the prevailing truth and from the established order."[135] Highly respected figures—emperors and empresses, retired emperors, holy men, and members of aristocratic families such as the Fujiwara— are rendered foolish or vulnerable. Humorous or bizarre forms are frequently opposed to serious tenets and official practices. In some instances, a tale may have developed years or even decades after the facts, reflecting earlier resentments or grudges, so that the liberation may have been completely psychological.

If, as generally thought, most people in the Heian and early Kamakura periods regardless of social class or occupation heard at least some tales, then setsuwa would have sometimes served as places where the minds and hearts of commoners, aristocrats of different ranks and roles, and Buddhist practitioners with various affiliations or none at all could meet. As with European carnivals, they could be considered communal space. If the theory that aristocrats were the only or main audiences of setsuwa is correct instead, we might view setsuwa as a hypothetical carnivalesque realm for aristocrats and Buddhists. Such a realm demands that aristocrats consider commoners and even allows them to imagine a commonality or connection with people from different socioeconomic classes—with people other Heian literature generally ignores and therefore renders invisible. The stories did not have to be true or free of biases to begin eroding the insularity of the aristocratic world. Setsuwa prove that almost any kind of person can be at the center of an interesting experience or event. Moreover, people have an equal chance at rebirth in the Pure Land. If some tales did in fact come from commoners, aristocrats could also learn from them, just as they did from Indian and Chinese people.

Many setsuwa can be treated imperfectly as carnivalesque realms, resembling but falling short of the Bakhtinian ideal. In *Rabelais and His World*, the carnival and the carnivalesque hold all social distinctions in abeyance and allow for the temporary destruction of the truths of society. The only truth about the world is its "unfinalizability": the state of nothing ever being completed or finished. Opposed to the official feast, "carnival was the true feast of time, the feast of becoming, change, and renewal. It was hostile to all that was immortalized and completed."[136] Its principle of laughter and high spirits "frees human consciousness, thought, and imagination for new potentialities."[137] The attacks on socially and politically dominant people, prevailing ideologies, and established hierarchies are not as extreme as in the carnival imagined by Bakhtin. Grotesque elements within the carnivalesque realm of setsuwa rarely result in "the suspension of all hierarchical rank, privileges, norms, and prohibitions,"[138] but they destabilize them.

Bakhtin sees a somewhat different purpose in the challenge of the grotesque to the existing order in "Forms of Time and of the Chronotope in the Novel."[139] Gary Saul Morson and Caryl Emerson called this second version of the principle "responsible carnival."[140] In *Mikhail Bakhtin, Creation of a Prosaics*, they explain that laughter and the carnival in that essay are "tied down to concrete personalities in a recognizably real space and time. . . . Carnival in this redaction is directed toward affirmative, positive, and humanist action to be undertaken within the historical process."[141] It is part of the transition from the medieval world to the Renaissance seen traditionally as a progressive step in European history.

The teleological sense of the carnival and of Rabelais has little relevance for the grotesque in setsuwa. Yet, the pretense of historical truth about recognizable people, places, and events marks the narratives. In numerous tales, the undermining of authority and dominant ideologies foreshadows actual social and political change, such as a society dominated by warriors and new or reshaped forms of Buddhist thought. It is affirmative, positive, and humanistic in how it moves toward shattering silences and giving more people voices.

Yet, "the claims Bakhtin offers for carnival laughter are themselves extravagant and 'Rabelaisian,'" write Morson and Emerson.[142] Peter Stallybrass and Allon White have somberly pointed out problems "concerning the politics of the carnival: its nostalgia; its uncritical populism (carnival often violently abuses and demonizes *weaker*, not stronger, social groups—women, ethnic and religious minorities, those who 'don't belong'—in a process of *displaced abjection*); its failure to do away with the official dominant culture, its licensed complicity."[143] These observations and others pave the way for alternative approaches to the carnivalesque by suggesting that the carnival differed from what Bakhtin imagined.[144] The idealism of Bakhtin is open to attack not in the least because people in power sanctioned the carnival. Similarly, appropriating an idealistic vision of the carnivalesque would cause problems in this study. Since people in positions of authority were probably instrumental in creating most setsuwa collections, the tales could not have been completely liberating. Although setsuwa broadened the horizons of the imagination and literature, their impact on social and political change was limited.

Bakhtin's insistence on festive laughter and on the absence of terror and gloom in the grotesque before the Romantic period also prevents us from adopting his theories without modifying them. The Japanese grotesque has many terrifying elements, as I assert particularly in Chapters 4 and 5 about *oni* (demons). Bakhtin refuses to give anything serious or terrifying a place in the medieval and Renaissance grotesque, but he concedes only that they function in the Romantic grotesque. Since I am working in a different tradition, it is not necessary for me to determine whether or not there is a horrific and fearsome grotesque in medieval Europe and the Renaissance. Bakhtin distinguishes between "the aesthetics of the grotesque" and "the aesthetics of the monstrous,"[145] but the monstrous is integral to the grotesque in classical and medieval Japan. The analyses of individual tales will show that monsters such as flesh-eating demons function along grotesque lines.

Determining whether something is liberating or restricting involves a certain degree of subjectivity. Although Bakhtin sees carnival laughter as liberating in its antinomianism, the carnival is not a permanent realm; certain dominant ideologies and other truths resurface once the festivities are over. In any society, powerful people may tolerate or enjoy a topsy-turvy state in certain social or literary spaces precisely because, being contained, it comes with the promise of the restoration of order. Yet, the same people would be terrified by the prospect of things not returning back to so-called normal. Such is the case with many aristocrats in Heian and Kamakura Japan when they comprehend the fragility of their privileged positions in society and begin to experience their world in decline.

The comic and the terrible tend to function similarly in setsuwa: both undermine authority by directing attention to the body and other material objects. Horror in the premodern Japanese grotesque differs from what

Kayser sees in the European context. His emphasis on an alienated and estranged world, where the familiar and natural suddenly become strange and ominous, is relevant to some tales—to those describing how forlorn, beautiful women or old, comforting women turn out to be demons among others. However, the grotesque in setsuwa does not show the bitterness and cynicism of the Romantic and modern grotesque. Demons belong to this world as much as to any other. Even destructive change is part of the natural order. As Bakhtin asserts, grotesque imagery is relatively in tune with the elements and cyclical time although, over the ages, it begins to draw "into its cycle social and historic phenomena."[146]

The spiritual force governing events and people to some, usually ambiguous, extent in many setsuwa is karma: an intrinsic part of being that is neither humane nor inhumane. Audiences and characters may experience fear in part because of their inability to understand fully the workings of karma. They see people affected by it, often negatively, but not always the causes. The desire to reduce the fear of the unknown would partially account for why the commentators in setsuwa frequently provide reasons for events and do not seem to mind when the narrative portion contradicts them. Explanations for phenomena that could instead be viewed as senseless and meaningless violence or change prevent people from feeling entirely alienated or estranged. Guidance offered at the close of the tales on how to avoid gruesome and tragic fates, such as by staying away from abandoned places, seems intended to give audiences a sense of control and suggests that frightening events did not make everyone feel helpless and hopeless.

SITUATING BAKHTIN, III: THE JAPANESE GROTESQUE, THE ORAL, AND THE FOLK

According to Bakhtin, grotesque imagery and the laughter linked to it originate in the realms of folk humor and oral tradition. They are later appropriated by artists and writers, and, with negative consequences, by political and religious institutions. The grotesque in setsuwa and the humor of certain stories most likely have some connection to folk and oral traditions. Unfortunately, we have no way of familiarizing ourselves with these traditions or even just with the oral tales.

Furthermore, suppose the oral version of a tale never existed. According to Thomas Raymond Howell Jr., a key factor in the creation of setsuwa collections was the desire to gather knowledge from canonical texts and to give a broader audience access to it by representing it in a non-hierarchical way closer to the experiences of people. This goal would have come into play especially in regard to Buddhist beliefs and perceptions. Howell sees the references to an oral genesis in tales as mostly simulated, masking this goal and the fact of setsuwa being "the result of writing."[147] Creators or compilers have narrators attribute stories to oral sources even in tales that were initially written and possibly even transmitted only through writing to make them more believable or to give them greater authority, further complicating the issue of oral versus written origins.[148]

Although Howell is likely correct about numerous setsuwa, we do not have enough reason to reject the idea of oral genesis completely. Every setsuwa is the result of writing at some point, but many still could have begun as a story told aloud. A small percentage seems to have started as a kind of gossip or *seken banashi*: stories told as if they happened to someone in the society of the first audience and circulated by word of mouth. The secular section of "Tales of Japan" probably includes this type since it contains many tales that cannot be traced to likely textual origins.[149] Moreover, certain tales may have been connected to the oral in ways not necessarily related to their origins. A compiler could have learned them from oral sources even if they were also written. Practices of reading or performing stories aloud would have added yet another dimension to the oral-written debate. Co-existing oral and written traditions must have influenced each other in complex ways. There is no reason to assume that compilers would turn to texts only and exclude oral sources in seeking knowledge, be it based in doctrine or experience. The danger for researchers can lie in either extreme: forgetting that we can only hypothesize about the role of oral traditions or in making too much of textual connections.

Even if we could link certain tales to an oral tradition, we would still have to determine if they are folk—that is, from the traditions and sensibilities of commoners. Tales imported from India and China through Chinese translations of sutras and other texts obviously did not emerge from Japanese folk traditions. Despite possible roots in the folk traditions of those cultures, they start in Japan as written. The first Japanese people to be exposed to them would have been literate, either aristocratic men or Buddhist clergy. If grotesque representations have precedents in *Kojiki* or other early works, any connection of them to the folk would be once or more removed from the source. Finally, tales often include details that commoners are not likely to have known, such as the name of an imperial physician. They may concern tensions between different aristocrats and aristocratic groups, between Buddhist monks and aristocrats, or between different types of Buddhists. As my analyses of many stories will demonstrate, certain individuals and groups among the elite apparently needed ways of transcending aspects of official discourse, which is not monolithic. These people could have drawn on folk traditions to create their own tales or may have appropriated grotesque elements from other texts with links to oral folk tradition, but it is impossible to know for sure. Questions about the relation of these representations to folk culture and the oral tradition lack satisfying answers.

CONCLUSION

Although many aspects of grotesque theory enrich our understanding of certain strange creatures and events in setsuwa, Bakhtin provides the most promising starting point for a study of the grotesque in setsuwa in his focus on the material body. Given the diversity of the narratives we call setsuwa, it makes sense to move beyond questions like "what is setsuwa" and instead consider prominent features of groups of narratives and the idiosyncrasies of individual tales. Since the genre of setsuwa is a single beast comprised of heterogeneous parts, we limit ourselves when talking about its illusive unified whole. We need many approaches to come to terms with the different aspects of it and the tales. And so, I will now turn my attention to the most unusual body parts.

CHAPTER 2

Fantastic Detached Body Parts

What could be more bizarre than body parts acting independently from bodies: severed heads biting at each other in a kettle of boiling water or a small hand beckoning from the knothole in a pillar? Where else but in literature can penises be magically detached without causing permanent injury to the men who lose them? These representations from *Konjaku* and *Uji shūi* have historical and political dimensions. The analyses of the three tales below will show how the detached body parts undermine and degrade people or institutions in or previously in positions of authority and thus officially exalted. While also being largely concerned with vulnerability and loss, the three tales are marked by a resistance to authority and, in this sense, provide "temporary liberation from the prevailing truth and from the established order" in a way similar to Bakhtin's carnival.[1] This tension is not apparent from a cursory reading, but becomes evident only by closely examining narrative details and by putting the tales into dialogue with other historic and literary texts.

Before turning to these tales, I will distinguish between the detached body parts studied in depth in this chapter and other types. While the specific fantastic representations of heads, hand, and penises discussed here contribute to defining the grotesque in the Japanese context, the same cannot be said of all dismembered or otherwise absent body parts in setsuwa and related works of literature. Some detached body parts point more to the tragic than the grotesque—and here I use *tragic* in the common sense of the word, as we might to describe our own news stories about the mutilations of innocent people. Consider the story of a young woman who leaves her child behind with beggars to escape being raped:

How a Woman Abducted by Beggars Abandons Her Child and Flees

Now it is the past; in [ ]² county, the province of [ ], two beggars are traveling through the mountains on the same path as a young woman, who walks ahead of them carrying a child. The woman realizes the beggars are approaching her and moves to the side to let them pass, but they both stop short.

"Hurry up and go," she says. Since they do not go ahead, the woman has no choice but to walk again in front of them. Then one beggar runs up and grabs her. She has no way to resist them, alone in the middle of the mountains.

"Please, what are you going to do to me?" she says.

A beggar replies, "Now, move over there. We have something to say to you."

Then he drags her deeper into the woods against her will, while the second beggar keeps lookout. When the woman says, "Please stop being so awful; I will listen to whatever you have to say," the beggar answers, "OK, great. And now, well, well."

Then the woman says, "How can you do such a thing to a person—even if we are here deep in the mountains? Please pile up the wood or something and hide us."

"Umm, that's right," thinks the beggar and begins cutting down thick tree branches. The second beggar thinks, "Won't the woman run away?" and stands right in front of her keeping guard.

The woman says, "I promise not to run away. But I've been having stomach troubles I can't control since this morning; I want to step right over there and do something. Please, just give me a moment." But the beggar says, "Absolutely not."

Then the woman says, "I'll leave this child as a hostage. I cherish this child more than myself. Everyone in this world, regardless of his or her status, understands how dear a child is to a parent. So, of course, I would never do anything like abandon this child and run away," and "It's just that I was about to stop and take care of my business when we were over there before because I couldn't bear my upset stomach any longer. I tried to let you two pass."

And so the beggar takes the child and holds him, thinking, "Whatever the case, she certainly won't abandon the child and run." Then he says, "Hurry up and come right back."

The women thinks, "I'll go far away and pretend to be doing what I said, then I'll leave my child and escape." She flees, running and running until she reaches a path.

Just then arrives a band of four or five warriors on horseback, carrying bows and arrows. Seeing the woman running and out of breath, they ask, "Why are you running like that?"

The woman says, "I am running away because of . . ." and explains.

"Where are those guys?" say the warriors and, following the woman's directions, ride their horses into the mountains. They find the wood piled up at the site she described, but the beggars are gone and the child is torn into two or three pieces, so it is too late to do anything.

The warriors admire the woman for thinking, "The child is indeed very dear to me, but still I won't let beggars touch me," and then abandoning her child to flee. Thus there are people among the lower classes with a sense of honor. And so the tale is told and passed down.[3]

Here, the butchered body is unsurprisingly lifeless. There is no question about whether or not the incident could have occurred. Although the warriors admire the woman for sacrificing her child to avoid her own physical degradation, the brutal murder of the child, especially without any karmic explanation, lacks the positive and regenerating aspect Bakhtin saw as fundamental to the grotesque. It is shocking that the commentator can offer only the sentiment of the warriors in conclusion.[4]

From the point of view of the compiler, commentator, or both, the main value of the story lies in its illustration of what a certain woman would do to avoid sexual assault by beggars. This focus diverts attention away from the horror of such experiences for women and children, yet the tale gives us insight into their vulnerability when traveling in the hills and mountains of Heian period Japan (794–1185, but the focus on the values of warriors suggests its second half). The tale raises many questions: Would an average Heian woman act in this way to preserve her honor or does the description of her words and behavior merely illustrate the values of warriors, the commentator, and other men? Would she have internalized the view, perhaps shared by the people in her society, of a sexual assault bringing shame to the victim? If a child is as dear to a parent as she asserts, how could she leave him or her behind? The story is about much more than the commentator acknowledges. There probably were women who lost children to heartless men on journeys through isolated places, but we have to listen beyond the didacticism of the commentator to hear their cries—or rather, shrieks of terror and despair. While the story appears to have been appropriated for other reasons, its tragic content may have also moved early audiences.

One possible way of reading subtle grotesque elements into the story would be to see intended irony in the final comments. Perhaps the absurdity of the focus given what happened is meant paradoxically to illustrate the horrific side of warrior values, which put honor before life and even enable a mother to sacrifice her beloved child rather callously. The commentator, compilers, and audience would then lament how such values permeate the lives of ordinary people, even of the lower classes, rather than embrace them.

While the view of honor endorsed by the warriors seems undermined by the tragic consequences of adhering to it, the realism of the murder and its discovery weaken any reading of the tale along grotesque lines. The loss of a child rather than the severed parts is what challenges the stance of the warriors. While the cruelty of the beggars is emphasized by the dismembering, an intact corpse would have been enough to raise questions about the warrior sense of virtue. This story is haunting because of the absence rather than inclusion of supernatural elements. A different reading would be required had the killers some connection to the world of spirits.

Many representations of severed heads can be found in setsuwa about warriors and *gunki monogatari* (longer martial tales), but most do not function in a grotesque mode. In episodes describing the beheading of people such as Taira no Masakado in a *Konjaku* tale or of warriors in *Heike*, the heads serve as trophies, often displayed on the prison fence or paraded through the capital.[5] They are generally realistic, underscoring the gruesomeness of the battlefield during the Heian and Kamakura periods. One decapitation in *Konjaku* involves a dispute between individuals. Minamoto no Yorinobu orders Taira no Sadamichi to behead a certain man who has offended him. Sadamichi initially decides to spare the life of the man, but later changes his mind when the man reacts to his kindness by suggesting that Sadamichi could not kill him anyway. The beheading of this man merely confirms the status quo.[6] Such representations cannot be considered grotesque because the boundaries between the realms of humans and other spirits and beings are never crossed. Additionally, the sense of violence and death these representations convey far outweighs any suggestion of transformation or rebirth.

Often a body part is left behind by a hungry demon (*oni*): the head of a king by a female creature in *Uji shūi*, the head of a government official who goes to work too early in *Konjaku*, and the head and finger of a new bride in *Nihon ryōiki* and *Konjaku*.[7] The grotesque in these examples cannot be explored mainly in terms of the remains of the victims since there is nothing magical or even unusual about them. Rather, it must be understood in relationship to the particular role of *oni* in challenging the human social order, a subject addressed in Chapter 4.

Lastly, the detached body parts studied in this chapter differ from those we see in the Buddhist hells portrayed in tales or in artwork such as *Scroll of Hells* (*Jigoku zōshi*). In one tale, an aristocrat finds himself in hell because he copied sutras for the deceased without first purifying himself or practicing abstinence. He faces the punishment of being sliced up into two hundred pieces, each with the ability to feel pain.[8] A scene in *Jigoku zōshi* depicts "monks who have broken the precept against killing. They are being chopped up as finely as sand by demons sitting at low table-sized cutting boards. When the demons chant '*katsu, katsu,*' the minced flesh gradually gathers and transforms into its original form. Then the bodies are again turned into mincemeat."[9] The painting shows the bodies at different stages in the process; there are detached heads and limbs strewn on the chopping boards. Such representations are less carnivalesque than many other grotesque representations because of their potential for instilling horror and fear in people. There is humor in them, too, but it is usually hostile or sadistic. To explore such representations in terms of the grotesque, we must draw upon pre-Bakhtinian theories addressing the terrible and fearsome, such as Kayser's, as I do later in the chapters centered on demons. Having briefly shown how fantastic detached body parts differ from those that are not magical, I will now move on to the analyses of tales.

BATTLING HEADS

In "How Moye of China Makes a Sword and Presents It to the King and How His Son, Broad-of-Brow, Is Killed," the severed heads function in conjunction with other representations to depict the toppling of a king. The fall of the king is only partially connected to the will of human beings—to the smith, Moye, and his son. It is accomplished instead predominantly through the power of a spirit. The tale ultimately suggests the triumph of resistance and revenge, even while most of the characters serving as instruments of these forces die. A translation of the tale reads:

*How Moye of China Makes a Sword and Presents It to the King
and How His Son, Broad-of-Brow, Is Killed*

Now it is the past; in China during the reign of [ ], there is a person called Moye who is a smith. At the time, the consort of the king constantly embraces an iron pillar because she finds the summer heat unbearable. Soon she becomes pregnant and gives birth, but one look reveals it is to an iron ball spirit. Thinking this odd, the king asks, "What on earth happened?"

"I have done absolutely nothing wrong. Being unable to endure the summer heat, I simply embraced an iron pillar. Do you suppose . . . that might have been why?"

Deciding that had to be the reason, the king has the smith, Moye, summoned, and orders him to make a precious sword with the iron that was born. Moye makes two swords with the iron entrusted to him and presents one to the king while hiding the other. When the king goes to store the sword he received from Moye, it cries incessantly. Perplexed by this, the king asks his minister. "Why do you think the sword is crying?"

The minister replies, "The sword is definitely crying for a reason. It must be one of a pair, husband and wife. I suppose the one cries yearning for the other."

When the king hears this answer, he is very angry and immediately has Moye summoned for punishment. Before the official has reached Moye's house, Moye speaks to his wife, saying, "I saw an evil omen last night. An official of the king is sure to come and will doubtless put me to death. If the child you are carrying is a boy, tell him to look in the pine tree on the southern mountain once he has grown up." Then Moye leaves through the northern gate, enters the southern mountains and hides within a huge tree. Finally, he dies there.

Afterwards, his wife gives birth to a boy. By the time the child turns fifteen, he has a one-*shaku* space between his eyebrows.[10] So, he is given the name Broad-of-Brow. His mother tells him all the details of his father's last request. He follows her instructions and looks to find a sword. He takes it, determined to take revenge on his father's enemies. Meanwhile, the king has a dream: a person in the land with a *shaku* space between his eyebrows is plotting to murder him. Awakening very fearful, the king immediately issues an imperial edict to be sent in all four directions of the land: "Somewhere in society, there is sure to be a person with a *shaku* space between his eyebrows. I will reward whoever captures him and brings me his head with a thousand pieces of gold."

Soon after, Broad-of-Brow happens to hear of this and flees deep into the mountains to hide. The fellows who received the proclamation are searching everywhere within their stride and reach, and in all four directions, when Broad-of-Brow encounters one of the king's men in the mountains. The official sees that he has a one-*shaku* space between his eyebrows. Delighted, he asks, "Are you the person known as Broad-of-Brow?" "I am he," is the reply. The official says, "We received an imperial edict demanding your head and the sword in your possession." Then Broad-of-Brow severs his own head with his sword and hands it to the official, who goes back and presents it to the king. The king rejoices and rewards the official.

Afterwards, the king hands the head of Broad-of-Brow over to the official. "We must quickly boil this head to a pulp." Following the king's orders, the official places the head in a kettle, where it boils for seven days, but does not even begin to disintegrate. The official reports what happened to the king, who thinking it odd, goes over to the kettle to check for himself. When the king looks, his own head falls off spontaneously, dropping into the kettle. The two heads bite at and fight each other to no end. Thinking it strange as he watches, the official throws the sword into the kettle to weaken the head of Broad-of-Brow. Instantly, the two heads both disintegrate. When the official looks in the kettle again, his own head drops off and falls into it. The three heads get all mixed up together and there is no way of telling them apart. So, a single grave is made and the three heads are buried together.

To this very day, the grave is in a district called Yichun. And so the story is told and passed down.[11]

The *Konjaku* compiler and several others place the story of Broad-of-Brow in clusters or collections of tales on filial piety because they focus on it as a story about a son avenging his father. Modern scholars often follow their lead in how they comment on the various versions of the tale.[12] However, this categorization minimizes the subversive implications of the plot—namely, the political violence implicit in the deception and murder of the king. Broad-of-Brow's behavior is less threatening when it is explained in terms of an officially sanctioned principle.

Nothing appears to be written on the *Konjaku* tale per se, but many scholars have contributed research relevant to the study of it. They treat it as part of a group: one tale of many, both Chinese and Japanese, in setsuwa collections and elsewhere.[13] These tales mention the swords and one or more of the following characters: the smith, the smith's wife, and the son with the wide space between his eyebrows. The name of the smith varies: besides being Moye, he is sometimes Ganjiang Moye or Ganjiang with a wife named Moye. These tales resemble the *Konjaku* tale in varying degrees, ranging from sharing a few plot elements to being almost identical. In the Chinese context, they are included in such texts as *Yuejueshu* (*The Book of Yue*, ca. 52 C.E.),

Wuyue chunqiu (*The Spring and Autumn Annals of Wu and Yue*, mid-first century C.E.), *Lieyizhuan* (*Arrayed Marvels*, ca. early-third century C.E.), collections of *Xiaozizhuan* (*Tales of Filial Children*, mostly adult sons, 100–600), *Soushenji* (*In Search of Spirits*, ca. 335–49), *Fayuan zhulin* (*Forest of Pearls from the Garden of the Law*, 668), and *Taiping huanyuji* (*Taiping Geographical Record*, ca. from 980).[14] In Japan, they are in *Hōbutsu shū* (*Collection of Buddhist Treasures*, ca. 1200), *Taiheiki* (*Chronicle of Grand Pacification*, ca. 1372), *Soga monogatari* (*The Tale of the Soga Brothers*, ca. 1400), and *Sangoku denki* (*Legends of the Three Lands*, between 1407 and 1446).[15]

The *Konjaku* tale closely resembles tales in two Chinese collections centered on filial children extant only in Japanese manuscripts. The first, *Yōmei bunko shozō kōshiden* (*Tales of Filial Piety* in the Yōmei collection), is a Kamakura period manuscript of a forty-five-tale text acquired in either the Heian or the Kamakura period. *Kiyohara-ke bon kōshiden* (*Tales of Filial Piety* in the Kiyohara house manuscript), is probably a revision of this text from a later period.[16] As with the *Konjaku* story, the tales in these two collections include the encounter of the consort and the pillar while other Chinese versions do not.

The research on this group, which I call "the Moye tales," is marked by an interest either in outlining the development of the tales or in determining what elements of a tale were appropriated from where. Yet, most scholars admit more data are missing than available. In "Kansho Bakuya setsuwa no tenkai" ("The Evolution of the Tale of Ganjiang and Moye"), Hosoya Sōko expounds one theory of how the tales evolved. The course of development she constructs can be roughly outlined as follows: The earliest extant tale in *Yuejueshu* celebrates the forging of excellent swords for the king by Ganjiang and another smith. The focus then shifts in the *Wuyue chunqiu* tale. That tale centers on the forging of the swords—on how Ganjiang and his wife struggle to make them for the king. In the next phase, tales introduce Broad-of-Brow and, along with him, the idea of a son seeking to avenge his father against the king. Included in many extant texts, the tale in this form supposedly merges with a separate tale explaining the origin of an actual grave—hence the ending of the story.

Hosoya concedes her explication is limited because of the probable loss of numerous oral and written texts over time, yet provides an exaggerated sense of progression and continuity between what survived. She also privileges the *Soushenji* tale, treating the earlier extant tales as stages in the process of that particular rendering. Her article exhibits the problems of attempting to trace precisely how individual tales developed, namely filling in too many blanks and adopting a teleological approach. Yet, she meticulously takes note of all the similarities and differences between tales, some subtle and easy to miss. Such observations can be used instead to explore how the king in the *Konjaku* tale is degraded. The details of one tale can deepen our insight into another by providing new possibilities for interpretation.

Broad-of-Brow does not die a victim by allowing the official to decapitate him but instead is empowered by doing it himself. His body then accomplishes the remarkable feat of standing and handing its own head, the trophy, over to the king's official. The power of the spirits, that of the deceased Broad-of-Brow, and of the iron, is manifested not only here, but also in the failure of Broad-of-Brow's head to dissolve. This resistance to the obliteration of identity, revealed by the face and particularly the brow with this young man, leads to the bizarre decapitation of the king.

A tale depicting the fall of an authority figure would have had relevance for Japanese audiences during the late Heian and early Kamakura periods, as they were experiencing the weakening of the aristocratic class and changes in the social order. The king is literally and figuratively decrowned: he loses both his head and status. Although the decapitation of the king takes place suddenly at the end of the tale, the undermining of his authority occurs gradually through the pregnancy of the consort, the withholding of the sword, the decapitation, and the burial of his head with the heads of the other two men, especially with that of his would-be murderer. As previously mentioned, the destruction of the king depends on both the spirit of iron and the determination of a son to avenge his father.

The encounter of the consort with the iron pillar is sexual. The inability of the woman to bear the heat may or may not suggest sexual excitement, but the fact that she becomes pregnant leaves the nature of her experience unquestionable. In *Yōmei bunko shozō kōshiden*, the consort in the nearly identical tale "plays" when embracing the pillar (*xi* in Chinese and *tawamureru* in Japanese).[17] Moreover, a line in *Kiyohara-ke bon kōshiden* reads: "The spirit of the iron has a feeling and the consort ultimately gets pregnant" ("Tiejing you gan, sui nai huairen / Kurogane no tama wa kanzuru tokoro ga atte, tsui ni kainin shi").[18] It is not clear who is doing the feeling here—the consort, the spirit, or both—but the pillar in the *kōshiden* and *Konjaku* is in some sense animate.

The sexual dimension of this tale seems partially connected to the fact that the earlier extant Chinese tales about the smith named Ganjiang or Moye are linked to the Iron Age as part of the metallurgical mythology of the two ancient states Wu and Yue. In *Iron and Steel in Ancient China*, Donald B. Wagner discusses the "view of the alloying of bronze as a sexual union" implicit in a *Yuejueshu* tale.[19] He then makes a connection between that tale and the *Wuyue chunqiu* tale about Ganjiang and his wife, Moye. The couple initially has trouble getting the metal and iron to "melt, sink, and flow."[20] Ganjiang explains that, long ago, metal and iron did not melt unless husband and wife entered the furnace together. Ganjiang and Moye do not take that drastic step, but Moye ends up throwing her cut hair and clipped fingernails into the fire, where "three hundred maidens and youths work the bellows and charge the coals."[21] Two swords—one yin and the other yang—are successfully produced as a result. In *Wudiji* (*The Record of the Wu Area*, ca. ninth century), the wife "enters the furnace herself to marry the Furnace Guard."[22]

The pillar's impregnation of the consort is an aggressive act against the king in *Konjaku*. When the king confronts the consort, she replies, "I have done absolutely nothing wrong." This response raises the question of what she is denying. The consort undermines the influence and authority of the king, revealing him to be someone whose actions lead to the birth of something he did not father. The Chinese compound for the newborn is *tiejing* 鉄精, a word that is defined in many ways: "powdered iron," "iron scoria or cinder," "iron essence," and "a spirit of iron."[23] The Japanese reading, *kurogane no tama*, suggests the additional interpretation of "iron ball." However, the rendering of the word as "ball," as in Ury's translation, does not give the whole picture since the iron is more than a material object.[24] When the king orders Moye to forge a sword, the iron is described as *shōjitaru kurogane*: "the iron that was born" or "is alive." The same Chinese character, *tama* or more typically *tamashii*, is frequently associated with a spirit. In tale 5 of *Konjaku* Book 27, it refers to a water spirit who rises from a garden pool as a small old man and touches the faces of sleeping people.[25] In the *Taiheiki* version of the Moye tale, the consort gives birth to an iron ball, *tetsugan*, which the king declares is a spirit, *seirei*.[26] The line in the *Yōmei bunko kōshiden* about the iron pillar and a feeling also indicates that seeing the *tama* as only a ball is insufficient: the consort would not be physically sensing the object before her pregnancy. The magical aspect of the story should not be lost in translation. At once a spirit and material object, the "child" suggests transformation. Given that the early versions of the tale have a connection to the Iron Age, one allusion is to how the discovery of iron changed the nature of agriculture and warfare.

Narita Mamoru attributes the success of the revenge to Broad-of-Brow's spirit. Depending on which Moye tale is in question, he perceives it as driven either by devotion or by an angry obsession intense enough to transform the deceased Broad-of-Brow into a vengeful spirit.[27] However, the weakening of the king begins before the appearance of the young man. If the spirit of Broad-of-Brow causes the beheading of the king and his official, it is only after another spirit has made that revenge possible. Who equalizes the men in death by rendering their heads indistinguishable from one another if not the spirit of the iron—the spirit of the sword? The presence of that spirit would partially or fully explain the many other extraordinary events in the story as well: the crying sword, the premonitory dreams of Moye and the king, the ability of the corpse of Broad-of-Brow to remain standing and hand over its own head, the failure of the decapitated head of Broad-of-Brow to disintegrate, the way the heads of the king and his official drop off, their biting and fighting, and the power of the sword to make them disintegrate.

It is not surprising to find swords in the symbolic landscape of a tale about the decrowning of a king. The process continues with the decision of the smith to hide one weapon. Moye's act of withholding further suggests that the king wrongly claims paternal rights to the iron. The subversive implications are apparent: can a king have command in a kingdom where the iron does not belong to him and where people are concealing weapons? The smith is summoned from a different land in some earlier Moye tales, so in them Moye's act may refer to tension between different Chinese states. In *Konjaku*, Moye seems to be a subject of the king since nothing indicates otherwise. His defiance can thus be linked to internal conflict—a more relevant issue for Japanese in the late Heian and early Kamakura periods.

The decapitated heads suggest conflicts depicted in Chinese histories. Hosoya connects the tale to a group of peasant insurgents who defeated the troops of Wang Mang (45–23 B.C.E.) and succeeded in gaining control of the lower basin of the Yellow River.[28] These rebels supposedly painted their eyebrows red to recognize each other. This theory would seem farfetched except that the Chinese character for red and the measurement used for the brow (*shaku* in Japanese) have the same pronunciation: *chi*.[29] In certain versions of the tale in Chinese collections of tales of filial piety, the smith's son has a one-*chi* space between his eyebrows but is named Red Nose. After being introduced, he is simply called Chi, the measurement. Hosoya attributes this switch to an orthographic error. She supports her hypothesis with the descriptions of the smith's son in *Lieshizhuan* (*Arrayed Lives of Great Men*, last century B.C.E.) and the previously mentioned *Lieyizhuan*.[30] In those books, the forehead is only three *cun* (Japanese *sun*) wide (about three and a half inches). At some point, someone may have accidentally or intentionally substituted the measurement for the color.[31] The possibility of this modification allows us to perceive one more connection. According to a reference in chapter 12 of *Taiping huanyuji*, a now non-extant text called *Beiwangji* (*Records of a Northern Journey*) states that a person called Red Eyebrows and another man assassinated King Hui of Liang. All three men were buried together at a place later known as the Grave of the Three Kings.

There is also a link between this tale and the biography of Wu Zixu in *Shiji* (*Records of the Historian*, 109–91 B.C.E.).[32] In chapter 36, the Lesser Tutor at court talks the king of Chu into marrying a woman initially intended for the prince and later convinces the king that the prince is planning to revolt out of resentment. The Grand Tutor, who is the father of Wu Zixu, defends the prince and condemns the Lesser Tutor, but his remarks only anger the king. The king hopes to kill Wu Zixu along with his father and brother but he manages to escape from the imperial envoys. He seeks to avenge his father and brother after the king of Chu unjustly executes them.[33]

Later in the biography, Wu Zixu becomes the enemy of the king of Wu. Broad-of-Brow's self-decapitation in *Konjaku* evokes the scene in *Shiji* when he cuts his own throat after this king condemns him to death.[34] Immediately before, Wu Zixu orders his retainers to hang his eyes on the eastern gate of Wu to enable him to watch the Yue soldiers destroy that state. The three heads in the *Konjaku* tale symbolize Wu Zixu and the two kings he angers. In addition, *Ishinpō* (*Prescriptions at the Heart of Medicine*), a Japanese medical text based on Chinese sources completed by Tanba no Yasuyori (912–95) in 984, indicates that Wu Zixu had a one-*shaku* space between his eyebrows.[35] The status of Broad-of-Brow is elevated by an allusion to this brave, determined man. The *Konjaku* does not describe Broad-of-Brow other than to mention the wide space between his eyebrows, but the ancient Chinese believed that this facial feature, exaggerated here, was characteristic of men of excellence.[36] The person who threatens the king is thus marked as someone with superior qualities. In many tales, the grave is even called the Grave of the Three Kings, indicating that the king's enemy is posthumously considered an equal.

Yet the defining feature of Broad-of-Brow also gives him away. The space between his eyebrows stands out in the king's dream and allows the official to identify him as the wanted man. The tale hardly celebrates the greatness of Broad-of-Brow as the head bearing that mark of distinction is boiled beyond recognition. Bakhtin's understanding of how praise and abuse function in the grotesque is helpful here. To him, they are "two sides of the same coin. . . . The praise . . . is ironic and ambivalent. It is on the brink of abuse; the one leads to the other, and it is impossible to draw the line between the two."[37] Along with Moye, Broad-of-Brow is praised and killed.

Once the official tracks Broad-of-Brow down, the king seems to have the advantage over the man of excellence. Then strange things happen. The ability of the headless Broad-of-Brow to hand over his own head is the first in a series of bizarre events focused on the severed head. The person who receives the head varies from tale to tale. He is not an official in the two *kōshiden* transmitted to Japan or in *Soushenji*, but instead a traveler who offers to help Broad-of-Brow avenge his father. Still a stranger, he is an enemy of the king in *Soga monogatari* and a friend of the deceased father in *Taiheiki*. As Hosoya suggests, Broad-of-Brow's suicide is more clearly an act of devotion in those texts: he cuts off his own head because the stranger promises to kill the king. The headless body does not fall over until the stranger reassures him in *Soushenji*.[38] This will to remain alive long enough to be reassured attests to Broad-of-Brow's sense of purpose in death. In contrast, it is unclear why the *Konjaku* Broad-of-Brow makes no attempt to escape or fight and is so willing to destroy himself.

The king is decapitated while checking on the head of his enemy. When the heads begin ferociously fighting each other, the official throws the sword Moye had hidden into the kettle. The *Konjaku* narrator states that the official hopes to weaken the head of Broad-of-Brow, reminding the audiences where his loyalty lies. Rather than side with the official, the spirit of the sword instead allows for his beheading. But although the spirit is politically aligned with Broad-of-Brow, it quickly becomes neutral. All the heads disintegrate. Moye and Broad-of-Brow die in their refusal to acknowledge the authority of the king, but their actions are not meditated. A mysterious and mighty force working through them orchestrates the decrowning. In other words, they are never more than instruments to be discarded once the mission is accomplished. The toppling of the king suggests political transformation, but whatever the new order, the deceased cannot benefit.

The grotesque may appear to favor the common people, rebels, and the underdogs of the upper classes when setsuwa focus on the elite, but any initial bias toward particular people or institutions is rarely sustained. It simply cannot be because once empowered, those people, too, invite debasement if they survive.

The next tale concerns a man destroyed politically before he flourishes. It only alludes to this political emasculation and speaks instead the language of nightmare, of helplessness, and of bittersweet torment.

THE BECKONING HAND

In this story, a mysterious little hand appearing at night from the knothole of a wooden pillar does not belong to a Kaguyahime (a tiny girl discovered inside bamboo) or a Momotarō (a baby boy hid within a large peach), as evoked by the concept of a tiny being dwelling inside a concealed space.[39] The hole and the characterization of the hand as a small child's link this tale to others about small people found in hollow areas, but here we have a nightmarish version of discovering a tiny creature in a would-be void.

How the Hand of a Child Reaches Out From a Hole in a Pillar at Momozono Mansion and Beckons to People

Now it is the past; present-day Sesonji Temple is still the Momozono Mansion. Nishinomiya Minister of the Left is living there, when it has yet to become a temple. There is an open knothole in a pillar southeast in the central room of the main hall. Upon nightfall, the hand of a small child reaches out from this hole and beckons to people! When the minister hears about it, he is very perplexed by its strangeness and alarmed. He ties a sutra over the hole, but even then, the hand continues to beckon. He hangs a picture of a Buddha over the hole but the beckoning continues. He experiments with many things in this way, but the hand simply does not stop. After two or three nights, it predictably beckons around midnight when everyone is fast asleep.

Meanwhile, another person decides to try something else: he pokes a single war arrow into the hole and the beckoning stops as long as the arrow remains inserted. And so next, he detaches the shaft and pushes just the arrowhead deep into the hole. From then on, the beckoning ceases.

When we think about this incident, it does not make sense. What happened surely must have been the work of a someone's ghost or the like, but even so, how could it have possibly feared the virtue of the war arrow more than the Buddhist image and sutra?

Indeed, when the people then hear what happened, they all think it odd and wonder in this way. And so the story is told and passed down.[40]

On one level, the tale of the beckoning hand alludes to the increasing importance of the warrior and foreshadows the rise of that class; the privileging of the war arrow over a sutra and a picture of a Buddha suggests an awareness of the increasing emphasis on military power and the limitations, at least in a realm of violent politics, of peaceful Buddhist remedies. When we consider that the person trying to stop the hand with Buddhist materials is a high-ranking aristocrat, the tale seems even more prophetic in its message. After all, the warrior will eventually threaten the aristocrat, not Buddhism. Since the narrator does not even name the man with the arrow, the focus here is on the loss of power rather than on its gain. The tale emphasizes failure even if our interpretation follows the lead of the *Konjaku* commentator and focuses on the Buddhist effort rather than on the aristocrat making it. The outcome contradicts those we find in Buddhist miracle tales or setsuwa illustrating the wondrous effects of simple faith in a sutra or a Buddhist image. Here Buddhism fails.

As with many other setsuwa, this tale is deceptive in its simplicity. The reading I offer above represents only one possibility for interpretation. Certain narrative details reveal additional information and sources of tension when considered in terms of their relevance in the larger context of Heian literature and history.

Among the most important of these details is the protagonist and sole figure identified in the tale: Nishinomiya Minister of the Left, a cognomen for Minamoto no Takaakira (914–82). A son of Emperor Daigo, Takaakira held many powerful positions in the government including Minister of the Right and Minister of the Left. As a Minamoto (a member of the imperial house made commoner), he was a threat to the northern branch Fujiwara. In 969, the government accused him of participating in a plot to have his son-in-law Prince Tamehira made crown prince—a move that would have led to Takaakira ascending to the position of regent once Tamehira became emperor and fathered a son, thereby shifting political control away from the Fujiwara to the Minamoto.[41] It is not clear whether such scheming ever took place or, if it did, whether Takaakira was involved in it, but Takaakira was appointed to the position of Provisional Governor General of Dazaifu (Dazai no Gon no Sochi): an assignment amounting to exile. This incident, the so-called *Anna no hen*, was part of the Fujiwara effort to maintain political power as regents.[42] Mention of Takaakira in the tale evokes this event and, more broadly, the efforts of the northern branch Fujiwara to suppress their rivals.

The Fujiwara connection also comes into play when considering the symbolic significance of the Momozono Mansion as the setting for Takaakira's bizarre encounter with the tiny hand. Not only does Takaakira prove unable to control the mysterious creature, but also, his failure occurs in a place associated with the northern branch Fujiwara—to the people who destroy his political career. Although the first proprietor of the Momozono Mansion was probably a son of Emperor Seiwa, Prince Sadazumi, the mansion was ultimately transferred to Fujiwara no Yukinari, possibly from his father Yoshitaka, who inherited it from his own father, Koremasa. It was Yukinari who had the mansion made into Seson Temple (Sesonji). While some scholars suggest that Yukinari inherited the estate from his maternal grandfather, Minamoto no Yasumitsu, tales in the setsuwa collections *Ōkagami* and *Shūgaishō* (*Collection of Oddments*, an encyclopedia started in the fourteenth century) indicate that members of the northern branch Fujiwara were among the people who owned the estate or resided there at different times.[43]

The mansion was located in an area called Momozono, outside the official boundaries of the capital, just north of Ichijō (First Avenue) and slightly west of Ōmiya Avenue but still in the east. It was one of several or more residences there. Although situated outside the Heian capital proper, those mansions housed people whose lives remained circumscribed within the Heian political sphere. In this sense, Momozono was one of many areas in Heian Japan collapsing the distinction between center and periphery.

The estate in the tale, the Momozono Mansion that will become Sesonji, suggests inauspiciousness because many people who either live there or are otherwise linked to it are ill fated. One of its inhabitants, Fujiwara no Koremasa, dies in 972 while only in his third year of regency from an illness that causes an unquenchable thirst. Two of his sons, Takakata and Yoshitaka, contract fatal cases of smallpox shortly afterwards during an epidemic.[44] Tale 84 (6:2) of *Uji shūi* conveys a sense of both Koremasa the unlucky man and Momozono the inauspicious mansion. It describes how the aristocrat finds an undecayed and unblemished corpse of a young, beautiful nun buried in a stone coffin on the mansion grounds. Although the failure of the corpse to deteriorate implies that the nun was born in the Pure Land, the discovery of her body does not benefit Koremasa; according to the last line of the tale, some people attribute his death to it. The same narrative begins with information about the Momozono Major Counselor or Fujiwara no Morouji, the man living at the mansion immediately before Koremasa. Morouji dies two days before he is supposed to hold a banquet there and his family consequently suffers economic hardship.[45]

We do not know when in history Takaakira lived or stayed at this mansion in Momozono, if at all. Some scholars speculate that Prince Sadazumi gave Momozono Mansion to Takaakira before it was passed on to Koremasa or that he lived there after his pardon in 971.[46] Others reject the possibility of him having resided there, suggesting that the storytellers confused the pre-Sesonji Momozono Mansion with another estate in the same area belonging to Takaakira.[47] At least three separate residences at Momozono are relevant here: the future Sesonji; a mansion belonging to Takaakira if it existed; a third, where, according to *Kagerō nikki* (*The Gossamer Years*, ca. 974), the principal wife of Takaakira, Aimiya, retreats as a nun following the exile of her husband and the arson of his mansion at Nishinomiya.[48]

Aimiya is the half-sister of Kaneie, the husband of the author of *Kagerō nikki*, and Koremasa.[49] Both men are members of the northern branch Fujiwara who serve as regents. The Momozono Mansion mentioned in this *nikki* belongs to her or her family, but it is unclear whether she inherited the estate from her father, Fujiwara no Morosuke, or her mother, Princess Gashi, a daughter of Emperor Daigo and a half-sister of Takaakira.[50] She leads a very sad and lonely life there. The aura of inauspiciousness at Momozono looms not only over the Sesonji Momozono Mansion, but also manifests itself in the unfortunate circumstances leading Aimiya to the area as well as in her emotional state there. Moreover, because Princess Gashi was a wife of Morosuke, subtle connections of the northern branch Fujiwara to this Momozono Mansion exist in *Kagerō nikki* regardless of which side of the family passed it down. This residence shares with the Sesonji Momozono Mansion unsettling connections to the aura of the area, Takaakira, and the Fujiwara. Perhaps Takaakira stayed briefly at this Momozono Mansion while visiting either Aimiya or Gashi. Assuming the storytellers were aiming for historical accuracy, the confusion about where Takaakira resided in Momozono may stem in part from the residence associated with Aimiya. Her negative connection to Momozono—that is, her move resulting from the political attack on him—reinforces the nightmarish quality of the setsuwa: the elements of helplessness and haunting.

It may even be poetic license rather than error placing Takaakira in the Sesonji Momozono Mansion. Either way, we should not be overly concerned with historical accuracy in studying this or other setsuwa because narrative details can make sense at the symbolic level and still be historically inaccurate. The more important question is whether we can uncover another kind of logic at work in the story. The Momozono Mansion most frequently linked to misfortune and also destined to become a temple is an appropriate setting for a story alluding to Takaakira's loss of power and lack of control.

Takaakira's defense—his use of a sutra and a picture of the Buddha—coincides with the historical narrative of his life as he takes vows in response to his exile.[51] The tale challenges his Buddhist effort. Marked as the better choice, the war arrow suggests that a violent act would have been the more appropriate, more empowering response for Takaakira, at least in the view of some people. It may also represent anger Takaakira represses in the act of becoming a monk. With this last comment, I am not suggesting that we can know how the historical figure (the so-called real person), Takaakira, reacted emotionally to his fate but rather that the tale can be viewed on one level as a psychological reality constructed by its creators and audiences.

The hand, usually in conjunction with the arm, is a stylized representation. Otherwise invisible demons often interact with the human world simply by revealing only this body part and reaching out.[52] Mori Masato illustrates this point with incidents in two *Konjaku* tales and an anecdote in *Ōkagami* further discussed in Chapters 4 and 5.[53] In the first *Konjaku* story (27:17), a couple is staying at the uninhabited Kawara mansion one evening when the door opens abruptly. A hand suddenly reaches out, grabs the woman, and drags her into the next room. The second (27:22) involves two brothers who are hunters. Their technique is to hide in trees and shoot at animals passing under them. One night they are waiting in ambush when a hand seizes the topknot of the older brother and begins pulling him up, only to be shot off by the younger brother's arrow. In *Ōkagami*, something grabbing at the sword of Fujiwara no Tadahira also turns out to be the hand of a demon.[54] As we see most clearly in this first example, demons tend to appear in places that humans generally leave uninhabited. In the story involving Takaakira, the small hand appears southeast in the central room (*moya*) of the main hall (*shinden*). Both the *shinden* and the *moya* are usually left vacant until needed for special, high-ranking guests. Furthermore, the small hand beckons at night or the time when spirit creatures usually become active because the world is "exempt from the order controlled by humans during the daylight hours."[55]

Yet, there are important differences between these hands and the beckoning hand. The hand of the child belongs to a benign spirit while demons are usually malevolent. Whereas the other hands pursue people and are clearly life threatening, the little hand is not especially harmful. It stays put, gently calling people toward it. Takaakira chooses to confront it, moving into its time and realm. In contrast to the beckoning hand, the other hands all appear to be adult. Why is the hand from the pillar a child's? I see two possibilities. Many of Takaakira's troubles have to do with a very young person: *Ōkagami* tells us that Prince Morihira is only nine (eight by our count) in 967 when he becomes crown prince although Takaakira's son-in-law Tamehira is by tradition the rightful successor.[56] As previously mentioned, this development prevents Takaakira, a Minamoto, from becoming the maternal grandfather of a future emperor and of thus securing the powerful position of regent. In evoking Morihira through the hand, the storyteller may be slightly exaggerating his small size and young age (*chisaki chigo no*[57]) to emphasize the powerlessness of Takaakira. As a second possibility, the small hand may also be associated with the Minamoto infant who would have become the emperor had the Fujiwara not prevented the realization of Takaakira's political dream.

Takaakira can no more stop his torment than he can the spirit. The hand evokes the children haunting him, but they are merely instruments of the people struggling for power. Adorable yet gruesome, harmless yet threatening, the little hand is ambiguous and a source of tension. It draws us to it, however eerie and repulsive in its bodiless form. It beckons. Who can reject the hand of a small child? At one level, the representation is a construction of a state of mind: how did Takaakira see Morihira or the infant who should have but could never fulfill his dream? Perhaps it was with both affection and repulsion.

The arrow's ability to subdue the hand underscores the impermanence of the haunting spirit, the Fujiwara influence, but the man wielding that weapon is not Takaakira. He and other aristocratic contemporaries of the Fujiwara cannot benefit from the future demise of this powerful lineage. The tale is historically correct in suggesting the weaknesses of both him and the Fujiwara. Whether or not the tale foreshadows the decline of the aristocrats in general or the Fujiwara in particular depends on when it was first created and told, facts we do not know. Even as a reflection on the past influence of the Fujiwara, the narrative speaks of the relationships of men at the top of political hierarchies with others only slightly below them.

The next tale, too, deals with the vulnerability of someone connected to the capital, although he is not famous. It could be gruesome with its focus on penis removal were it not so absurd and humorous.

DISAPPEARING PENISES

What can we make of *Uji shūi* and *Konjaku* tales dealing with disappearing penises? At one level, they illustrate rivalry between the capital and the provinces by depicting how something in the provinces retains its mystery and cannot be transmitted to the capital. Although the tales focus on magic, the sketch of an elegant room and a beautiful woman in its first part reveals the materialistic side of the competition. The room impresses the protagonist, Michinori, a palace guard of the Takiguchi (a unit attached to the emperor's private secretariat or *kurōdo dokoro*), largely because it is not what he expects to find in a country mansion located so far from the capital.[58] While comically undermining the view of the Heian capital as culturally superior to the provinces, the tale also suggests other struggles over what people or practices have authority. The last part of this section will examine the tension between Buddhist and non-Buddhist practices evident in only the *Konjaku*.

Japanese scholars believe that the *Konjaku* and *Uji shūi* versions of this tale are based on the same source, probably the non-extant *Uji dainagon monogatari*.[59] Although these two tales are nearly identical in plot, they differ in significant ways. I provide a translation of the *Konjaku* tale below and later mention differences between the two texts relevant to the discussion.[60]

How a Palace Guard of the Takiguchi Unit Goes To Collect Gold during the Reign of Emperor Yōzei

Now it is the past; during the reign of Emperor Yōzei, palace guards of the Takiguchi unit are sent to Michinoku as gold collectors. A guard named Michinori, who has received the imperial order, stops overnight on the way at a place called [ ][61] in Shinano Province.[62] He is staying at the home of the district official who waits to receive him and later treats him with boundless hospitality. After the evening meal and related things are finished, the head of the household, the district official, leaves the house accompanied by his retainers.

Unable to sleep in a strange home, Michinori quietly gets up to have a look around. Peeking into the room of the district official's wife, he sees folding screens and standing curtains set up in a row. *Tatami* is neatly spread and two-level shrine-style shelves along with other things are pleasingly arranged. Hidden incense must be burning somewhere because a rich fragrance fills the air. "So, such things exist even way out in the country." Michinori is struck by the elegance of the room. When he takes a closer look, a seemingly flawless woman about twenty years old, with pretty hair, a slender figure, and a well-shaped forehead is gorgeously lying there. When Michinori sees this, he can hardly pass by. Since no one else is around, he can act without restraint and go to her without anyone reproaching him. He quietly slides open the door and enters.

No one even asks, "Who's there?" The room is very bright because there is a standing oil lamp on the other side of the curtain. Michinori deeply regrets having such indecent feelings for the official's wife, especially after the district official had received him so wholeheartedly. When seeing the appearance of the woman, though, he is unable to control himself.

He reaches the woman and lies beside her, but the woman is not terribly surprised. As she lies covering her mouth with her sleeve, her face is even more splendid close up. Michinori feels immeasurable delight. It is around the tenth day of the ninth month, therefore she is not wearing many layers of robes but rather an unlined kimono made from light purple figured cloth and dark red trousers. The incense perfumed into her clothes has left its fragrance on everything. Michinori removes his robe and tries to slide a hand to her breasts through the opening of her robe. The woman pulls her robe closed a few times but because she does not resist very strongly, he is able to get his hand in. Meanwhile, his penis begins to itch, so he examines himself—to find only hair there. His penis is gone. Startled and suspicious, he searches himself thoroughly, but he might as well be searching through a head of hair as there is absolutely no trace of anything. In great shock, he forgets the splendor of the woman. The woman smiles slightly as she watches the man groping around confusedly with a bewildered look.

The man finally rises quietly and goes back to his own bed, unable to comprehend what happened and feeling very strange. He searches again for his penis, but it is not there. Baffled, he calls one of his close retainers and, without giving him the details, says, "There is a beautiful woman in there. I was with her myself and it was no problem. You go ahead, too." Delighted, the retainer also goes to her. A while later, he returns. Seeing the bewildered look on the retainer's face, Michinori thinks, "The same thing happened to him." When he calls yet [ ] other retainers and sends them in with encouragement, they also come back with perplexed expressions and upward gazes. Michinori sends seven or eight retainers off in this way and all return with the same look.

The dawn breaks while Michinori is repeatedly thinking about the strangeness of what happened. Within his heart he is grateful to the head of the house for giving him such a hearty welcome the previous night, but given the odd and incomprehensible thing that followed, he forgets everything and leaves hurriedly at dawn. After the men have gone about seven or eight *chō*, a voice calls after them.[63] They look to see someone coming on horseback. Glancing at the rider, they realize he is the retainer who served them their meal at the mansion. He has come carrying something wrapped up in white paper.

Michinori stops the horse and asks, "What is that?" The retainer answers, "This is something the district official told me to give you. How can you go, disposing of something like this? This morning we prepared breakfast for you just as people should for guests, but you were in such a hurry to leave that you and your men left these behind. We gathered them together and I came to give them to you." He hands the package over. "What in the world," thinks Michinori. When he opens the package to have a look, he discovers the nine penises of the men bunched together and wrapped like mushrooms. Dumbfounded, Michinori calls his retainers to gather and have a look. All eight retainers come thinking something is strange. They look and there are nine penises. Suddenly all the penises vanish. The retainer who brought them the package had left immediately after giving it to Michinori. Now all the retainers talk at once, saying: "Such a thing happened to me" and when they check again, the penises are where they belong. From there, they go onto Michinoku, collect the gold and, on their way back, go again to the house of this district official in Shinano to stay overnight.

The district official is delighted because they shower him with all kinds of gifts, including horses and silk. Yet he asks, "Why did you think to give me all this?" Michinori walks up closely and says to the district official, "This is quite embarrassing to ask, but [as you know] a very strange thing happened to me during my last stay here. What was it about? I am asking you because I am extremely perplexed about it." Since the district official had received so many things from Michinori, he now spoke without hiding anything. "Yes, that: When I was young, an aging official of a remote district in this province had a young wife.[64] I was trying to sneak a visit with her when my penis disappeared. Thinking this very mysterious, I did everything I could to show my kindness and sincerity so that I could learn from him. If you are serious about wanting to master this [art], first hurry to the capital and present all the imperial items you are carrying. Then return here on a special trip, so that you can study with a peaceful heart." Michinori vows to do so. He returns to the capital to present the gold and then goes back [to Shinano], having requested a vacation.

He brings with him appropriate gifts for the official, who is very pleased to receive them. "I'll teach him everything I know," he thinks and says, "This is not easy to learn. To prepare, you must first practice strict abstinence for seven days and thoroughly purify yourself, performing daily ablutions. So tomorrow begin by abstaining." Michinori then starts practicing abstinence and purifying himself with daily ablutions. On the seventh night, the district official and Michinori travel deep into the mountains without anyone else. They travel to the bank of a large river, where they take the vow: "I will not for all eternity believe in the Three Treasures," perform various feats, and take oaths too wicked for words.

Afterwards, the district official says, "I'm going upstream. You are to catch whatever comes floating downstream in your arms: demon or god." So saying, he leaves to go upstream. Shortly after, the sky upstream clouds over and thunder roars. The wind gusts, rain falls, and the current of the river rises. Moments later, when Michinori looks upstream, he sees a snake with a head so huge a man could barely encircle it with his arms. Its eyes shine with pupils like metal balls. The bottom of its neck is crimson while the dark blue and green-blue top gleams as if painted. Although he had been told to "catch whatever comes down the river," Michinori is terrified and lies down in the grass to hide. Shortly after, the district official returns. "How did it go? Were you able to catch it?" Michinori replies, "It was horrifying, so I did not catch it." "How regrettable. You will never learn this [art] that way. Even so, let's try one more time," he says and leaves.

Moments later, Michinori looks and sees a four-*shaku*-tall boar baring its teeth.[65] With bristling fur, the boar rushes toward Michinori as if to eat him. Sparks fly out from the rocks crushed beneath its weight. Although quite frightened, Michinori moves closer and embraces it, thinking "this is the end." He finds himself holding a three-*shaku* decayed piece of wood. Now, he is filled with deep regret and anger at himself. "The first creature must have been this sort of thing. Why didn't I just catch it?" he is thinking when the district official returns. "You have lost your chance to learn the magic of making penises disappear, but I suppose you can learn how to transform insignificant objects into something else. I will teach you that," he says. Michinori regrets his failure to learn how to make penises disappear.

He returns to the capital and the palace. At the Office of the Takiguchi Guard Unit, he bets other guards that he will succeed in transforming all their worn-out boots into puppies. Or he changes old straw sandals into three-*shaku*-long carp and makes them dance, alive, on a tabletop.

Soon the emperor hears about Michinori and summons him to the Black Door Hall to have himself taught the art. Later he will do things like make a miniature Kamo festival procession move across the horizontal bar of his standing curtain.

But people in society do not talk much about this thing. This is because everyone criticizes someone in the position of emperor for practicing an art forever against the Three Treasures. Given that such practice is a grave transgression even for insignificant people of lower status, perhaps the emperor's choice to engage in it explains why he ultimately went insane.

This must be what it means to worship *tengu* and slander the Three Treasures. It is hard to become part of the human world. Coming across the teachings of the Buddha is even more difficult. And yet, when someone rejects the Buddhist way and heads toward the world of evil, after by chance being born into the human world and coming across the Buddhist teachings, it is precisely the same as entering a mountain jewel mine and returning empty-handed, then losing one's life by embracing a stone and entering deep waters. And so, it definitely should be stopped. And so the story is told and passed down.[66]

A brief discussion of this tale appears in the article "Black Hair and Red Trousers: Gendering the Flesh in Medieval Japan" by Hitomi Tonomura. Her focus is on how Michinori and his men experience the magical loss and recovery of their penises, ending with the men being restored to normal—that is, on roughly half the entire tale, excluding the comments of the *Konjaku* compiler. While the first half works as an independent story, cutting it off from the second, where Michinori loses the chance he has to learn and transmit this skill to the capital, changes its meaning. The representation of the detached penises must be considered in relation to magic and secret transmissions. The profession of the protagonist reflects this interest. Although the emperor sends the Takiguchi guards on a practical mission in the story (which takes place before the actual guard unit was established by Emperor Uda, r. 887–97), in history, the Takiguchi palace guards had spiritual significance. According to Karl F. Friday, they had mainly "magical and exorcistic military functions" such as ritually twanging bows "to drive away evil spirits and disperse ghosts."[67] The representation of Michinori and the other men as victims of someone else's magic and of Michinori's difficulty in learning magical skills mocks the real Takiguchi.

Moreover, since the second half of the tale reveals that the district official performed this magic using his wife as a medium, the confiscation of the penises is ultimately about the vulnerability of men to other men rather than to women. We need to consider the importance of the bond between the district official and Michinori, because, as Tonomura writes, *Konjaku* tales in which "the penis figures prominently," help establish a "collective male identity . . . reinforced through the sharing of a common male culture centered on the penis."[68] The idea that the penis "represents vulnerability, a thing to be controlled or taken away"[69] can be explored in terms of the second half of the tale as well. To describe the collective male identity, male culture, and type of vulnerability depicted in the tales, we need also to look at who is in the position of control.

Had Michinori merely sought to learn whether other men would mysteriously lose their penises when trying to penetrate the district official's wife, he could have sent one or two of his retainers in for the test. Why does he make certain all of them are deprived? Can it be because doing so makes his suffering easier? Is it because he cannot bear the thought of any of his men having something he does not? Perhaps he now needs to assert control over other people, having been manipulated precisely when he thought his desire was going to be met. Part of this collective male identity has to do with degradation and the potential each man has for being humiliated in the same way. It does not involve sharing the experience, at least not until the crisis is over, since the men do not confide in each other while lacking penises but only when their parts are reattached.

While the disappearance of a penis could be an event in a horror story, here it is funny. Bakhtin discusses laughter at length, describing it as liberating, purifying, and empowering. It marks a "victory over fear"[70] and is a defining feature in his vision of the grotesque. The sixth tale in *Uji shūi* also comically addresses the idea of a missing member. There a Buddhist priest tries to convince Middle Counselor Morotoki that he has cut off his own penis to sever his worldly ties. The priest exposes himself to prove his assertion, but in truth he has somehow twisted and tied his penis back, then pasted hair over it. Morotoki reveals the deception by ordering a very young page to caress the holy man in the genital area. The crowd watching breaks out in laughter.[71]

In contrast, the sexual organs of women in setsuwa are almost never treated comically. Tonomura discusses the vagina as "a focus of physical vulnerability" and an "explicit site of male revenge and control."[72] Hagiographies of a certain Nun Sari in *Nihon ryōiki*, *Sanbōe*, and *Hokkegenki* include a representation approaching the idea of detached female genitals.[73] The beautiful devout nun is described as vagina-less, in part to indicate her degree of spirituality. This representation may be liberating to a woman celibate for religious reasons as it suggests the absence of or control over sexual desire. In the words of Bernard Faure (who also views this representation as ambivalent) in *The Red Thread: Buddhist Approaches to Sexuality*, "she has the ideal, 'closed' body of the bodhisattva."[74]

Faure sees a negative side of this representation in the sense it gives of Nun Sari as "not even a woman."[75] Yet, since being a woman is not desirable in Buddhism, being less than a woman cannot be bad. Her incomplete body can also be read as part of the discourse in Buddhism that, as Ōgoshi Aiko notes when examining the cultural paradigm of Buddhism, teaches "women to hate being women and to wish to rid themselves of their female form."[76] Ōgoshi is referring to the concept of the need for women to transform into men to enter the Pure Land, but the connection made between spirituality and Nun Sari's missing genitals also suggests the undesirability of the female form.

Why is the penis more likely to be portrayed in a playful manner? In the tale about the disappearing penises, the representation of the penis frees the male audience to laugh about fears of impotency, losing one's penis, and as we will see, inadequacy in other areas as well.

In the second half of the tale, the narrator moves from the loss of a body part to the loss of a chance at mastering a desired art. The story continues to describe the plight of a man who falls short of achieving his goal, only now the loss is less personal and its significance for society slightly greater. The magic of making penises disappear has a tradition, as the district official himself mastered the magic after being mysteriously deprived of his penis when, as a young man, he was visiting the official of an even more remote region. The art seems to have more value precisely because the official learned it far away from the capital. Moreover, Michinori has to dissociate himself from the official sphere to study it, returning to the mansion only after he has completed the imperial mission.

The acquisition of magic is depicted as a serious, religious activity undertaken with a pure, tranquil heart and fixed mind. Yet, the way Michinori comes to be interested in this magic and the type of feat he seeks to master put the very suggestion of solemnity into question. The district official is not described as a monk or a priest and his disciple is hardly seeking enlightenment or immortality. Instead, the narrator mocks the master-disciple relationship and the idea of sacred transmissions by linking the bizarre sexual encounter and the detached penis to the idea of a spiritual effort.

The *Uji shūi* tale never indicates that a particular religious tradition, such as Buddhism or Daoism, is being lampooned or criticized. The practitioners make wicked vows on the riverbank, but in contrast to what we find in *Konjaku*, do not reject Buddhism in particular. While in *Konjaku* Michinori and the district official swear never to believe in the Three Treasures, there is nothing overtly threatening or harmful about the magic in *Uji shūi*. It does not permanently damage anyone, nor does it seem to have any lasting consequences for society. The vows in *Konjaku* never to believe in the Three Treasures are there to indicate that magical removal of penises threatens Buddhism. They seem included mainly to justify the counterattack coming as the sermon at the end of the tale.

If *Konjaku* and *Uji shūi* did draw these tales from the same written source, the *Konjaku* compiler possibly added the vow against the Three Treasures to emphasize the threat of non-Buddhist magical traditions. He probably put in the last paragraphs of that version as well. Many tales in *Konjaku* have extant earlier versions, but only rarely do we find in them anything resembling the final remarks of the *Konjaku* commentator. If both *Konjaku* and *Uji shūi* are based on an earlier non-extant text, then we cannot assume that the ideology in *Konjaku* versions is older simply because that collection was likely compiled first. As D. E. Mills notes, Kunisaki Fumimaro believes that the *Uji shūi* version is older because "*Konjaku* adapts the wording of tales to accord with its standard narrative technique, whereas *Uji shūi* does not."[77] A group of people committed to Buddhism—perhaps the monks who compiled *Konjaku* according to one popular theory—took a tale initially having nothing to do with Buddhism and appropriated it to fit their own belief system.

After a week of abstinence and daily ablutions, Michinori is tested. He must catch the demon or god coming down the river. Despite his status as a Takiguchi palace guard, he proves himself a coward by hiding from the huge serpent. How humiliated he must be when, upon grabbing the frenzied boar, it transforms into an insignificant, rotten piece of wood! The man from the capital is no match for the district official. Having already been subjected to the strange loss and recovery of his penis, Michinori now has to suffer a spiritual and intellectual emasculation. The district official offers to teach him the lesser art of transforming insignificant objects into something else, which the emperor, in turn, learns from Michinori. In this way, Michinori manages to master some magic and transmit it to the capital, but not the magic the district official would have taught a better student. The higher magic remains in Shinano while the lesser art travels to the Heian capital. Since Shinano has the superior magic, no one can call the province inferior.

The *Uji shūi* tale ends on the humorous note about the miniature procession, without any condemnation of the magic. In contrast, the *Konjaku* commentator asks the audience to judge the magic harshly, creating a discrepancy between the tone of the tale before and after the mention of Emperor Yōzei's interest. Yōzei (868–949, r. 876–84) is the insane emperor forced to abdicate after killing the son of his wet nurse.[78] The commentator attempts to capitalize on this piece of history by providing a Buddhist explanation for it: he turned his back on the Three Treasures. The tale thus becomes a Buddhist lesson, complete with scriptural references to *Sutra of Meditation on the Correct Teaching* (*Zhengfa nianchu jing*) and possibly *Sutra of Buddha Names Preached by Buddha* (*Foshuo foming jing*).[79] However, an emperor enjoying a simple, second-rate, magic seems more frivolous than wicked. The jump from the depiction of him delighted by a tiny procession traveling across the top of a curtain to someone who has entered the world of evil because of this type of interest seems extreme, even forced. There is a gap between what most of the tale tells us about the magic and the links to evil the commentator suggests.

The *Konjaku* story is in a cluster of tales in Book 20 about *tengu*, a spirit-creature associated with the slim hawk known as a kite but whose physical features are vague at this time.[80] The placement of the story provides insight into how the compiler hoped to control its messages, especially since the narrative never mentions a *tengu*. Haruko Wakabayashi has argued that *tengu* in *Konjaku* "practice heretical teachings and challenge the Buddhist priests. . . . These *tengu* which use 'heretical magic' not only symbolize evil in its religious sense, but also represent social evil, or the other religious groups in conflict with Buddhism."[81] The *Konjaku* commentator accuses Emperor Yōzei of worshiping these creatures. From a Buddhist point of view, magically removing penises and transforming insignificant objects into something else would constitute heretical teaching. In the tale preceding this story, a priest has mastered this second type of magic. Wakabayashi sees him as exemplifying people "who choose to study a non-Buddhist practice, the *gejutsu*, and worship *tengu*."[82] *Gejutsu* literally means "the outside teaching."[83] An art can be described with that word only in contrast to Buddhism. That term is never used in the tale about the disappearing penises, but the sense of it is added with the inclusion of the sermon and the placement of the tale. Buddhists could easily appropriate this story because any fascinating non-Buddhist art can be labeled a threat.

The final comments in *Konjaku* obscure the power struggle at work throughout the tale—namely, that of the capital versus the provinces. The great wealth and power of the provinces would increase with time. So while the story is set in the reign of Emperor Yōzei, it has relevance to the situations of the late Heian and early Kamakura periods. Michinori initially travels to the provinces to collect a payment for the emperor. His journey thus appears to affirm the authority of the court, dominated by aristocratic families. However, he ends up in situations that render him physically and spiritually impotent. The incapacitation is not permanent, but makes the man and the capital less than ideal. Magically removing penises is an act of rendering others vulnerable and of making them aware of their weakness. Even a single provincial district has this power over the capital.

CONCLUSION

In the three tales analyzed in this chapter, fantastic detached body parts are sites of tension between conflicting desires and ideologies. An ancient Chinese king rules, but forces that are more powerful move people toward resistance and the desire for his head. As the northern branch Fujiwara rise to power, they necessarily crush the dreams of other aristocrats to become regents. Not surprisingly, then, Heian storytellers have left us with a tale suggesting how Takaakira is haunted by the children whose identity and fate shape his own. The last tale portrays bonding and competition among elite Heian men and their territories. These body parts are positioned to undermine people in the highest positions of authority, but they do so without privileging anyone else. They highlight the vulnerability and loss of the protagonists. In the tales of Broad-of-Brow and Michinori, degrading someone is akin to disfiguring him: to severing a body part. For Takaakira, it comes in the form of a child's body part without the child. The missing child, the emperor-grandson, would have been a political extension, a limb, of himself. These setsuwa give us deeper insight into the Heian literary imagination, commanding our attention because they are bizarre, highly imaginative, and rich in their multiple layers of meaning.

CHAPTER 3

Curious Sexual Encounters

In grotesque realism, reducing people in status or dignity is often a downward movement enacted on the body. "To degrade," writes Bakhtin, "also means to concern oneself with the lower stratum of the body, the life of the belly and the reproductive organs; it therefore relates to acts of defecation and copulation, conception, pregnancy, and birth."[1] In setsuwa, these bodily functions have a prominent position in subverting authority, but whereas eating and conceiving are sometimes linked, defecation and procreation are not. This chapter explores grotesque representations of copulation, conception, pregnancy, and birth in setsuwa. It demonstrates how such representations minimize the role of the female body in these acts when compared to the male body or transform active bodies into something non-human.

The chapter concentrates on five tales. The first describes how a discarded turnip used by a man in masturbation impregnates a woman. Both of the next two deal with ghosts and demons sexually attracted to women: the first depicts the sexual involvement of a demon with an empress and the second, a ghost interrupting the sexual activity of an emperor and his consort, and then demanding the woman for himself. In the fourth tale, a snake performs oral sex on a married monk as he dreams about an encounter with a beautiful woman. Since the representations in the dream evoke other associations of women and snakes, the last part of the chapter before the conclusion looks at the most famous tale with this link: a story of a monk pursued by a woman turned snake and cremated alive in the bell at Dōjōji Temple. As my analysis indicates, the burning of the man by the snake coiled around the bell can be viewed as a grotesque sexual consummation.

The first four tales of this chapter, particularly the story involving bestiality, are somewhat crude and might even be viewed as distasteful or mildly obscene. They lack the humor that made discussing the disappearing penises in Chapter 2 relatively easy. Therefore, before beginning to analyze them, I would like to pause a moment to mention the uneasiness I often feel in coming to terms with the unpolished sexual elements of setsuwa. In "Rabelais and Obscenity: A Woman's View," Carol Bellard-Thomson addresses a similar issue:

> I have also wondered about the reason why (as the daughter of a former Methodist lay-preacher, with all the intellectual freedom that entails) I was able not only to accept the obscenity in the Rabelaisian text, but to enjoy it and to find it profoundly significant. And the reason I wonder about that attitude is closely related to the fact that I am a woman. Somewhere in my mind runs a thought that says, because I am woman, I should find obscenity, particularly of a sexual nature, upsetting or, at the very least, unacceptable.[2]

My background differs from that of Bellard-Thomson: my parents (particularly my mother, since my father died when I was six) were always trying to gain access to newer and freer ways of thinking. Therefore, my dilemma is not quite the same. I am not surprised at myself for my interest in this earthy side of Japanese literature or for finding the details of these and other setsuwa with a similar leaning interesting, profound, and significant. The tales are not repulsive to me because they reveal the conflicts of needs people sometimes experienced, such as the Buddhist demand for celibacy and a purity of mind vying with physical desire and fantasy.

Blatant sexual imagery troubles me when it is linked to violence, but my discomfort does not always prevent me from trying to understand it. Aware that some people expect women to find other types unpleasant as well, I worry about being misunderstood. Yet, this concern does not prevent me from doing what seems important. I am more disturbed by how previous generations of scholars minimize or ignore these kinds of representations along with highly suggestive language in, for example, *waka* and *monoga-tari*, as part of the effort to portray Heian literature as aesthetically pure. Bakhtin stresses that much of the grotesque is ugly, monstrous, and hideous only because we judge it "from the point of view of 'classic' aesthetics, that is, the aesthetics of the ready made and the completed."[3] Overcoming such biases is necessary for appreciating the tales discussed below and ultimately for placing them within the context of premodern Japanese literature.

The common usage of the word "grotesque" to mean "ugly" can cause us to forget that the acts of copulation, pregnancy, and birth are integral to Bakhtin's definition of the grotesque and carnivalesque, especially if we view those things as potentially wonderful. In the popular tradition, which Bakhtin sees as giving rise to the grotesque and carnivalesque, "woman is essentially related to the material bodily lower stratum; she is the incarnation of this stratum that degrades and regenerates simultaneously. . . . She debases, brings down to earth, lends a bodily substance to things, and destroys; but, first of all, she is the principle that gives birth. She is the womb."[4] Bakhtin equates woman with nature, but to him the female body is also cultural. It is the source of the tradition producing pleasure and laughter, thereby exposing the sterility of so-called high, official culture. Of course, the idea of woman as womb is problematic, however positive some of its implications in Bakhtin. The time when the womb generates life, if at all, is relatively short. If women are wombs, how do we account for those of us who do not give birth or for the rest of us during all those years, most of our lives, when we are not reproducing? Bakhtin appropriates an attitude about women that is often oppressive and turns it into something occasionally empowering and positive.

In setsuwa with clearly Buddhist intent, such as *ōjōden*, sexual activity is generally viewed negatively because it hinders both men and women from rebirth in a higher realm or men from enlightenment. Hence, a woman married at some time during her life who achieves birth in the Pure Land (*ōjō*) is usually separated from her husband by his death or by choice before dying herself. Or, she may have an unconventional "marriage" with no sexual relations, as does the wife of a governor of Ōmi in a *Gokurakuki* tale.[5]

In many sutras, *śāstras* (religious treatises), and tales, certain women are treated as the equivalent of sexual activity. This association has no positive aspects because sex can keep people from enlightenment and is consequently an undesirable experience in most Buddhist frameworks. Whereas nuns and the mothers or sisters of the men in question would usually be excluded from this view, women perceived as potential sexual partners are blamed for maliciously keeping men from spiritual advancement by "tempting them to passion and thus cutting off any seeds of Buddhahood they might have planted (*busshu shōmetsu*)."[6] The version of the *Flower Garland Sutra* (*Avataṃsaka sūtra*) read by Nichiren describes these women as "messengers of hell who can destroy the seeds of Buddhahood. They may look like bodhisattvas, but at heart they are like *yaksha* demons."[7] Similarly, a version of *The Great Nirvana Sutra* (*Mahāparinirvāṇa sūtra*) states: "Women are Great King Māras, and they consume all living beings. In this life, they ensnare men and hinder their enlightenment, and they become enemies in the life to come."[8]

Even in Buddhist setsuwa, though, traditional attitudes toward the female body and heterosexual sex are occasionally subverted. In one *Konjaku* tale, the god of luck, Bishamonten (Vaiśravaṇa), helps a poor monk by appearing as a temple boy (or sending him a being in that form) who transforms into a woman and becomes sexually involved with the monk. She gives birth to gold, and then conveniently vanishes so that he can prosper. It is not surprising to find Bishamonten in this role since he is worshipped as the god of treasure in addition to being a Deva King who protects the Buddha. Yet, the idea of sex and gold for personal use contradicts traditional Buddhist values, especially since a monk is involved. Nonetheless, the female human body, though not really human, is a means to good fortune rather than an evil threat. Other tales as well question the view of heterosexual sex as an obstacle to spiritual development—for example, in a *Goshūi ōjōden* tale, when a promiscuous woman pursues the way of the bodhisattva by turning no man away and by treating all equally. She uses sex to practice the Buddhist ideal of nondiscrimination (showing "equal compassion to all, without distinguishing between high and low, rich and poor, or young and old"[9]). However, during sex, she is intentionally cold to her partners and emotionally detached from them. According to Keller Kimbrough, this behavior can be seen as a form of "ascetic self-abasement" because the woman is not motivated by lust and experiences no pleasure.[10] Since the lovers of this woman ultimately feel shame and stop visiting her, it is possible that her behavior helps them develop spiritually as well (that is, as long as they are disillusioned enough not to seek out other women). In the end, the woman is reborn in the Pure Land.[11]

Yet, the type of tale that criticizes women is far more common. In *Shūi ōjōden*, a monk continues to diligently practice meditation despite his relationship with a woman who performs all the duties of a wife. Upon falling gravely ill and realizing death is imminent, he asks the other monks to keep his condition a secret from her. Later, when the woman learns her husband has died, she reacts with a temper tantrum, rolling on the floor and screaming wildly. As it turns out, she had been pursuing the monk through various lives in order to obstruct his attainment of enlightenment. Finally, she exclaims, "How infuriating! In this life he has gained release despite my intentions. Where shall I go?"[12] In a similar tale in *Sangoku denki*, she even transforms into a green demon and ascends to the sky.[13] Such attitudes seem initially intended for Buddhist monks, who would have a stronger psychological defense against sexual desire when adopting them, and not for the general male population.[14] As Buddhism spread outside the monasteries or into different lifestyles in and outside Buddhist circles, negative views of women grew more problematic and oppressive to women. In part because of their influence, sexual relations are also sometimes viewed ambivalently in secular tales. Bizarre things occur.

AN ORAL CONCEPTION

The pregnancies and births of ordinary people are not usually celebrated in the tales, perhaps because of the harsh realities of life, especially for the poor. Nor are women identified as the primary source of life. Many tales direct our attention to spirits, men, demons, dogs, and even vegetables as chief participants in procreation while the female body is merely a recipient or vessel. *Konjaku* tale "How a Person Traveling East Has Intercourse with a Turnip and Causes a Child to Be Born" describes an accidental insemination. Spun around a man masturbating with a turnip and the consequent birth, it suggests that some people thought women could become impregnated orally. Less obviously, the tale additionally refers us to the problem of unexpected pregnancies. The child is accepted from the beginning, unlike the abandoned or nearly abandoned infants in several other tales. The young mother has the support of her family in contrast to a pregnant woman discussed in Chapter 5 who serves at a great house but is alone.

How a Person Traveling East Has Intercourse with a Turnip
and Causes a Child to Be Born

   Now it is the past; a man is traveling from Kyoto to the eastern provinces. The name of the province or district is not known, but while passing through a certain district, he suddenly experiences intense sexual desire and wants a woman to the point of being almost crazed. He cannot calm his heart and while he is pondering what to do, he notices something called greens growing tall within a fence near the roadside. The roots of the turnips are thick, it being the tenth month. The man suddenly gets down from his horse, enters the area enclosed by the fence, picks one big turnip, hollows out a hole, and penetrates it until he ejaculates. He then throws it in the enclosed area and leaves.

Some time later, the owner of this garden goes there accompanied by many women servants and his little girl, who is fourteen or fifteen years old and has no experience with men. While they are picking greens, so, too, is the girl. Walking and playing near the fence, she discovers the turnip thrown by the man. "Look, here is a turnip with a hole carved into it. I wonder what it is," she says, carrying it and playing with it for a while. Then she scrapes off the withered part and eats the turnip. The owner soon brings all the servants back to the house.

Afterwards, the girl begins to feel sick for some reason. Her parents worry because she does not eat and seems ill. They say things like "What could be wrong?" As the days and months pass, they realize she is pregnant. Quite surprised, they interrogate her, "What exactly did you do?" The girl says, "I never went near a man. But a bizarre thing happened: on a certain day, I found a strange turnip like so and ate it. From that day on, I began to feel odd and this is what happened." Her parents neither understand nor believe her explanation. When they ask around, even the servants in the house say, "We never saw her go near a man." So as time passes with everyone baffled, the pregnancy finally reaches full term. Everything goes smoothly and the girl gives birth to a very splendid boy.

Since there is nothing anyone can say or do after that, the girl's parents raise the child. In the meantime, the man who went east is traveling to the capital, having spent many years in an eastern province. He passes the garden on his way back, accompanied by many people. Just as before, it is around the tenth month and the father and mother of the girl are picking greens together with the servants. The man is chatting with people as he passes by the fence. In a loud voice, he says, "Oh yes. I passed by here years ago when I was going to the provinces. I wildly desired an opening and, not being able to control myself, went inside this fence, picked a huge turnip, carved a hole into it, and satisfied that feeling by penetrating it. Then I went and threw it within the fence." The girl's mother, who is standing inside the fence, hears him clearly. She remembers her daughter's words and, thinking what happened miraculous, goes outside the fence, calling "What was that? What was that?" The man thinks she is reprimanding him for stealing a turnip. "I was joking," he says and tries to make a quick escape. Now weeping, the mother says, "There is something very important I must question you about. Please answer." She must have some reason for this, thinks the man. Then he says, "I have nothing to hide. Nor have I committed any grave wrongdoing. I did what I did because I'm an ordinary man. I happened to blurt it out on the impulse of telling a story." Upon hearing this, the girl's mother cries and, still in tears, leads the man to the house. The man is suspicious, but he goes to the house because she insists.

Just then, the woman says, "Such and such a thing actually happened, so I want to compare you and that child." When she brings the child out and looks over the man and child, there isn't the slightest difference between the two. At this moment, the man, too, is moved. "Well, to think that there is also this kind of fate. What should we do, then?" The woman says, "It's up to you to decide" and calls the mother of the child. He looks at the woman and notices that she is wholesomely pretty despite being of a lower class. She is about twenty years old. The five or six year old child is a very splendid boy. Seeing them, the man thinks, "When I return to the capital, I have no parents or relatives such as these to rely on. My connection with them is so deep. I'll make her my wife and stay here." He solemnly makes a decision and, just like that, marries the woman and stays there. This is truly a rare thing.

Therefore, if semen enters a woman's body, a child will be born as he was in this case, even without a man and woman having intercourse. And so the story is told and passed down.[15]

Displacement of the female body with other bodies and mystical forces figures prominently in the conceptions of holy figures. In *The Karma of Words*, William LaFleur shows that births of divine beings into lower forms of being take place "outside of the sphere of the usual"—outside ordinary sexual relations, the birth canal, or the female body—because each "must be attended by circumstances and effects that attest to the extraordinary nature of the event."[16] He gives the example from *Nihon ryōiki* of Nun Sari, who was born from a ball of flesh.[17] Even Queen Māyā dreams that her son, Śākyamuni, enters her body through her right side the night he is conceived.[18] Still, the characters are hardly divine in the tale about the turnip. Instead, the extraordinary nature of the event is used to illustrate the power of both semen and karma, which results in the birth of an ordinary boy and brings two people together who otherwise might never have met.

As a means of satisfying sexual desire and a medium in impregnation, the turnip blurs boundaries between humans and vegetables. Similar gray areas can be found elsewhere in premodern Japan, for example, in the concept of all things, including vegetables, having a Buddha-nature (*busshō*) and the ability to attain Buddhahood (*jōbutsu*).[19] Although Buddhahood and accidental pregnancy are dissimilar, the temporary substitutions of a vegetable for a man and a woman, as the radish acts as both female and male genitals at different times, fits in a worldview allowing for vegetables to become Buddha. Some people may have reasoned that if vegetables can attain the highest level of spirituality available to humans, so, too, would it be possible for them to have bodily experiences resembling ours. Although the girl eats the turnip in the story, that act is indirectly sexual since the vegetable contains semen and its consumption results in pregnancy. Eating also replaces sexual activity elsewhere in setsuwa when, as we will see in the next chapter, a demon consumes a woman expecting intimacy with a man.

Why a turnip (*kabura* or *kabura no ne*)? The girl can be associated with the qualities of the vegetable: bland tasting but nutritious.[20] Apparently from relatively humble origins despite the presence of servants in her home, she does not offer the man prestige or anything else outside the ordinary. The man decides to stay with her because she provides sustenance in the form of a connection to family: supportive in-laws and a son. A turnip is a root, suggesting a link to the soil or stability.

Yet, turnip or *kabura* may also have erotic implications apart from its use in the tale, as it definitely does at a later time. In *Shikidō ōkagami* (*The Great Mirror of the Art of Passion*, 1678), Fujimoto Kizan (1626–1704) writes, "*Turnip* refers to a novice. . . . This should be evident in the expression 'like eating turnips' in reference to tasteless food."[21] Drawing from this statement, *Kokugo daijiten* (*The Extensive Dictionary of Japanese*) gives one definition of *kabura* as "a novice because of the simple, plain taste of the vegetable. Someone unaccustomed to amusements with prostitutes."[22] While the *Konjaku* does not refer to prostitution, this understanding of the word in the Edo period may have developed from an earlier time—from a similar but different usage. After all, *kabura* is connected to sexual behavior in the setsuwa. Someone may have been poking fun at the idea of a man having abundant sexual energy but no human partner: a novice in resorting to a vegetable as a sexual partner. Who can be more potent than he who ends up impregnating someone through masturbation?

While uncontrollable circumstances shape the lives of both the man and the girl, the story emphasizes as a defining force the behavior and experience of an ordinary if momentarily desperate man. All that follows the masturbation can be traced back to it. Although the pregnancy cannot occur without the girl ingesting the semen, she does so unknowingly. In contrast, the man acts with relatively more deliberation, carefully choosing and carving the vegetable, then throwing it back into the garden. He does not intend to impregnate anyone, but he decides to behave sexually. Furthermore, although the man lacks control over the consequences of his actions, he determines how much they will affect his future.

The tale has a subtle side about girlhood despite this focus on the man, but it is not from a girl's perspective. There is tension between girlhood innocence and emerging desire caused by the efforts of the parents (and perhaps also of a certain sector of Heian society) to preserve or prolong the former and negate the latter. The story omits the female body from genital sex. If the girl/woman has any sexual dimension, it is defined in terms of eating and giving birth. Her mouth becomes a passionless vagina and eating a bland food becomes intercourse. In this way, she jumps to motherhood without first becoming sexual and is given, not the sensations that would accompany that change, but the nausea of early pregnancy.

The depiction of the man entering a fenced-in area is significant. The fence simultaneously suggests protection and vulnerability, as apparent in the first poem of *Nihon shoki* and *Kojiki*, in which the god Susano-o builds a palace surrounded by fences for keeping his wife, or in *Genji* and other classical works, where men catch glimpses of girls and women through fences.[23] The space, with the girl or woman inside, is partially protected by the structure. In the setsuwa, the man ends up having access to both, thereby demonstrating his invasive power. His sexual fluids are powerful enough to change the body and life of the girl even before meeting her. The girl benefits in the story since the man ends up socially bound to her through his actions, but even the narrator comments "this is truly a rare thing." He may be referring to the entire series of events that lead up to the marriage, but the decision of the man is included. Even the narrator seems to admit that a man would rarely choose to marry and stay with a girl he has accidentally impregnated. The suggestion of what might have happened in similar circumstances minus the turnip is implicit in the tale.

Not all setsuwa portray reproductive women as passive in shaping the future for themselves or society while their mates have more control. Rather, representations of the female body often undermine male authority. However, the significance of a more active woman is often minimized by the presence of another agent at work alongside her. In Chapter 2, I touched on the subversive role of such representations when discussing the king's consort in the tale of Broad-of-Brow. More can be said about her.

The iron spirit ball can be further understood in terms of its additional definition of "scoria" (*kanakuso* or *kane no sabi*). The child of the consort alludes to the scoria obtained while forging and shining swords, a process once believed to require the sacrifice of women to the furnace god. This substance was supposedly an elixir believed "to cure a hundred diseases and turn gray hair black."[24] The consort similarly uses her body to produce something with the power of transforming things, but she does so through a pleasurable act and without destroying herself. Her child is the material used to kill the king, who in an earlier version in the *Wudiji* is the indirect cause of the death of a woman.[25] (Without the king's demand for swords, no woman would have to be sacrificed.) The *Konjaku* consort thus participates in avenging the women sacrificed for the production of swords. It is tempting to view this birth as celebrating the power of the woman, but, as I demonstrated in the preceding chapter, the spirit of the iron works through her. The procreating body has limited potential as a site of resistance because it depends on something else to be impregnated. As a result, the threat or challenge to human male authority in setsuwa often comes in the form of a man, a spirit, or a creature working through or in conjunction with a female body. Although connected to reproduction here, the female body may function along the same lines in other roles. In the next tale, it is an object of sexual desire and also a site for expressing discontent.

DEMON INTERCOURSE

Setsuwa often describe the dangers of spirits and creatures who enter human space through sexual involvement with men and women. The two tales examined below, the first from *Konjaku* and the second from *Gōdanshō*, are both concerned with ghosts or demons attracted to elite women. The first is entitled "How Empress Somedono Is Tormented by a Tengu," although no *tengu* appears in the tale. The priest who attaches himself to Empress Somedono becomes a demon (*oni*) after death. The tale seems to have been placed in a cluster of tales about tengu because most mountain priests or monks who transform into creatures become tengu rather than oni. Instead of dealing with an exception, the compiler may have imagined this particular oni as a type of tengu. Another reason for the confusion between a tengu and a demon may be in the connection of this story to another in the "Tales of China" section. It involves a holy man who becomes a king of tengu after he dies in exile, having been punished for impregnating an imperial concubine.[26] Generally speaking, though, oni are more likely than tengu to figure in tales involving sex between a male creature and a woman.

The word *nyōran* in the Japanese title of the tale about Empress Some-dono, "Somedono no kisaki tengu no tame ni nyōran seraruru koto," is open to interpretation. It is translated here as "tormented" in accordance with its standard definition.[27] In this context, it may also have connotations of forced or otherwise destructive sex, as suggested by Robert Brower's rendering of it as "violated."[28] Something like "confusedly seduced" would best reflect what happens in the story. Although the demon is said to deprive the empress of her senses before charming her into sex, the tale does not indicate that the empress suffers with him in that form or is later horrified at what happened, as *torment* and *violation* suggest. The idea of torment in the title may even refer to stories portraying the empress as possessed in a non-sexual way; the entire title and not just the substitution of a tengu for a demon may come from knowledge of other tales, discussed below. In any case, the body of the empress is used to upset the order of things rather than her. Discussions of her suffering cannot be taken very far since there is no indication of it.

How Empress Somedono Is Tormented by a Tengu

Now it is the past, when the person called Somedono no kisaki, daughter of the regent Minister Yoshifusa, is the mother of Emperor Montoku. Her beauty is especially splendid. Now, this empress is constantly being tormented by evil spirits, so various ritual prayers are performed. All the monks known in the world for their miraculous powers are summoned and assembled. These exorcists perform the ritual prayers, but without the slightest effect.

Incidentally, at the summit of Mt. Kazuraki in Yamato Province is a place called Kongōsen. On that mountain lives an eminent holy man who has practiced there for many years. He makes his bowl fly away to return with his meals and his jar do the same with water. While he is there practicing in this way, his miraculous powers are unparalleled. And so, because of what becomes his great reputation, the emperor and the minister (father of the empress) hear about him. "Let's summon him and have him pray to cure the illness of the empress," they think and have an edict issued telling him to come. When the envoy goes to the holy man and informs him of the order, the holy man declines many times, but he finally goes because of the difficulty of disobeying an imperial order. He is summoned to her presence to chant incantations and the results are truly miraculous. One of the ladies-in-waiting suddenly goes mad, wailing and shouting. A spirit has possessed her and is running about screaming. As the holy man chants more and more forcefully, the woman is bound and beaten. An old fox comes out from her bosom, runs around, then falls over and lies there unable to run away. Then the holy man has someone tie the fox up, whereupon he reprimands it. Upon seeing this, the minister rejoices to no end. The empress recovers in one or two days.

The minister rejoices at this. "Your Holiness should stay for a while," he says, so the priest accepts the invitation and stays for a while. Since it is summer, the empress is wearing a single, unlined kimono, when the wind blows open the august hanging curtains and the priest catches a glimpse of her through that gap. The holy man sees her classically beautiful form with the eyes of someone not used to the sight. His heart is suddenly agitated and his liver falls to pieces, giving rise to a deeply passionate desire for the empress.

Since nothing can be done, he is tormented with yearning; it is as if his chest were ablaze. He is unable to bear thinking about it for even a moment, so his heart weakens and he loses his ability to reason. Careful that no one is around, he enters behind the curtains and firmly embraces the waist of the empress lying there. The empress is alarmed and bewildered. She breaks out in a sweat and is terrified, but it is difficult to resist with [only] the strength of an empress. The holy man humiliates her with all his might and her ladies-in-waiting, seeing this, scream out loudly.

The imperial physician, a man called Taima no Kamotsugu, is also in the palace to treat the illness of the empress, having received an imperial edict. He is in the courtier's hall when he hears the sudden screams. Alarmed, he races toward them just as the holy man is coming out from behind the curtains. Kamotsugu grabs the holy man and reports this incident to the emperor. Enraged, the emperor has the holy man bound and thrown into prison.

Imprisoned, the holy man does not say a single word to anyone and, gazing up toward the heavens, vows in tears, "I will die immediately, become a demon, and as long as the empress is in this world, be intimate with her whenever I desire." The prison director hears this and tells it to her father, the minister. The minister is alarmed, so he reports it to the emperor, whereupon the holy man is pardoned and returned to his mountain.

Now the holy man has returned to his mountain and cannot bear these feelings. He calls upon the Three Treasures, in which he has faith, praying fervently to have regular access to the empress. Even so, he resolves to become a demon just as he originally vowed, perhaps because of the unlikelihood that his other wish will be realized in this life. He doesn't eat and consequently dies of starvation in about ten days. Then, he suddenly becomes a demon. As for his appearance, he is [almost] naked and his head is bald. His height is as much as eight *shaku* and his skin is black as if it were lacquered.[29] His eyes appear as if they have metal bowls in them; his mouth is opened wide with teeth like swords planted in it and tusks protruding from the top and bottom. He wears a red loincloth with a mallet stuck in his waist[band].

Suddenly, this demon is standing beside the curtains in front of the empress. When people actually see him, they completely lose their senses and are distraught; they run away, falling down in confusion. When the ladies-in-waiting and such see this, some faint and others lie down, covering themselves completely with their robes. No ordinary people see him since this is not a place where they can go.

Now because the spirit of this demon bewitches the empress and makes her crazy, the empress is most genteel, smiling sweetly and hiding her face with her fan, then going behind the curtains and lying down with the demon. When the ladies-in-waiting listen in, the demon is saying how, day after day, he has only been forlorn with his yearning for her and other such things. When the empress laughs haughtily in delight, the ladies-in-waiting and others all run away. After some time, around sunset, the demon comes out from behind the curtains and leaves. The ladies-in-waiting think, "What could have happened to the empress?" and hurry in, but nothing is unusual and she is sitting there as if she does not realize that such a thing has happened. Still, the expression in her eyes reveals a little fear. When this incident is reported to the emperor, he laments deeply, feeling sorrow even more than alarm and fear. "What will become of the empress?" he says.

After this, the demon comes daily in the same way, but the empress still does not feel her heart or liver go to pieces in fear, nor does she have a change of heart; rather, she merely thinks of the demon as someone charming. And so, when everyone within the palace sees what is happening, their pity, grief, and laments are boundless.

Not long after, this demon possesses someone, saying, "I will definitely avenge myself for my grudge against Kamotsugu!" Hearing this, Kamotsugu is struck with terror in his heart, and he suddenly dies shortly afterwards. In addition, Kamotsugu has three or four sons who all go insane and die. And so, seeing this, both the emperor and minister (father of the empress) are quite terrified and have many of the best monks earnestly pray for the conquering of this demon. Perhaps because of their various prayers, this demon stops coming after about three months, so the heart of the empress slightly improves. When she is back to her usual self, the emperor rejoices, saying "I'll check on her condition again," and there is an imperial visit to her palace. It is more touching than ordinary imperial visits, with the hundred officials all in attendance and no one absent.

The emperor immediately enters the palace, meets with the empress and says touching things with tears in his eyes. The empress, too, is deeply moved. Her appearance is as it had previously been. Just then, that same demon suddenly leaps out from a corner and goes inside the curtains. While the emperor watches flabbergasted, the empress rushes behind the curtains in her usual way. A while later, the demon leaps out on the south side of the palace. All one hundred officials, from ministers to courtiers on down, distinctly see this demon. As they stand frightened and confused, the empress comes out behind the demon, lies down with him and does unspeakable and unsightly things without any scruples where all those people can see. When the demon gets up so does the empress, and they withdraw behind the curtain. Unable to do anything, the emperor returns home lamenting.

And so, eminent women should listen and never become intimate with a holy man like him. This incident is very sensitive and its telling demands reserve; however, it has been told and passed down for the knowledge of future generations as a strict warning against intimacy with holy men.[30]

Fujiwara no Akirakeiko (also known as Akiko or Meishi, 829–900) is called the Somedono Empress (Somedono no kisaki) because she lived at the Somedono mansion during her widowhood. The oldest version of this setsuwa about her is in *Zenke hiki* (*Secret Records of the Miyoshi Family Lineage*), a collection of strange tales compiled by Miyoshi no Kiyoyuki (847–918) between 910 and 918, most likely during the last two years of his life or no later than eighteen years after the empress's death. *Zenke hiki* is not extant, but three stories and references to their source survive in later texts such as *Shingon den* (*Lives of Esoteric Masters*, 1325). The possibility that these stories are later creations cannot be ruled out, but if they are authentic fragments as believed, then this story was recorded when the northern branch Fujiwara were still about a century away from reaching the zenith of their power.

According to the *Zenke hiki* tale, an elderly lady-in-waiting to Empress Somedono told the story to Kiyoyuki in 899, a year before the death of Somedono.[31] Whether or not the source and date are true, they raise the possibility of the tale having been orally circulated and recorded while Somedono was still alive. Moreover, 899 would mean that Kiyoyuki heard it only three years after a scandal erupted involving the daughter-in-law and cousin of Somedono. The history *Fusō ryakki* (*Concise Chronicle of Japan*, early to mid twelfth century) includes an account of an affair Fujiwara no Takaiko (also read Kōshi, 842–910) had with a certain Priest Zenyū of Tōkōji. The date 899 may have found its way into the Somedono tale because it falls close to the official response to the affair: the stripping of Takaiko's rank of imperial consort in 896.[32]

In other words, the creator of the Somedono tale may have drawn elements from the lives of both women. While the affair of Takaiko and a Buddhist priest is considered fact, Somedono is a better candidate for a protagonist in a story about a supernatural sexual encounter because of her mental fragility or "possessions." Furthermore, an emphasis on Takaiko's relationship with a Buddhist priest in later years would have detracted from the portrayal of her as a young lover of the famous man of great passion, Ariwara no Narihira (825–80), in *Ise monogatari* (*Tales of Ise*, ca. 905) and elsewhere (discussed in Chapter 4).[33] In the logic of setsuwa, it makes more sense to attribute a scandalous affair with a Buddhist priest-turned-demon to the older, already haunted woman.

The tale about Somedono has sparked the interest of many scholars and at least one fiction writer. Terry Kawashima interprets the "demonic mind control as an excuse for polyandry," enabling the empress to engage in an extramarital affair without threatening her social position or life.[34] Although this excuse can be understood as undermining authority by allowing Somedono to escape a punishment resembling Takaiko's, the political implications of a union between a holy man and an empress must also be considered. In *Akujo ron* (*On Evil Women*), Tanaka Takako responds to numerous discussions of the tale, including those of Baba Akiko, Iizawa Tadasu, and Tanabe Seiko.[35] She resists the emphasis of these scholars on crazed passion and their concern with mainly deep feelings of the priest/demon for Somedono. Another scholar who reads a kind of "love" (*ai*) into the relationship is Minamoto Junko.[36] In contrast, Tanaka sees the incident as revenge for the loss of the political power of a particular priest, Shinzei, otherwise known as Kakinomoto no Ki (800–860) and the rivals of the Fujiwara.

Relying heavily on tales about the non-sexual possession of Empress Somedono by Priest Shinzei, Tanaka insists on specificity, criticizing the reading of Komine Kazuaki in *Setsuwa no mori* (*The Forest of Setsuwa*) for not focusing on the eminent holy man as Shinzei.[37] She and others associate the priest in the story with the *Konjaku* and *Zenke hiki* demon because he is linked with Somedono elsewhere. The Buddhist figure in those older tales was probably not intended to correspond to a historical figure since many holy men practiced on Mt. Katsuragi, but it did not take long before Shinzei replaced the unnamed priest in the minds of people.

Many scholars discuss a related tale in *Sōō kashō-den* (*The Biography of Priest Sōō*, early tenth century and later) and *Shūi ōjōden* along with other versions in many additional texts.[38] That tale describes how Priest Shinzei possesses the empress as a celestial fox or as a tengu. It focuses on how Priest Sōō (831–919) exorcizes the creature and discovers its identity through a meeting with Fudō Myōō (Acalanātha), the Buddhist divinity of wisdom and fire. Somedono is merely the victim. However entangled with such stories later, the *Konjaku* tale is different. It involves both the karma of prohibited passion and an angry spirit whereas the *Sōō kashō-den*-type tale depicts only the latter. Nor is the possession of the empress sexual in that tale.

Research tying the possession of the empress to Shinzei includes at least one version of how Somedono depends on the rival of Shinzei to have her son, Korehito, succeed to the position of emperor. The story appears in many places, including *Gōdanshō*, *Heike*, *Hōbutsu shū*, and *Soga monogatari*.[39] Shinzei backs a member of Ki lineage, Prince Koretaka, whereas Korehito is supported by Priest Shinga in *Gōdanshō* and Priest Eryō in *Heike*. Horse races and sumō matches determine who will become emperor. The priest behind Korehito launches a rumor of his death, thereby tricking Shinzei into performing his rituals with less fervor than usual. Later, the wrestler representing Koretaka loses when that same rival makes an offering of some of his own brains. In the *Kakuichi* text of the *Heike*, Somedono gets Eryō to smash open his head by sending numerous messengers expressing fear that the wrestler representing her son will lose. Her role in the defeat of Shinzei is thus more prominent there than in texts lacking that detail.[40] However, the account of this succession dispute predating the *Konjaku* tale, in *Gōdanshō*, does not mention Somedono.

When scholars put this tale into dialogue with the tale about the fox possession in the *Sōō kashō-den* and elsewhere, they attribute the possession to a political grudge against the empress concerning this rivalry. Drawing from Tanaka, Bernard Faure writes: "Obviously, the unfortunate Somedono empress is a mere pawn in a political conflict about imperial succession that goes beyond her: she is chosen because she is the most vulnerable link in the adverse lineage. Her (imaginary) rape is transformed into an expression of her lustful nature."[41] In his view, the hostility toward Somedono is displaced anger at Korehito for winning the succession dispute. The dispute has been used to explain the sexual incident in *Konjaku* as well. However, since that tale comes from *Zenke hiki*, the stories of the competition to become emperor postdate it considerably and could not have been popularized before the late Heian period. They are consequently limited in determining why Empress Somedono is debased through a sexual representation.

We have to be equally cautious when considering the significance of Shinzei to the *Konjaku* tale. Since Shinzei is aligned with Koretaka, his demonization links him to others supporting the Ki *uji* (lineage group). Narihira also backs Koretaka because the destinies of the Ariwara and Ki are intertwined. (Narihira is married to the prince's cousin.) In a *Konjaku* tale discussed in the next chapter, he becomes an unwitting accomplice in the demonic consumption of a woman who can be identified as Takaiko. Along with Shinzei, Narihira can be seen as representing a force against the Fujiwara. Yet, until Shinzei is clearly identified as the spirit who possesses Somedono, sexually or otherwise, then the associations between him and Narihira through representations of demons are similarly latent, waiting to emerge and develop with time.

An error in *Konjaku* stating that Somedono is the mother of her historical mate, Montoku, suggests that Somedono's past and present connection to the northern branch Fujiwara is more important than her role as mother of Korehito. No mistake is made about her paternal roots: she is correctly identified as the daughter of Fujiwara no Yoshifusa (804–72), who gives rise to the dominance of the northern branch Fujiwara as the first regent not from the imperial family. Of course, the two issues are not separate: as future Emperor Seiwa, Korehito was Empress Somedono's contribution to the Fujiwara legacy. While her line ends with the deposition of Emperor Yōzei and installment of Emperor Kōkō, the genealogical connection of the emperor to her father's family (via his brother) is restored through Fujiwara no Mototsune. As the adopted son and biological nephew of Yoshifusa, this cousin insures the success of the line by maintaining his influence as regent almost until his death and by ultimately becoming the grandfather of two emperors.[42]

According to Komine, "the *tengu* of Shinzei becomes intertwined with a legend about an *oni* precisely because of the grudge against the authority" of the northern branch Fujiwara.[43] The *Konjaku* demon represents the Ki or other lineage groups or branches of Fujiwara politically destroyed or suppressed. Additionally, Somedono is an easy target as the grandmother of Emperor Yōzei; she can be defamed without direct insult to a reigning emperor since the role of her direct lineage in the imperial line ends with her grandson. The competing *uji* can attack without incurring the full wrath of the northern branch Fujiwara, who are probably ambivalent about this empress themselves. Although the regent's house would not have created such a crude tale to slander one of its own matriarchs, especially since Somedono is the daughter of Yoshifusa, they may have allowed its circulation because of their embarrassment about the violently insane Yōzei.[44] This tale would then exemplify the appropriation of a story initially intended to undermine authority by that authority.

The opposition to powerful figures begins with the priest viewing the empress and going through her curtains. The frightened empress resists him, but his behavior resembles that of aristocrats who glimpse a woman through an opening in a curtain or a fence, an act called *kaimami*. The transgression of the priest has more to do with what people expect of someone in his position than with rape, which we usually determine by a lack of consent. Although Buddhist institutions challenge the authority of the imperial house and the Fujiwara elsewhere in setsuwa, this figure cannot be seen as representing them because he resists their official stance on chastity, even calling on the Three Treasures to help him satisfy his lust. In contrast, the priest who exorcises Empress Somedono in a similar *Uji shūi* tale can be seen as challenging the world of Heian nobility along Buddhist lines. There, Priest Sōō from Mudōji Temple on Mt. Hiei is summoned to the palace because of his reputation as a great exorcist. The empress and her attendants initially have him intone his prayers on the veranda because they are repulsed by his shabby dress and demonic appearance. Sōō leaves after successfully exorcising the empress despite an invitation to stay. When the emperor issues an edict acknowledging his miraculous powers and appointing him as bishop (*sōzu*), he responds, "How can a beggar like me become an official in the Bureau of Priests?"[45] Summoned yet again, he refuses to go because "people are looked down upon in the capital."[46] Unlike the priest in *Konjaku*, Sōō remains within a Buddhist framework in denouncing the world of the aristocrats. His behavior affirms the Buddhist value of renunciation. Whereas Sōō indirectly criticizes the snobbery of the aristocrats and the elite way of life through his choices, the holy man in *Konjaku* is entirely iconoclastic, challenging the values of both Buddhist clergy and aristocrats.[47]

From another perspective, the *Konjaku* tale reads as a criticism of mountain asceticism by other Buddhist practitioners, especially those associated with temples in the capital. By the early Heian period, *yamabushi* and *hijri* had begun to gain the respect of aristocrats, including emperors and retired emperors. Their increasing popularity may have been threatening to monks and nuns associated with established institutions. Located south of Kyoto on the border of Yamato and Kawachi provinces, the Kazuraki mountain range is one area where mountain asceticism developed; the founder of what is called Shugendō, En no Ozunu (otherwise named En no Gyōja and En no Ubasoku, 634–701) is thought to have been active there after his exile for the misuse of magic.[48] Or the tale might be a warning against the charlatans and hypocrites among those people who practiced mountain austerities.

The depiction of Empress Somedono engaged in sex with a demon may be read at one level as a degradation of both the Fujiwara and the imperial house. Anyone who did not benefit from the dominance of the Fujiwara would have had reason to reduce them to a body, simply there to be penetrated while others indulge in the vicarious pleasure of humiliating them. The violence of the representation would have appealed to some men even in later times, when the heyday of the regent house had passed or even to the enemies of warrior government (Shogunate) founder Minamoto no Yoritomo (1147–99), if we accept the generally embraced theory that Yoritomo's lineage is descended from Somedono's son, Emperor Seiwa.

With the creation of the demon-lover, the tale reveals that the mental and physical state of the empress is profoundly altered in a way dissimilar to ordinary sexual arousal. The grotesque nature of the tale is largely contingent on the one lover being the terrifying transformation of a dead person. He becomes something acceptable or perhaps even beautiful in the eyes of Somedono in contrast to the perception others have of him as monstrous. A passage in the medical book *Ishinpō* by Tanba no Yasuyori (912–95) deals with the concern of ghosts or demons becoming sexually involved with women. Despite the differences between the medical description of this condition and the case of Empress Somedono, there is enough common ground between the two to warrant taking the *Ishinpō* into consideration. The book is believed to have been an authoritative source in the medical field during the Heian period before *Konjaku* was compiled and possibly around the time the tale was being orally circulated. Below is a response to the question of what causes illness involving sexual intercourse with demons:

> Because of a lack of interunion between *Yin* and *Yang*. When the tension of sexual desire increases, ghosts (demons) appear and the woman begins to have sexual intercourse with them. The manner in which [the ghosts] (demons) perform intercourse is superior to that of an ordinary person. The longer this is practiced, the more confused and secretive the woman becomes. She never understands the seriousness [of this] and dies a lonely death. The way to treat this malady is to let the woman have sexual intercourse with her man day and night without stopping. The man must not release the semen. She will be cured in seven days. . . . To leave her alone without treatment is murder for she will certainly die in a few years. Should proof of this matter be desired, go into the wilderness of deep mountains and great marshes and concentrate on the longing to combine *Yin* and *Yang*. After three days and three nights the body will experience quick transitions of chills and fever, mental confusion and blurred vision. A man will see a woman and a woman will see a man. The dreamlike act of sexual intercourse will feel far more pleasurable than that performed with ordinary humans. But this condition is a sickness difficult to cure. It is simply the effect of

loneliness and depression and of being overwhelmed by evil spirits. In future generations this will happen again and again.[49]

Two additional prescriptions are then suggested: for girls and aristocratic women who cannot be treated with continuous intercourse because of their rank, burning sulfur can be used to fumigate the genitals while the patients swallow powdered deer horn. Regular dosages of powdered deer horn—one cubic-inch spoonful three times a day—can also be taken.

In the published English translation of *Ishinpō*, the word *oni* is translated only as *ghosts*, but I add the word *demons* in parentheses. (The translators included the bracketed words.) Since the author, Yasuyori, borrows heavily from Chinese medical books and wrote in *kanbun*, we should take the Chinese meaning of *gui* (oni) into consideration. In ancient China as in premodern Japan, relatively benign spirits of the dead overlap with threatening and malevolent spirit-creatures. As Michel Strickmann has written: "ghosts and demons alike are generically called *kuei* [*gui*], and the boundaries between the two groups seem to be quite fluid."[50] Spirits of the deceased that are not worshipped are demons, but the term can also refer to the deceased worshipped only by their descendants and not by large groups of people as gods. *Gui* can roam the world causing various calamities or not be threatening at all.[51] The harmful nature of the spirits is stressed with demon intercourse. How would the Heian aristocrats have read this passage? The Chinese character read as *oni* usually refers to demons in Japan, although such spirits could have also been ghosts since people feared trouble caused by spirits of the dead.

Descriptions of such possessions may strike us as attempts to explain erotic dreams. It would be wrong, though, to reduce the ghost-demon entirely to this psychological phenomenon. In both *Ishinpō* and *Konjaku*, the main issue for the authors is not autoeroticism, but the fear of outside influences. The female body becomes a site of invasion. The passage suggests that men and women will react similarly when simultaneously focusing on and depriving themselves of sex. Elsewhere, the *Ishinpō* states that men can suffer from ghost or demon intercourse, but the ailment appears to be more devastating to women since no section centers on its effects and cures for men.[52] Loneliness makes people vulnerable to the ghost-demon, but the creature is not viewed entirely as a manifestation of that loneliness and desire. It is also an external force. Whereas the disease devastates the individual in the medical text, the threat endangers the existing social order in setsuwa.

Ishinpō shares with the tale a similar interest in the possibility of ghost-demons becoming intimate with women. A creator of the tale about the empress and the oni may have been familiar with the malady of ghost-demon intercourse because many manuscripts of the medical book circulated during the Heian period.[53] Medical knowledge was probably transmitted orally as well. A connection between the passionate priest and the realm of court medicine is made within the tale itself as the imperial physician reports the degenerate priest to the emperor. The demon avenges his former self by causing the death of this man, Taima no Kamotsugu. The tension between these two figures suggests competition of the court physicians trained at the university (*daigaku*) and provincial schools (*kokugaku*) with the Buddhist priests treating illness.[54]

The demon intercourse experienced by the empress differs from the medical description in that the loneliness of the holy man rather than of the empress causes the affliction. In Heian Buddhism, sexual abstinence helps to preserve the monastic community, keeping it separate from the familial social relations practiced in society at large. But celibacy was problematic for many Japanese monks. As an overview of Japanese Buddhism indicates, "from approximately the ninth century on, monks had been taking secret wives, and it was a known practice among monks of Mt. Hiei."[55] The affair of Takaiko and Zenyū has already been discussed, but there were many real and fictionalized accounts of Buddhists attracted to court women. Homosexuality was often more accepted than heterosexuality because it did not complicate the lives of monks by creating outside attachments, including children.

The grotesque tone of the tale begins to materialize after the priest declares he will become a demon and then, dead, returns in that form to seduce the empress. Almost everyone at court is horrified and rendered powerless, including the emperor. For the empress, though, the encounters have something fundamentally in common with the medical book scenario: they feel good. The paradox of ghost or demon intercourse lies in its being more pleasurable than human contact. The *Ishinpō* warns that these encounters will cause physical decline and death, threats that lead people to seek a cure. Yet *Konjaku* never mentions this kind of danger. How is the encounter threatening if Empress Somedono enjoys it without being harmed? Crossing socially and politically defined boundaries is supposed to be negative, but here the empress is happy.

Boundaries between human and demonic spirits are also between the known and unknown. The official stance attempts to temper if not silence the voices of people who travel beyond the realm of control. United, a politically important aristocratic woman and a priest have the potential to redefine politics and religion in Heian Japan. How much worse it would be were the same woman and a demon collaborating against the authority of the imperial house, the Fujiwara, and the Buddhist establishment. The precedent for a high-ranking woman and a Buddhist acting as a political unit is Empress Shōtoku (also called Kōken, 718–70) and the Buddhist priest Dōkyō (700–72). Empress Shōtoku succeeded to the throne after her father abdicated and ruled for about ten years until abdicating herself in favor of Emperor Junnin. She retained enough power to depose of Junnin and give Dōkyō the titles of Chancellor (*Daijō daijin zenji*), previously conferred only on members of the imperial family, and Dharma master (*Hō-ō*). In 767, Dōkyō attempted to become emperor but was prevented when the empress sent a government official to Usa to consult with the deity Hachiman. The response indicated that the emperor had to be a member of the imperial family descended from the gods, so Dōkyō was disqualified.[56] Had the empress been less cautious, lacking second thoughts about who should be in power and respect for protocol, Buddhism and its relationship to the government would have developed differently. Yet, scholars rarely wonder why the empress decided to confer with Hachiman (actually, other humans) instead of making the decision herself. While her actions led in part to Dōkyō's rise to power, she also had a role in his fall in that her hesitation was the beginning of it.

Nor do the accounts of this event consider that the empress may have initially shared with Dōkyō a vision of a Buddhist state, a land led by people committed to both the country and Buddhism.[57] According to Tanaka and Faure, many medieval representations of her focus on her insatiable lust, often graphically suggested by descriptions of the genitals of both the empress and the priest as unusually large.[58] Such representations divert attention away from how these two people may have been using their minds. Modern interpretations often depict Shōtoku as a victim of loneliness and longing with Dōkyō taking advantage of her neediness. In the *Foundation of Japanese Buddhism*, we read: "The Empress was a lonely, unmarried forty-five year old woman obsessed with religion. It was simply a matter for an unscrupulously ambitious priest to manipulate her."[59] Both views detract from the possibility that the empress was trying to change the existing political regime. Although the modern readings seem less crude and more compassionate than the premodern representations, they suggest she did not have her own vision and aspirations. While the ruling empress was expected to remain celibate, a sexual relationship might have been overlooked if it were not overtly political—for example, if it were with someone, such as a servant, who had limited ability to profit from it. Had the desires of the empress been primarily physical, she could have found a secret, innocuous, lover.[60]

The threat of the relationship of Empress Shotoku and Dōkyō was about more than unsanctioned sexual pleasure. It was that Dōkyō as emperor would no longer have been subordinate to imperial rule and the existing order of familial authority would have been altered.

His fathering a son would have changed the imperial line. Even a bond between an empress and monk without a sexual dimension could be dangerous because the loyalty of the empress was divided.

While evoking the relationship of Empress Shōtoku and Dōkyō, the story of Empress Somedono and her demon lover undermines the significance of high-ranking aristocratic women forming close bonds with eminent Buddhists. The tale lampoons the power of the connection by depicting the empress under a trance and not responsible for her actions. As long as the empress is incompetent, the threat to the social order of the aristocrats remains external. Political ambitions are reduced to sexual desire. In contrast, the political actions of men are not generally attributed to loneliness and the desire for a relationship. What if Somedono were in her right mind and the demon were human? The question is there, implicit in the attempts to bury it.

A *Gōdanshō* tale (3:32) about how the ghost of Minamoto no Tōru (822–95) challenges the authority of Retired Emperor Uda (867–931) alludes to the concern about sexual relations with demons or ghosts as well. Here, the female body serves entirely as the site of conflict between men.

How Minister of State Tōru Grabs the Waist
of the Cloistered Emperor of the Kanpyō Era

Minister Sukenaka has related the following: The Cloistered Kanpyō Emperor and Kyōgoku no Miyasudokoro travel to the Kawara Mansion, viewing the mountains and rivers. Night falls and the moon shines. He has the cart mats taken out to use as seats. He is doing what is done in the bedroom with Miyasudokoro when a person in the storehouse of the Shinden opens the door and comes out.[61] The cloistered emperor demands an explanation. "I am Tōru," the person responds. "I want you to give me Miyasudokoro."

The cloistered emperor answers, "When you were alive, you were a retainer. I was your emperor. What a reckless thing to say. You ought to leave and go back where you came from." Frightened, the ghost suddenly grabs onto the waist of the retired emperor. Miyasudokoro loses consciousness, the color disappearing from her face. All the imperial soldiers are outside the central gate and the emperor's voice cannot be expected to reach them. However, a boy ox herd is very close by. The emperor calls that child and has all the people summoned, and his cart is drawn up. Miyasudokoro is helped getting in. She has no color in her face and cannot rise. She is helped in the cart and taken back. The cloistered emperor summons Priest Jōzō and has him perform incantations for her, so soon she is revived.

In accordance with karma accumulated in a previous life, the cloistered emperor became the sovereign of Japan. Even without the status of emperor, he reveres the protection of the gods of heaven and earth. He chased the spirit of Tōru away. In front of the door are traces of his sword: traces of a pursuit ordained by a guardian deity. Moreover, some people say such things as, "When the cloistered emperor is behind his rattan blinds, the ghost of Tōru dwells around the rail."[62]

Kawara-no-in was a luxurious mansion on the east side of the capital, between Fifth and Sixth Avenues and beside the Kamo River. It was known for its garden, designed to resemble the famous scenic spot Shiogama in Michinoku and as a place where poets and statesmen gathered. The belief that it was haunted may have come in part from the fact that "the occasional heavy flooding of the Kamo River caused it to deteriorate rapidly."[63] Sutras were recited there on the fourth day of the seventh month of 926 to pacify the spirit of Tōru. After the death of Uda, it became a temple.[64]

The ghost visitation at Kawara-no-in assumes more meaning when we consider facts about the people involved.[65] Emperor Uda and Minamoto no Tōru were both members of the imperial family made commoners: Tōru was the son of Emperor Saga and Uda (Minamoto no Sadami) was the son of Emperor Kōkō. That change proved temporary for Sadami. In 884, Emperor Kōkō divested his children of imperial status under pressure from the regent, Fujiwara no Mototsune, to remove them from the line of succession, but the court restored it to Sadami in an unprecedented move three years later. According to *Ōkagami*, Tōru aspired to become emperor toward the end of 883, claiming rights to the position when a council was held to depose the insane Emperor Yōzei, but Mototsune used Tōru's status as subject to resist him.[66] Kōkō was selected instead, in part because his mother was a Fujiwara. Tōru ended up serving Emperors Kōkō and Uda as Minister of the Left. Uda's remarks to the ghost, then, are historically true but ironic.

"When you were alive, you were a retainer," he says, "I was your emperor."
It could have been the other way around given the histories of the men.
Tōru had reason for resentment.

The careers of both Tōru and Emperor Uda were shaped by the struggle
between the northern branch Fujiwara and the courtiers of other lineage
groups (some of whom were from different branches of Fujiwara), but the
emperor was in a better position than Tōru to resist Fujiwara dominance.
Uda would appoint people who were not members of the Fujiwara to high-
ranking and influential political positions. His interests were at odds with
those of Mototsune, the regent to an adult emperor (*kanpaku*) and most
powerful person at court at the time of his succession. This conflict was
apparent from the very beginning of Uda's reign, during the so-called Akō
incident. After Uda became emperor, he was supposed to issue edicts in accordance with his late father's wishes requesting that Mototsune continue
as regent. The recipient of such an edict customarily turns down the first.
The second edict insulted Mototsune because of the substitution of the title
akō for *kanpaku*. A scholar named Sukeyo, who significantly was a Fujiwara,
informed Mototsune that *akō* is only an honorary title conveying no real
power. Already disturbed by Uda's reliance on other non-Fujiwara government officials, Mototsune used the switch in terms to express his displeasure. In the end, Uda placated Mototsune by blaming the man who drafted
the edicts for the word choice and by promising to punish him. Uda also
accepted a daughter of Mototsune as a consort. It was apparently Tōru who
convinced Uda to capitulate.[67]

A month before the Akō incident ended, in the fifth month of 888, Uda
relied on Tōru, his Minister of the Left, to get things under control at court,
but to no avail.[68] In the tale, the ghost of Tōru also seems ineffectual—
remarkably weak compared to others of his type. As Mori Masato points
out: "In most cases when a person treaded unprepared into a haunted place
he would arouse the wrath of the supernatural creatures living there, and
generally lose his life."[69] The portrayal of the ghost evokes the representation
of Tōru in historical sources as someone more likely to adapt than resist.
After 888, Tōru is the only other official of ministerial status besides Mototsune, but he presents no opposition to the Fujiwara.[70]

The woman caught in the middle of this struggle between ghost and
man is Kyōgoku no Miyasudokoro: Lady (of) Kyōgoku. She is Fujiwara
no Hōshi (dates unknown), a daughter of Fujiwara no Tokihira (871–909).
Tokihira is the rival of Sugawara no Michizane (845–903), whom Emperor

Uda supports politically as long as possible. Hōshi, whose title Miyasu-dokoro indicates that she is an imperial concubine, is linked to Emperor Uda and the Kawara-no-in in *Yamato monogatari* (*Tales of Yamato*, ca. 938–1011). Episode 3 depicts her announcing plans for a celebration of Emperor Uda's sixtieth birthday. In episode 61, Uda has a special apartment set up for her in the Kawara-no-in and leaves many concubines behind in another palace to be with her. The brief story, which includes an exchange of poems, then shifts to the plight of the neglected women.[71]

Given the connections of Hōshi to Uda and the mansion, it seems logical that she is the woman with Emperor Uda when the ghost of Tōru confronts him. That her father is Tokihira adds another dimension to the tale. Why are Uda and Tōru struggling over possession of a northern branch Fujiwara woman? Tōru's demand for her suggests a desire to connect to the Fujiwara, since, in Heian politics, ties between men are forged in part through access to the female body. Historical sources show Tōru resigned to the power of Mototsune and the Fujiwara in contrast to Uda. On the other hand, how-ever strong the sexual attraction between Uda and Hōshi, their bond must have been complex and charged with political meaning. Robert Borgen writes in his book on Michizane, "Tokihira's relations with the imperial family were less than ideal."[72] Tokihira had difficulty retaining "what for the Fujiwara had become their customary close relationship with the reigning emperor," and a problem "manipulating a blood relative into the imperial line."[73] When Tokihira's rival, Michizane, is exiled, the Retired Emperor Uda tries to help him only to be barred from the palace. Given the way Uda struggles against Fujiwara influence and his strained relations with Tokihira, the depiction of this woman as preferred seems odd. If Uda did favor her at some point, it could have been an attempt to ingratiate Tokihira. His feel-ings about accepting her would have been mixed. In the tale, Uda refuses to give the Fujiwara woman to Tōru. He prevents the ghost from taking her, perhaps as he would have prevented the living Tōru from entering the realm of the Fujiwara had he been able.

Konjaku tale 2 of Book 27, tale 151 of *Uji shūi*, and tale 27 of Book 1 of *Kohon setsuwa shū* describe a similar meeting of Emperor Uda and the ghost of Tōru but do not mention the lover.[74] The element of confrontation in them is also toned down. That version indicates Emperor Uda inherits Kawara-no-in after Tōru dies. In *Konjaku* and *Kohon*, the ghost appears and complains about the lack of space now that Retired Emperor Uda, too, lives under his roof. He even suggests the retired emperor leave. Unperturbed by a spirit, the emperor argues the house now belongs to him and the ghost vanishes. The spirit is even less threatening in *Uji shūi* as it expresses concern about not being able to serve Uda properly. Since scholars do not believe there is a direct textual connection between the *Gōdanshō* tale and the tales in these later collections, we cannot attribute the differences in the stories to rewriting and hence censorship of a particular text. Yet, we are left wondering why a rendering similar to the *Gōdanshō* tale was not chosen for other compilations.

Along with the *Gōdanshō* tale, the *Konjaku* and the *Uji shūi* tales praise Emperor Uda in the closing. They focus on his superior qualities, suggesting "he is hardly an ordinary human being."[75] Such praise should be interpreted with the larger, historical picture in mind. If Tōru suggests acquiescence to the Fujiwara, then Uda's ability to stand up to the ghost alludes to the triumph over that tendency. The resistance of Emperor Uda to the Fujiwara can be interpreted as courageous despite his ultimate failure.

The praise for Uda in *Gōdanshō* may be connected to the political involvement of that collection's compiler, Ōe no Masafusa (1041–1111), with Retired Emperors Go-Sanjō and Shirakawa as superintendent or *bettō* in the cloistered governments of both. Ōe was proud of his academic ancestors, none of whom was a Fujiwara. The tale about Uda standing up to a ghost demonstrates the extraordinary existence of an ex-emperor and someone who was not a Fujiwara. Yet, the ghosts of the people who gave into the Fujiwara did not easily vanish. Emperor Uda ironically has a Fujiwara woman saved in the tale. She and the others persist as conduits for political relationships between the imperial house and the Fujiwara.

A TRANSFORMED FEMALE BODY

Buddhism traditionally instilled or sometimes reinforced in men a fear and contempt of women and heterosexual sex to keep them in the monastic community. Before the Kamakura period (1185–1333), when new forms of Buddhism permitted monks and priests to marry, the loss of semen to a woman was the potential loss of Buddhahood. The next tale, number 40 in *Konjaku* Book 29, conveys a negative view of the female body consistent with much Buddhist thought, but the woman is a dream manifestation of the man's desire. It has some other interesting twists as well.

How a Snake Who Sees the Penis of a Napping Monk
Dies after Receiving and Swallowing Semen

Now it is the past; there is a young monk in the service of a preeminent priest. This monk has a wife and child. He accompanies his master to Mi-idera, where, come afternoon and it being summer, he feels sleepy. Since the monastery is huge, he wanders to a place away from everyone and falls asleep using a ground beam as his pillow. Sound asleep and with no one to disturb him, he sleeps long and dreams: A beautiful, young woman approaches and lies beside him. He penetrates her again and again until ejaculating. Startled the monk suddenly awakens and looks down to find a snake about five *shaku* long beside him. He quickly jumps up in fright, and then looks again: the snake lies dead with its mouth open. Shocked and disgusted, the monk glances down at himself and notices his robe is wet with semen.

"Hum, how odd. Could it be I was actually penetrating a snake as I slept dreaming of sex with that beautiful woman?" he thinks as fear overcomes him, almost knocking him senseless. When he looks at the open mouth again, the snake has vomited semen.

He thinks, "What on earth. . . . This is what must have happened: I'm fast asleep, the snake notices my erect penis, approaches it and takes it into his mouth, all the while making me feel as if I'm having sex with a woman. And then when I ejaculate into the snake, it dies unable to bear it." The monk is shocked and disgusted by this realization. He leaves the room and, in private, gives his penis a good washing. "Can I mention this to anyone?" he thinks. "If I tell people about this trifling thing and leave it for them to judge, they may all start calling me "the monk who has sex with snakes." So, he keeps his mouth shut. But this experience strikes him as so bizarre, he ultimately tells a close friend and colleague, and that monk, too, is terribly frightened.

Well then, you shouldn't take naps alone in remote, empty places. But, no other strange things happen to this monk afterwards. It's true what they say about beasts not being able to bear human semen and definitely dying when receiving it. Apparently, even the monk has been sick with anxiety for a while. And so the story is passed down by people hearing it from the second monk as the first monk told it to him.[76]

Since the *Konjaku* tales predate the open acceptance of married monks, the reference to the monk's marital status alludes to his moral laxity or his lack of full commitment. Implicit in the narrative is a contrast between this monk and the man he serves, described in the Japanese as *yamu koto naki*, literally meaning without a stop or limit and, in this context, conveying the sense of preeminence in devotion and practice. The young monk hardly emulates the high priest when he wanders off to a remote room of the spacious

Tendai monastery, Miidera, for a midday nap. His vulnerability to illusions is manifested in his dream and sexual excitement. In *Konjaku* as in most other medieval Japanese texts, no sharp distinction is made between waking reality and dreams. As LaFleur explains, Buddhists in particular "made it their business to point out that it is not a matter of a black-or-white difference between waking consciousness and dream consciousness but rather of both of them being *on a continuum* of consciousness."[77]

The monk immediately heeds to physical urges in the dream. Wet dreams are not offenses in the Vinaya (the scriptures concerned with monastic discipline and moral behavior) and commentaries: they do not represent a loss of control over the mind because the semen is emitted unintentionally.[78] The central issue here cannot be a loss of celibacy since sexual acts during sleep are not considered morally wrong (although experiences in dreams are generally considered very important for other reasons) and the man is already married. It must be the extent of the monk's desire, illusory as the dream woman herself, and thus his vulnerability. Nothing is said of the woman, solely a product of the monk's eroticism, except that she is young and beautiful. These are two characteristics men in setsuwa inevitably desire in their partners. Without any distinguishing marks, she does not attract attention as a character but instead exposes the bodily nature of the monk.

Here, the monk is not held responsible for being unable to transcend desire. Although the act occurs in a dream, the understanding of why it happens, merely because the woman is present, resembles many descriptions of sex in tales involving conscious men. The snake causes the monk to engage in sexual intercourse with two different partners: itself and the imagined woman, but the man experiences the snake's mouth only as a vagina. The narrative progresses through the substitution of one body part for another: vagina to snake's mouth and then, once the monk awakes, from mouth back to the idea of female genitals. If the vagina is the mouth of a snake, then the rest of the animal, too, is in some sense female. The dead snake vomiting semen shocks, disgusts, and frightens the monk. Normally having the capacity to give life, semen is poisonous when ejaculated into the wrong creature or the wrong cavity. There may also be an implicit warning against oral sex, at least when a woman is involved.

Even so, the idea of coitus is implicit in the representation of the snake. Are there any phallic aspects to this snake, otherwise linked to the female body? The verbal phrase used to describe the vomited semen, *hakiidashitari,* refers to a forceful and sudden ejection and echoes the behavior of the monk. In addition, this tale and the preceding tale (number 39) are linked by the representation of a snake sexually excited by human genitals. The snake is unquestionably phallic in "How a Snake Becomes Desirous When Seeing a Vagina, Emerges from His Hole and Is Killed with a Sword." There, a young woman traveling by foot suddenly has to urinate. When she squats behind an earthen wall, a huge snake comes out of a hole in it. Terribly frightened, the woman freezes and cries for four hours, even while the snake returns to its hiding. A man passing by eventually helps the distraught woman by striking the animal dead with his sword when it again sticks his head out. He assumes the snake was sexually excited.[79] Taken together, the exposed woman, the snake in the hole, and the idea of the animal being aroused suggest sexual intercourse. Tales 39 (woman and snake) and 40 (man and snake) mirror each other. The phallic animal and the "real" vagina of tale 39 contrast with the symbolic vagina and "real" penis in 40. Yet the second tale also represents a progression: male and female genitalia merge in the single body of this animal.

In the tale of the sleeping monk at Miidera, the reaction of the man to the open mouth of the dead snake suggests feelings about women and sex embraced by many Nara and Heian period Buddhists. Women represent evil, relentless desire, and the loss of control. The vagina is repelling in its association with the snake's mouth. The bestial attack on the penis of an unsuspecting man alludes to the view of women as physical creatures who pursue men sexually to prevent them from attaining enlightenment. Women may slither up toward unguarded men and suck their potent energy away from them with their snake-mouth vaginas or, since the imagery also suggests oral sex, with their mouths. In discussing "the zoological peril to male sexuality" in traditional Chinese stories, Michel Strickmann notes that premodern Chinese men seem to have "a primal and obsessive fear of . . . being devoured, or sucked dry."[80] The tale about the napping monk reveals that some premodern Japanese men had similar apprehensions and fantasies with its focus on orality and secretion.

Given this implicit warning, the remarks of the commentator come as a surprise. He merely cautions against sleeping alone in isolated places and fails to acknowledge the Buddhist implications of the tale: the precept forbidding sexual behavior or the negative view of women. The *Konjaku* compilers were certainly aware of the Buddhist stance on women and their bodies, given the nature of many other tales in the collection, but did not turn this story into an authoritative statement on the dangers of the female sex. They did not even place it in the Buddhist part of "Tales of Japan." That choice, the final remark of the commentator, and the fact that Japanese monks often had sexual partners or secret wives, suggest that many people were not entirely persuaded by the Buddhist attacks on the female body and heterosexual sex. Even religious figures must have been influenced by belief systems and practices other than Buddhism, including those of the courtier since many were aristocrats by birth. Nonetheless, the grotesque representations of this tale express more than the final comments.

The snake assuming the form of a woman in the dream evokes the woman-turned-snake in the story of Dōjōji Temple, famous because noh and kabuki plays are based on it. In the *Hokkegenki* and *Konjaku* tales, a woman tries to seduce a young monk traveling to Kumano. The young man promises to return after his pilgrimage and comply with her wishes, but then avoids her by taking another route home. Discovering this deception, the woman rushes into a separate room, closes the door, and dies. A huge snake soon emerges from the room and pursues the man, who escapes to Dōjōji Temple, where he seeks help. The monks there take the bell down from the belfry and hide the young man within it, but the snake breaks through closed gates and locked doors, finds the bell, and coils around it. Its venom sets the bell on fire, reducing the monk to ashes as the bell even melts a bit. Later, in a dream of an old senior monk of Dōjōji Temple, the deceased in the form of a huge snake explains that the female snake controlled him and caused him to be reborn as its mate. He requests that the Tathāgata chapter of the *Lotus Sutra* be copied for him and the woman. When this request is fulfilled, the two spirits are born in separate Buddhist heavens, she into Trāyastriṃśa Heaven (*Tōriten*) and he into Tuṣita Heaven (*Tosotsu*). The *Konjaku* commentator warns about the evil in the hearts of women and stresses the importance of avoiding them.[81]

This story, too, reveals ambivalent feelings of many men toward women at this time. Despite the salvation of the woman, it is deeply embedded in misogynistic forms of Buddhist thought, supporting the views that women have the potential to obstruct the enlightenment of men and are evil enough to do so intentionally. Their own spiritual development is unlikely because of the strength of their passions and illusions, far exceeding those of men.

The sentiment in the tale seems split between making the monk responsible for his fate and blaming the woman.[82] The sizes of the snakes people become often reflect the offenses committed during their lives. The spiritual chastity of the young man is suspect despite his ability to resist the sexual advances of the woman since he ends up becoming quite a large snake, even larger than his partner. Besides, he resorts to deception. Yet, the spirit of the former monk argues that the poisonous female snake controlled him and consequently caused his rebirth in his present form. Instead of embracing this ambivalence, the *Konjaku* commentator reinforces the negative attitude toward women by blaming them for the failures of men.

That the woman escapes the body of a snake does not reflect positively on her since we never see her desiring enlightenment or pursing any spiritual goals in the setsuwa versions of the story. Rather, her release from that physical form despite a lack of effort attests to the miraculous power of the *Lotus Sutra*. Besides, the new abode of the woman, Trāyastriṃśa Heaven, is inferior to that of the man, Tuṣita Heaven. This difference reinforces the inferior status of the female spirit. No birth in a Deva Heaven is the same as enlightenment or birth in the Pure Land. Spirits born in one of these realms must become human again before achieving enlightenment. This feat is difficult because lifetimes in Deva Heavens are long and comfortable, and the departure from them, painful.[83] Although both heavens are one of six in the world of desire (*saṃsāra*), all bodhisattvas are born in Tuṣita Heaven before appearing on earth as Buddha. The heaven where the young monk ultimately resides was the dwelling of Śākyamuni before he appeared in the world. It is also where the future Buddha Maitreya (Miroku) awaits. Along with Amida's Pure Land, Tuṣita Heaven attracted religious people in the Heian and early Kamakura periods, as demonstrated by a comparison of the two realms in *The Essentials of Rebirth in the Pure Land* by Genshin (942–1017).[84]

Focusing on the demonic feminine, Susan Klein has considered these setsuwa in connection to the noh play *Dōjōji*. Her perspective is largely psychoanalytic, but she also carefully examines the historical contexts. In general, I see psychoanalytic theory as culturally and temporally specific and resist all but the most cautious use of it in interpreting Japanese literature. Yet, certain representations can assume similar symbolic meaning in different societies and historical periods. A given story ultimately determines whether or not such an interpretation makes sense and, if so, how. Klein emphasizes the phallic nature of the woman transformed into a snake, stating that it is obvious to post-Freudians that the female body "is transformed into a living phallus."[85] Additionally, she writes: "In the *setsuwa*, we can see masculine desire being projected onto the female body, a projection that enabled men to deny those negative aspects of their own sexual nature which had to be eliminated for enlightenment to occur: the woman as female snake (that is, simultaneously phallic and female) embodies the animal nature of both masculine and feminine sexuality."[86] In the Freudian/Lacanian reading, to have power is to be phallic.[87] Authority and control on the part of a woman probably would have been perceived as a transgression into a male realm and therefore threatening. However, since the ability to hinder men from enlightenment actively and consciously is feminine in the Buddhist context, I hesitate to associate the power illustrated in the tale with the phallus or maleness, or at least not exclusively. Why not look for a representation that underscores the female quality of certain types of power?

Klein directs our attention to feminine representation by mentioning that temple bells are symbolic of wombs in Japanese esoteric Buddhism, but, at that point in the article, she has left the setsuwa behind to focus on the noh plays *Kanemaki* (*Enwrapping the Bell*, ca. fifteenth century) and *Dōjōji* (ca. late fifteenth–early sixteenth century).[88] The transformation of the woman into a snake occurs within the bell in those plays, but the womb imagery functions in the setsuwa as well. The idea of a hollow space, such as the inside of a bell (or, a cave as mentioned in the Introduction of this book), as symbolic of the uterus is also apparent in psychoanalytic theory. In "Symbolism in Dreams," Freud writes:

> The female genitals are symbolically represented by all such objects as share their characteristic of enclosing a hollow space which can take something into itself: by *pits*, *cavities* and *hollows*, for instance, by vessels and bottles, by receptacles, boxes, trunks, cases, chests, pockets, and so on. Ships, too, fall into this category. Some symbols have more connection with the uterus than with the female genitals: thus, cupboards, stoves and, more especially rooms. Here room-symbolism touches on house-symbolism. Doors and gates, again, are symbols of the genital orifice.[89]

Although I would caution against seeing a connection to female body parts whenever an object with a hollow space is mentioned (just as I would see-ing all elongated objects as phallic), the transformation of the woman into a snake within the bedchamber in the setsuwa is symbolically charged: if we see the room as evoking the womb, then it is an appropriate place to meta-morphose and from which to be reborn. Furthermore, although the male snake does not emerge from the ashes in the tale, the potential for another life is realized in his death inside the bell. The spirit of the young monk must be released within those flames for the next life.

In a grotesque mode, a reverse birth takes place. In contrast to an infant emerging from the womb, the man is taken into it and never separates from the maternal body. Reduced to ashes, the man inside the corporal mother vanishes from this earth. The understanding of the bell as a female body is supported by the actions of the snake—by its coiling around the bell as if embracing it or her, and striking the dragonhead for four to six hours, an action alluding to sexual intercourse, however exaggerated the time frame. The phallic nature of the female snake is compromised when the animal winds itself around the bell, assuming a circular and thus feminine shape and containing the container. The young monk is then trapped within two layers of female flesh, his own self the phallus.

CONCLUSION

Representations of copulation, conception, pregnancy, and birth are defining features of the grotesque in setsuwa. Women are not idealized as the source of life, as Bakhtin argues they were in the European popular tradition. As we saw in the story involving the turnip, the emphasis of a tale often shifts to the role of men and other creatures or objects. The female body frequently functions as the central point for conflict between men. This tendency is especially apparent in the two tales dealing with ghost-demon intercourse.

Yet, issues concerning women and female bodies surface in what seems a more consciously male-centered narrative. Empress Somedono is cast as a victim of the priest-turned-demon, but another story concerning how women may have used their bodies to resist authority emerges when we consider the possible motivations someone had in assigning her that role.

In Buddhist setsuwa, the female body is condemned for drawing men to it; women are blamed for pursuing men and destroying their chances of enlightenment. Certain Buddhists could cope with their own unwanted eroticism only by making women rather than their own bodies (or the combination of the two) the source of it. Yet, many men likely could not truly understand or accept this misogyny. As the *Dōjōji* tale suggests with its depiction of the monk both as victim and victimizer, for some Buddhists, the urge to blame women vies with the desire to take at least partial responsibility for one's spiritual failures. Furthermore, evidence indicates that the idea of celibacy was not entirely successful in Heian and medieval Japan. In the lives of aristocrats, including monks who had elite backgrounds, it had to compete with the idea of passion as an art. The representation of the snake sucking the penis of the monk points us back to the dream—to the reality of desire. The grotesque can be erotic through the power of suggestion.

CHAPTER 4

Who Eats Whom?
Flesh-Eating Demons
and Political Power Struggles

In *The Grotesque in Art and Literature*, Kayser identifies monsters as a main theme of the grotesque. It prevails in Europe during the fourteenth through sixteenth centuries in the many portrayals by Hieronymus Bosch, the Brueghels, and other artists of "The Temptation of St. Anthony." (In these paintings, St. Anthony resists demonic creatures, who representing evil and spiritual conflict, torment him.)[1] Among the creatures Kayser sees as a source of inspiration for later artists and writers are devils in the Judeo-Christian sense (with horns, tails, and hooves) as well as strange animals and truly bizarre beings "which, often lacking a torso, are composed of human and animal parts."[2] He uses the term "monster" broadly to mean threatening and destructive creatures with frightening and usually invented appearances. Yet something invisible, partially visible, seemingly ordinary or beautiful can be a monster, too. Joseph Campbell once stated, "By monster, I mean some horrendous presence or apparition that explodes all of your standards for harmony, order, and ethical conduct."[3] In his view, gods in "the role of destroyer," such as Vishnu at the end of the world or the Judeo-

Christian God as creator of hell, qualify as monsters. Often the ghastly nature of such a spirit is not apparent until after it has struck.

In classical and medieval Japan, *oni* (demons) are arguably the most prominent monsters. They are essential figures to the Japanese grotesque, crossing both physical and conceptual boundaries, directing attention to the body and bodily life, debasing authority figures and challenging official discourses. These spirit-creatures appear most powerful when viewed collectively over time as they function within particular tales on a smaller scale than the monsters Campbell has in mind. Rather than having cataclysmic effects, they erode the fabric of certain sectors of society, usually that of the aristocrat, by challenging one or at most several standards at a time. The actions and effects of these creatures in setsuwa are intricately connected to the tensions accompanying political and social change in Japan.

The most common demons in setsuwa are uncultivated, threatening, and horrific creatures who manifest latent hostility toward dominant people and institutions more consistently than other types. Yet, other types are also important. They include a delightful and relatively gentle bunch: clownish figures who mimic aristocrats in some of their interests. With their fine appreciation of poetry, music, and dance, these creatures affirm aesthetic pursuits even while mocking them and hinting at the ugly and monstrous side of the refined Heian elite.

We see them as demons dwelling at the gate to the capital, Rajōmon, or the gate to the Greater Imperial Palace, Suzakumon, in collections including *Gōdanshō*, *Konjaku*, *Jikkinshō*, and *Kokon chomonjū*.[4] The stories in these collections also involve aristocrats and either a poem or musical instrument, a *biwa* (lute) or *fue* (flute). In the following anecdote from *Gōdanshō*, a Chinese-style (*kanbun*) poem stirs the feelings of a spirit:

On the Mildness of Spring, recited by Miyako no Yoshika
at a private imperial banquet:

The mist lifts; the wind combs the hair of the budding willow tree
The ice melts; its waves wash the beard of old moss[5]

According to the elders, an unnamed horseman recites this poem while passing Rajō Gate on a moonlit night. A voice from the second story of the gate says, "Touching, touching." The splendor of the composition naturally moves demons and gods.[6]

The remark about how the splendor of the poem profoundly affects demons and gods evokes the famous lines in the Japanese and Chinese prefaces of *Kokinshū* (*A Collection of Poems Ancient and Modern*, ca. 905): "Poetry is what effortlessly moves heaven and earth, causes invisible demons and gods to feel beauty and sorrow (*aware*), softens the relations between men and women, and stills the hearts of fierce warriors."[7] In *Gōdanshō*, the words of the spirit—"*Aware, aware*" ("Touching, touching")—strengthen the allusion to *Kokinshū*.

Kokinshū annotators and translators often take *onigami* (also read *kijin* and translated above as "demons and gods") to mean "gods and spirits"[8] or "spirits of the deceased and deities" (*reikon to jingi*).[9] Spirits of the deceased can be demons, but the term can include other *oni* as well. According to the standard dictionary *Kōjien*, *onigami* does not refer to two separate types of spiritual beings but to only "fierce and frightening gods; *kijin*."[10] The same dictionary defines *kijin* as either "spirits of the deceased; souls and divine spirits of heaven and earth" or "fierce and terrifying demons. *Bakemono. Henge*" ("monsters" and literally "the metamorphosed" or "the transformed").[11] The creatures haunting gates are best described as *bakemono* or *henge*, but they are not quite terrifying. The line between raging god and terrifying demon is thin when it exists at all as they both act with uncontrollable, destructive behavior. The demons dwelling at gates in these tales have instead a gentle side, sharing with gods and humans the ability to be moved by music and poetry. They speak to people, give them things, and often have a concrete form.

The association of demons with gates becomes clearer and more fixed with time. In the thirteenth-century collection *Jikkinshō*, the same Miyako no Yoshika (834–79) recites the first line of the poem while passing the gate, whereupon a voice from an unseen source completes it. When Yoshika shares both lines with the famous scholar and politician Sugawara no Michizane (mentioned in the preceding chapter), Michizane responds by attributing the last line to a demon.[12] In another Kamakura period tale collection, *Senjūshō*, a red demon leans a head of white hair down from the gate.[13]

Konjaku tale "How the Lute Genjō Is Snatched by a Demon" describes the recovery of a *biwa* named Genjō during the reign of Emperor Murakami (r. 946–67).[14] It is missing from the palace when the virtuoso Minamoto no Hiromasa (918–80) recognizes its elegant sound coming from the upper story of the gate Rajōmon. He realizes that the performer is a demon because no human can achieve such mastery of the instrument.[15] The demon lowers Genjō by a cord to Hiromasa, who then returns it to the emperor. In *Gōdanshō*, *Jikkinshō*, *Kokon chomonjū*, and the collection related to music called *Shichiku kuden*, the Suzakumon demon returns Genjō only after Buddhist ceremonies are held to retrieve the instrument.[16] Tales with similar plots involving the Suzakumon demon and famous people (Narihira among them) appear elsewhere as well. In *Gōdanshō* (Book 3:50) and *Jikkinshō* (Book 10:20), the instruments are flutes (*fue*) rather than lutes.[17]

An *Uji shūi* tale about an old woodcutter embarrassed by a huge wen on his cheek illustrates the ability of certain demons to appreciate a good dancer. One day while in the mountains, the woodcutter gets caught in a storm and seeks shelter in a tree hollow. Moments later, one hundred or so demons described as red, black, green, one-eyed, or mouth-less gather to drink saké and be entertained by a young demon dancer. Although the performance is very good, the chief wishes aloud for a truly special show. The old man, apparently possessed, suddenly springs from the hollow and surprises the crowd with a spectacular dance. Afterwards, the demons magically remove his wen to make sure he will return at the next party. They consider it lucky and assume he would want it back. The old man encourages this error by pretending to be upset. It happens that his neighbor has a wen on his left cheek. Hearing about the experience of the first man, the second hides in the tree hollow in hope of receiving the same painless surgery. The demons appear and meet their guest, whom they never realize is another person. When the man turns out to be a clumsy dancer, they "return" the wen of the first man, so that the second man ends up with a blemish on both cheeks. Although the narrator concludes with a moral about envy, the story also portrays the ability of some demons to distinguish between talent and its lack.[18]

While some demons are charming, humorous, or even benevolent, most depictions of them in setsuwa initially appear to coincide with Kayser's understanding of the grotesque as somber and terrifying. These demons tend to be heartless and hungry for human flesh. They usually remain mysterious, the reasons for their appearances and behaviors given only indirectly when at all. In contrast to later accounts of demons, the demons of setsuwa frequently triumph or avoid retaliation. Human conquests of demons become frequent only later, as in the Muromachi period story about the defeat of Shuten dōji, the demon of Ōeyama.[19]

To Kayser, the world of the grotesque is unfathomable and completely hostile. "The ambiguous way in which we are affected by it results from

our awareness that the familiar and apparently harmonious world is alienated under the impact of abysmal forces, which break it up and shatter its
coherence."[20] His view assumes a homogeneous audience. After all, what
is familiar and harmonious to one group of people can be oppressive to
another. Tales about demons often voice the resentment and suggest the
desires of people who are otherwise silenced, so that even the most dreadful
have redeeming qualities. Destruction, death, and change within the tales
need to be considered from a number of angles, not simply in terms of good
and evil or gain and loss defined from one perspective.

In Chapter 3 we saw how the demon-lover of Empress Somedono undermines both imperial and Buddhist authority by transgressing boundaries
between the court and other realms and by acting upon unsanctioned sexual
desire. While the tale reveals much about how some oni function, it would
be a mistake to view any one demon as typical. Fundamentally spirits, they
can appear as transformed humans, spirits in human form, or even malicious objects, such as a flying plank of wood that kills a retainer sleeping
without his sword, among other things.[21] Although setsuwa contributes to
the increased stylization of oni in Japanese art, literature, and drama, there
is no quintessential oni in the Heian and early Kamakura periods.

In this chapter and the next, I continue to examine demons as grotesque
representations. Central to these chapters are flesh-eating demons and gender issues—specifically, how concepts of male and female are developed and
employed in representing demons and humans in relation to them. This
chapter focuses on the significance of demon hunger and how the act of
consumption undermines or affirms the political authority of men. Most
demons examined here assume male or unspecified forms, contrasting with
those in Chapter 5, who are female or assume female forms.

The research on demons in Japanese is extensive. In the twentieth century, many scholars wrote on oni in folklore, literature, art, and cultural history, covering a vast range of material from premodern Japan. My analyses
of certain setsuwa involving oni should be understood within this larger
scholarly context. Therefore, before shifting my focus to individual tales, I
begin by briefly discussing how twentieth-century scholars have viewed oni.
I narrow the discussion by concentrating on how Baba Akiko categorized
them in *Oni no kenkyū* (*Research on Demons*). Baba conveys a sense of earlier
influential views of demons by incorporating them into her own, and other
scholars often quote her or acknowledge her impact on their research.

Early twentieth century folklorists writing on premodern Japanese demons envisioned and pursued what Baba calls an "original image": indigenous spirit-creatures who emerged before Indian and Chinese concepts of demons were introduced along with the Chinese character for *oni* (*gui*).[22] In several texts, Yanagita Kunio mentions oni along with *tengu*, foxes, monkeys or apes, and legendary mountain men and women (*yama otoko* and *yama onna*) in connection with real mountain inhabitants and their beliefs, practices, and lifestyles.[23] In building on Yanagita, Baba and others do not question the appropriateness of Yanagita's findings to understanding ancient, classical, and medieval Japan despite the focus of most of his research on an oral tradition thriving in remote villages during his lifetime. Perhaps because Yanagita himself assumes a significant degree of transhistoricity in his work, others, too, fail to consider the discontinuity between representations in the premodern and modern worlds.[24] Their discussions of demons are occasionally flawed by the uncritical appropriation of his views.

Another famous folklorist, Orikuchi Shinobu, sees demons as vast spirits of the mountains or, in concrete form, as giants who descend from them.[25] In setsuwa, oni are commonly described as standing around seven or eight feet. Orikuchi also argues that demons are subordinate gods who defend other, greater gods. This relationship resembles that of buddhas and many initially non-Buddhist deities, but it cannot be attributed to Buddhist influence alone—indigenous beliefs and practices must also be at work.[26]

Writing in the early sixties, the cultural historian Kondō Yoshihiro examines the role of demons in a variety of literary, historical, and religious texts. He briefly addresses the question of the origin of the Japanese demon, arguing that the fear and reverence people felt toward destructive natural phenomena such as hurricanes, volcanoes, lightning, and earthquakes led to the creation of demons. He is responding to Meiji scholar Ishibashi Gaha, who also connects the forces in nature to demons but instead emphasizes the link of demons to illness, especially contagious diseases, and to death. Kondō believes that link came after demons had already been associated with natural disasters.[27]

In insisting on indigenous origins, these scholars encourage us to look beyond features of oni clearly appropriated from Chinese and Indian cultures, especially Buddhist. Unfortunately, they take that effort to the extreme. Drawing from Nietzsche, Michel Foucault writes the following on why "the pursuit of the origin (*Ursprung*)" does not work:

> It is an attempt to capture the exact essence of things, their purest possibilities, and their carefully protected identities, because this search assumes the existence of immobile forms that precede the external world of accident and succession.. . . . However, . . . there is "something altogether different" behind things: not a timeless and essential secret, but the secret that they have no essence or that their essence was fabricated in a piecemeal fashion from alien forms.[28]

Demons seem never to have had a pure form or stable identity; as far back as we can see, they have always been incompletely described and transforming. To attempt to trace them back to one source (or one type of source) is to ignore the complexity of the imaginations creating them. Even if there were a single point of origin, a certain fear or idea that gave birth to the first demon, the quest to determine it would be blocked by the loss of oral cultures and the nonexistence of written texts from Japan before it began appropriating things from other cultures.

Baba Akiko begins *Oni no kenkyū* with the question "What are *Oni*?" rather than "What are the origins of *Oni*?"[29] Her answer consists of five categories. Occasionally problematic, this scheme nonetheless conveys a sense of the diversity of the creatures considered oni and of the complexity of the issue.[30]

The first category consists of ancestral spirits or spirits of the earth who visit during times of prayer or celebrations and are either good or harmless. The oldest form of oni, this group comes from the ancient and medieval Chinese understanding of *gui* as spirits of the deceased who return to this world.[31]

Her second category of oni derives from the mountain ascetics who developed and spread Shugendō (mountain asceticism) during its formative stages, possibly dating back to the early Nara period.[32] These creatures are most commonly tengu. While descriptions of tengu and oni can overlap, it is more productive to distinguish between them. Their differences are suggested by the placement of tales in *Konjaku*. Whereas oni appear throughout *Konjaku* and especially in Book 27 in the so-called secular section of "Tales of Japan" (Books 21–30), tengu are predominantly in Book 20, which

Wakabayashi asserts is "designed to tell the history and structure of forces working against the Buddhist Law."[33] As creatures leading people astray and causing them harm, tengu are demons in the broadest sense (as are animal spirits). I place them with animal spirits in Chapter 6.

In the third category are demons from the Buddhist tradition, including *yakṣas*, *rākṣasas* (*yasha* and *rasetsu* in Japanese), demons of hell, and ox- or horse-headed demons. Yet, religious connections to creatures are often very loose. The plots of stories reveal more about the relationship of a demon to Buddhism than the appellation. Furthermore, while the Chinese characters for some demons came to Japan through Buddhist texts, the terminology was originally Sanskrit and dates back to Vedic times. Certain characteristics of these creatures, including the flesh-eating behavior of *rākṣasas* and *yakṣas* also correspond to what we find in Hindu mythology.

More speculative, the fourth category consists of people who willingly become demons through their choice of lifestyle: certain exiles, ex-convicts, outcasts, and thieves. The prosperity of the Heian court produced a dark side, too, with many people and lifestyles sacrificed for the benefit of the elite. Some victims turned to destructively deviant behavior such as robbery, rape, and murder. Baba sees these people as demons, especially when they belong to bands, as do many demons in the Muromachi period (1392–1573).

Occasionally, a tale raises the possibility that a criminal is not human or establishes a less direct connection between the deviant human and the supernatural. In "About an Unknown Woman Robber" a woman employs sadomasochistic tactics to recruit a guard into a gang of robbers. At first, she provides him with days of sensual and sexual pleasure as well as material gifts. Once he is dependent on her, she introduces sessions in which she first whips him severely and then nurses his wounds. The man has participated in numerous robberies and has lived with the woman for two or three years when, one day, his attendants ride off with his horse. He borrows another horse but cannot find the woman, his house, or the storehouses with the stolen goods.[34] The narrator wonders if the woman is really a *henge no mono*. In its broadest sense, *henge* means a transformed being— "something that has taken on a different shape, such as a ghost, goblin, spectre,"[35] or a similar being including oni. This is apparent in a section of *Kokon chomonjū*, entitled "Henge," which comprises stories about the metamorphoses of demons, tengu, foxes, boars, a cat, and other creatures.[36] Here, it makes sense to consider the woman robber as demonic. However,

Baba extends the meaning of demon to include characters described only as human—for example, the beggars and thieves in *Konjaku* Book 29 who are also often rapists and murderers. In my view, we should not refer to violent criminals as oni indiscriminately. If such connections are not made in the tales, calling people demons does not enhance our understanding of their behaviors or situations. My own discussion of demons focuses on those creatures clearly distinguishable from humans by magical powers or mysterious events. All but one of my references to demons correspond to the use of the term oni in the tales.

Baba's last category is people transformed into demons by excessive grudges or indignation and the desire for revenge. The Buddhist priest attracted to Empress Somedono is an example, presumably because Baba sees him motivated more by anger at the people and institutions denying him access to the empress than by the intensity of sexual desire. Such demons overlap with vengeful spirits (*goryō* or *onryō*) and spirits of the living and the dead who possess individuals (*ikisudama* or *ikiryō* and *shiryō*). In contrast to these invisible spirits, this type more often has a visible body.

Baba distinguishes sharply between the female demon in noh, the *hannya*, and the demons imagined before its creation. With the *hannya* comes a philosophy of the demon, by which Baba means the creation of the internal nature of the demon and the systematic inquiry into it. This nature expresses a complex, anguish-filled historical age in medieval Japan that mirrors the torment of oppressed women.[37] Her view of *hannya* draws from the noh master Zeami Motokiyo (1363–1443), who emphasizes the connection between humans and demons when explaining the style of demons portrayed by the Kanze school of noh. In one of his treatises, "Shūgyoku tokka" ("Finding Gems and Gaining the Flower"), he writes:

> A real demon cannot be seen in our actual world. Even though an image of a demon may appear in a picture, for example, there exists no definite model on which that picture can be based. Therefore, an actor creates a general conception, avoids presenting a character who appears merely wild, gives a certain softness to his motions, and deceives his audience into believing that they have seen a real demon. Such is the Sphere of Accomplishment as it pertains to demon roles. One such appearance is called Delicacy within Strength, or, as it is sometimes referred to, "the Appearance of a Demon, the Heart of a Human."[38]

In the *kanbun* passage, the phrase translated above as "the Appearance of a Demon, the Heart of a Human" is *kyōki shinnin*, written with the characters for *form*, *demon*, *heart*, and *person*.[39] Baba renders the phrase in Japanese as "although the appearance is of a demon, the heart is of a human."[40]

The work of scholars frequently reflects Zeami's vision of demons with a human heart. While the attribution of human feelings to demons does not begin with Zeami, noh plays contribute to that understanding. In "'Oni' no kanashimi" ("The Sorrow of Demons"), Ikegami Junichi argues that medieval demons belong in the category of medieval people and focuses on their loneliness, sorrow, and shame. Although one of his examples is from *Kankyo no tomo*, an early Kamakura period collection, most others come from later eras, especially the Muromachi period.[41] Descriptions of the feelings or thoughts of demons are rare in earlier setsuwa.

To Baba, earlier demons are limited by their folkloric links. She clearly favors demons of later periods: the *hannya* and other oni she believes depict an internal landscape and the mood of an age. In contrast, she sees the tales of *Konjaku* Book 27 as "merely relating the details of events in the simplest language despite being a treasure-house of demons."[42] This assertion and her privileging of the *hannya* and post-*hannya* demons indicate that she does not fully comprehend the suggestive power of detail in setsuwa. She misses the richness of the tales. This failure is by no means complete since her keen observations and analyses of the tales reveal a tremendous amount of insight. A storyteller or writer does not have to depict the inner workings of the mind for a tale to be psychological. Events can suggest interior landscapes of individuals or groups without explicit descriptions of feelings or thoughts. The desires and fears of people shape the demons of setsuwa as they develop.

DEMON HUNGER

While many characteristics of demons are grotesque, their hunger for humans is perhaps the most suggestive. The grotesque body transgresses its own limits in the act of eating: "it swallows, devours, rends the world apart, is enriched and grows at the world's expense."[43] In analyzing Rabelais, Bakhtin is concerned with the human appetite and the banquet; eating is consequently joyous, a process in which man "triumphs over the world, devours it without being devoured himself."[44] The same cannot be said generally of consumption in setsuwa.

People fail to be completely victorious even in tales where they are eating rather than being eaten. In a well-known (demon-less) tale about a fifth-rank retainer (*goi*) and yam gruel, the prospect of eating to satiation results in ambivalence or disillusion. After overhearing the *goi* wish aloud that he could eat his fill of yam gruel, Fujiwara no Toshihito takes him on a journey to his father-in-law's mansion in Tsuruga, a port town in Echizen (present-day Fukui Prefecture).[45] The peasants there are each ordered to bring a huge yam with odd proportions (about five feet by three and a half inches). Five or six cauldrons with a capacity of five *koku* (twenty-four bushels) are set up for preparing yam gruel. By the time the cooking is finished, the very thought of eating the porridge disgusts the *goi*. Toshihito ultimately lavishes him with gifts of clothing, silk, and a horse, so he triumphs in that sense. However, the feast itself is a soggy failure for the *goi*, who gets what he thinks he wants only to discover he cannot enjoy it.[46] Elsewhere in setsuwa, the festive meal has disastrous results, especially when it involves meat since Buddhism prohibits killing animals. In one tale, a sheep slaughtered for a farewell dinner turns out to be the reincarnation of the host's deceased daughter. Upon learning the identity of the animal, the father falls ill and dies.[47]

Given that consumption by humans has mixed meaning in the tales, how about the consumption of humans? What is the significance of the flesh-eating demon? Tales depicting the threat of attacks by such demons express more than a fear of death or murder since a particular kind of demise by a certain type of creature is involved. They also have subversive and redeeming qualities. While we would not expect to find joy, these tales can convey a sense of human triumph. (Of course, it would not be from the standpoint of the victim.) In what ways is the act of consumption an affirmation of the underdogs of society or a decrowning of people who are resented by others because of their power? How might the people of Heian and early Kamakura Japan have enjoyed their monsters?

Let us look briefly at an earlier time. The first oni in the extant literature appear to be the hags Izanami dispatches to pursue Izanagi when, having traveled to the land of Yomi, he shames her by glancing at her decaying and maggot-infested corpse. These creatures are called *shikome*, written with *manyōgana* (Chinese characters used mostly phonetically) in the *Kojiki* and with the characters for *minikui* (ugly) and *onna* (woman) in the *Nihon shoki*. *Shiko* is also a reading for the Chinese character *gui* (along with *mono*), as the pronunciation *oni* does not appear until the Heian period.[48]

The earliest report of a demon consuming a person in the extant literature is a passage on the township of Ayo in *Izumo no kuni fudoki* (*The Topography of Izumo Province*, ca. 733):

> The Township of Ayo: located 4.4 miles southeast of the district office. According to the elders, long ago a certain person cultivated and guarded land reclaimed from the mountainside here. One day, a one-eyed demon comes and begins to eat the tiller of the field. At that moment, as the man's father and mother hide in the bamboo grove, the leaves there shake. While being devoured, the man says "ayo, ayo." Consequently, [the place] is called Ayo.[49]

Since the verb for *shake* is *ayogu*, some scholars interpret the cry of the man, *ayo*, as meaning something like "Watch out. You're making it rustle."[50] The gender of the demon is unspecified. Although the victim is a man, the idea of the devoured woman will appear shortly in setsuwa. Even before then, a deceased woman and possibly her death are loosely connected to a demon. In *Nihon shoki*, a demon wearing a bamboo hat is seen watching the funeral of Empress Saimei (594–661, r. 655–61 and 642–45 as Kyōgoku) from Mt. Asakura. In some interpretations, the creature caused her demise.[51]

In two versions of a tale with subtle but important differences, one from *Nihon ryōiki* and the other from *Konjaku*, a woman is consumed either before she expects to have sexual intercourse or during it. Below is a translation of the *Konjaku* tale.[52]

How [Parents] Regret Their Daughter Was Eaten by a Demon Because They Were Lured by Treasures

Now it is the past; there is a person who lives in eastern Amuchi Village, Tōchi district, Yamato Province. The household is very rich and their family name is Kagamitsukuri no miyatsuko. They have one daughter with perfectly beautiful features. Moreover, she does not seem to be the daughter of such country bumpkins.

Since she is yet to marry, suitable fellows from the vicinity court her. However, she flatly refuses them and, after many years pass, another man insists on marrying her, but she rejects him, too, and remains unpersuaded. Meanwhile, this suitor piles up numerous treasures in three carts and sends them to the woman. Seeing them, her parents are suddenly lured by the treasures and feel assured. And so, the father and mother permit the union in accordance with the man's request. They choose an auspicious day and the man arrives. He immediately enters the bedroom and the couple has intercourse.

Shortly after, around the middle of the night, the girl shouts three times, "Oh, it hurts. Oh, it hurts." When they hear her voice, the father and mother share the same thought. "Having sex must hurt because she isn't used to it yet," they say and sleep.

When the daughter does not get up the next morning, the mother approaches her room and calls to wake her. Perplexed because there is no answer, the mother goes closer to have a look: only the head and one finger of her daughter are there. The rest of her body is missing. Blood is everywhere.

When the father and mother see this, they cry and grieve without end. They hurry to look at the treasures sent, but these have become various kinds of horse and ox bones. When they check the three carts where the treasures had been loaded, they have become silverberry wood. "Did a demon turn into a person, come, and eat her? Or did a god become angry and cause a terrible curse to befall us?" they wonder. While they are deeply grieving, the people in the vicinity hear what happened and gather. Upon seeing the things, everyone feels a sense of awe. Later, the parents offer a Buddhist memorial service for their daughter. They place their daughter's head in a box and, on the seventh of the month, set it before the Buddha and have held a service with a vegetarian meal.

When we think about it, people should not be lured and taken by treasures. The father and mother were filled with regret and sadness, believing this [loss] was the result of their being lured by treasures. And so the story is told and passed down.[53]

Evidence of demon consumption of a person when there are no witnesses is stylized in setsuwa: only one or two body parts, frequently a head, remain when a demon has finished its meal. All or most of the corpse is usually left behind in tales about other types of murders. In the story, discussed in Chapter 2, of the woman who abandoned her child to flee beggars, the warriors discovered the pieces of the child.[54] In the tales about the murdered newlywed, a supernatural being is clearly involved; had the murderer been merely human, his gifts would not have transformed into bones.

The misogynistic implications of this tale can make its redeeming qualities difficult to see. Yet, we cannot determine the way such representations function and the full scope of their messages without suspending our disgust, horror, and anger at how they link sex, violence, and the female body. In truth, representations of women as victims in tales tend to direct our attention to men. Female characters are often constructed to make points about male characters and their challenges, so that trying to glimpse real women of the past through them can be difficult. Women are depicted as easy prey, making not even the slightest attempt to defend themselves, while most men are at least able to grapple with their attackers. This difference is obvious in a *Konjaku* tale focusing on the struggle of a man and a demon although it is a woman who has been seized. The couple is traveling from the eastern provinces to the capital, where the man hopes to purchase an upgrade in his status: the fifth rank. When the inn they plan to stay at has no vacancies, they make the mistake of going to the uninhabited Kawara mansion. Many days have passed when, one night, a door is pushed open and the hand of a creature reaches out, grabs the woman, and drags her into the next room.

> Alarmed, the husband screams and tries to stop it from pulling her. It drags her inside in an instant, so he rushes up and tries to pull open the door. The door shuts immediately and cannot be opened. He then tries pulling open the lattice doors and sliding open the others this way and that way, but how can he open them when they are all locked from the inside? The husband gives up in alarm, then runs here and there, pulling on the doors of the north, south, east, and west sides of the building, unable to open any.[55]

The story does not depict what the woman experiences as her husband tries to save her. The struggle centers instead on barred points of access, with the locked doors also suggesting how the body of the woman is closed off to the man. The man must prove his power over the demon by saving the woman. He races to a nearby house for help, but ultimately ends up taking an axe and chopping his way inside the room, only to find his wife hanging dead from a pole used for drying clothes. People later agree a demon sucked the flesh and blood out of her. (The representation is unusual in that the body remains.) The woman is the victim, but the main issue is the vulnerability of the man. Here and in many other tales, the female body is the site of conflict between men or men and other forces. The battle in this tale is related to the unworthiness of the man for the rank he hopes to obtain. That he does not receive the rank because of his merits or genealogy but instead seeks to purchase it alludes to his inferior nature. Nor does he seem suited to stay at the Kawara-no-in. The former mansion of Minamoto no Tōru and later Retired Emperor Uda is too good for him even if believed haunted.[56]

The bride also dies at the mouth of a demon, but is that story really about her? To begin answering this question, we can consider how a song of the type called *waza-uta* in the opening of the *Nihon ryōiki* version relates to the narrative. Often believed to be omens, *waza-uta* are "popular songs frequently used for purposes of satirical political comment."[57] Here is a possible reading in (romanized) Japanese of the difficult *waza-uta* prefacing this story, followed by a translation:

Nare o zo yome ni hoshi to tare, Amuchi no komuchi no Yorozu no ko.
Namu, namu ya. Hijiri sakamo sakamo mochi susuri, nori mōshi, Yama no chishiki amashi ni, amashi ni.

Who says he wants you for his bride, Yorozunoko of Amuchi Village—child of myriad families from here and there?
Gracious, gracious, mountain ascetics imbibe an entire *koku* or so of saké, then preach the Buddhist law. And the knowledge in the mountains is too much, too much.[58]

When Kimoto Michifusa wrote about this song in 1942, no one had yet figured out its meaning after *namu, namu*. His interpretation depends on a reading of the characters different from the passage quoted above.[59] It was at one time influential, having been quoted in the older Iwanami shoten edition of *Nihon ryōiki* and footnoted in the English translation of the text by Kyoko Motomochi Nakamura. In Kimoto's rendering, the song blames the death of Yorozunoko on her own lack of insight, with its last lines meaning: "The bridegroom came with decorated horses and oxen loaded with wine / if Yorozunoko had been wise, she would not have incurred her own death."[60] Whereas most later scholars believe that *nori mōshi* (法万字師) refers to the preaching or chanting of the Dharma (Buddhist law), Kimoto reads the same characters as *ho ma ushi* or "decorated horses and oxen" with *ho* (*hō*) referring to treasures. The mountain ascetics who appear in readings by later scholars are absent in his transliteration and the subject of the sentence is instead the suitor. In addition, Kimoto sees the characters 夜万能知識 as *ya*, an exclamatory particle belonging to the previous phrase, followed by *Yorozu no chishiki* (the wisdom of Yorozu) in contrast to more recent readings in which the same phrase is understood as *yama no chishiki*.

According to this interpretation, the song explains or summarizes what occurs. *Waza-uta* often do, in fact, provide an explanation or summary. Rather than point to something in the future, they frequently reveal information about a past event. If the song above is to foreshadow the tragedy, the meaning Kimoto gives would have to be hidden within another, more obvious message, such as in the above translation.[61]

The song may be an attempt by people affiliated with officially sanctioned Buddhist institutions to criticize and discredit certain mountain ascetics. *Nihon ryōiki* compiler Kyōkai was himself a priest at a major temple,

Yakushiji. Shortly before the story supposedly takes place, efforts are made to prohibit Buddhists not affiliated with government-sanctioned temples from taking orders or from otherwise acting in a religious capacity. In 717, the government issued *Sōniryō* (Rules and Regulations for Monks and Nuns).[62] In the song, the mountain ascetics are portrayed as untrustworthy, drinking in excess, and preaching while intoxicated. The exclusion of them is in this way justified.

When interpreted in the context of the entire song, the last comment, "the knowledge in the mountains is too much, too much," also indicates sexual indulgence. The name of the young woman, Yorozunoko, means "ten thousand (a myriad) children." The phrase modifying the name, *amuchi no komuchi no*, can be understood as "from this Amuchi Village" or as corresponding to the modern *achira kochira*: "here and there." Consequently, *Amuchi no komuchi no Yorozunoko* can refer to either a single person, "Yorozunoko from this Amuchi (Village)" or "a myriad children from here and there."[63] Buddhist precepts demanded that monks and nuns refrain from sexual activity, but the general population would probably not have cared either way unless the behavior of these men and women had some impact on their lives. The song draws in other people by presenting this transgression as a potential threat to children. "The knowledge of the mountains" is a synecdoche substituting for mountain ascetics. The song warns people to be wary of these monks, depicting them as licentious.

Baba sees the tension between the mountain ascetics and the government as carrying over into the narrative portion of the tale. The suggestion that a demon ate the woman refers us back to the mountain ascetics mentioned in the song. As with the Somedono tale, the *Nihon ryōiki* version attacks mountain ascetics by associating them with demons.[64] The song discredits the mountain ascetics and their spiritual pursuit by representing them as a source of hostility and tension. They are shown unable to live up to their own standards. The negative energy flowing from them can be attributed to their ambivalence about the central government, which sometimes resulted in overt resistance. Significantly then, the Kagamitsukuri were closely associated with the government.

In ancient Japan, the Kagamitsukuri served the Yamato rulers as *tomo-no-miyatsuko*, local elite vassals who oversaw groups of workers (*be*). They produced mirrors and likely also spears or other objects forged or cast from metals. At least one guild of mirror-makers, possibly the Kagamitsukuri, was closely associated with the powerful Mononobe *uji*, Shinto priests and armorers for the imperial family before the Soga crushed them in 587.[65] Although the relationship of the Kagamitsukuri with the government would have changed at that time and with mid-seventh century efforts to centralize the government, such as the Taika Reform in 646, they remained members of the elite. According to *Nihon shoki*, they were granted the title *muraji* in 683, indicating that they enjoyed a high position in the political hierarchy, were landholders, and claimed descent from a founding god.[66] Since the tale describes this family as wealthy, they must have retained some of their former status during the reign of Emperor Shōmu (r. 724–49), when the story takes place.

Another source of hostility in the tale is the rejected men. In *Konjaku*, the treasures seduce the parents. This change shifts the responsibility for the death of the woman from her to her parents. It is the mother and father who permit the union in response to the man and then choose the day for it. The suitors here are clearly local inhabitants, possibly resembling the fifth-rank suitor from Higo who, in *Genji*, hopes to marry Tamakazura while she is still living in Hizen.[67] The woman from the Kagamitsukuri no miyatsuko family does not strike others as being raised by country people. The Heian elite would have seen such people as lacking in culture and refinement, but this is not the case here. As with Tamakazura, who is raised most of her childhood in what is now Kyushu, the daughter of the Kagamitsukuri family is not a product of her environment. Another storyteller might have portrayed the family as resisting the suitors because they want the best for their child, but here they are shown acting out of selfishness and greed.

The hostility of men or male beings—whether mountain ascetics, suitors, or the demonic husband or god—is instrumental in the realization of karmic law. Both tales present the death of the young woman as predetermined. *Nihon ryōiki* suggests that the woman, her parents, or both, suffer because of resentment from another life, while the emphasis in *Konjaku* is on immediate retribution, with the tale placed in a sixteen tale cluster about that kind of karma.[68] However, knowing the death is inevitable differs from understanding why it takes a particular form. Certain connections of the tale to myth and *kami*-worship reveal some things regarding the symbolic significance of death by a flesh-eating demon.

In addition to producing mirrors, which had religious and symbolic significance, the Kagamitsukuri were involved in the ceremonial worship of the gods. They are considered descendants of Ishikoridome-no-mikoto, the goddess who in *Kojiki* creates a mirror to lure Amaterasu out of the heavenly cave. Ishikoridome-no-mikoto is also linked to smithery—in the *Nihon shoki* she creates a copper sun-spear. In several books, Ōwa Iwao mentions Kagamitsukuri-make jinja, one of three shrines associated with the Kagamitsukuri family (*uji*) and located near what would have been Amuchi Village, where the tales are set.[69] The one-eyed smith god, Ama-no-ma-hitotsu-no-mikoto, was worshipped there.[70] This information helps to explain the choice of family in the tale as they are connected to what becomes a vicious creature.

Although the one-eyed smith god is not portrayed as violent in *Nihon shoki*, one-eyed demons, as do others, come to be associated with murders and the consumption of people. Most violence involving them is described in folktales from or after the Edo period (1600–1868) or otherwise connected to beliefs and practices documented then or later. However, the previously mentioned demon who eats the mountain farmer in the *Izumo no kuni fudoki* is also missing an eye.[71] Ōwa considers that creature a mountain god, hence the location of the event, and the man as a sacrifice, with his death insuring a bountiful harvest.[72] At the very least, his death allows for the naming of the area. Through associations to the one-eyed god, textual connections exist between the concept of sacrifice and the consumption of the woman from the Kagamitsukuri no miyatsuko family.

However, Ōwa pushes his argument too far. There are links between the Kagamitsukuri, Ama-no-ma-hitotsu-no-mikoto, violent one-eyed demons and gods, and the devoured young woman, but he goes on to argue that the Kagamitsukuri *uji* chiefs sacrificed young women to Ama-no-ma-hitotsu-no-mikoto as sexual partners or wives.[73] There is no proof. Certain ancient texts suggest that human sacrifice took place in Japan; both *Weizhi* (*Wei Dynasty Chronicles*, ca. 297) in its description of the land of Wa (Japan) and *Nihon shoki* recount incidents of live attendants being buried with the corpse of the person they served, but archeological evidence of such deaths is lacking.[74] Even if we had evidence that people were killed in this way, we still would not know whether other types of human sacrifice also took place and, if so, when, to what extent, and for how long.

Besides, sacrifice as an offering to a god usually implies the presence of someone who acknowledges the god and willingly gives it something. The behavior of the demons determines death in the *Nihon ryōiki* and *Fudoki* tales. By using the term *sacrifice* (*ikenie*) in describing what happens in them, Ōwa implicitly defines it along these lines: as indirectly and unwittingly causing the death of a cherished person in the attempt to gain something. The parents are unaware they will lose their daughter for what they believe are treasures. Their so-called sacrifice is a consequence of wrong choices, misguided behavior, and karma. Similarly, in *Izumo fudoki* (where we find the first victim of a flesh-eating demon in Japan), no one decides on the death of the tiller for the common good, the naming of a village, and an abundant crop. Ōwa's interpretation forces us to ask: can there be a sacrifice without a sacrificer? People do not offer demons human flesh in setsuwa; these creatures simply take their meals.

Ōwa weakens his argument by equating the victims in the *Nihon ryōiki* tale, the *Izumo fudoki* tale, and other stories from later historical periods with human sacrifices, but is correct in noting connections between sacrifice and flesh-eating demons. We know ritual sacrifice has a place in the imaginations of at least some Heian Japanese, whether or not it was actually practiced. A tale discussed at length in Chapter 6, "How the Spirits of Mimasaka Province Give Up Living Sacrifices Because of a Hunter's Scheme," depicts how, each year, the people of Mimasaka Province offer a young virginal woman to what they believe are two deities. Since this type of ritual appears in setsuwa, it is not surprising to find more abstract notions of giving up, losing, or murdering a person for the perceived greater good.

The meal of a demon can represent an assault on a practice or ideology. Marrying a daughter to a particular person for the sake of several family members, as the Kagamitsukuri no miyatsuko attempt in the *Konjaku* tale, was a common strategy in premodern Japan. When this tale is considered in conjunction with other tales involving the consumption of women, the criticism of this practice seems aimed not only at one set of parents but also more generally at families who destroy opportunities for others by strategically choosing partners for their own daughters. Women are the ultimate victims when they are eaten. However, the hostility directed toward them is displaced. The sexual tone of the violence in the tales—the substitutions of demon for lover and murder for would-be intimacy as well as the suggestion of oral sadism—can be partially explained in terms of the match-making and marriage politics of the time. One way to hurt politically prosperous families would have been to destroy their daughters. Since doing so was not usually possible, the attack is instead carried out symbolically when demons consume women in scenes initially suggesting a sexual bond—that crucial tool for political advancement.

The familial unit best known for its success in strategically arranging marriages for its daughters was the northern branch Fujiwara, from which the *sekkanke* (the regent's house) emerged dominant. The patriarchs were able to secure positions for their daughters as imperial consorts. Once a Fujiwara woman gave birth to a son and he became emperor, the maternal grandfather of the emperor would govern as regent, called *sesshō* if the sovereign was a minor, or assist the adult emperor also as regent but called *kanpaku*. Members of the *sekkanke* monopolized other major governmental positions as well, limiting posts for other courtiers, even men belonging to sublineages of the northern branch Fujiwara.[75]

The resentment of the northern branch Fujiwara and their strategic use of marital bonds become apparent when we consider a *Konjaku* tale about the consumption of a potential lover of Narihira in conjunction with a similar episode in *Ise monogatari*. The murder of the woman by the demon is again sexualized. It occurs at a moment when the human couple could be intimately involved were it not for impending danger.

The *Konjaku* account reads:

How a Woman of Middle Captain Ariwara no Narihira is Eaten by a Demon

Now it is the past; there is a person called Middle Captain Ariwara no Narihira of the Right Imperial Bodyguards. Celebrated as a man well versed in amorous affairs, he decides to become lovers with every woman in society famous for her beauty, ladies-in-waiting as well as the daughters of renowned people, without leaving anyone out. Hearing that the daughter of a certain person has features and a form so splendid as to be unparalleled in this world, he yearns very passionately for her with all his heart. Her parents say, "We plan for her to wed a high and noble mate." Because they cherish and protect her, Middle Captain Narihira is unable to do anything until he secretly abducts this woman through some kind of scheming, whatever it is.

However, there is nowhere to take and hide her immediately. Narihira is wondering what to do when there, in the vicinity of Kitayamashina, is an old mountain villa, dilapidated and uninhabited. A log storehouse stands on that estate with both of its doors fallen on the ground. Even the planks of the veranda are missing on the house, where people once resided. Since there does not seem to be any way to enter it, the man leads the woman inside the storehouse, bringing a thin mat with him, and has her lie on it with him. Just then, thunder suddenly roars and lightning flashes. The Middle Captain pulls out his sword and pushes the woman behind him. As he stands brandishing his sword, the thunder eventually stops and dawn breaks.

Meanwhile, there is no sound of the woman's voice. Thinking this strange, the Middle Captain turns his head and looks: only the head of the woman and the robe she was wearing remain. Ghastly terrified, the Middle Captain flees to escape, without time even to retrieve his robe. Later on, he learns the storehouse is for capturing humans. And so, what happened must not have been caused by the thunder and lightning. Was it not the work of a demon living in the storehouse? And so, people should never stop at places they know nothing about—much less even think about staying at them. And so the story is told and passed down.[76]

Here, the reason for rejecting Narihira is given. The parents mention the type of union they are seeking for their daughter: "yamugoto nakaramu mukotori o semu," translated above as "we plan for her to wed a high and noble mate." *Mukotori* means "the reception of a male mate" or "marriage."[77] The marriage would literally "have no end" or be "unsurpassable." Although *yamugoto nakaramu* modifies *mukotori* rather than simply *muko*, it also refers to the type of man sought. According to the *Konjaku* annotators of one edition, the parents are telling Narihira they hope to make their daughter an imperial consort.[78] This interpretation is probably based on information given in the similar account in *Ise monogatari* section 6 since *yamugoto nashi* is not reserved for describing crown princes or emperors.[79] Even without reference to that text, the use of *yamugoto nashi* sets up a contrast between Narihira and the desired groom.

Where does Narihira fall short? The parents of the woman would not have viewed his fame as a skilled and voracious lover negatively as Heian society considered the pursuit of multiple relationships proper for aristocratic men. Instead, his position in an inauspicious genealogical line is problematic.[80] His paternal grandfather, Emperor Heizei (774–824, r. 806–9), abdicated after less than four years in power because of illness, but he soon became the key figure in the so-called Kusuko incident: a failed attempt by his favored attendant Fujiwara no Kusuko and her brother Nakanari to reinstate him at the Nara capital. When Heizei lost the dispute to his younger brother Saga, Prince Abo, the father of Narihira, was banished to Tsukushi for fourteen years. Narihira and his brothers were later all given the surname Ariwara. Prince Takaoka, younger half-brother of Abo, was removed from the position of crown prince. Kusuko was pressured to poison herself. Her family had been the *Shikike* (ceremonial branch of the Fujiwara), but they were exiled for having served as advisors to Heizei and permanently weakened as a result.

Although the paternal grandmother of Narihira was of low status, his own mother, Princess Ito, was a daughter of Emperor Kanmu (737–806, r. 781–806). Had birthright been the only consideration, Narihira might have secured high rather than middle-ranking political positions. As it happened, he went no further than provisional Middle Captain of the Right Imperial

Bodyguards and provisional governor of Mino, carrying the prescribed rank for the first office of junior fourth rank, lower grade. While a man did have to be a member of a leading family to serve in one of the three highest positions in the Imperial Bodyguards (major, middle, and lesser captains), the most prized post in the headquarters was Major not Middle Captain.[81]

Unlike the suitors courting the daughter of the Kagamitsukuri no miyatsuko, Narihira is hardly a provincial aristocrat. The response of the parents in *Konjaku* degrades him, considering his family background and the glimpse history and the imagination give of what his political career might have been had his grandfather been reinstated two generations earlier. When Narihira abducts the woman in *Konjaku*, he acts against the wishes of her parents. Who are the mother and father to reject him and set such high standards for their daughter? Episode 6 of the *Ise monogatari* answers this question and also strengthens our sense of the pursuit and abduction of the woman as an act of defiance. We should keep in mind that historical accuracy is not the issue here; it cannot be because most of the so-called facts come from stories. Rather, the accounts in *Ise monogatari* and *Konjaku* allow us to speculate about certain emotions and attitudes in Heian Japan.

The *Konjaku* compiler probably did not draw his material directly from *Ise monogatari* but from another, non-extant, source.[82] The differences between the two texts are great, including the central role of the poem in *Ise monogatari* versus that of the plot in *Konjaku*. Nonetheless, putting the *Ise* episode into dialogue with the *Konjaku* tale makes sense because of what the two texts share in terms of plot and detail. Would the episode in *Ise* have influenced the understanding early audiences had of the *Konjaku* tale? The answer to this question is both no and yes, assuming that the audiences of setsuwa consisted of members of many sectors of society. While illiterate commoners who heard the story through preachers or traveling entertainers would not have been familiar with *Ise monogatari*, the literate would have known the text in some form. A line in *Ōkagami*, written around the year 1119 or nearly the same time *Konjaku* was likely compiled (ca. 1120), reads: "Is there anyone nowadays unfamiliar with *Kokinshū*, *Ise monogatari*, and so forth?"[83] It is consequently important to take the *Ise* episode into consideration when interpreting the *Konjaku* tale.

The section in *Ise* reads:

It is the past, when a certain man is still around. For years, he has been courting a seemingly inaccessible woman, but finally he abducts her, escaping into the pitch-black night. The man is leading the woman along the

Akutagawa River when she asks, "What is that?" referring to the dew on the grass. They have far to go. It is growing late, a terrible thunder crashes, and rain pours down. So the man pushes the woman deep inside a decrepit storehouse, unaware demons inhabit the place, and stands guard at the door with his bow in hand and his quiver on his back.

While he is wishing for morning to come quickly, a demon suddenly gulps the woman up. "Ohhh" the woman shrieks, but the thunder prevents the man from hearing her. As dawn gradually breaks, the man looks inside. The woman he had brought there is now gone. He stamps his feet in a tantrum and weeps, but to no avail.

Shiratama ka	When my darling asked
nani zo to hito no	Are those white jewels
toishi toki	Or are they what?
tsuyu to kotaete	Had I only answered "the dew"
kienamashi mono o	and vanished

This happens when the Empress of the Second Ward is in attendance upon her cousin, an imperial consort. Because she is extremely beautiful, a man abducts her, carrying her off on his back. Her older brothers, the Horikawa minister and, the oldest son, Major Counselor Kunitsune, still minor officials then, are on their way to the palace when they hear someone crying dreadfully. They stop the man and return the woman. They are the demons mentioned. This incident occurs when the future empress is still very young and only a commoner, or so it is said.[84]

Here the abducted woman is Fujiwara no Takaiko, mentioned in Chapter 3 as a lover of Narihira when young and of a Buddhist priest later in life. Daughter of Fujiwara no Nagara and Fujiwara no Takaharu, Takaiko is adopted by her uncle, Yoshifusa, along with her brother Mototsune, the Horikawa minister mentioned in the episode. Mototsune becomes regent when Yoshifusa dies in 872 because Yoshifusa has no biological son. The Fujiwara achieve the goal of making Takaiko an imperial consort to Emperor Seiwa (850–80, r. 858–76), son of her cousin Somedono, who is also the imperial consort mentioned in the *Ise* episode above. Takaiko gives birth to the future Emperor Yōzei. When the child succeeds to the throne in 876 at age nine, Mototsune serves as *sesshō* (regent to a minor).

We can connect the association of Empress Somedono and Takaiko with demons to how their sexual behavior defies the political use of their bodies by the Fujiwara and the imperial house, although both women ultimately fail in their resistance. Kawashima describes Takaiko as "a woman who is portrayed as having met (demonic) resistance and suppression in her attempts to have relationships with more than one man—be it at one time or in succession."[85] The death of the woman in *Konjaku* then is retribution for her involvement with Narihira. This intriguing explanation raises the possibility that Takaiko was a willing participant in the encounter. However, the tale is ambiguous about whether the so-called abduction is consensual. The response of the woman to abduction is not given in either *Konjaku* or the narrative portion of *Ise monogatari*. Only in the explanatory passage of the *Ise* episode are we told that the woman is crying dreadfully. However, we have no way of knowing what about the incident disturbs her. Does the man force her to go with him? We are told he carries her off on his back in the last passage but she is following him in the first. Of all the things a woman might say to an abductor, her question about the dew is not particularly agitated. (Dew has sexual connotations.) Does she fear the reaction of her family? Or is something else happening to make her cry? The storytellers would have been clearer about the role of the woman had they wanted to emphasize her wrongdoing. If she were a victim, would she have to suffer retribution?

The narrator of *Ōkagami* treats the affair of Narihira and Takaiko as historical, suggesting that Takaiko could not have become an imperial concubine in the usual manner because of it. Yet, it is unlikely that the leading Fujiwara family would have left their luck to fate—to a chance meeting of Emperor Seiwa and Takaiko. So-called biographical information has limited use because most of it concerning the affair comes from other sections of *Ise* and *Yamato monogatari* (section 161). In addition to section 6, sections 3 and 5 of *Ise* name Takaiko as the object of the affections of Narihira. She is also believed to be the woman he visits in section 4 and the woman mentioned in sections 26, 29, 65, and sometimes 100. Section 76, in which the Empress of the Second Ward (Takaiko) appears, and its poem in *Kokinshū*, are often read as evidence of their relationship.[86] As a result, scholars such as Tsunoda Bun'ei believe Takaiko and Narihira were indeed lovers.[87]

We know with more certainty that the personal life of Takaiko later conflicted with the wishes of the authorities. As mentioned in Chapter 3, she was stripped of her position of imperial consort in 896 because of her involvement with Priest Zenyū, only to be reinstated posthumously in 943.[88] If the demotion took place at the time of the relationship or slightly later, she would have been in her early fifties when involved with the priest. There are no records of her motivations, but, in addition to physical attractions, she may have been exerting independence or expressing discontent.[89] She could not have been happy about how things turned out. Her son, Emperor Yōzei, had been forced to abdicate in 884 after beating the son of his wet nurse to death. He went on to live in an official residence as retired emperor, but his reputation for violence continued to grow. Although Takaiko continued to live well materially, it must have been extremely painful to be his mother.[90] Any hope she had for him or of continuing her line with a grandson was dashed by his behavior. Since Takaiko had already lost almost everything, what would keep her from becoming sexually involved with whomever she pleased, even if it upset powerful men?

The affair with Narihira raises the possibility that her discontent started earlier, when she was young. She must have known what she meant to the dreams of her uncle Yoshifusa and her brothers. If she also had high aspirations for her family, then why would she become involved with Narihira? Perhaps she resisted being a political pawn or, more likely, it was a mixture of passion and resistance. Could she have wanted to assist Narihira (either consciously or subconsciously) in the weakening of the Fujiwara?[91]

Since Takaiko's family would have had political reasons for keeping her from Narihira, Narihira's abduction can be read as an attempt to oppose the Fujiwara, political demons who continued to victimize him and his family.[92] Although Narihira died at least twenty-five years before the creation of *Ise monogatari*, the northern branch Fujiwara were still rising to power in the early tenth century, so the suggestion of resistance to them in that text still has direct relevance to certain aristocrats. When Narihira transgresses political boundaries by stealing away with Takaiko, he enters not only into a concrete domain of the demon, the abandoned building, but also into the philosophical, aesthetic, and ideological space of the grotesque. He challenges social and political assumptions and practices, using the body as an instrument of disruption.

The demon in the *Konjaku* tale ironically supports this struggle, but not to the benefit of Narihira. Although the woman is unnamed in *Konjaku*, the consumption of a lover of Narihira by a demon refers literate people to the last passage of *Ise* episode 6, recalling Takaiko, the death imagined for her, and the denial of it ever having occurred. The representation of a woman actually consumed by a demon superimposed on that of Takaiko or vice versa suggests hostility aimed at the Fujiwara and their political strategies. In *Konjaku*, there are no protective brothers to intervene. Here the Fujiwara family hardly comes across as a formidable challenge, as in sections of *Ise* regarding the affair. Whereas they prevail in *Ise monogatari*, the death of the woman in *Konjaku* alludes to their vulnerability, which, historically speaking, would have already been witnessed.

Who or what demon is able to defeat both the Fujiwara and their rivals, replacing with new tensions the power struggles that helped to create and maintain the aristocratic world? It must be the force of social change—the increasing role of the retired emperors in ruling the country and the rise of the warrior class. Since *Konjaku* was compiled in the late Heian period, its compilers and audiences would have already begun foreseeing or experiencing major changes in society. Tales set in the past would have been shaped in part by the contemporary concerns of compilers whether the stories were newly created, recorded from an oral tradition, or appropriated from earlier texts. There would have been no impulse to repeat stories without meaning for the new writers and audiences within the context of their own lives. The basic issue of opposing those in power who are also in some sense oppressors would persist.

Some demon tales in *Konjaku* and *Kokon chomonjū* appear also in histories. The tale below, from the "Henge" section of *Kokon chomonjū*, shares an almost identical plot with accounts in *Nihon sandai jitsuroku* (*Veritable Records of Three Reigns of Japan*, ca. 901) and *Fusō ryakki*.[93] However, since the differences that do exist between the histories and setsuwa are significant, we should avoid lumping the accounts together.[94]

How Something Transformed Appears on Pine Grove, East of the Hall of Military Virtues during the Eighth Month of Ninna 3 (887)

On the seventeenth day of the eighth month of Ninna 3, a certain person tells the following to a traveler: Three beautiful women are walking east on the west side of Pine Grove, east of the Hall of Military Virtues. Beneath the pines appears a man with elegant features, who takes the hand of one woman and converses with her. After some time, even their voices can no longer be heard. Surprised and thinking this strange, the women go to look, whereupon they find the hand and feet of the woman lying severed on the ground. Her head is nowhere in sight. The night watchman at the headquarters of the Right Gate Guards of the Right Military Guards hears about this incident, then goes and looks to find that the corpse is missing. This must be the act of a demon.

The next day, a sutra recitation is held, the monks from various temples having been summoned. They work through the night in the east and west corridors of the Court of Government. A rumpus sounds around midnight, so the monks go outside the building and look, whereupon it suddenly gets quiet. Nothing whatsoever is there. "Indeed, what brought us out here?"

they all ask each other, but no one knows the answer. They must have been deceived by a creature [*mono*]. We hear that incidents such as these were numerous within the palace and the capital during this month.[95]

In the histories, the corpse is not the only thing missing when the guard goes to the scene of the brutal murder: "the people at the site" (the other women) also disappear. Moreover, the narrators do not attribute the murder to the demon but instead tell us that the people of the time do. The "historic" accounts also include the following statement: "During this month, on the palace grounds and within the capital, there are thirty-six groundless eerie fabrications like these being spread word of mouth by people; we cannot give a detailed account of the others."[96]

"Eerie fabrications" corresponds to *yōgo*, written with Chinese characters meaning "monstrous talk" 妖語: yō as in *yōkai* ("spooks") and *go* referring to "speech." In other words, the historians are documenting a story of a haunting spirit in circulation but rejecting its truth. The *Kokon chomonjū* narrator asserts a demon killed the woman whereas the narrator of the histories denies the reliability of the report.

The *Kokon chomonjū* tale and the accounts in histories share a focus on the public sphere. Yet, the latter address the threat to the government and society on a larger scale than the setsuwa. When we look beyond the entries for the seventeenth of the eighth month, the larger context gives us a picture of Japan in the late seventh through eighth months of Ninna 3 (887) as plagued by calamities and strange events. Many people die during earthquakes; swarms of winged ants appear more than once in the capital; the Bureau of Divination issues warnings about imminent strong winds, flooding, and spreading fires. Herons, possibly associated with death, are spotted on buildings and gates within the imperial grounds and Emperor Kōkō dies on the twenty-sixth day of the eighth month.

The sutra reading is probably held because of a combination of problems experienced by the court and the country. No explicit statement connects it to the woman's death and the consequent pollution of the imperial palace. Perhaps the histories document two separate events occurring on the same day, the telling of the tale and the sutra reading, linked only loosely by the supernatural element. If this is the case, it is the *Kokon chomonjū* compiler, Tachibana no Narisue (dates unknown), who creates a causal relationship between the events, turning them into one story and tightening the connection between the oni eating the woman and the *mono* distracting the monks.

In the *Kokon chomonjū*, the horrific death of the woman on the imperial palace grounds is one reason the monks are called to recite the sutras. The government sponsors the sutra reading to appease both the spirits of the living and deceased as well as to suppress the demon. In contrast, the *Konjaku* version never mentions monks and sutra readings. Here is its translation:

How a Demon Becomes a Person and Eats a Woman
at Pine Grove, the Imperial Palace

   Now it is the past; during the reign of the Komatsu Emperor, three young women are gathered together on Pine Grove by the Hall of Military Virtues, walking toward the palace. The moon is quite bright, it being the night of the seventeenth of the eighth month.
   Just then, a man appears from beneath the trees. He pulls one of the passing women toward him and, taking her hand, talks with her in the shadow of the trees. The two other women say, "The conversation will be over in a minute and she'll come" and stand there waiting. After quite a while, they still don't see her and the voices have ceased. They go to look, bewilderedly thinking, "What could have happened?" Neither the man nor woman is there. "Where could they have gone?" the women think as they take a closer look: lying on the ground are just a severed hand and a foot. The two women flee in horror. They approach the headquarters of the gate guards and tell one of the gate guards about the incident, whereupon the shocked gate guards go to the site and look. Nothing approximating a corpse is scattered about, instead only a foot and hand remain. People gather around and look, creating a tremendous uproar. They say, "This was caused by a demon who transformed into a person and ate the woman."
   And so, if a woman is called by a man, a stranger, at a place better avoided, as in the case here, she should not go thoughtlessly with him. She ought to be very careful; and so the story is told and passed down.[97]

With the closing comment, the compiler shifts the focus of the tale from the public sphere to personal danger. The advice is practical since Heian women were sometimes at risk when venturing off by themselves or when trusting men who courted them. Nevertheless, the recycling of this tale to illustrate this message is odd. Why is the threat to women attributed to creatures disguised as aristocratic men rather than to the men themselves? Placing the blame on non-human forces is means of denying that real men caused the dangers. The fear instilled by the possibility of being attacked would have helped to keep Heian women behind screens and otherwise under control.[98]
   Demons appear on the imperial grounds in other tales set around this time as well. "How a Controller Attending the Early Morning Meeting Is

Eaten by a Demon" in *Konjaku* describes how, during the reign of Emperor Seiwa, a clerk in the Council of State (*sakan*) discovers that a demon has eaten a superior, a controller (*ben*). The victim had arrived before anyone else to the early morning meeting, which, commencing before dawn, requires lit torches. Yet, the building is strangely dark when the clerk appears and calls for a servant from the Bureau of Grounds to bring a lamp. He finds only a bloodied head with patches of hair, a courtier's scepter, shoes, and a fan with the work plan inscribed on it in the controller's handwriting. Although the word *oni* does not appear in the tale, the remaining head is evidence a demon has struck. The tale title and the position of the tale in the collection also indicate that the *Konjaku* compiler or perhaps a later editor envisioned a demon culprit.[99] As tale 9 of Book 27, the section comprised mostly of tales about malevolent supernatural beings, it falls between the story of the woman eaten at Pine Grove and another, also in *Fusō ryakki*, about an unspecified creature who steals lantern oil from the Jijūden (the original imperial residence) during the reign of Emperor Daigo (r. 897–930).[100]

 Fusō ryakki and *Kokon chomonjū* also overlap in their accounts of oni. In both, demonic footprints are discovered on the palace grounds on the twenty-fifth day of the fourth month of Enchō 7 (929).[101] Signs of demons on imperial grounds in histories and setsuwa set in the late ninth and early tenth centuries may have been related to the political atmosphere of the time. In response to increased violence and instability in the country, the court took countermeasures to achieve greater peace and stability, thereby maintaining the wealth and status it achieved largely by exploiting the majority of the population.[102] The government had to increase the use of police forces to prevent the rebellions of insurgents already undergoing discipline in Mutsu, Dewa, Kōzuke, Shimozuke, Awa, and other provinces in 886, a year before the consumption of the woman at Pine Grove. Baba sees a relationship between the thirty-six incidents involving demons mentioned in the histories and mounting resistance toward the central government. In her view of the Pine Grove attack, the three women represent the relaxed hearts of the politically powerful while the victim also symbolizes their vulnerability.[103]

 The late ninth century is also marked by tensions between aristocrats of different prominent lineages (*uji*) as well as between members of those same groups and the imperial house. Recall how the efforts of Emperor Uda to rely less on the Fujiwara and more on other aristocrats contributed to the so-called Akō incident.[104] Tales about the presence of demons and demonic attacks on the palace grounds are one way of shifting attention away from in-house hostilities. Threats to the stability of the government are cast in terms of supernatural rather than human events, so that the palace, too, can be extraordinary and connected to spirit realms, even in its bleakest moments.

Resistance to the aristocrats and their government conveyed through tales involving demons in official spaces would have been relevant to later audiences as well. It would have resounded with people living during the dramatic social and political transitions of the second half of the Heian and early Kamakura periods, from the decline of the Fujiwara regent house to the increased influence of ex-emperors as the imperial house fought for control and then to a warrior centered society.[105] In analyzing a tale, we should always take the date or time functioning as part of the setting into consideration: among other things, it prevents us from generalizing or universalizing too much. Yet, we should also keep in mind that the people who recorded and compiled setsuwa were often far removed from those times. The opening phrase of the *Konjaku* tales, *ima wa mukashi* or "now it is the past," negates what it asserts: the past may be experienced in the present as the present but is still something other than the "now" of another, vanished, time.

Since demons are active in histories as well as in setsuwa collections, it is important to consider whether the approach to them differs consistently depending on the genre. Which texts suggest that people believed in demons, if any? In which are the creatures fictional? If, for example, accounts of them were almost always dismissed in the histories but presented as "real" in setsuwa, we would have a basis for arguing that some literate people in classical and medieval Japan saw them as imaginary. Unfortunately, questions about how premodern Japanese people thought rarely have simple answers. While my research on demons in so-called historical sources is not extensive, the narrators of the passages I have studied seem to reject only individual accounts of the creatures or simply refrain from judging them. In other words, the existence of demons is never in itself challenged. Such is the case with the demon at Pine Grove. The following two entries from the *Nihon kiryaku* (*A Condensed History of Japan*, late Heian period) are also examples.[106] The first account below is under the twenty-fourth day of the seventh month of Kanpyō 1 (889) and the second, the ninth day of the seventh month of Tentoku 2 (958):

A certain person says, "People-eating demons from Shinano entered the capital." That is, in the capital, children see people who appear to be Buddhist priests and call them demons. Then the children all run and hide. Demons appear in this form or as little boys according to others. This is what is said. The report must be an eerie fabrication.

There is a madwoman. She takes the head of a dead person and eats it in front of the Taiken Gate. Afterwards, ill people who occasionally lie under the various gates are sometimes eaten alive. Everyone in society thinks the woman is a female demon.[107]

In the first passage, the narrator rejects the report of flesh-eating demons having entered the capital from Shinano but neither challenges the possibility nor declares that demons do not exist. In the second passage, the narrator gives us only the reaction of the contemporaries of the mad woman (*kyōjo*). (*Society* or *yo* refers to the people who know of the woman at the time of the report in 958.) No clue is given as to whether or not the person or people recording the entry agree with this view. As with setsuwa, a communal voice (the people of the time) rather than a narrator often declares a demon has struck. Along with tales, histories suggest that there were people who took demons to be real.

This ambivalent stance toward the creatures does not change in the Kamakura period, at least not in *Tsurezuregusa* (*Essays in Idleness*, ca. 1330). In entry 50, author Yoshida Kenkō writes about rumors that a female demon has been brought into the capital. Everyone tries to get a peek at her and, although no one has any success, no one calls the report untrue. Only later do people refer to it as false, but even then, the report of a demon is associated with something adverse: it is seen retrospectively as foreboding short-term illnesses.[108] Perhaps the writers and compilers of histories were among those people uncertain about the existence of demons in the world. Or, they may have felt obligated to affirm only those magical realities that had gained official acceptance by the Bureau of Divination and the like.

These two passages also provide a glimpse of attitudes toward cannibalism, which may or may not have taken place in Japan. There seem to be no references to widespread cannibalism during the Nara, Heian, or Kamakura periods in the extant sources. The first passage quoted above indicates only that there may have been isolated cases of it, but we cannot be sure since so-called historic accounts are often fictive or otherwise unreliable. In the second passage, the behavior of eating human flesh distinguishes the woman as other than human, a demon, since no attempt is made to explain or somehow excuse it (was she herself starving?) or to suggest that others might act similarly under certain circumstances. In both passages, the flesh-eating demons are said to come from outside the capital. The provinces are frequently associated with a degree of barbarism in literature as well.

Elsewhere, the provinces are not remote enough; demons and cannibalism are often associated with people and places from abroad. As early as the reign of Emperor Kinmei in *Nihon shoki*, people who arrive at Sado Island in a boat from abroad are described by islanders as non-human and as demons. These visitors, called the *Mishihase*, plunder Umu Village, on the east side of the island. Many scholars believe they are the Tunguses (ancestors of the Manchu).[109] In *Shōyūki* (*Diary of the Ononomiya Minister of the Right*, 982–1032), a *kanbun* diary by Fujiwara no Sanesuke (957–1046), the islanders on Iki and Tsushima report that the Nüzhen (an ancient Chinese nationality) consume people. They are described as invaders of both these islands and Chikuzen in the entry dated the twenty-fifth day of the fourth month of Kannin 3 (1019).[110] In a *Konjaku* tale entitled "How Chishō Daishi Travels to Song China and Returns with the Law of Exoteric and Esoteric Teachings," the land called Ryūkyū is described as "a country where people are eaten."[111] In other words, the inhabitants are either flesh-eating demons or cannibals.

Despite the effort of certain writers to portray demons as coming from outside the capital or Japan, it is a mistake to view demons as diametrically opposed to the structured world of the aristocrats. In "Konjaku Monogatari-shū: Supernatural Creatures and Order," Mori Masato asserts that the demon was "a creature who invades the inside from without . . . that creature which existed outside the order formulated and supported by human beings (the worlds of politics, culture, daily life and the like), and that creature which invaded this order and attempted to destroy it—that creature was a demon."[112] Since demons frequently serve the interests of the people in or vying for power, they cannot simply represent confusion or chaos—that which, according to Mori, comes into conflict with "order, authority, and centralism."[113] Instead, they are insiders because of their place in the imaginations of literate people, who often defined power in relationship to them. Who grapples with demons and to what degree a person or institution controls them if at all are crucial questions. While demons often reach out from an invisible world or leave only footprints or blood behind as evidence of their existence, their realm exists within the hearts and minds of the people who speak, write, and hear about them.

The worthiness of an individual to rule is defined in terms of a demon conquest in "How Sōkara and Five Hundred Merchants Go Together to the Land of the Rākṣasīs," a tale from both *Konjaku* and *Uji shūi*. An Indian man called Sōkara and five hundred merchants are searching for treasures by sea when the wind blows their ship south to an unknown island inhabited by beautiful women who unbeknownst to them are demons (*rākṣasīs* and *yakṣīs*). Ignorant of the danger, the men marry and enjoy happy, erotic lives. Then one day when the women are napping, Sōkara discovers an enclosed area filled with corpses and living men trapped to be eaten. He and all but one of his men escape from the island with the help of Avalokiteśvara (Kannon), who responds to their prayers. The bodhisattva transforms into a huge horse and carries the men on her back as she gallops through the sea. (One man is unable to overcome his passionate attachment and consequently falls into the waves.) The demon-wife of Sōkara appears later in India, quite angry at having been abandoned. She complains to the king, who is then struck by her beauty. He spends days in the bedchamber with her, heedless to warnings, until at last, she devours him and flies away into the clouds, leaving behind only his bloody head. The crown prince sanctions Sōkara and his men to attack the island and, once the demons are destroyed, bestows it on Sōkara to govern.[114]

The fates of Sōkara, the king, and the crown prince demonstrate that men who prove themselves more powerful than demons are exceptional and deserving of reward. In addition, sovereigns lose their power when they fall prey to their passions and ignore sound advice. Stated another way, there are appropriate and inappropriate forms of imperial authority: the inept king dies and is replaced by a crown prince who is more qualified, as indicated by his support of Sōkara the demon conqueror. The outcome of events attests to the sublime status of the crown prince and of Sōkara. Since the earliest extant versions of the tale are Chinese, appearing in *Da-Tang xiyuji* (*Great Tang Record of the Western Region*, ca. 646) and other Chinese texts, it would not be out of cultural context to say they have the Mandate of Heaven.[115]

An anecdote in *Ōkagami* also emphasizes the role of imperial authority in subduing demons. During the reign of either Emperor Daigo or Emperor Suzaku, Fujiwara no Tadahira (880–949) is carrying out an imperial decree when a demon reaches out from the dais curtains of the Shishinden, the main ceremonial building of the residential compound of the emperor, and grabs his scabbard tip. Tadahira summons up courage and responds: "Who stops a man on his way to the council chamber with an imperial decree? You will regret it if you don't let go," then draws his sword and grasps the shaggy hand with its long knife-like fingernails. The demon is frightened away.[116] The opportunity Tadahira has to confront demons comes from his connection to imperial authority, most immediately in his delivery of an imperial decree. However, the connection is more broadly manifested in the various offices he holds during his lifetime: Minister of the Right, Minister of the Left, and Chancellor (*Daijō daijin*), as well as regents (both *sesshō* and *kanpaku*) for two emperors, nephews Suzaku and Murakami.[117] Just as Sōkara destroys an entire land of demons, Tadahira proves to be victorious as an ancestor of the northern branch Fujiwara line, whose connection to the imperial family initially grows stronger with time.

In the tale about the island of female demons, the affirmation of Avalokitéśvara juxtaposes the affirmation of the crown prince and Sōkara. The bodhisattva responds to the prayer of the merchants by helping them escape. Similarly, the conquests of demons in other tales frequently function to prove the efficacy of Buddhist beliefs and practices. Calling upon Kannon or the *Lotus Sutra* is the most common means of seeking protection from demons, and all types of people use it. In a tale in *Hokkegenki* and *Konjaku*, a young Buddhist priest ensures his own safety by reciting the *Lotus Sutra* when an ox-headed demon comes to attack whereas an elderly priest who does not react quickly is torn to pieces.[118] In another tale from *Hokkegenki*, the first Chinese character from a copy of the *Lotus Sutra*, *myō*, prevents a demoness (*rākṣasī*) from eating a government official from Higo Province. In the *Konjaku* version of this last tale, the man is saved by *myō* because he calls on Kannon for help, but the character advises him to devote himself to the Buddha and recitation of the *Lotus Sutra* in the future.[119] Less frequently employed is "Mystical Verse of the Honored and Victorious One" (*Uṣṇīṣa vijayā dhāraṇī* in Sanskrit and *Sonshō darani* in Japanese), a tantric formula from the sutra of the same name used as a protection against evil.[120] A triangular link exists between the Nocturnal Procession of One Hundred Demons (*Hyakki yagyō*), aristocrats, especially the Fujiwara (Takafuji, Tsuneyuki, and Morosuke), and this formula.

Tales describing the nocturnal procession can be found in more than nine collections. The idea of a parade of creatures also captured the imaginations of artists—for example, in the Muromachi period (1392–1573) scroll painting *Hyakki yagyō emaki*.[121] Whereas this scroll focuses on abandoned objects such as clothing or instruments that have spontaneously transformed into demons after one hundred years, the tales do not usually specify the type or origin of the demonic participants. They vary in the amount of visual description provided. In the encounter of Fujiwara no Tsuneyuki (836–75) with the procession, *Konjaku* merely states that the creatures "have every sort of horrific form."[122] Several other texts tell us that some creatures have three arms, others have one leg, and still others have one eye. In *Uchigiki*, there are both one- and three-eyed demons.[123] The creatures appear carrying lit torches on or around midnight on specific nights, but setsuwa seldom give the exact date.

The Fujiwara encounter more demons than any other aristocratic family.[124] Tales about their encounters, especially as witnesses of the nocturnal procession, convey both the prominence and instability of its members. In the following anecdote from *Gōdanshō*, the "he" of the opening is Ōe no Masafusa (1041–1111), who supposedly provided the material for *Gōdanshō* in conversations with Fujiwara no Sanekane (1085–1112).

> He also says: When both Ono no Takamura and Fujiwara no Takafuji are Middle Counselor and Middle Captain, they encounter the nocturnal procession of one hundred demons in front of the Suzaku Gate. Takafuji climbs down from his cart when that happens. The one hundred demons of the nocturnal procession look at Takafuji and apparently cry out "The Spell of the Honored and Victorious One!" Takafuji does not realize that his wet nurse concealed "The Spell of the Honored and Victorious One" inside his robe. At the time, Takamura shows Takafuji the spirits out of kindness because he feels indebted to Takafuji.[125]

The passage does not explain how showing the procession to someone is an act of kindness or the nature of Takamura's debt to Takafuji. Nor does historical information help. Takamura lived from 802 to 852 and Takafuji from 838 to 900. The men supposedly encounter the nocturnal procession of demons when both are serving as Middle Counselors (*Chūnagon*) and Middle Captains (*Chūjō*). However, Takamura held neither office. Takafuji was never a Middle Captain and did not become a Middle Counselor until 897, forty-five years after the death of the older man. It is highly unlikely that the men shared any post since Takafuji was only fourteen when Takamura died and is not known to have held any major political position until 865, when he became a Chamberlain (*Kurōdo*). Yet, the last line conveys the sense that it is a privilege to view the nocturnal procession. The privilege is clouded in ambivalence because, in the next account, Takafuji damages Takamura's ox cart out of apparent resentment at having been shown the demons.[126] The glimpse he gets of the procession may be a gift, but one he does not appreciate receiving.

The motif of the wet nurse who protects the young man she once nursed appears in the story included in many collections of how Fujiwara no Tsuneyuki encounters the creatures of the nocturnal procession.[127] The young man frequently wanders out at night to be with a lover, having become sexually active even before the official ceremony marking his puberty (*genpuku*). He sees the terrifying creatures in front of the Bifuku Gate, but avoids harm because of his concerned wet nurse. A year earlier, she had her brother, a Buddhist priest skilled in esoteric rituals, write out the formula so she could sew it into the collar of his robe. This tale has a tighter plot than the *Gōdanshō* account, but Takafuji and Tsuneyuki are protected from demons in the same way.

In *Ōkagami*, Fujiwara no Morosuke (908–60) also encounters the nocturnal procession. He is traveling with his attendants one night on Ōmiya Avenue when struck by the presence of these demons. His attendants have no idea what is happening as he takes steps to protect himself and the others from them: lowering the blinds, shouting orders to unyoke the ox, prostrating himself, ordering the others where to stand, and, most importantly, reciting the *Uṣṇīṣa vijayā dhāraṇī*. They fail to see or sense the demons. Similarly in the tale about Tsuneyuki, the creatures do not affect a page and groom accompanying the young man.

Baba attributes the encounters of Fujiwara men with demons to latent grudges other aristocrats held against that family, the consequent instability of their position, and the superficiality of the harmony they achieved. Yet, as she points out, some tales suggest that people need the proper cultivation to view the creatures.[128] Seeing them can attest to the privileged position or superiority of an individual or group. In "How Kamo no Tadayuki Teaches the Path to His Son Yasunori," ten-year-old Kamo no Yasunori (917–77) is able to see demons at an exorcism performed by his father, a yin-yang diviner. Struck by the talent of the boy, Tadayuki (died ca. 960) thinks:

> I am the finest of all in the world who have taken this path. Yet, as a child, I could not see spirits in this way. Only through training was I finally able to see them. That he instead can see these spirits with his young eyes surely must mean he will become someone great. He will certainly not be inferior to the people from the age of the gods.[129]

Tadayuki has great expectations for his son and teaches the boy everything he knows about divination. In illustrating the precociousness of Yasunori and the ability of his father to appreciate it, this tale celebrates the Kamo family as the finest yin-yang diviners. Although the reason people are shown seeing or otherwise encountering demons differ, this ability can mark them as extraordinary if they come through the experience unharmed. Outstanding genealogical connections are often an important factor in determining their fates.

CONCLUSION

The grotesque in ancient through medieval Japan cannot be understood without examining the role of oni in setsuwa. As the relationships of oni and aristocrats demonstrate, the monsters embraced by a society can help illuminate the perceptions, internal struggles, fears, and aspirations of its members. Buddhist elements, such as criticisms of mountain ascetics or the use of Buddhist formulas to ward off demons, often figure largely in the tales about oni as well, and consequently give us some insight into perceptions people had of the effectiveness of Buddhist beliefs and practices in protecting against danger or explaining mysteries.

What could have been more terrifying to Heian aristocrats than people and events threatening to limit their possibilities for social and political advancement or to destroy their way of life? In many setsuwa, forces of change are manifested in oni, pervasive monsters in various forms or formless who erode the standards and values of the elite or of subgroups within the upper class.

As instruments of decrowning, these same creatures can be heroes to people who are not benefiting from the practices or systems under attack. A main threat of oni lies in their hunger for human flesh. This hunger and the success of creatures in satisfying it serves to undermine or affirm the political authority of men in setsuwa. While it is often difficult to find redeeming qualities in such tales, the violence of oni can express the otherwise suppressed discontent of people and elucidate their hopes and desires. The depictions of demons as terrifying and destructive are empowering because the undermining of one group of people often suggests the liberation of another, even when the release does not conform to historic reality.

Consumption by demons has symbolic significance. Flesh-eating creatures in setsuwa are connected to myths and *kami*-worship (later referred to as Shinto) such as the one-eyed demon who consumes a tiller in *Izumo no kuni fudoki* and Ama-no-ma-hitotsu-no-mikoto.[130] The idea of sacrifice comes into play. The threat of being eaten has to do with the weakening or death of the victim or the powers he or she represents for the sake of another, stronger, force. One particularly frightening aspect of such an attack is that the victim does not simply die. The prey nourishes its attacker, having become part of the larger body, whether a political system favoring men over women, one aristocratic family over others, or warriors over aristocrats. At the same time, no group can dominate completely since the people in power depend on the oppression of others and are consequently in a precarious position themselves. As they struggle to maintain their privilege and authority, new demons inevitably come along.

Oni are not always diametrically opposed to the aristocratic way of life or institutional Buddhism. Many tensions played out in setsuwa are between members of different elite families in both the provinces and the capital. Who encounters demons and what happens to them as a result often indicate privilege and power. Finally, monsters can be tamed or converted to serve the interests of authority. We see this strategy especially in sutras and tales taken from them, or, more generally, in the way Buddhism appropriates demons from other traditions as defenders of Buddhist law.

Demons affirm and undermine the positions of men. While some tales touch on concerns of particular interest to women, tales with female demons or demons in female form more often raise such issues.

CHAPTER 5

The Feminization of Demons

Women often function as objects of sexual and gastronomic desires in setsuwa involving *oni*. As seen in Chapter 4, these two types of appetites merge in the stories, among the most violent, describing how demons consume women expecting courtship or sexual relations with men. Yet, depictions of demons victimizing women represent only one of many ways women are associated with demons in premodern Japan. Demons gendered female in setsuwa tend to be active in contrast to the usually passive figures of women victimized by demons. These creatures frequently suggest the discontent of Heian women as well as the possibility of resistance in a world more oppressive of women than of men. They are potentially empowering figures for women, but the view of them as undesirable and threatening undermines their strength as an affirmation of women. The latent power of women is acknowledged but considered unacceptable and suppressed.

What is a female demon? The gender of so-called female demons is rarely fixed; setsuwa usually suggest such demons have another, gender-less, identity. Only one tale in *Konjaku* describes the change of an unquestionably human woman into a demon: "How the Mother of Hunters Becomes a

Demon and Tries to Devour Her Child." "How a Woman Giving Birth Travels to South Yamashina, Encounters a Demon, and Escapes" may also depict such a transformation, but the story leaves open the question of whether a mountain woman actually turns into a demon who threatens a newborn.

Whereas some Buddhist texts portray women as inherently evil, many tales point to the existence of lethal female impersonators rather than intrinsically wicked women.[1] The final remarks of the *Konjaku* tales, which frequently seem tacked on to pre-existing narratives, often shift the focus away from the idea of threatening spirits in the guise of women to evil women. The negative attitudes toward women in Buddhism colored the interpretations of commentators. Their bias can be seen in their failure to associate demons in the form of men with the intrinsic nature of men although, as we have seen, many equally dangerous male human impersonators also lurk about.

How can we argue that such representations demonize women when the creatures are clearly revealed as impostors—something other than women despite their temporary forms? In the Heian period, oni of an unspecified gender are often feminized. Incarnated, they draw from representations of women idealized according to Heian cultural standards: delicate but fleshy aristocratic young women with long, full hair, a perpetually forlorn expression, and perfect features. Moreover, the dynamic of being hidden versus being seen figures prominently in the depictions of both women and demons. The first section below explains this connection. It focuses on certain juxtapositions of aristocratic women with demons in literature predating the compilations of most setsuwa collections but not necessarily the creation of individual tales. The section addressing setsuwa follows. It centers on demons gendered as female with a study of four tales from Book 27, including the two mentioned above.

Associations of women with demons begin early in extant works, such as with the hags who pursue Izanagi in the land of Yomi in *Kojiki* and *Nihon shoki* and the demon who watches the funeral of Empress Saimei in *Nihon shoki*, mentioned in Chapter 4. They continue through present-day literature and popular culture, differing greatly but not entirely from era to era. We should attempt to distinguish between trends that predate or are contemporaneous with the tales and those that come later lest we develop myopic vision: relying on an understanding of demons in literature created after the early Kamakura period to interpret the significance of creatures in setsuwa. While looking at associations of women and demons in later texts can give us insight into how demons are gendered in setsuwa collections, scholars often see connections that exist only because they have knowledge of subsequent creatures. Similarly, we can be tempted to base our understandings of certain tales on later versions when it usually makes sense only to see the influence of older tales on newer.

WOMEN AS HIDDEN DEMONS OUTSIDE SETSUWA

In "Mushi mezuru himegimi" ("The Young Lady Who Loves Insects," ca. 1055–1185?), the daughter of the Major Counselor and Inspector of the Provincial Administrations (*Azechi no dainagon*) defies social convention by collecting insects. Contrasting with the Young Lady Who Loves Butterflies next door, this woman collects and observes insects that frighten the young women in attendance on her. Especially fond of caterpillars, she tries to understand "the depth of the caterpillar heart" (*kawamushi no kokoro fukakisama*).[2] She resists the pressure of contemporary fashion by refusing to pluck her eyebrows or blacken her teeth and her color choice in clothing is atypical. In another uncustomary move, she calls for boys of low birth to serve her because they do not mind handling the insects. She quotes from Chinese poetry and writes *waka* in *katakana* rather than in *hiragana*, the form desirable of a young aristocratic woman. Her behavior deeply upsets not only her ladies-in-waiting but also her parents, who think the hairy insects ghastly, but are most concerned about the damaging effects of their daughter's tastes and interests on her reputation. However defiant, the young woman remarks, "Demons and women are best not seen."[3]

A major component of the link between women and demons in Heian literature is the tension between the need to be hidden and the need to be perceived, either visually or through other senses. Demons are most powerful when they are emerging from the state of being disguised or concealed. There would be no encounters between people and demons, nor could the creatures have any political impact, if demons did not first make some aspect of their identities known. Once revealed, they are themselves vulnerable; with every action comes the risk of being destroyed. Women, too, are frequently delineated in literature in terms of the interplay between invisibility and partial or full visibility. Whereas demons tend to reveal all or part of themselves, women are generally shown to be the objects of the male gaze. *Kaimami*, the act of peeping through a gap in a fence or another barrier at someone (usually a man at a woman), exemplifies this dynamic.[4] Although the Young Lady Who Loves Insects emphasizes the state of being concealed with her remark about women and demons, being seen and acknowledged is as important in her story as it is in others.

The resistance of the Young Lady Who Loves Insects is rooted in strong convictions and logic. The young woman disapproves of how aristocratic women make themselves up and affectation in general.[5] Her perspective is a critique of the conventional sense of courtly beauty and taste developed in *The Pillow Book*, *Genji*, and many other classics. "The way people love flowers and butterflies is shallow and absurd!"[6] she bluntly remarks. People are most admirable when they are sincere and search for "original forms," written as *honji*, a Buddhist term usually referring to "the original Buddhist deity of which a Shinto god is said to be the manifestation."[7] Whereas we see caterpillars as developing into butterflies and therefore at a less advanced stage of growth than them, the Young Lady Who Loves Insects views the butterfly as a manifestation rather than a transformation of the caterpillar.[8] The emphasis is not on the butterfly but on the caterpillar because it does the changing. There is also a practical side to this preference: as she points out, silkworms are useless once they become butterflies. (They are actually moths, but the story makes no distinction.) Here the butterflies work as a metaphor for conventional court ladies.

What do demons have to do with this critique? When the young lady remarks "demons and women are best not seen," she attempts to avoid the gaze of her parents and people in society who normally would not view her. Why not say simply that women are best not seen (without the juxtaposition)? The link between women and demons makes sense because both women and demons are forces shaping the male-dominated political realm while also dwelling mostly in their own space. "Hidden" women represent latent energy and are demon-like as potential sources of social and political change. They need to be controlled for men to establish political alliances through courtship and marriage.[9]

Although others may find the young lady who loves insects disagreeable, she does not see herself that way. The association of women with demons in her story is empowering even while self-derogatory. However, her resistance concerns us with the dream of acceptance despite being unusual and perhaps of even being influential because of it rather than with the desire of more presence in public life. She wants the freedom to pursue her odd interest and ignore contemporary fashion within the confines of a protected space. Therefore, we should not be surprised by her willingness to participate in the practice of sequestering women by conforming to the notion that women should not be seen.

The potential of "The Young Lady Who Loves Insects" to be subversive is largely unrealized. The story ends abruptly with the promise of its continuation in a second section that either went unwritten or is no longer extant. The writer, believed by some scholars to be a woman, appears ambivalent about the protagonist herself.[10] While she succeeds in creating a strong and interesting character, the narrator undermines the strengths of the Young Lady by considering her behavior pitiful.[11]

The author was perhaps unsure about where to go with the story. Most people react to the unconventional woman with criticism and hostility. In contrast, one nobleman is interested upon hearing about her eccentricity. He initiates an exchange of poems by sending her an artificial but authentic looking snake made from a sash along with a poem about crawling beside her. Later, he observes her through a lattice fence and is struck by her beauty despite her strangeness. Yet, the narrative does not develop into a story of how the odd woman wins the unconditional acceptance of the man. Along with the narrator, he and his men lament her bizarre taste and behavior, seeing it as especially inappropriate because of her good background and looks.

Suppose the story continued. Would the caterpillar woman have given into external pressures, she herself becoming a lovely but dull and useless butterfly? Could she have continued to endure in Heian society as a nonconformist, even though women of her class needed for support wealthy and high-ranking men—in contrast to those low-class boys who would have grown up and become even fonder of her? She might have become a nun, but doing so would not have given her the freedom to be herself. Perhaps the ending of the story went unwritten because the author could not conceive of a conclusion that would preserve its force and beauty.

The Young Lady Who Loves Insects is a grotesque figure in many ways. In the Heian context, her natural looks connect her to the earth and to the lowest creatures. Her bushy eyebrows and white teeth must have been quite repulsive to Heian readers. She collapses the distinction between beauty and ugliness and between high and low: the caterpillar is more intricate than the butterfly; the boys of low birth are brave, delightful, and fun whereas the refined nobleman is a crawling snake by reason of his own imagination. The young woman personifies the caterpillar, as she herself suggests. Her initial response to the suitor in a poem states that they will probably meet in the Pure Land if their destiny is to be together because becoming entwined is difficult when one is near or in the form of an insect.[12]

In this reaction to the advance of the nobleman, the young woman completely avoids the possibility of sexual involvement. The insect has trouble becoming entangled, but then she proposes meeting in the Pure Land, hardly the place for carnal love. This initial response coincides with her resistance to behaving and dressing as other aristocratic women. Buddhist beliefs and practices can provide an argument against the roles Heian aristocratic society expects women to play—including that of lover. I do not mean to suggest that women were interested in Buddhism only as a means of avoiding other things. The Young Lady Who Loves Insects incorporates Buddhism into her aristocratic life, as demonstrated by her recitation of the *nenbutsu*, a mindful chant of the name of Amitābha (Amida) Buddha, when she believes the imitation snake sent to her is real. Yet, she also uses it as a defense—to distance herself from the nobleman and the Heian conventions for intimacy.

Whereas the writer of "Mushi mezuru himegimi" links women to the demons through the idea of remaining out of sight, Sei Shōnagon (ca. 966–after 1017) connects herself to them by focusing on the experience of being revealed. Both women and demons move from a hidden state to partial exposure. In one section of *Makura no sōshi* (*The Pillow Book*), Sei does the peeking (*kaimami*) after Empress Sadako (or Teishi, 976–1000) suggests that she spy through a space between a pillar and a folding screen. The person watched is another woman, Fujiwara no Motoko (the Lady of Shigei Sha, 981–1002), who is a younger sister of the empress. She arrives on a special visit a month after being installed as the consort of Crown Prince Okisada (future emperor Sanjō, 976–1017, r. 1011–16). Sei is observing all the details of this auspicious event hidden from view when someone pushes aside her cover. Referring to herself as *kaimami no hito*, she writes: "Kaimami no hito kakuremino toraretaru kokochi shite" (The person peeping feels as if she has been robbed of the straw raincoat concealing her).[13] Here "the person peeping" corresponds to "I." Sei is associating herself with those demons said to wear magical straw coats (*kakuremino*) rendering them invisible. Ivan Morris brings out this point in his translation by making the reference to demons more explicit: "The screen behind which I had been peeping was now pushed aside and I felt exactly like a demon who has been robbed of his straw coat."[14]

Sei hurries to another hiding place: a space behind a bamboo blind and a curtain of state. She continues to spy but is again revealed because the train and skirts of her robe stick out from under the blind. When Michitaka (953–95), father of the empress and her sister, asks reproachfully whom he has glimpsed, Empress Sadako tells him, but she attributes the behavior to Sei's curiosity rather than admit it was her idea to have Sei watch. Sei must be hidden or at least inconspicuous to observe carefully the details of the visit and later record them.[15] The vantage point initially allows her to write about the visit almost as someone separate from it. Still, her position does not really make her an outsider since she is always shaping the events: without her eye, there would be no narrative and with a different eye would come another account. Moreover, the description of the visit is framed within the story of the role of the observer. The anecdote ultimately turns to how Sei is discovered by the people she views—to how she moves into their consciousness. Tales about demons generally show a similar movement, except that we are told nothing about their world before they enter the realm of human awareness.

Along with a bamboo hat such as the one worn by the demon who watches the funeral of Empress Saimei, the straw raincoat can denote that its wearer is from, going to, or temporarily associated with a non-human and magical realm. The hat and coat are usually a set, whose symbolism has fascinated Orikuchi and others. Whereas many scholars drawing from Orikuchi associate the hat and coat with a visitor from the spirit realm (*marebito*), the outfit can also be treated more generally as traveling clothes indicating the transcendence of the boundaries of mundane life—a ritualistic disappearance or sequestering, including death.[16]

Does the bamboo hat and coat conceal or reveal people and spirits? Rather than emphasize one dynamic over the other, it makes sense to follow the lead of Ōwa Iwao and take the middle ground: the dynamics of revealing and concealing merge in the outfit which, connected to birth and death, marks the divine or supernatural qualities of the wearer.[17] For Sei, a writer who fluctuates between the roles of observer and participant and whose work depends on that fluidity, the image of the straw coat underscores how her work distinguishes her from most other ladies-in-waiting. She makes her appearance and leaves a lasting impression on her world and ours because of her changing position. She is revealed when others think it best women be concealed and so defies silence—resisting becoming just another court lady. She magically keeps alive the atmosphere of the salon of Empress Sadako, yet her very being is almost as elusive as that of a demon. Her straw coat,

Makura no sōshi, reveals bits and pieces of her character, but it is difficult to say that we know her after reading her book.

Women are tied to demons elsewhere in Heian literature as well. In *Yamato monogatari,* the courtier Taira no Kanemori (?–990) indirectly refers to two girls living in the remote province of Michinoku as demons. The following poem appears in section 58 as well as in *Shūi (waka) shū* (*Collection of Poetry Gleanings,* ca. 1005–06):

Michinoku no	Demons secretly
Adachigahara	dwell in Kurozuka
Kurozuka ni	on Adachi Field
oni komoreri to	in Michinoku Province
kiku wa makoto ka	Is this, what I hear, true?[18]

A legend about the Michinoku demons must have been circulating at the time. However, Kanemori also playfully refers to the girls as demons since he cannot see them either. He even requests to marry one girl, but her parents refuse him because of her young age. There is no mention of Kanemori even catching a glimpse of the girl, as Genji does of the young Murasaki. What, then, is the source of his attraction—this love at no sight?

Kanemori may have been politically motivated. He is a great grandson of Emperor Kōkō (830–87, r. 884–87), but his father was given commoner status as a Taira, just as the father of the girls was a grandson of Emperor Seiwa (son of Somedono) made a Minamoto.[19] During the Heian period, the imperial family, especially the retired emperors, and the Fujiwara employed commoners of royal blood politically. Given the surnames Taira or Minamoto, these men emerged as powerful forces in their own right. Members of the so-called *zuryō* class, they served as provincial governors and managers of private proprietorships (*shōen*).[20] Since genealogical backgrounds were usually important components of romantic attachments in Heian Japan, it would have been significant when one household of marginalized royalty established intimate ties with another. Although the Taira represented is not the Kanmu line (the military elite who ultimately secured temporary leadership of the country), the tale suggests that families who had lost much of their influence in the capital and at court might gain strength by uniting with others in the same predicament.

The demons dwelling in the fields of the provinces are the dormant forces of change. Hidden women from families with wealth and authority in remote places could be influential or used instrumentally by men. According to the narrative, the young woman ultimately forms a bond with another man and Kanemori is dismayed upon hearing of her return to the capital with someone else years later. For Kanemori, then, the potential connection with the woman and her family is never realized.

The association of the hidden girls with demons may also refer to the feelings Kanemori would experience had he access to the girls. His demonization of them suggests that he sees them rather than something internal (or the combination of his own yearning and them) as the cause of his sexual response and chaotic emotions. In the poem, Kanemori celebrates the idea of confronting women as demons. His attitude contrasts with the Buddhist reaction equating sexually attractive women with evil. Either attraction or repulsion (or both) can motivate men to link women or even girls with demons.

In a poem incorporating the phrase *kokoro no oni* (demon of the heart), Lady Chikuzen of the Shijō mansion (ca. 1025–98), otherwise called Mother of Prince Yasusuke (Yasusuke ō no haha), suggests that a man is transposing the demon in his heart onto her. Daughter of a provincial governor of Chikuzen and poetess Ise no Tayū, Lady Chikuzen served as a lady-in-waiting for Fujiwara no Hiroko (Kanshi, ca. 999–1025), who ultimately became an empress consort of Emperor Go-Reizei (1025–68, r. 1045–68). The poem is in Lady Chikuzen's collection of one hundred and fifty-four poems focused on her time in service.[21] It is a response to another by Fujiwara no Mototoshi (?–1142) included in his collection without hers. He initiates the exchange upon hearing that she remains concealed inside a carriage parked outside his inner gate, listening to the Buddhist service given at his mansion.

Tada hitotsu	Just one
kado no hoka ni wa	is parked
tateredomo	outside my inner gate
oni gomoritaru	But it is a carriage where
kuruma narikeri	a demon secretly dwells[22]

As Baba comments, Lady Chikuzen does not arrive in a way befitting her social status; the poem seems to indicate that she has not brought much of a retinue and her carriage is simple. Dignified and tough, she tries to hide her identity, perhaps to concentrate better on the sermon. Mototoshi is sensitive to her quiet mood, but he is also trying to get a reaction from a woman who may be otherwise inaccessible to him.[23] If a room has been set up according to custom, with screens allowing women to listen to the sermon out of view, she chooses not to go there.

The reference to the demon suggests potential explosive energy and chaos. The poem has erotic undertones, possibly alluding to the Kurozuka demons and the message Kanemori sends the girls in Michinoku. Just as Kanemori gently pokes fun at the girls, so too does Mototoshi tease this woman by comparing her to a cloistered demon.

The response to Mototoshi's poem appears only in *The Collected Poems of Yasusuke ō no haha* and is missing from most discussions of women and demons.[24] Here is a possible reading:

Minori koso	The person riding
kono kuruma ni wa	secretly dwells in this carriage
komoreru ni	precisely because of the Dharma
kokoro no oni wa	How is it you call *me* tormented
ware to nanoru ka	a demon of the heart?[25]

"Minori" has several meanings: a "body or person riding," the Dharma, and a taboo involving coming into contact with starch (*nori*) on the day of the snake (*mi*).[26] The poem indicates all three things—the body, the Dharma, and the taboo—are secretly contained in the carriage. In this way, Lady Chikuzen suggests that she remains in the vehicle to observe ritual seclusion (*monoimi*) because of the taboo and that she does not have to leave the carriage to ride with the Dharma—that is, to experience the sermon.[27] "Minori" may also allude to the chapter of *Genji* in which Murasaki dies and Genji resolves to take vows, perhaps having something to do with the end of a bond between a man and a woman and the turning away from passion to religious concerns. While acknowledging the demon, the poet contrasts it with her own body or self, thereby rejecting the idea that she resembles it. With the rhetorical question, she urges Mototoshi to consider the demon of his own heart.

This message with its phrase *kokoro no oni* evokes a famous poem by Murasaki Shikibu. The preface to that poem indicates that the poem is a response to a painting of a possessed woman undergoing an exorcism. The husband of the victim is reading sutras while a young priest binds down the man's former wife who has died and become a demon:

Naki hito ni	Although the deceased
kagoto wa kakete	is made the pretense
wazurau mo	Does not the torment
ono ga kokoro no	truly lie in
oni ni ya wa aranu	the demons of the heart?[28]

"Demons of the heart" can refer to the following: phantoms born of fear, doubt, and suspicion, often referring to a woman's feelings toward her estranged lover; suffering caused by carnal attachments; a guilty conscience.[29] Rather than see the painting as representing the jealousy of one woman toward another, Murasaki expands the term to include the emotions of the people blaming the deceased. In the standard interpretation, the husband is transposing his feelings onto his former wife—the possession is linked to the man, who may be further disturbed by his own conscience.[30] However, the poem does not indicate exactly who attributes the possession to the deceased woman and suffers torment: the husband, the priest, the poet, the artist, the viewers of the painting, or, as Doris Bargen has asserted, the possessed woman.[31]

At another level, the poem states more generally this kind of thought: we blame the dead for our torment, but are we not really haunted by something within ourselves? A second poem serving as the response to this poem asserts that since the poet's own heart is in darkness, she "must clearly see the shadows of demons (oni no kage)" elsewhere.[32] In other words, people who experience emotional suffering (internal demons) are better equipped to see the same in other people and perhaps empathize with them. However, they must first acknowledge rather than deny the demons in their own hearts.

While not quite as insightful as Murasaki, Lady Chikuzen similarly takes the association of a woman with a demon and suggests that it refers us back to the person making it. Rather than passively accepting the label of demon, she instead realizes that men often create in women what they fear to confront in themselves.

Section 58 of Ise monogatari further demonstrates that men sometimes flirted with women by calling them demons. The man of deep feeling and skilled in the sexual arts (Narihira) has a house built beside an imperial residence where many attractive women are in service. The women teasingly banter "What a job for a great lover!" when they spot him overseeing the rice harvest in the fields.[33] He retreats inside, but the women recite a Kokinshū poem about a house neglected for generations. The man tells them in another poem that the only eerie thing (uretaki wa) about the mansion is the demons swarming around it—that is, them. The joking continues with the women offering to help the man gather the fallen ears, whereupon his answer, also a poem, conveys the suggestive message that, were poverty forcing them to gather the gleanings, he would happily join them in the fields. In short, the association of women with demons is part of an erotically charged exchange of poems. Given his reputation, the claim that he does not enjoy the gathering of women outside the mansion sounds false.

Even so, the labeling of women as demons is not entirely positive because it indicates that certain men or men at certain times experience the expression of sexual interest by women as unpleasant and even demonic. Time and place are everything: after all, the man is in the fields trying to work when the crowd of women appears. The man himself fails to distinguish between the behavior of the women as distracting and therefore demonic and the women themselves as demons. Implicit in the section then is a generalization about the nature of women. No attempt is made to identify what about sexual energy is problematic for men. Similar negative connotations may be part of why Lady Chikuzen resists the image of the demon.

In the above examples, the associations of women with demons have redeeming aspects. To identify with demons as does the Young Lady Who Loves Insects or Sei is to embrace a certain kind of freedom and knowledge. It means retreating to think in unique ways about things from insects to abstract ideas and social values. Even when Kanemori, Mototoshi, and Narihira associate women with demons, they are coyly initiating a poetic dialogue without cruel intentions. The pejorative connotations come as a side effect and are often related to a sense of what is appropriate for certain times and places. Although the associations of women with demons in setsuwa usually degrade women, demons gendered female and women who become demons have a positive side inasmuch as they affirm discontent and the will toward change. A creature threatening to eat someone demands a response.

DEMONS IN FEMALE FORM

Setsuwa usually portray demons in the form of women as young, beautiful, and sexually attractive. As we saw with the tale of Sōkara in the last chapter, a Sanskrit term for such a creature is *rākṣasī* (*rākṣa* for males), which means "a lower form of demon, flesh-eating and hideous."[34] In Japanese, they are called *rasetsu* or *rasetsunyo* (*nyo* being the character for woman). A demon may also transform into an old woman. An elderly female demon associated with the mountains is called a *yamauba, yamanba, yamahaha,* or *onibaba,* whereas a similar but younger figure is sometimes called *yamaonna, yamahime,* or *yamamusume.* Such terms for mountain figures are usually used in literature created after setsuwa, as in the noh play *Yamanba* or in folk tales (*mukashi banashi*) and secondary literature about female demons.[35]

According to Ema Tsutomu, demons and ghosts (*yōkai*) appearing as men are more abundant than those appearing as women before the Muromachi period and creatures in female form increase after the Ōnin War (1467–77), ultimately becoming twice as many as the male.[36] I have already pointed out that most so-called female demons in setsuwa are something other than female. They resist our understanding them in terms of a heterosexual binary largely because the tales are often unclear about the gender, indistinguishable from the sex, of demons in their violent moments.[37] What gender is a demon that appears as female and male or as female and gender-less? Most setsuwa do not even describe the body of the demon. Moreover, even when a person becomes a demon, it is not always obvious that he or she retains his or her sex/gender. Tales suggest demons are something other than what they describe but give little access to those identities.

Demons are theoretically sex-less spirits who materialize in various forms. In setsuwa, they can convey messages as creatures with concrete bodies whose gender is strategically changeable as they undermine authority and dominant modes of thought. The analysis of the tale below will center on understanding this fluidity and how it operates as part of the grotesque.

How the Demon of Agi Bridge in Ōmi Province Eats Somebody

Now it is the past; one day, when the governor of Ōmi, a man called [ ], is in that province, many vigorous young men are gathered at his mansion. They are telling stories of the past and present, engaging in various amusements—games such as *go* and *sugoroku*—and eating and drinking saké when one of them says, "In olden times, people used to cross the Agi Bridge in this province, but somehow, word has spread that no one who goes there can get across it, so no one tries." Apparently rejecting this talk, an easily excitable man who speaks impressively and is considered quite skillful says, "I'll cross that bridge. I'll get over even if a horrid demon is there, just as long as I'm riding the finest bay of His Lordship's mansion." Then all the other men gather around and together say, "Fantastic! Ever since word [about the demon] got out, everyone has been taking a different route instead of the more sensible direct one; now let's find out if this thing is true or false. And let's test the mettle of this gentleman." They egg him on in this way, so that the man feels even more provoked and everyone begins to argue.

Because he has boasted in this way, the men vehemently argue with each other. The governor hears them and asks, "What in the world are you shouting so about?" "We are speaking about such and such," they answer in unison. The governor replies, "You're a man who fights for truly point-less things! As for my horse, go ahead and quickly take it." The man then says, "It was a crazy joke. I feel ashamed," but the other men gather around provoking him with "Coward, coward. Weakling, weakling." The man says, "Crossing the bridge isn't difficult, but I feel ashamed because I seemed to covet His Lordship's horse." The other men say, "The sun is high. You're too slow, too slow." They saddle the horse, bring it out and compel him to take it. The man feels as if his chest is being crushed, but since this is something he himself proposed to do, he smears a large amount of oil on the rump of the horse, tightens the cinch securely, slips the loop of the whip on his wrist, and, dressed in light clothing, sets out mounted on the horse.

Eventually approaching the foot of the bridge, he is so terrified that he feels ill, his chest [constricting], yet he continues because it is too late to turn back now. The sun, too, is approaching the edge of the mountains. The man has a vague feeling of hopelessness—all the more because of the sur-roundings: there is no sign of anyone anywhere and the village also appears far away, the smoke from its houses faint. He continues, feeling a lack of purpose all the while, when in the middle of the bridge, though he had been unable to see it from afar, is a person.

He looks in terror, thinking, "This must be the demon." A woman dressed in an unlined deep purple robe over a delicate pale lavender robe and a long crimson divided skirt, shyly covers her mouth with her sleeve, a vaguely forlorn expression in her eyes. The glance she casts at him is also moving. She has not come on her own; rather someone seems to have left her behind. She is leaning against the railing of the bridge and, upon seeing someone approach, appears embarrassed yet happy. When the man sees this, he loses sense of why he has come and where he is going. "I'd like to sweep her up on this horse and ride away with her," he thinks, so overcome with feeling that he almost falls off his horse.[38] But then he realizes, "It must be a demon since this kind of person would not normally be here" and firmly decides, "I'll keep going." With his eyes shut, he whips the horse to move faster.

The woman waits, thinking, "Now, he'll come say something to me," but he passes without a word. "Oh, you sir. Why do you pass me so coldheart-edly? Someone abandoned me at this horrid, unforeseen place. Please take me to the village," she says.

Without even hearing her out and so frightened that the hair on his head and body seems to thicken, he urges the horse to move faster and travels as if he were flying. "Oh, how cruel!" says the woman in a voice that shakes the earth. As she chases after him, he thinks, "I was right." He prays: "Please help me, Kannon!" When he whips the amazingly fine horse and gallops, the demon chases after him, pulling at the rump of the horse, grabbing and grabbing with its hands. No matter how it pulls, it cannot seize the horse because of the oil smeared on it.

While urging the horse on, the man looks back and sees the demon. Its face is vermilion and has one eye as broad as a round cushion. The demon is about nine *shaku* tall and has three fingers on each hand. Its knife-like fingernails are five *sun* or so long.[39] Its body is a verditer green and its eye is like amber. The hair on its head is as tangled as mugwort. Looking at the demon, the man feels his heart and liver crumble; his fear has no bounds. He reaches a village, perhaps because he fervently invokes the name of Kannon as he gallops. At that moment, the demon says, "Very well, things may be this way now, but don't think we won't meet again," and vanishes into the air.

The man arrives at the mansion on horseback at dusk, gasping for breath and in a state of shock, whereupon the fellows there stand up in a rumpus, asking, "What happened? What happened?" The man only falls into a deeper daze and cannot say a word. Next, everyone gathers around, caring for him and calming him down. Even the governor is worried and asks what happened. When the man tells them everything, the governor says, "You may die pointlessly for engaging in a meaningless dispute" and lets him keep the horse. The man returns home with a triumphant expression. He tells his wife, children, and attendants to their faces what happened and they are terrified.

Shortly after, there is a spirit in his house. When they ask a yin-yang diviner about this curse, he performs divination and says, "On a certain day, you must observe a grave taboo." When that day arrives, the man consequently closes the gate and strictly adheres to confinement in his house.

This man has one younger half brother from the same mother who had previously gone to serve the governor of Michinoku, taking their mother down there with him. On the day of the taboo, he returns and knocks on the gate.

"I am adhering to strict ritual confinement. I will meet with you the day after tomorrow. Stay at someone else's house until then," the man calls out.

The younger brother calls in, "That won't do at all. It's already dark. I will go somewhere else myself but what should I do with the large amount of baggage? Today is ominous, so I came intentionally. Our elderly person has already passed away, so I have come myself to tell you."

The man thinks of his caring and dear parent of so many years, his chest [tightens with sorrow], and he says, "Could the reason for this taboo be to hear of this? Open the gate quickly." He lets his brother in, crying with grief.

First he gives his brother something to eat in the antechamber, and then the men talk and cry, facing each other. In black clothes, the younger brother sits there talking through tears. The wife of the older brother sits behind a screen listening to them. Whatever is said, the older brother is suddenly wrestling with his younger brother, tumbling about, on the top, then on the bottom. Seeing this, the wife of the older brother says, "What's going on? What's going on?"

The older brother has the younger brother pinned beneath him. He says, "Get the sword by my pillow and bring it to me."

"How absurd! Are you out of your mind? What do you think you're doing?" she says and does not bring the sword. Again he says, "Get it now! Or do you want me to die?"

While he is calling out, the younger brother on the bottom pushes his way over on top and suddenly bites off the head of the older brother. The younger brother leaps up and starts to leave, but then he turns back, faces the wife, and says, "I'm delighted." When she sees his expression, it is the face of the demon her husband had said chased him on the bridge. He disappears without leaving a trace. At that time, all the family members including the wife weep and wail in confusion, but can't do anything to change things in the end.

And so, the wisdom of a woman results in evil. The people look at all the things that the second man had brought and the horse, but everything has become bones and skulls. All who hear about what happened criticize the man, saying "How foolish for him to have ultimately lost his life for a pointless confrontation."

Later, various rituals are performed and the demon disappears. It is no longer there. And so, the tale is told and passed down.[40]

While the description of the creature reveals it is no longer human when chasing the man, its vermilion face, single round amber eye, long knife-like fingernails on six fingers, bluish-green body, and towering statue are neither feminine nor masculine. To complicate the question of gender, the demon of Agi Bridge later appears as the younger brother of the first man with the sad news of their mother's death.

This tale has a place in the history of later texts. Some studies discuss the significance of the demon at Agi Bridge to stories and plays in *Heike*, *Taiheiki*, *Soga monogatari*, and noh involving Watanabe no Tsuna (953–1025) or other demon-quellers and, depending on the story, sometimes also Hashihime (Lady at the Bridge).[41] I need not repeat that emphasis here because those studies value the setsuwa about Agi Bridge mostly for its contributions to these subsequent works.

The significance of the setsuwa for its creators and early audiences could not have been in what it would later inspire. We might look instead at the ties of this demon to earlier or contemporaneous creatures. While the demon at Agi Bridge appears to be the oldest extant example of a demon impersonating a woman waiting or abandoned at a bridge, it also remains connected to other gender-less creatures. Most demons described before the early Kamakura period have at least one physical feature in common with other extraordinary beings despite being somehow unique. The single eye of the Agi Bridge demon links it to two figures mentioned in Chapter 4, Ama-no-ma-hitotsu-no-mikoto and the demon who eats the tiller in *Izumo no kuni fudoki*, as well as to other one-eyed creatures. Its three-fingered hands suggest a connection between demons and monstrous birds as well as dragons. Monstrous birds and dragons are usually depicted with three claws on each foot and are associated with thunder, as are demons.[42] Such hands are precedents of the hands of many later demons. The skin of demons is typically the color of lacquer or pigment: black, vermilion, or green. Demons are also generally taller than humans.

The earliest visual images of demons in both China and Japan indicate that loose, wild hair had long been associated with gods and demons.[43] The Agi Bridge tale tells us the demon has hair tangled as mugwort. A similar representation appears in the "Parables" section of the *Lotus Sutra*. When the disciple Śāriputra asks the Buddha why he previously preached the existence of three paths to salvation if there is really only one, the Buddha answers with the parable of the burning house to justify his use of the doctrine of the three vehicles or expedient means.[44] The story is subsequently reiterated in verse, with details changed or added. Described as old and decaying in the prose, the house in the verse becomes more vividly one of horrors, stinking of excrement and urine and populated not only with people but also with carnivorous animals and demons feasting on corpses.

> Again, there are other sorts of demons
> those whose heads are shaped as ox heads
> some eating human flesh
> still others devouring dogs
> their hair tangled as mugwort.[45]

The simile in the tale, "kami wa yomogi no gotoku midarete"[46] ("hair tangled as mugwort") appears to come from here, though possibly via other tales.

In another tale, the same phrase describes the hair of an incarnated god of thunder: a fifteen- or sixteen-year-old boy who destroys a pagoda three times to help his friend the mountain earth deity resist being built upon. Finally, a priest subjugates him by reciting the *Lotus Sutra*.[47] The boy/god demonstrates the thin line between god and demon. Since *kami* can be destructive and oni constructive, the two cannot be distinguished as good versus evil. Famous Heian and Kamakura period statues of the demonic thunder and lightning god, Raijin, also merge the two, as does an ebullient screen painting of Fūjin (the wind god) and Raijin by seventeenth-century artist Tawaraya Sōtatsu.[48] Although these art works are from later periods, the fusion of god and demon is apparent even in *Kojiki*, in the reckless god Susano-o. The tousled hair suits a wild, uncontrollable force, as does the incarnation of thunder as an energetic and well-meaning but destructive boy. Baba even notes a connection between the shoulder-length hairstyles of children and five demons associated with Ōeyama whose appellations appropriately end with *dōji* (male child).[49]

The scene describing Genji undergoing the ritual hair cutting at his coming-of-age ceremony reveals the beauty of the loose hair of a child.[50] Such an emphasis gives the hair of children more in common with that of women than of men. For both women and children, loose hair and the absence of a cap are marks of being outside the bureaucratic ladder. Along with demons, they exist in a world run by men without being fully part of it.

Unkempt hair suggests the sensual and sexual realms as well. Women in literature of the mid-Heian period such as *Genji* and in picture scrolls focusing on mid-Heian times but from a slightly later period, such as *Genji monogatari emaki* and *Makura no sōshi emaki*, portray aristocratic women wearing their hair long and loose.[51] Such hair was considered attractive and erotic. Conversely, its eroticism would have rendered it repulsive and even demonic to some Buddhist practitioners.

Still, what could unbound hair have to do with old women? According to *Nihon shoki*, the emperor passed a decree on the twenty-third day of the fourth month of Tenmu 11 (682) stating that men and women must tie back their hair.[52] An edict passed on the fifth day of the fourth month of Tenmu 13 (684) states: "Women forty and older may do as they please in regard to both tying up their hair or not and riding astride or side saddle. Also as an exception, court and shrine shamanesses (*kannagi*) and priests (*hafuri*) are exempt from tying up the hair."[53] Long, loose hair was suggestive of the afterlife. It was associated with spirits of the dead who took the form of gods and demons.[54] A similar edict recorded in *Shoku Nihongi* (*Sequel to Chronicles of Japan*, 797) and passed twenty-one years later in 705 (nineteenth day of the twelfth month of Keiun 2) applies only to women: "The women beneath heaven, except those of the group serving the gods, the attendants of the Itsuki Shrines, and old women, must all tie up their hair."[55] Here, aging women share with people involved with gods and demons through *kami*-worship the privilege of being allowed unbound hair. (A woman over forty was old because the life expectancy of people who had survived infancy around this time was probably forty.[56]) Given the symbolic significance of unbound hair in connection to shamans and priests, the loose hair of these women may indicate a similar link to spirits and the afterlife. This link would in turn contribute to later associations of women and demons and to the gendering of demons as female.

Through hair, *Konjaku* tale "How a Thief Climbs to the Upper Story of Rajō Gate and Sees a Corpse" links an old woman and a young woman together and to the demonic. A thief discovers a white-haired old woman plucking the hair from the corpse of a young woman on the upper story of the Rajō Gate (or Rasei Gate, later called Rashōmon) and thinks that they both must be demons or dead people (*shi'nin*). Upon drawing a sword and rushing in on them, he realizes that the creature collecting the hair is merely an old woman. Terrified, she explains that she brought the corpse of her young mistress to the gate because there was no one to bury it and is collecting the long hair to make a wig. The thief strips the old woman and the corpse of their clothes, and then leaves with the garments and the hair. According to the commentator, people often left corpses on the upper story of the Rajō Gate (Rajōmon) when they could not afford burial. The story was supposedly first passed on when the thief told it to someone.[57]

The actions of the old woman are practical albeit repelling. Her deceased mistress could not have been financially secure if she left no means of providing for her burial, and a person serving her would have done very poorly as a result. Tresses of beautiful hair were highly valued during the Heian period, as suggested by a scene in "Yomogiu" ("A Waste of Weeds"[58]) a chapter of *Genji*, when Suetsumuhana gives a faithful servant a tress of her own hair as a memento before permanently parting from her. Since many people were unable to grow their hair as long as was fashionable, switches were in high demand.[59] Tangled in the hair of a dead person is the potential for new splendor and passion. A woman needing a switch and her lover may have been able to feel enhanced beauty and joy precisely because of the hair of the dead woman (as long as they did not know or think about its origin).

The tale forces its audience to rethink this standard of beauty. What woman would want to wear a switch if she could visualize someone picking it strand by strand from the head of a corpse? As for men, the image could have appealed to only a necrophiliac. While the narrative centers on the old woman initially mistaken for a demon at the Rajō Gate (a place where people expect demons to appear), it also leads us from her to the head of the deceased young woman through the image of the hair. The long, beautiful hair is associated with death, the gruesome behavior of plucking strands, and greed. The desire to survive, the probable motivation of both the old woman and the thief, is shown in a dismal light. The old woman at Rajōmon is clearly demonized. Of course, demons could not be feminized without women also being demonized, but the movement toward demonization has its positive side: it allows the suffering and discontent of women to be expressed and acknowledged. Through an old woman perceived as a demon, audiences could learn that attendants had to resort to desperate means when left impoverished after the unexpected death of the person they served.

In cases where "real" demons (not humans mistaken to be demons) are involved, *male* or *female* can refer only to the body and roles a demon assumes in a particular situation. In the Agi Bridge tale, the impersonation of the man is of a particular person, the younger brother of the daredevil. In contrast, the young and beautiful melancholic woman waiting at the bridge approaches an archetype. She alludes to similar figures in other texts, most notably in *waka*, beginning with poem number 689 in *Kokinshū*, and the *Uji* chapters of *Genji*. Almost all of the early literary representations of this figure predating *Konjaku* are of Hashihime of the Uji Bridge, whom many scholars see as exemplifying hashihime worship of the period.[60] These figures are deities (usually tutelary goddesses of bridges), pining lovers, or a blend of both.[61]

The frequent transformation at bridges of demons into female form may have resulted in part from the merging of two separate motifs: the beautiful woman waiting at the bridge and threatening spirits at bridges.[62] Terrifying associations with bridges are tied to fears of spirits of the dead. There may have even been an early practice of burying people considered wicked at crossroads or the foots of bridges "in the hope that the pressure of heavy traffic would keep them in their graves."[63] Buddhists could easily appropriate the combined motifs to warn men about the evils of women. The lady of Agi Bridge turns out to be lethal. True to Buddhist thought, her eroticism is an illusion. She threatens to become an obstacle to the goal of crossing this bridge, just as women in other tales are obstacles to enlightenment. The bridge is generally symbolic of spiritual development, although the attempt at growth here is misguided.[64]

Yet, there are other possible reasons why a deity or a lover might end up demonized. The association of women or female deities with demons makes sense when we consider the force the objects of the two different passions, the one sexual and the other religious, exert over the hearts and minds of people. Most lovers and deities have the potential to become monsters. When the actions of deities do not coincide with the wishes or expectations of the worshippers, the harmony and order of those people can be easily shattered. A lover who becomes the source of anguish suddenly or over time can also be perceived of as cold and cruel.

Indeed, the demon at Agi Bridge was possibly once associated with positive energy. The man who raises the concern about the blocked bridge begins by pointing out that it could be crossed at one time. Was there previously no demon? Perhaps there was a spirit whose nature changed. This second possibility seems likely since the representation of the waiting woman alludes to a tutelary goddess. The spirit as a demon is still protecting the bridge, only now to the extreme—no longer for the benefit of the provincial elite but against them. Its hostility toward the elite is apparent in its pursuit of a man close enough to the governor to socialize in his home and borrow one of his best horses. The man himself is apparently a lower-ranking member of the provincial elite since he has attendants and lives in a mansion.

What the demon attacks is a man on the horse of another person: a man representing more than himself. Were it not for the governor, he would have had a way out of the dangerous adventure since riding the best bay in the mansion is the condition he sets for success. As much as the governor criticizes the young man, he is partially responsible for the encounter with the demon because he lends him the horse. The other young men, presumably from similar backgrounds as the daredevil, are also key figures here. The man acts for the group, meeting their challenge almost against his own will.

The oiling of the rump of the horse is a key in the preparation. This act ties the event at the bridge more tightly to the first part of the story. Through the horse, connections between the young man and the governor as well as between the great mansion with its boisterous gatherings and the bridge are firmly established. In preventing the access of aristocrats to a realm that it or another spirit once safeguarded for aristocrats, the demon resembles and foreshadows the Seiwa Genji, Hidesato-ryū Fujiwara, the Kanmu Heishi, and other warrior households. These groups began in the service of the aristocrats but ultimately claimed all or part of the geographical and ideological realms they protected as their own. Hardly sudden, their rise was occurring in small degrees all along.[65] With the Agi Bridge, the loss is not yet final since the commentator informs us that later efforts, exorcisms, or other rituals performed by Buddhist monks, successfully rid the bridge of the demon. Yet it is only a matter of time until new spirits, the warriors and their haunts, take control.

In the end, the protagonist depends too much on human strength. He first provokes the demon by racing over the bridge. We cannot attribute his success to the oiled rump or his resistance to the woman because he also calls on Kannon. When the demon visits him in his home, he relies on his wife in hope of conquering it with his sword. He forgets to invoke Kannon, the *Lotus Sutra*, or another spiritual power, and dies without that help.

The tale reveals ambivalence about who is to blame for the death. In the opening, the governor initially criticizes the man for engaging in a pointless struggle. When the man returns to the mansion triumphantly, the governor realizes that his actions may still ultimately prove fatal. In contrast, the warning against women who act on their own wisdom is given after the story is all but over, reflecting only one view of who is responsible. Moreover, the tale does not end with a verbal attack on the woman. Instead, the man is criticized a second time: in the view of the people, he dies for getting involved in a pointless confrontation, a stance that echoes the warnings of the governor rather than the judgment of the commentator.

Besides, given the circumstances, the argument that the woman should have listened to her husband is weak. The guise of the demon fools even the brother of the person impersonated, so how could the sister-in-law not be deceived? Few people would want to help a man kill his brother or give a weapon to a person already stirred. The demon depends on the most natural responses from his victims: the man's emotional response to the lie of his mother's death gives the demon entry into the house in the first place. Moreover, because the tale indicates that the choices of the man are foolish and fatal, the demon and the wife can be seen as instruments of karmic justice. As is often the case, the commentator focuses on only isolated parts of the story in an attempt to shape the interpretation of the audience. It is as if he could neither miss the opportunity to express a misogynistic sentiment nor cope with severe criticism of a man without balancing it with the condemnation of a woman. According to the narrative, though, the man brought his terrible fate upon himself.

The next tale more successfully blames a woman for jeopardizing a man who faces a non-human force. It also fuses the ideas of a beautiful woman waiting at a bridge with dangerous creatures at bridges. However, the women are described simply as malevolent spirits rather than as oni.

How Ki no Tōsuke of Mino Province Meets Female Spirits and Dies

Now is the past; there is a person called Fujiwara no Takanori, the former governor of Nagato. While provisional governor of Shimotsusa Province, he supervises a place called Ikutsu Villa in Mino Province in the service of the regent. There is a person named Ki no Tōsuke at that villa.[66]

Among the many people there, Takanori grows accustomed to relying on Tōsuke. And so, Tōsuke is promoted to long-term night attendant and guard (*tonoi*) at the Higashisanjō Palace [in the capital]. When that term ends, Tōsuke gets leave to return home. On his way to Mino, he crosses the Seta Bridge. There a woman stands holding the train of her kimono. Tōsuke looks at her and thinks, "How weird." He is about to pass when the woman says, "You sir, where are you going?"

And so, Tōsuke dismounts from his horse and answers, "I am going to Mino."

"I would be greatly obliged if you would take something there for me. Would you be kind enough to do me that favor?"

Tōsuke answers, "I can do that for you."

"I am delighted," says the woman and takes out from inside the bosom part of her kimono a small box wrapped in silk. "When you take this box to the foot of the Osame Bridge in the Village of Morokoshi, Katagata District, a woman should be at the western end. Please give it to her."

Tōsuke has an eerie feeling and thinks, "I've been given a pointless task," but he finds it difficult to refuse because there is something terrifying about the woman. Taking the box, Tōsuke says, "Who is the woman coming to wait at the foot of the bridge? What province is she from? If she is not there, where shall I go to find her? And who should I say is giving this?"

The woman says, "If you just go to the foot of that bridge, that woman will appear to receive it. There will definitely be no mistake about it. She is certain to be there. But beware: you must never, never open this box and look inside."

None of the retainers accompanying Tōsuke see this woman, but only that, strangely, their master dismounts from his horse and stands there without any reason. The woman leaves when Tōsuke takes the box.

Afterwards, Tōsuke rides his horse and arrives at Mino Province. Only he forgets to stop at the foot of the bridge when passing over it and returns home without delivering the box. Suddenly remembering, he thinks: "How terrible. She has not taken the box," and then: "Now, I'll just have to make a special trip to look for the woman and give it to her." He places the box high up on a piece of furniture standing inside the walk-in closet. The lover of Tōsuke with her extremely jealous heart happens to see Tōsuke put the box away and concludes: "He purposely bought something in that box in the capital to give to another woman. I suppose he put it there to hide it from me." When Tōsuke is out, she secretly takes down the box and looks inside. It contains many gouged out eyeballs as well as numerous severed human penises with a few strands of pubic hair still attached.

Seeing this, the lover is shocked and terrified. When Tōsuke returns, she calls him in panic and shows him the contents of the box. Tōsuke says, "Oh no. A certain someone said: 'Please don't look inside.' Something terrible might occur!" Overcome with terror, he ties up the package as before and immediately brings it to the foot of the bridge mentioned by the first woman. He stands there, whereupon another woman indeed appears. Tōsuke hands her the box and tells her what the first woman had said.

The woman takes the box and says, "Sir, you opened this box and looked inside!" Although Tōsuke replies, "I certainly did nothing of the sort," her expression turns to one of great displeasure and she says, "You have acted terribly." She accepts the box despite the extremely furious look lingering on her face, so Tōsuke goes home.

Later, Tōsuke says, "I don't feel well" and lies down. To his lover he says, "And you pointlessly opened the box—the box the woman forcefully said 'please do not open'—and you looked inside." The man dies shortly after.

Well then, the jealously of female lovers is deep. Their empty doubts result in this kind of bad fortune for their male lovers. Because of jealousy, Tōsuke inconceivably lost his life without just reason. While [jealousy] is an ordinary behavior of women, all the people who hear what happened criticize this female lover. And so, the story is told and passed down.[67]

Known for its demons, *Konjaku* Book 27 also includes other extraordinary creatures not referred to as oni: ghosts, other types of spirits, wild boars, and foxes. Therefore, if we choose to view the women at the Seta and Osame Bridges as oni, it should be only in a broad sense because of their diabolic influence on the lives of the human couple. The idea of beautiful women waiting at bridges is reworked in this gruesome tale about the box that, in the logic of tales, must be opened precisely because doing so is forbidden. The story further shapes the idea of malevolent spirits in female form by adding the component of so-called female jealousy. In this sense, the tale foreshadows stories in later setsuwa, *gunki monogatari* (martial tales), *otogizōshi* ("companion books" or Muromachi period tales), and noh showing the transformation of jealous women into demons.[68] However, here in contrast to later stories, the jealous woman does not transform into a demon; the demons are physically though not psychologically separate from her.

Perhaps the spread of certain Buddhist attitudes toward heterosexual relations and women contributed to the rise of demons impersonating women at bridges in place of figures affirming *kami*-worship or passion. However, this general explanation, which works also for the Agi Bridge tale, does not address the significance of specific representations. Of all the odd things that might be hidden away, why penises and eyeballs? Both organs suggest the male role in sex. While the penises are obvious, the eyeballs appear to point to both the male gaze and the testes. Because the box contains these items, it must allude to the vagina. Thus, the lover is not wrong in sensing a connection of the package to something sexual outside her relationship with the man.

It is sex intertwined with violence. Why would spirits, who are quite capable of delivering things on their own, want the man to transport the box unless they are also sharing him in some mysterious sense? Why are things set up so that the human woman in the tale is tempted and drawn into their evil doings?

The severed body parts and the consequent death of the man are a displacement of the anger and resentment of the woman. Given access to a box that she cannot help but open, she is forced to view items that reflect her own feelings. A hurt lover might indeed hope for the worst at first, desiring at the level of fantasy and perhaps for only a moment, to gouge out the eyes, castrate, or even kill the person she sees as the source of her pain. In light of the tale, it is not the jealousy, resentment, or anger of women per se that Heian men fear but rather the possibility of their confronting and acting on hostile emotions (even if only verbally) rather than repressing them—of opening the forbidden box containing ugly truths and looking hard at them. The curiosity of the woman and her desire to know where she stands even if her suspicions prove unfounded is what ultimately kills the man.

The tale also points to the discontent of women who suspect their lovers or husbands favor someone else. (Since polygamy was the norm and had to be accepted by women to some degree, the discovery of another woman in itself would not have been surprising.) At the same time, it attempts to discourage women from being motivated by their unhappiness—caused by anger, conflicted emotions rooted in attachment or love, and the fear of being deceived or of losing economic support—by showing how doing so results in punishment. After all, the woman in the tale ends up losing someone whose attention she craves. His death only makes his absence permanent, the very opposite of what she desired, so that she presumably regrets her behavior and the emotions behind it. Along with the tale of the demon at Agi Bridge, this story suggests that many Heian men felt threatened by the prospect of women making decisions and acting on them independently. Jealousy is accepted as an ordinary emotion for women, so the problem cannot lie in it alone. Rather, doing something with it is deviant and dangerous. Both tales also demonstrate the autonomy of women and the impossibility of men having full control. The storytellers unwittingly acknowledge the power of women to shape the course of events and suggest men's fear of it.

HELPFUL YET HARMFUL: THE AMBIVALENT ASSOCIATIONS OF OLD WOMEN WITH DEMONS

In *Konjaku*, only one unquestionably human woman becomes a demon. Since the protagonist in "How the Mother of Hunters Becomes a Demon and Tries to Devour Her Child" is the mother of men, we can assume that she has been human for a lifetime in contrast to creatures who temporarily assume a female form.[69] Two professional hunters who are brothers travel deep into the mountains to hunt in their usual way, waiting up in separate trees for the chance to shoot arrows at animals passing beneath them. On this moonless night, something reaches out and grabs the older brother by his topknot, and then pulls him upward. When he feels for the hand, it turns out to be withered, emaciated, and human. Afraid a demon is about to devour him, he calls to his brother for help. In this way, the motivation of the creature is ascribed to it by the man and later backed by the commentator.

The younger brother succeeds in severing the hand of the demon with a forked arrow. The men then decide to return home, taking the hand with them, although they have not killed anything. At this point, more than halfway through the story, their elderly mother is introduced into the narrative. Scarcely able to get about, she is moaning from her room.[70] When she will not tell them what is wrong, they light a torch and check the hand. Seeing it belongs to her, they open her door, respectfully ask if it is hers, and then throw it at her. The woman dies shortly after and her mutilated wrist confirms their suspicions. Since the demon is not described, we cannot know whether it is supposed to have had a fully materialized form. Was the hand attached to the rest of the old woman or to something else? The demon may be a bodiless spirit moving through the dark and manifesting itself as a hand, but the body of the woman is ultimately wounded.

A hand (probably with the arm) is often the only part displayed by a demon in setsuwa. Usually unrecognizable, it rarely establishes the identity of the creature as someone with close bonds to its victim, as it does here. The tale focuses on the experience of the sons, so that the horror of the attack is intensified by the discovery of the identity of the creature.[71] Despite the violence of the demon, the representation is not merely part of an effort to vilify women. To the contrary, the tale suggests a woman would have to become something other than herself to act against her children. The assault makes sense precisely because the attacker is a demon rather than a human.

Once we know that the demon is an elderly mother, her transformation suggests the mental and behavioral changes caused by dementia (*oihore*)—especially the hostility, sometimes including physical violence, exhibited by certain victims of what we now consider a disease. While the representation of the old woman as demon should not be reduced to merely a medical issue, the desire to label the baffling behavior of many elderly people may have been a factor in shaping this tale. The old mother as demon seemingly voices the frustration, anger, and ambivalence of grown children faced with the task of caring for a parent whose mind and body are deteriorating. The commentator connects the aging process to the deteriorating mind with the remark, "parents who are extremely old always turn into demons and, in this way, try to eat even their own children."[72] While it is significant that the parent here is female, the use of the word *parents* (*oya*) suggests that, in the mind of the commentator, aging men and women are equally likely to transform in this way and that children dealing with elderly parents have similar experiences regardless of whether the aging person is a father or a mother.

The view of an elderly parent or a close relative as a burden appears elsewhere in *Konjaku* as well. In a tale of "Tales of India," a land in India exiles people over age seventy to another country. The practice continues until an old woman hidden by her son saves the country from attack by providing the means to answering questions posed as challenges by a hostile neighboring land.[73] In "Tales of China," a tale demonstrates that elderly fathers are also vulnerable. Angry with his father for not dying fast enough, a man has his son Hou Gu help carry the old man on a litter deep into the mountains, whereupon they abandon him. Hou Gu brings the litter back with him. When his father asks him why, Hou Gu explains that he will need to use it again when the time comes to abandon his own father. The man then rushes back to the mountains to get his father and never again fails to be filial.[74] The inclusion of this tale in *Konjaku* indicates that the care of an elderly father becoming an onus fell within the realm of possibilities for late Heian Japanese people. Yet, while the burden of caring for the elderly is not gender-specific, no *Konjaku* tales with Japanese settings describe the problems associated with caring for an aging father.

We have instead the famous legend of Obasute-yama (Mt. Abandoning-an-Aunt) in *Yamato monogatari* and *Konjaku,* which provided inspiration for the noh play *Obasute* by Zeami, the poetic travel account *Sarashina kikō* (*A Journey to Sarashina,* 1689) by Bashō, and the modern short story *Obasute* by Inoue Yasushi (1907–91) among other works.[75] In the tales, a man abandons his fragile aunt on a mountain after his wife convinces him that the old woman is mean-spirited. Upon his return home, he feels grief and remorse. He recites a poem about gazing at the moon shining on Mt. Obasute in Sarashina, and then goes to retrieve the woman.[76] The story does not hold the man responsible for his decision; rather the emphasis is on how his hateful wife slanders the aunt and suggests abandoning her. Without excusing the deception and cruelty of the wife, we can acknowledge that she experienced the care of the old woman as an unbearable hardship. The tale rings true psychologically—a younger woman might grow weary of caring for a dependent, elderly woman and sometimes wish her gone. However, the fantasy of abandoning the very old, which may also be rooted in the pain of watching someone dear decline further and die, is acted out through the male figure.

The tale protects the male conscience by attributing the negative feelings to the female force: we are assured of the devotion of the nephew even though he turns his back and walks down the mountain, deaf to the cries of his helpless old aunt. Likewise, the tale of the demon-mother allows men to release negative feelings toward an aging mother without fully acknowledging them. Through the character of the young woman, women must confront the potential people have for the cruelest feelings toward old dependent relatives. Facing these feelings might have encouraged them to assume responsibility and exercise control.

Why does the threat of harm to adult children by parents take the form of consumption? The simplest answer here is that demons usually attack by devouring people. Additionally, the imagery of being eaten by a senile mother may allude to feelings grown children have toward elderly parents as their care becomes more demanding. Even the most loving children might occasionally see the parent as a monster threatening to swallow their lives.

In discussing the place of the *yamauba* figure of fairy and folk tales in the Japanese psyche, Kawai Hayao relates the imagery of a mother eating her child to an overabundance and therefore a psychologically oppressive amount of affection on the part of the mother (or sometimes grandmother).[77] Although Kawai is dealing predominately with relatively recent stories and contemporary people, his ideas can help us a bit in thinking about the relationships of mothers and children in ancient through early medieval Japan. While the hunter-brothers are adults, in contrast to his examples, and the mother shows no sign of being too loving, the element of the children somehow stifled by their mother is apparent in the tale. The destroyer here is aging and the loss of affection.

According to Kawai, contemporary Japanese people have complex feelings toward their mothers (just like people in the United States and elsewhere), but expressions of negative feelings or neglect of Mother are generally taboo. In his analysis, the frequent occurrence of negative images of *yamauba* in *mukashi banashi* (even while the figure has both nurturing and destructive sides) compensates the extraordinarily high evaluation of motherhood in modern Japan.[78] *Mukashi banashi* allow for people, especially children, to experience negative feelings toward Mother otherwise forbidden or discouraged.

Similarly, in *The Uses of Enchantment: The Meaning and Importance of Fairy Tales*, Bruno Bettelheim discusses how the image of the wicked stepmother in Western fairy tales enables children to feel anger toward their mothers and even temporarily despise them without experiencing unmanageable guilt. Young children can cope with being disciplined and denied certain things by splitting the mother or sometimes grandmother figure into the good mother (who is often dead or a fairy godmother) and the wicked mother (who is often the stepmother or something transformed, such as the wolf in "Little Red Riding Hood"). It is acceptable to have negative feelings toward the bad figure in the fairy tale. As children mature, they are supposed to be able to accept and deal with the complexity of Mother and other people.[79] Although I reject most of the assumptions and views of Bettelheim, which are rooted in Freudian thought and generally hostile toward mothers, this particular explanation of why representations of mother figures are divided into good and evil in fairy tales aids in understanding the multiple layers of negative views of women in setsuwa.[80]

While the focus of Bettelheim is also on children, adults, too, often cope with feelings about other people by dividing them into clear-cut categories.

Moreover, fairy tales came from adult imaginations and were not intended only for the very young, having been created even before the concept of childhood. Therefore, without suggesting that premodern Japanese people had childlike minds, I raise the possibility that the setsuwa about the mother of the hunters offered male audiences coping strategies and catharses resembling what Kawai and Bettelheim proposed. Of course, the issues leading to the mixed feelings of either young or adult children would differ depending on the historical period, culture, and experiences of individuals.

Unfilial behaviors or attitudes would probably have been the main cause of feelings of guilt regarding parents in the late Heian and early Kamakura periods. That filial piety was an issue then is evident in, for example, the inclusion of numerous tales about the subject in both the "Tales of China" and "Tales of Japan" sections of *Konjaku*.[81] Through the tale about the mother of the hunters, men could experience irrational anger at their mothers for aging and becoming needy and resent the burden of looking after them without feeling overwhelmed with the sense of being bad sons. The cause of their hostility is placed outside them—on time and nature. Men can vicariously hurt their mothers because aging has turned the mothers into something similar to threatening demons, and people are expected to lash out at demons in defense. The severed hand of the mother is a poignant image because mothers use their hands in nurturing their children. The cutting off of the hand that may have once fed, washed, held, and rocked the men as babies and boys—the hand they have no difficulty recognizing—foreshadows the death of the mother. Once severed, it is no longer there to reach out, not even as a menace. The same is true of the mother in death.

While the mother-turned-demon can be seen as a threatening figure, the tale also emphasizes the weakness of the woman. She is a needy person who must be watched. Even if we agree with Terry Kawashima that, as a mother, she is a reassuring presence to her sons or think she must have been in the past, her presence at the time of the tale also has an unsettling aspect.[82] She is a constant reminder of human fragility and mortality. The transformation from a reassuring presence to something else had to have been a process rather than a sudden event, culminating with the attack. Depicting the last stages in life as a demonic transformation may have eased the pain of the final separation. It is hard to let go of a beloved parent but not a demon.

How might the transformation benefit the old woman and suggest the concerns of others in her position? She is briefly empowered, lashing out at society and threatening the order, which she herself helped to maintain by raising devoted sons who look after her in old age and see to her burial. The tale briefly allows for discord between the mother and sons—for disruption in the social order. Although the harmony is restored with the death and burial of the woman, her expression of discontent and its threat to society resound.

With limited information, we can only hypothesize about why an elderly woman might have enough suppressed hostility to enable her metamorphosis into a monster. The tale does not inform us how long the sons have been caring for her or how she lived when physically more able. Some women might have been resentful because of a lifetime of forced dependency requiring submission to men: to their fathers before marriage, to lovers and husbands when in their prime, and to sons in old age.[83] Anger at aging, declining health, and impending death may have led to the transformation as well. Strongly attached to life, this mother would not die gently and quietly, as her sons would have undoubtedly preferred.

Finally, the Obasute-yama tale and others suggest that it was common for people to lose respect for old women in their families and devalue them. Such stories reminded people of the need for continued filial piety and respect for elders. In one *Uji shūi* tale, a sixty-year-old woman cares for a sparrow after a boy breaks its leg by hitting it with a rock. Her children and grandchildren ridicule her until something wonderful occurs: the bird repays her kindness by rewarding her with a magical calabash seed that grows into a fruit-bearing plant. Dried into gourds, some of the fruit become an endless source of rice, making the woman and her family very wealthy.[84] In the tale of the mother of the hunters, the sons do not show any concern for their mother despite their mutilation of her hand. Although she attacks one of them first, they might show compassion once she returns to her room and is no longer a threat. Instead, they simply throw the hand at her and slam the door. The experience of being devalued and limited by others or simply by one's own frailty may have caused feelings of hostility in some elderly Japanese women.

The otherwise repressed anger and resentment of women could be expressed through depictions of women transformed as demons. Awareness of this possibility must have contributed to later storytellers creating female characters who overtly wish for such a change. Women display the will to become demons in a *Kankyo no tomo* tale, "How a Deeply Resentful Woman Becomes a Demon While Still Alive," in the previously mentioned story of the Lady of the Uji Bridge in the sword sections of *Yashirobon Heike* and *Taiheiki*, and in the noh play *Kanawa* (*The Iron Crown*, ca. late fourteenth–early fifteenth century).[85] While demonic transformation is not portrayed in a positive light, such representations suggest a fantasy of gaining control in a situation. Whatever the repercussions, becoming a demon must have been preferable to being unheard or invisible. Ironically, men usually envision this change for women. Even so, the desire to be a demon is not far removed from the identification with demons of Sei and the young insect-loving lady. In the male-authored works of the late Heian and medieval periods, a female sensibility or at least one sympathetic to women seems to survive, although often buried, despite the pervasive misogyny marring it.

The representation of the mother of the hunters alludes to unreleased emotion and energy as well as to decay and destruction. Her final outburst points to an unwillingness to accept things as they are. Naturally suffering from her own passion, the female demon is an affirmation of life and the attachment to its struggles and disappointments. The essence of her being directly opposes many Buddhist values. In this way, she and the old woman at Rajōmon share something in common with the figurines of old, senile but pregnant hags discussed by Bakhtin in *Rabelais and His World*:

> In the famous Kerch terracotta collection we find figurines of senile pregnant hags. Moreover, the old hags are laughing.[86] This is a typical and very strongly expressed grotesque. It is ambivalent. It is a pregnant death, a death that gives birth. There is nothing completed, nothing calm and stable in the bodies of these old hags. They combine a senile, decaying and deformed flesh with the flesh of new life, conceived but as yet unformed. Life is shown in its twofold contradictory process; it is the epitome of incompleteness. And such is precisely the grotesque concept of the body.[87]

While the connection between "senile, decaying and deformed flesh with the flesh of new life, conceived but as yet unformed" is not as explicit in the representations of old women / demons in setsuwa, those characters do suggest among other things productive, life-affirming forces.

Many feminist critics are interested in Bakhtin's understanding of the Kerch terracotta figurines. Mary Russo asserts that this image is problematic for the feminist reader, being "loaded with all of the connotations of fear and loathing around the biological processes of reproduction and of aging."[88] She further criticizes Bakhtin for failing "to acknowledge or incorporate the social relations of gender in his semiotic model of the body politic, and thus his notion of the Female Grotesque, remains in all directions repressed and undeveloped."[89] However, Lisa Gasbarrone questions Russo's understanding, arguing that Bakhtin approaches these figures as positive and would not have experienced fear and loathing toward any biological process. She gives Bakhtin the benefit of the doubt, refusing to assume "that fear is the only response men have to pregnancy and the womb" and sees the ambivalence of these figures for Bakhtin as connected to the process of aging.[90]

While agreeing with Gasbarrone that Bakhtin would not have experienced fear and loathing toward the figurines, I believe that the ambivalence Bakhtin has in mind has to do with the simultaneous aging and pregnancy: to the idea of a new life forming within an elderly *female* body—a body not far from death. Furthermore, the reading by Russo draws attention to the limitations of the female grotesque perceived as such by men. The question remains: does the idealization of such an image enhance the situation for women? That is, are women being seen or constructed in a brighter light?

Along with the figurines of the hags, women associated with demons in setsuwa convey mixed messages and cannot be viewed as either positive or negative. As with other grotesque representations, such creatures are necessary for voicing discontent because people cannot draw attention to their struggles otherwise. However, the very need for them reflects certain conditions in society unfavorable to women. Moreover, to identify women as demons or demons as women is to contain their power. Doing so limits the number of people who would see a connection between their situations and those of the creatures. Many women in the early audiences of setsuwa were likely to see only the surface message of how demons are despised. Or, just as Russo saw fear and loathing in the Kerch terracotta hags described by Bakhtin, so too might they have been affected by what initially appears as only a negative male response to the aging female body. There is another reality, though: female demons were desired and needed. The very act of grappling with these monsters is a sign of attachment and dependency—perhaps even of a distorted form of love.

"How a Woman Giving Birth Travels to South Yamashina, Encounters a Demon, and Escapes," raises the question of whether threatening demons or people mistaken for them can be constructive forces. The tale demonstrates that demons do not always pull toward chaos and confusion, but can also lead toward order and compassionate resolutions. The perception of them as violent can have odd twists.

A young woman employed at a mansion discovers she is pregnant. Without anyone to turn to for help, she plans to give birth in the mountains, abandon the baby, and then return pretending nothing happened. She travels far and, at last, comes across a dilapidated house on the ruins of a mountain estate. Since it appears to be uninhabited, she decides to give birth there. Oddly, an old, sympathetic woman appears and cares for her. Her kindness leads the young woman to believe the Buddha has sent someone to her aid. After the birth, the mother decides to keep her newborn son. While still recuperating, she thinks she overhears the old woman comment on how delicious the baby looks. She flees with her son and servant, convinced that the woman who cared for her is really a demon. Once back in society, she arranges for someone to look after the baby while she continues working. Only years later, after she has grown old, does she tell anyone of her encounter with a demon.[91]

The tale offers no conclusive evidence on the identity of the old woman. The phrase introducing the comment about how appetizing the child appears is "this woman stares and seems to say" (*kono onna uchimite iu naru yō*). It is unclear whether the remark is real or imagined by the young woman, especially since she is not fully awake when she faintly hears it. Nor is a transformation of the old woman into a demon shown. As for the commentator, he relies on the impression of the young woman by asserting that someone who makes such a remark would have to be a demon. Perceptions of truth rather than some notion of objective truth are at the heart of most tales. We have to accept the possibility that the old woman is a demon because to discount the perspective of the young woman is to destroy the story. Yet, the question remains open. The ambiguity reveals that the true nature of the old woman cannot be known and throws the young woman's first impression of her as kind into question.

Meera Viswanathan sees the two women as representing "the dialectic of female resistance, in which we see not so much an opposition between female characters as an internal struggle between production and consumption, between the sacrifice of self and the assertion of self, between order and anarchy." She reaches this conclusion after demonstrating how the tale is governed by "a carefully balanced structure of reversals," including the countering toward the end of the tale of "the inhumane aspect of the pregnant woman's character . . . by the old woman's unnatural penchant for young male flesh." As the analysis demonstrates, the tale lends itself to symbolic interpretations.[92]

While suggesting an internal struggle experienced by some Heian aristocratic women (and perhaps others, as Viswanathan emphasizes), the tale also speaks of the outside world since psychological and philosophical conflicts occur within given societies and are shaped by them. The tale addresses a concrete problem with tremendous external implications: unwanted pregnancy and ultimately unwanted children, since safe abortion was not an option in Japan even in the Edo period (1600–1868) and certainly not in Heian times.[93] Abandonment as a form of infanticide is not unique to premodern Japan.

Related to this issue is whether the mother in the story changes her mind because the baby is a boy.[94] However, rather than having two separate plans for the infant depending on its sex, the woman simply decides before the birth to reject him or her. Nor can we assume that girls were more likely to be abandoned than boys during the late Heian period without more evidence. According to *Shūi ōjōden*, the future monk Gensan was abandoned by his troubled mother after a difficult pregnancy.[95]

Konjaku tale "How a Dog Stealthily Comes to a Child Abandoned at Tachii Gate and Suckles Him" also demonstrates that male babies were sometimes rejected despite their sex. One morning a traveler notices a newborn boy who does not appear to be of the lowest social class abandoned by the Tachii Gate. Although the man feels sorry for the crying child, he has things to do. The next morning, he is surprised to see the baby alive and apparently content as he had expected dogs to devour him. This supposedly busy man goes to the gate again on the third morning and hides to watch what is going on. A big white dog feared by other dogs comes and suckles the baby. The same thing happens for two nights until the baby finally disappears. Since the dog never shows up, the man concludes that the animal took the baby elsewhere because she was aware of the human presence. The commentator is optimistic, imagining that the dog is a Buddha or a bodhisattva who continues to care for the child.[96] From a modern perspective, the story is chilling. What happened to the compassion of the humans: of the mother and the man? How can the commentator fail to criticize the man for not helping the baby? This tale suggests among other things a relaxed attitude about the life of an unwanted newborn. There appears to be no moral or legal obligation to save him.

Finally, in *Konjaku* tale "How a Person from Yamato Acquired Someone's Daughter" a wealthy and influential woman who cannot have children acquires a baby girl after the wicked wet nurse of the baby's half sister has the baby abandoned in hope that dogs will devour her. The adoptive mother-to-be does not inquire about the sex of the baby, but she worries that the biological mother is from a low class.[97] Genealogy is more important than gender here.

The woman in the *yamauba* tale has no reason to prefer a boy, as might a farmer in need of strong helpers. Nor does the tale suggest that she is thinking about future economic support when changing her mind. There must be another reason why she keeps the baby.

Demons tend to be stereotyped as destructive forces, but the behavior of the old woman ironically encourages the mother to accept responsibility for the welfare of the child. The young woman would have been more likely to abandon him had she given birth in a cold, lonely place. Although she wisely takes along a serving girl to assist her, it is the old woman who nurtures her and provides simple comfort. For many women who desire a baby, the pain of labor is bearable only because they are anticipating the joy of having a newborn. How does an anxious and fearful woman cope? Is she prepared to hold and nurse an unwanted baby in her mental and physical exhaustion or during hormonal changes or even postpartum depression? Articles about abandoned or murdered newborns often appear in our own newspapers. When discovered, the mothers are frequently very young women who bore the nine months and labor alone and lacked support afterwards. Perhaps they would have reacted differently to their babies had someone like the old woman of the mountains been there to care for them. Call her a demon, but she makes a difference in the life of that Heian woman and saves the child. Indeed, the outcome of the story supports the young woman's first impression of the old woman as Buddha-sent.

The old woman of the mountains also reinforces the maternal bond by appearing as a threat and instilling in the mother a desire to protect her son as demonstrated by her quick escape and her appeal to Buddha. Amazingly, only good results in the encounter of the two women. Yanagita and Kawai emphasize the two-sided nature of the *yamauba*—that of child eater and granter of good fortune. Kawai writes: "As Kunio Yanagita stressed, it is absolutely erroneous to judge one-sidely that Yama-uba is merely a monster. The Japanese long ago saw both positive and negative sides in her and sometimes regarded her ambivalently."[98]

CONCLUSION

The female demons in setsuwa are complex. Viewing them in terms of the grotesque allows us to see in them much more than a generalized dislike or distrust of women. The apparent misogyny of such tales is a thin veil for other, deeper fears. Even when the Buddhist concern with sexual desire as an obstacle to enlightenment comes into play, as it so often does, the focus on female demons (or more precisely demons in the form of women) provides a means for men to confront their own anxieties about losing control, of which giving into sexual desire is only one form.

Women and demons are juxtaposed not only in setsuwa, but in other Heian literature as well. Sei and the Young Lady Who Loves Insects each identify with demons differently, but they see in themselves something akin to the imagined creatures. This sense is linked to the interplay of invisibility and visibility in the lives of Heian aristocratic women—to the need of being both hidden and seen. Furthermore, women could declare a degree of spiritual and psychological independence from the rest of society by identifying with demons. For passionate aristocratic men, associating women with demons is teasing and playful—a way of expressing erotic interest. However, as the response of Lady Chikuzen to the poem by Mototoshi suggests, women did not always appreciate this type of advance. Their resistance may be rooted in the differences in the reasons why women associate women with demons and why men do.

The main point of setsuwa about female demons is not to convey negative attitudes toward women. In the tales involving young, attractive women who turn out to be demons (*rākṣasīs*), the creatures are clearly something other than female merely in the guise of women. They remain closely tied through other physical characteristics to creatures not temporarily gendered as female.

Demonized women such as the old woman at Rajō Gate and the mother of the hunters have the potential to raise issues that would have been of particular concern to women or members of Heian society who could not speak for themselves (such as children and the elderly). They also challenge assumptions of the Heian elite and others. Although the commentator in the Agi Bridge tale warns against the wisdom of women, the narrative demonstrates that foolish pride and misdirected energy doom the man. The creatures waiting at bridges in female form have a role in meting out karmic justice.

What does a demon gain by transforming into a woman? Or rather, what can be expressed through a so-called female demon that would not be conveyed through a male or unspecified creature? Men often use the figure of the young, forlorn aristocratic woman—the Heian ideal of femininity—to expose their own longing and vulnerability. In most setsuwa, intimate relations are not shown to be worthy ends in themselves as they are in other genres but are frequently used to demonstrate the foolishness and cruelty of people, particularly of men. Heterosexual relations are also symbolic of other forms of desire and misdirected energy. What a demon acquires in the body of a beautiful, young woman is the potential to attract a man, reveal his shortcomings, and punish him for them.

What does a demon gain by transforming into an old woman? One answer is trust. The pregnant woman is grateful for the old woman in the mountains because she can initially rely on her. Whatever effects they intend to have on humans, creatures can best succeed by first establishing a connection. They do so by appealing to the needs or desires of people. Demons associated with old women allow people to experience a gamut of feelings, not only hatred and repulsion but also attachment, familial love, and loss. Consequently, ambivalence about the fundamental nature of demons marks the tales involving them.

CHAPTER 6

Animal Spirits

Animal spirits in setsuwa often function as grotesque representations in ways similar to demons, but each type also has distinct characteristics. No amount of reading in zoological studies can prepare a reader for this aspect of the animal kingdom since many have only the names and appearances of real animals. One spirit creature, *tengu*, even has its own name; in setsuwa, it frequently transforms into a small hawk or kite, but differs from the ordinary bird. When an animal spirit is mentioned, we get a sense of a spirit materialized as something we should know but do not quite recognize. Perhaps Japanese people in classical and medieval times did not have a fractured sense of these creatures. A fox was a fox. Or was it?

In this chapter, sections are focused on foxes, monkeys, a tree with bird spirits, snakes, wild boars and raccoon dogs, and tengu. The treatment of tales below differs slightly from that in previous chapters. Most sections provide a sweeping sense of a type of animal spirit in grotesque roles. In order to cover more ground, they explore the significance of the details of tales in less depth than elsewhere in this study. However, there are several exceptions where closer readings are given. All the stories illustrate well the kinds of tensions and transgressions I have been discussing all along.

FOX SPIRITS

"Mention *to bewitch* and the word fox is what first comes to mind," writes Komatsu Kazuhiko when discussing a medieval picture scroll *Tamamo no mae sōshi* (*The Scroll of Lady Tamamo*), depicting the legend of a fox disguised as a beautiful, brilliant woman who wins the favor of Retired Emperor Toba (1103–56, r. 1107–23) and then tries to kill him through illness.[1] *To bewitch* here is *bakasu* in Japanese, which can be translated also as "to deceive" or "to trick." Deception artists, foxes are constant reminders of the non-human realms of existence. They shake any sense people have of stability in the world. Yet, in many tales about foxes, pinpointing what or who is under attack or why can be difficult. Why would one fox assume the form of a huge cedar tree only to be shot dead? Why would another endanger itself by transforming into a young girl and hitching a ride on the horses of men, only to leap down and run away in fox form after a short distance?[2] The functioning of foxes as grotesque representations is often impersonal. Their great need to deceive can lead them to risk even their lives for a few moments of success.

We have seen how demons suggest the fragility of the Heian court and especially of the Fujiwara. How secure can the world of the elite be when they murder officials and aristocratic women on the palace grounds? Among other things, *oni* are manifestations of the anxiety and fear of aristocrats who sense the precariousness of their prosperity, but they are not the only menacing presences in the Heian capital and at the heart of aristocratic life.

In the very brief *Kobiki* (*Fox-Haunting Record*), Ōe no Masafusa describes five incidents of haunting by foxes in the Heian capital during the third year of Kōwa (1101). In the first account, foxes serve people banquet meals of rice and vegetables fashioned out of horse dung and cow bones, first in front of the Suzaku Gate and later behind the Department of Rites and Ceremonies (*Shikibushō*) and in front of the gates of houses belonging to high-ranking nobles and warriors. In the next record, they drive away in the carriage of one Minamoto no Takayasu in the form of aristocrats, three men and two women. This ultimately causes the death of the ox boy who steers the cart. He grows ill after discovering that a red fan given to him by the creatures has become a bone and lives only a few more days. Although the horrified Takayasu decides to burn the carriage, a man who appears in a dream, apparently one of the fox spirits, urges him not to destroy it. Ironically, the foxes then reward Takayasu for lending them the cart with the appointment of librarian the following year. Disguised as horsemen in the next story, fox spirits escort Emperor Horikawa (1079–1107, r. 1086–1107) as far as the Suzaku Gate, a popular spot for these creatures. They cover their possibly vulpine faces and refuse to give their identities when asked. A fox appears in another tale as an aristocratic woman who attempts to make a famous high-ranking priest, Precept Master Zōchin (1036–1109), ill by inviting him to an imitation feast, again prepared with dung. Finally, a fox transformed into a man purchases a house in Kyōgoku, the Shichijō District of the capital, only to destroy it and use it for burial materials at Toribe Field Cemetery. His payment of gold, silver, and silk for the house turns out to be old straw sandals and clogs, tiles, pebbles, and animal bones and horns.[3]

Several downward movements take place in this short work. The foxes undermine people simply by appearing in their lives and causing trouble. The higher the societal position of the victim, the greater is his debasement. The locations chosen by the animal spirits also have hierarchical implications: the undermining of aristocratic life is especially keen when it takes place on or near the palace grounds, beside the work places and homes of aristocrats. The image of exquisite food that turns out to be dung in two of the accounts takes us from high to low on the body: from the mouth to the bowels and from nourishment and pleasure to poison and suffering caused by illness. Few things could be more humiliating than to discover that the delicious food one ate is excrement. The very idea destroys the association of banquet food with luxury and celebration.

The foxes also trick the aristocrats by giving them seemingly valuable things that are really repulsive or useless, belittling the materialism of aristocrats similarly to demons. Yet, the ultimate loss is in the last account. The price Takayasu must pay for the position of librarian exceeds the loan of the carriage as it includes the life of a servant boy. The child becomes a sacrificial object chosen by the spirits themselves in the political advancement of his master. A strange sort of redemption takes place.

The spells and deceptions of foxes range from benign to pernicious. At one extreme is the fox acting as a messenger for Fujiwara no Toshihito in the tale, mentioned in Chapter 4, about the fifth-rank retainer (*goi*) who wishes for his fill of yam gruel. Traveling to the mansion of his father-in-law in Tsuruga with his retinue and the *goi*, Toshihito catches a fox racing along the beach. He orders it to inform his family that he is coming with a guest and to have them send two saddled horses to a place called Takashima at ten the next morning. When horsemen greet the party at the specified place and time, we learn that, on the previous night, the fox possessed the wife of Toshihito in order to convey the messages.[4] In *Uji shūi*, the fox is rewarded with yam gruel. He gobbles it up in mocking contrast to the *goi* who can no longer eat much.[5] In another tale, a man returns a small white magical ball after snatching it from a fox-possessed woman. The grateful fox later protects the man when he encounters trouble.[6] In these tales, the relationships between foxes and humans exhibit a mutual affinity and closeness that we do not usually find in the interactions of humans with demons. These animal spirits are endearing.

At the other extreme is the tragically horrid *Nihon ryōiki* account of how a fox avenges her cubs after a man leaves them skewered by the entrance to her den. The angry animal gets hold of the man's child by transforming into the grandmother and then slaughters the baby as the man did her cubs.[7] The death of the baby can be attributed not only to the fox, but also to the cruelty of the man, as apparent in the comments of the *Nihon ryōiki* compiler, the monk Kyōkai, who uses the incident as an example of immediate retribution.[8] The baby appears to have no independent karma since the murder is an attack on the father. Kyōkai does not condemn the fox or mourn the loss of the innocent child. Yet another tale relates how a fox shot in its hindquarters with an arrow avenges himself by running to the house of the attacker with a torch in its mouth, transforming into a man, and setting the place on fire.[9] In both cases, the fox reacts to being tormented. Foxes rarely inflict great harm on humans otherwise.

Some victims of foxes lose their sense of place and believe they are somewhere else. A servant abandons her child at an isolated heath, thinking that she is at a house rented by her master.[10] Elsewhere, a certain Kaya no Yoshifuji of Bitchū Province, described as "naturally lustful" (*tensei inbon*) and temporarily separated from his wife, meets a beautiful young woman who truthfully identifies herself as no particular person. She takes him to a splendid house filled with people of all ranks. He begins a new life there, forgetting his former wife and children, and even fathers a son. Meanwhile, his affluent brothers wonder about his whereabouts and whether he is still alive. When they carve a wooden statue of Kannon and petition it for help, Yoshifuji crawls out from under the storehouse, the dwelling of many foxes, to return to his former world. He has been there for thirteen days rather than years.[11]

Although Yoshifuji might have starved beneath the storehouse had the relationship with the fox continued, the fox appears to be genuinely interested in him as a companion, sexual partner, and father of her son. The commentator uses the tale to encourage dedication to Kannon, but the audience would probably observe that Yoshifuji felt fulfilled. What does it matter if this heightened experience—marked by deep feelings, satisfaction, joy, and even commitment—is based on an illusion, as is most of life according to Buddhists anyway? Why are the tricks of foxes bad if a man can experience a long, happy life through them, however short and empty according to the reality of another realm?

Foxes often transform into beautiful women and seduce men, but in contrast to demons, form emotional bonds, and sometimes even give birth to half-human children. In a *Nihon ryōiki* tale, the child of a man and a fox ultimately becomes "the ancestor of the Kitsune-no-atae clan in Mino Province."[12] His parents had had a harmonious relationship, spoiled only by a barking puppy that frightened his mother and forced her to reassume her vulpine form. The bond of a man and a fox-woman is also very deep in "How a Man Copies the *Lotus Sutra* for the Salvation of a Fox after Her Death." She dies so that he, her lover, can live and he insures her rebirth in a Buddhist heaven by copying and dedicating part of the *Lotus Sutra* to her.[13] The danger of engaging in such a relationship must be attributed to the fundamental nature of spirits: intercourse with them almost inevitably puts humans at risk. However, foxes are not necessarily malicious.

The association of the fox with the acts of bewitching, tricking, shapeshifting, and otherwise deceiving coincides with the characterization of them as tricksters in "The Trickster in Japan: *Tanuki* and *Kitsune*" by Brenda Jordan. As part of an exhibition catalogue, the essay explores the folkloric background of the fox in relation to certain seventeenth- through nineteenth-century works of Japanese art.[14] Although it focuses on the Edo period, the concept of trickster is relevant to the fox in setsuwa and to the grotesque in general.

Studies of tricksters include clowns, fools, and similar figures important to the history of laughter as described by Bakhtin. He writes: "Clowns and fools, which often figure in Rabelais' novel, are characteristic of the medieval culture of humor. They were the constant, accredited representatives of the carnival spirit in everyday life out of the carnival season."[15] They were also "herald[s] of nonfeudal, nonofficial truth."[16] The medieval festivals central to Bakhtinian thought are discussed by C. G. Jung in "On the Psychology of the Trickster Figure," a commentary to *The Trickster: A Study in American Indian Mythology* by Paul Radin. Jung sees the same customs Bakhtin considers grotesque as demonstrating "the role of the trickster to perfection."[17] Jordan defines *trickster* in a Jungian sense as "a part of our subconscious which does not respond to logic or reason, and which by virtue of its unexplainable deeds is difficult to understand," and "as a reflection of certain mischievous and sometimes evil elements of the human personality."[18] However, both Jung and Radin assume the existence of universals such as a "transcendental human psyche"[19] whereas most contemporary scholars acknowledge the importance of assuming dissimilarities in the minds of people of different cultures, eras, and socioeconomic classes. Grotesque representations in setsuwa are necessarily connected to the psychology of the multiple creators of the tales, but we should assume differences between the premodern Japanese psyche, or rather psyches, and our own. Still, it makes no sense to discount any possibility of similarity. Grotesque representations in setsuwa can suggest mischievous or evil elements of Japanese people during and around the Heian period that sometimes resemble those of people in other times and places.

Moreover, many qualities of the fox spirit coincide with concepts of the trickster developed by scholars after Radin and Jung. While unable to do justice to them in this study, I will give an example. One trickster-like quality of the fox spirit and other creatures in setsuwa is apparent in the view of anthropologist Mary Douglas. She sees the trickster "as having a social function of dispelling the belief that any given social order is absolute and objective."[20] Here, the concepts of the grotesque and the trickster overlap.

Nevertheless, the fox spirit is a conventional creature despite being a "deceiver and trick-player" at times.[21] Nothing about the marriages of foxes and humans is unusual except the identity of the foxes, who would continue to live as wives if possible. These animal spirits conform in other ways as well. In "About the Move of Imperial Advisor Miyoshi no Kiyotsura," fox spirits attempt to scare Kiyotsura from taking residence in an old mansion. They cause faces and about fifty tiny men on horseback to appear. Next, a woman visits Kiyotsura through their magic. She appears gorgeous until she takes the fan away from her face to reveal a red nose and long silver fangs. The seemingly beautiful woman who turns out monstrous exaggerates the possibility of a Heian aristocrat discovering that the hidden woman who attracted him with her voice and correspondence is actually homely. With the red nose, she evokes Suetsumuhana in *Genji* with fangs added as a horrific touch.[22] After these attempts fail, the fox patriarch appears as an old man and politely petitions against the move of Kiyotsura into the house, long the dwelling of fox spirits. Kiyotsura argues that people have the right to deed their houses to others and faults the spirits for frightening people away. When he threatens them, the old man concedes that Kiyotsura is right and apologetically blames the spooks on his disobedient children. He then asks permission to move to a university gate. In this way, the fox spirits adhere to a sense of hierarchy. They view people who stand up to them as superiors worthy of respect. The sense of hierarchy may differ in the eyes of the fox spirits and the man, but it exists for both. Kiyotsura declares, "True demons and gods understand justice and are frightening precisely because they do not distort it. . . . No doubt about it: you're an old fox living here and frightening people away."[23] In this view, foxes fall low in the ranks of spirits.[24]

SIMIAN EMOTIONS

Whereas the affinity or respect of foxes for humans is important in some tales, the similarities in the feelings and behaviors of monkeys and humans often figure prominently in others. Monkeys can be grateful: when a woman prevents a neighbor from stoning a monkey, the animal repays her by protecting her child from eagles.[25] The kindness of monkeys is also evident in genres other than setsuwa: in the *Utsuho monogatari*, monkeys help a mother and her young son survive for years in the woods of Kitayama by bringing them fruit, vegetables, and nuts to eat.[26]

Translated below, *Kokon chomonjū* tales 700 and 717 exemplify stories that demonstrate how deeply monkeys feel. They suggest the resemblance of simian emotions to those of humans without overtly personifying the monkeys (by having them speak, for instance) or by depicting their transformations into a human form.

> *About the Monkey Caught Alive by Takeda Tarō Nobumitsu*
> *Also, How a Monkey Who Is Chased Up a Tree by Gorō Nobumasa*
> *of the Same Family [Son of Nobumitsu], Tries to Avoid Being Shot*
> *with an Arrow by Pointing to a Doe*
>
> Around the summer of the year Jōkyū 4 (1222), Takeda Tarō Nobumitsu is hunting on Asama Plain in Suruga Province when he chases a band of monkeys across the plain shooting arrows at them, killing three and catching three alive. Upon returning home, he attaches a rope to the live monkeys and places the dead monkeys in front of them. One live monkey gazes intently at one dead monkey, embraces it tightly, and then dies itself.

The dead monkey had to have been its wife or something. How pitiful. A prisoner kept by Takeda and taken on that hunting trip truly saw this happen, they say.

Along the same lines, Gōro Nobumasa of the same family chases a huge monkey up a tree while hunting. He is about to shoot the monkey dead when it points a finger at something it wants to show him. Finding this behavior unsettling and strange, Nobumasa hesitates before shooting to kill and looks for a moment. The monkey continues to point its finger. Nobumasa sends someone to investigate the spot, and it turns out a huge doe is lying there. The monkey must have been telling him to shoot the deer and spare him. So informed, Nobumasa shoots the deer dead. Although he should have let the monkey go, he then shoots it, too. From time to time, Nobumasa says, "This thing seemed pitiful to me, so I copied a sutra."[27]

How Lay Monk Tarō of Buzen Province Is Moved by the Mutual Love of a Mother Monkey and Her Baby and Stops Killing Monkeys

There is a certain lay priest Tarō, a resident of Buzen Province. Before he had taken vows, he often shot monkeys. One day, he is passing through the mountains when a huge monkey appears. He chases it up a tree and shoots, striking it when it is in the fork between two branches but not killing it. It is about to fall from the tree when Tarō sees it try to place something where the branches fork: a baby monkey. Itself injured and about to fall to the ground, the monkey tries to help the baby it carries by attempting to place it between the branches of the tree. But the baby monkey clings to its mother and will not let go. Although the mother monkey tries over and over again, the baby monkey still clings, until they both fall to the ground together. For a long time afterwards, Tarō stopped shooting monkeys.[28]

In all three accounts, the emotions of monkeys highlight the cruelty of humans. Killing monkeys seems awful enough, but what motivates Nobumitsu to show the carcasses to the live animals? He feels no pity for the monkey that dies broken hearted at the death of its mate. This insensitivity reflects his character. Significantly, a prisoner witnesses the coldhearted behavior. Since, other than Nobumitsu, the prisoner alone knows what happened, the audience can imagine that he passed down the story first. A prisoner would have been unable to criticize his captor or guard directly, but the tale provides an unflattering portrait. Perhaps Nobumitsu treated other prisoners as he did the monkeys and a truth about human victims lies behind the tale.

In the next section of the setsuwa, Nobumasa resembles his father in his ruthlessness. An unscrupulous and greedy man, he cannot restrain himself and take less than what is available. As a result, the monkey inadvertently gives Nobumasa more to kill when trying to save itself. How sincere can this violent man be when he copies a sutra for his victim, especially since the tale does not indicate that he subsequently stopped hunting? As for the monkey, its decision to point out a doe is ironically human-like. A real monkey could not come up with any plan to save itself and would only flee. Yet, more than a few humans would point out someone else to be killed when the arrow is aimed at them. That victim would likely be someone unguarded, even half asleep—like a deer lying peacefully in the brush.

Tarō's change of heart in the third account is more convincing than Nobumasa's because Tarō stops hunting. In many stories, people grow remorseful at killing an animal after some aspect of its death evokes empathy or pity. In an extremely disturbing setsuwa entitled "How Ōe no Sadamoto, the Governor of Mikawa, Takes the Tonsure," Sadamoto suggests that a pheasant be cooked alive. He then watches or otherwise participates in the vile acts of plucking it and cutting it while it still flutters around crying tears of blood so that, feeling sorrow and remorse, he will be motivated to take vows.[29] In yet another story (with several versions), a hunter takes vows after witnessing the attachment of a duck to the mate he killed.[30] Tarō does not seem to become a lay priest immediately after the deaths of the monkey mother and babe. He may even return to hunting monkeys before beginning religious life, since the tale says that he gave it up for a long time rather than forever. Even so, since the tale opens by introducing Tarō as a lay priest, the experience must have contributed to his decision to take that path.

The emotions of the monkeys as suggested by their behaviors give us an understanding of the human characters, so that the focus is on people. Other animals in setsuwa also have anthropomorphic feelings. In a cluster of tales about animals in the "Tales of India" section of *Konjaku*, a touching story tells of a lion who gives some of his own flesh to save baby monkeys temporarily in his care. In another, a tortoise falls to his death because he cannot keep his mouth shut.[31] Animals are also frequently reincarnations of beloved humans. The difference between them and humans is clearly a matter of births: a sheep about to be slaughtered for a feast turns out to be the child of the host and a slain deer is the mother of the hunter. Other stories, too, qualify as the worst nightmares of meat-eaters.[32] Still, monkeys stand out from other animals because of their natural likeness to humans. If they are personified, it is not usually completely.

In a pair of *Konjaku* tales, evil monkeys about to consume people use cooking and carving utensils as well as salt. Their human-like eating habits suggest cannibalism when, posing as gods, they demand human sacrifices. At the same time, they are clearly distinguished from human beings through their incomprehensible chatter. The central issue in both stories is the threat of false gods—and by extension, the people endorsing them.[33] The tales return us to the associations between marriage, consumption, and sacrifice discussed in Chapter 4. The tension in the tales is rooted in conflicting beliefs and practices and, more specifically, in the question of what should be worshipped. Grotesque elements include the focus on human sacrifice and the demand for a virginal or otherwise pure woman.[34] The concern with the absence of sexual activity ironically directs us to the lower half of the female body because initially the young woman is defined largely in terms of it. Since both tales are long, I translate the first and summarize the second. The first appears also in *Uji shūi* as tale 119 (10:6) with a few important differences in content discussed below. Here is the *Konjaku* version:

How the Spirits of Mimasaka Province Give Up Living Sacrifices Because of a Hunter's Scheme

Now it is the past; there are two gods named Chūsan and Kōya in Mimasaka Province. Chūsan has the body of a monkey and Kōya of a snake. Once a year, a living sacrifice is prepared as an offering to them. A young girl, a virgin who is a native of the province, is given as that sacrifice. This [practice] has existed for a long time, from olden times until the present, and has never been neglected.

And so, there are people in that province (though what people does not matter) with an absolutely beautiful sixteen- or seventeen-year-old daughter. Her mother and father love and cherish her very much and would give their lives for her, but she has been designated as the living sacrifice. Chosen at the festival this year, she is to be nourished and fattened for one year from that day and offered at the same festival next year.

After their daughter is selected, the father and mother ceaselessly lament and grieve, but because they have no escape, the life [of the daughter] comes closer to its end with the passing of the days and months. With hardly any time left for the parents and child to spend with each other, the three can do nothing but count the days and cry together with sorrow.

Around this time, a person comes to that land from an eastern province because of some karmic affinity.[35] He does what is called "dog mountain": the occupation of raising numerous dogs and going into the mountains to hunt by having them bite boars and deer to death. Furthermore, he is a person with an extremely fierce heart, afraid of nothing. After being in the land for a while, this man hears about the sacrificial practice.

Then he goes to the home of the parents of the sacrifice with something
to discuss. While sitting on the veranda waiting to be called in, he peeps
through a gap in the latticed shutters: reclining there elegantly is the woman
kept as the living sacrifice. She is beautiful, with fair skin, an endearing form,
and long hair, appearing not at all as the daughter of country folk. Seeing
her lying there weeping with tangled hair and a look of distress on her face,
the easterner is deeply moved and feels great regret. Finally, he meets her
parents and they talk about various things.

One parent says, "Our only daughter has been selected for such and such
a thing, so we live each day in sorrow and worry all night. We are saddened
beyond measure as the day of our final separation approaches with the passing of each day and month. And to think there are such lands! What sin
could we have committed in our former lives to be born in this place and to
be faced with this miserable fate?"

When the easterner hears this, he says, "There is nothing more precious
to people of this world than life. Moreover, there is no treasure greater to
people than a child. That, in spite of this, your only daughter will be turned
into mincemeat before your eyes is truly lamentable. Better to die yourselves.
How can there be anyone who would not confront the enemy and risk dying
in vain?[36] We fear buddhas and gods because our lives are dear to us, and
value especially the lives of our children. And, that lady is now virtually
dead. Since she is to die anyway, give her to me, won't you? I will die in her
place. Give her to me and do not feel anguish."

Hearing this, a parent asks, "And then, just what do you intend to do?"

So the easterner says, "Well, I have an idea. Do not tell anyone that I am
at this house. Simply say that you are engaging in ritual purification and
stretch a sacred hemp yarn festoon here."

A parent says, "If it would mean our daughter does not die, I do not care
if I lose my life."

This easterner secretly becomes intimate with the young woman. While
he is living with her as his wife, he grows to feel that separating would be
difficult. He selects two dogs used for "dog-mountain" which he has raised
for many years and tells them, "Okay, you guys take my place." Diligently
training the dogs, he has them secretly fetch live monkeys at isolated places
in the mountains. He concentrates on teaching them how to chew them up.
Monkeys and dogs are naturally hostile to each other, but when he trains
them in this way, the dogs have only to see a monkey and they bite it to
death, and do so with many. When he has completely trained the dogs in
this way, he sharpens his sword well and carries it with him.

The easterner says to his wife, "I intend to die in your place. Death be
what it is, I am saddened by our parting." The woman does not understand,
but her sense of pity is boundless.

When the appointed day arrives, the shrine officials and numerous other
people show up to fetch [the woman]. They have brought a new long chest

and they place it in the bedroom, saying, "Get in this." Wearing only a hunting robe and trousers, the man climbs into the chest, sword at his side. His two dogs jump in and lie on either side of him. The parents carry out the chest as if their daughter is inside. Then people carrying spears, *sakaki* branches, bells, and mirrors [gather] as clouds and lead the way bellowing [incantations].[37] Fearing what would happen, the wife finds it pitiful that the man is taking her place. The parents think, "We don't care if we are killed later. Even if we come to die the same death, we cannot but do this now."

The crowd brings the living sacrifice to the shrine, chants dedicatory prayers, and opens the gate of the shrine fence. They cut the cords tied around the chest, place the chest down inside the gate, and leave. After closing the gate to the fence, the shrine officials sit in a row on the other side. When the man opens the lid of the chest just a crack and peeks out, he sees a seven or eight foot tall monkey sitting on the seat of honor. Its teeth are white and its face and rump are red. To his right and left sit monkey after monkey, about a hundred in all. They screech and chatter, raising the eyebrows on their red faces. In front of them, a huge carving knife has been placed on a cutting board. Everything is there: vinegar, salt, saké, and more salt. It looks as if they are about to eat venison or something else cooked.

A few minutes later, the huge monkey on the seat of honor stands up to open the chest. Just as all the other monkeys stand up and open it with him, the man suddenly comes out and says to the dogs, "Sic them!" The two dogs leap out, bite the huge monkey and knock him down. The man draws his icy sword, grabs the chief monkey and forces him down on the chopping board, knife held to his head. "So, this is how you kill people and eat their chopped flesh! I'll cut off your head and feed it to the dogs." As he speaks, the monkey's face grows redder and his eyes blink. He shows his white teeth in a snarl, and then in tears, rubs his hands together. Refusing to forgive the monkey, the man still holds the sword at its head and says, "I'm going to kill you today for eating the children of so many people year after year. Yes, I'll do it this very minute! If you are a god, kill me." Meanwhile, the two dogs are biting many other monkeys to death. Those managing to survive climb trees or hide in the mountains. They call out for other monkeys to gather, screeching and shouting until the mountains echo, but in vain.

At the same time, the god possesses one of the shrine priests and announces, "Henceforth, I will never accept a living sacrifice like this; I will never kill anything again. Moreover, I will not blame the man for conquering me. And I will not harm the girl chosen for the sacrifice, nor her parents and relatives. Just save me!" All the shrine priests come inside the shrine and say to the man, "The August God has thus spoken. Set him free," and "We are obliged to you." But the man will not free the monkey. "I don't care about my own life, but I will kill him in revenge for all the people. So, let us all die together," he says and will not let him go. But since the monkey prays and desperately makes vows, the man says, "Very well, but from now on, don't do anything like this again!" When he frees the monkey, it escapes to the mountains.

The man returns to his home and he and the woman live forever after as husband and wife. The woman's mother and father rejoice to no end about their son-in-law. Moreover, nothing bad ever happens to this family. This, too, must be the effect of positive karma accumulated in a previous life.

Afterwards, living sacrifices are abolished and the province is pacified. So the tale is told and passed down.[38]

In "Konjaku monogatari shū no 'kokka zō'" ("The Representation of the State in *Konjaku*"), Maeda Masayuki argues that *Konjaku* reveals an idealistic concept of the state manifested on two levels: in terms of control of the emperor and the imperial court over the people and in terms of the position of Japan in what was seen as the (Buddhist) world. We can modify his view by understanding "state" in the Heian period as the growing attempt of the aristocratic government to centralize power and to give the country a more unified identity. The tale translated above deals with the first level since the struggle is against gods worshipped in Mimasaka Province. The *Konjaku* compiler represents Japan as a great unified land at the domestic level with tales illustrating how threats to order within the state can be controlled or destroyed. The undesirable elements include criminals, supernatural beings, and "negative" aspects of the remote regions (in relation to the capital)— here, the eastern provinces.[39] Yet, the surfacing of those very forces and elements some storytellers seek to suppress undermines this portrait. Threats to order cannot be fully controlled or destroyed.

Significantly, the endings of the *Konjaku* and *Uji shūi* versions are not identical.[40] In *Konjaku*, the monkey escapes to the mountains, all living sacrifices are abolished, and the province is pacified. In *Uji shūi*, the monkey remains enshrined and the sacrifice of wild boars and deer replaces that of humans. The well being of the province is not mentioned. Both tales show the desire to wipe out "evil religions" (*jakyō*): religions in the remote regions incompatible with the social system, politics, and morals of Heian society. According to Maeda, *Konjaku* brings this effort to the level of the state whereas the *Uji shūi* tale reveals respect for the autonomy of the provinces and remote areas as well as for things characterizing them as independent from the state. In short, the complete rejection of the shrine gods in *Konjaku* reveals a desire to put the area (and others) under central rule.[41]

The tale suggests that local beliefs and practices not sanctioned by the state were a source of contention. We have no way of knowing whether sacrificing maidens was ever practiced in Mimasaka. However, an obviously evil ritual was either chosen or created to generate a negative picture of local beliefs and customs. Most Heian and medieval Japanese audiences would have approved of an end to human sacrifice whereas the same kind of intrusion would have been much harder to justify were the targeted ritual benign to humans. The Mimasaka people are portrayed as victims of the gods. Their apparent helplessness warrants intervention.

Yet, how can we view the story as alluding to a conflict between the aristocratic government seeking to centralize and local religious leaders when the hero has no connection to the government? If the power struggle fueling the tale is between these two groups, then the inclusion of the easterner might be an attempt to make the suppression of the government less obvious. People cannot protect their beliefs and practices when they do not know the identity of their attacker or even that they are being assailed.

Casting the struggle in terms of Buddhist and non-Buddhist practices is similarly complicated because the Buddhist aspects of the story are weak. The main non-Buddhist elements are the gods. According to Ikegami Jun'ichi, their names, Chūsan and Kōya, allude to shrines where gods connected to agriculture were worshipped.[42] Nothing more is said about the snake god in the tale, but the roles of monkeys as gods and spirits can resemble those of snakes. In *Kojiki* and *Nihon shoki*, the god Susano-o meets an old couple weeping because a huge serpent has devoured all but one of their eight daughters. He asks for the last daughter and transforms her into a hair comb, which he wears—hence her name, Kushi-nada-hime (Wondrous/Comb Princess of Inada). The two marry after he gets the serpent drunk and slays it.[43] In the Chinese collection *Soushenji*, a young girl saves herself from a virgin-eating serpent with a sword and a dog and becomes queen.[44]

What is Buddhist about the tale of the evil monkey gods? In contrast to *Uji shūi*, *Konjaku* mentions the effect of karma twice (although the first occurrence is debatable): a karmic connection brings the man to Mimasaka and the ultimate well-being of the family is the result of karma. The abolishment of all living sacrifice in *Konjaku* also coincides with the Buddhist precept against killing. However, these Buddhist elements appear to be added to an already finished tale since they are not significant to the plot. One element of the tale even seems to contradict Buddhist thought: the hero is a hunter. I will discuss below a more obviously Buddhist tale with a hunter as hero, but there the hunter functions as a contrast to a holy man.

The tensions between local beliefs and Buddhism would be more obvious were the hero a Buddhist monk instead, but then he could not marry the woman. Or could he? The protagonist in "How Living Sacrifices to Monkey Gods Are Stopped in Hida Province" starts out as an itinerant monk, but ends up in almost the same predicament as the easterner in the previous tale. Lost in the mountains of Hida Province, the monk finds himself in front of a huge waterfall resembling a rattan curtain. While he is praying to the Buddha for help, an old man wearing a straw hat appears, jumps into the waterfall, and vanishes. Fearing the mysterious man is a demon who will return, the monk decides to avoid the pain of being consumed by killing himself. He beseeches the Buddha for assistance in the next life and then takes the plunge, only to discover that the waterfall is in fact a curtain.

A path leads to a village on the other side. Many people argue over who gets to keep the monk, but the district governor awards him to an acquaintance of the man who led him from Japan through the waterfall. The numerous servants and retainers of the household treat the monk very well. He initially refuses the chicken and fish they serve him because of his vows, but the old man tells the monk to eat what he is given and to grow his hair because he is to marry his daughter. The monk follows orders out of fear but worries what the Buddha will think.

Married life agrees with the former monk: he puts on weight, is finally able to wear a topknot, and adores his wife. His father-in-law continues to feed him well, but his wife grows weepy. In fact, the man is being prepared as a human sacrifice in place of her. Seven days before the sacrificial festival, ceremonial ropes are stretched around the house and the man is purified through enforced fasting. When the appointed day arrives, he is bathed and dressed in a beautiful robe. His hair is done with care. The atmosphere at the shrine is festive, with food, drink, music, and dance, but, in the end, the man is left stretched naked on a large cutting board. Only two people, he and his wife, know that a dagger obtained from his wife is hidden between his thighs. Huge monkeys appear from the numerous sanctuaries. Just as one monkey is about to carve him, the man springs up and attacks the chief, who screams and wrings his hands. The former monk ties the gods to trees, burns the shrines, and parades the gods through the streets. The gods turn out to be real monkeys whom the man easily torments, beats, and drives off into the mountains. Seeing the power of his son-in-law, the old man suggests that he be revered as their new god. The former monk thus becomes the head of the village on the other side of the waterfall, with everyone devotedly at his service.[45]

What happens to his commitment to Buddhism? The tale seems set up perfectly to show how a great man brings Buddhism to a land of spiritually misled people. However, this hero makes no attempt to introduce Buddhist ideas and practices to the unknown world. He spares the lives of the monkeys, but does not otherwise indicate his adherence to Buddhist values. Is it too much to expect such a man, now happily married and with a privileged position in society, to renounce everything and return to his isolated life? Some men might be able to make that choice but what of the more typical? Of course, the move of the man away from Buddhist devotion to a secular life explains why this tale is not in the Japanese Buddhist section of *Konjaku*.

The weapon that empowers the ex-monk is suggestive: not the *Lotus Sutra* or Kannon or something along those lines but a dagger. His wife gives it to him, indicating her role in determining their future and alluding to their intimacy, and he hides it appropriately close to his genitals. The marriage is supposed to lead to his death but, with the help of the woman, becomes instead the reason for his survival and success in the village. How striking that the change in the life of the monk is positive! While the local belief and practice is condemned, Buddhism is not shown to be the solution to evil.

Nor does the next tale idealize Buddhism. Instead, it makes the struggle between institutional Buddhism and certain forms of *kami*-worship evident by illustrating that some gods not yet affected by Buddhism (and possibly indigenous) are not violent until provoked.

BIRD SPIRITS AND A TREE

"How Empress Suiko Founds the Original Gangōji" is set during the reign of Empress Suiko (r. 592–628), not long after the defeat in 587 of the Mononobe, the military family (*uji*) who led the resistance against Buddhism. Even so, it raises issues that are also relevant in the twelfth and thirteenth centuries. Buddhism spread rapidly in Japan at both times, although commoners were less affected by it in ancient Japan. In both periods, older religious understandings often had to be changed or destroyed to accommodate Buddhism. The tale points to strife between Buddhism and traditions established earlier. It suggests that some people remained loyal to deities not appropriated by Buddhists and were threatened by the Buddhist influence.[46]

The tale is an *engi* (a story recording how a temple is founded) and additionally a *reigendan* (a miracle tale about the mysterious responses of buddhas or gods). It consists of two separate sequences of events, each leading us through a different puzzle and resolution, with only the founding of the temple and the concept of mysterious things occurring in the process linking the two parts. The first half focuses on how a Buddhist monk deals with the spirits of a zelkova tree who murder to defend their home while the second is about the mysterious identity of an old man who disappears after he reveals how to fit a Buddhist statue through a temple entrance too small for it. *Nihon shoki* mentions the problem of the oversized statue.[47] I translate and discuss the first part of the tale because the tree spirits, who appear as birds, function in a grotesque mode.

How Empress Suiko Founds the Original Temple Gangōji

Now it is the past; during the reign of Empress Suiko, Buddhist law flourishes in this land and there are many people building temples. The empress regnant, too, orders [Kuratsukuri no tori] from Paekche to cast, using copper, a sixteen foot statue of Śākyamuni, and then decides to have a temple erected in Asuka Village for enshrining this Śākyamuni Buddha.[48] But when the building of the temple begins, someone notices a huge zelkova tree too old to even guess how long it has been growing there on the chosen construction site. An imperial order decrees, "Quickly chop it down and get it out of the way; then lay the foundation for the temple." While the court official in charge oversees the construction work, the event and the tree [*missing text*]. [ ] screams out, "Get rid of [ ]," so everyone runs away and is gone.[49]

Some time later, the official is forced to be even more decisive about having the [tree] chopped down, [ ], too far. Once again, he orders a man to chop down the tree, but since this man also dies suddenly after striking the tree only two or three times with a axe and broad hatchet, the chief official has the next man approach the tree very cautiously. Like the others before him, this man, too, drops dead. Seeing this, all the co-workers throw down their axes and hatchets and run for their lives without even worrying about the consequences. Some time later, they say, "No matter what the punishment, we just won't approach that tree now, anymore. After all, we can't serve the imperial court if we're dead!" Their fear and confusion are boundless.

At that time, a certain monk wonders, "Why on earth do people die when they chop at this tree?" Then he thinks, "There must be some way of finding this out." So, one night when it is pouring rain, he puts on a straw raincoat and a bamboo hat and goes out alone, timidly tiptoeing up to the edge of the tree, pretending to be a traveler seeking shelter from the rain under the branches, and remains close to its hollow. It is already the middle of the night when he hears many human voices coming from high inside the hollow. He hears someone say, "We stopped all those guys who came one after the other like that to chop our tree down by kicking them all to death. But even so, we won't be able to go on like this forever, without it ever being cut down." After this voice, another one speaks, "Whatever happens, we'll just kick them to death each time. Since there is no one in this world who doesn't value life, people will stop coming to cut down the tree." Then still another voice says, "If someone encircles the tree with a sacred hemp yarn festoon, recites the *Nakatomi no matsuri*, and has a woodcutter mark the tree with an inked string before cutting it down, we are doomed." Then all the voices speak at once, "Oh no, how true." The voices all begin moaning together. Soon the birds begin to chirp, and the voices then cease. "That's great to hear," thinks the monk as he tiptoes away.

Later on, the monk reports what he heard to the empress regnant, impressing the court and making them very happy. They follow the monk's suggestions and encircle the tree with a hemp festoon, scatter rice around the base of the tree, make offerings of cloth streamers, recite the *Nakatomi no harae* for the purification ritual, and summon a woodcutter to have him mark the tree with an inked string before chopping it down. No one dies in the process. As the tree gradually begins to tilt, five or six birds as big as copper pheasants rise from the branches and fly away. After that, the tree falls. It is cleared away completely and the base of the temple is built. The birds go to live somewhere in the southern mountains. When the empress regnant hears this, she feels sorry for the birds and immediately has a shrine built for them. The building is still a shrine today, located south of Ryūkaiji Temple.[50]

Certain plot elements of this story may have been appropriated from a *Soushenji* tale in which Duke Wen of Qin orders his men to fell a catalpa tree growing atop a certain offertory. Whenever the men chop it, the ax wounds heal and close. The forty men end up exhausted. Thirty-nine go home to rest, but a weary and injured man sleeps under the tree. There, he hears the voices of spirits. As in the *Konjaku* tale, one voice reveals the method necessary to fell the tree, but it is not through the same ritual.[51]

The Japanese zelkova (*tsuki* or *keyaki*) in the tale of Gangō Temple is a tall flowering tree visited by gods. It produces samara or key fruit provided with a membrane or wing, to which the bird imagery may allude. Accounts of the reigns of Empress Kōgyoku (642–45) through Emperor Jitō (690–97) mention the worship of this kind of tree.[52] In the tale, the zelkova tree represents non-Buddhist beliefs and practices.

Sacred from ancient times, trees function as strange or otherworldly realms (*ikyō*), pathways to such realms, devices for transformation, or places where gods and buddhas reside. Gods also descend to pine and cedar trees and use them as temporary residences (*yorishiro*).[53]

An early example of the link between trees and deities is in the *Kojiki* story of the god Ō-kuni-nushi-no-kami. Speak of sibling rivalry! He and his eighty brothers all want to marry the same goddess, but she chooses him. The envious brothers manage to kill Ō-kuni-nushi-no-kami twice, but he is revived each time. Their second means of murder is to fell a huge tree, drive a wedge into it, stuff him into the split in the wood, remove the wedge and crush him to death between the two sides of the tree. They renew their ruthless pursuit after he is freed and revived by his mother, but he escapes through the fork of another tree.[54] Trees are central in the death and escape of this deity, but spaces between their parts matter even more.

Just as men's attraction to and repulsion from women are often localized to the orifices of female bodies, so too is the awe and fear of trees frequently centered on their holes or spaces. Power and magic can be found in them. In *Utsuho monogatari*, Nakatada and his mother live happily for many years within an *utsuho*—a tree hollow or possibly a small cavern-like structure formed from huge cedar trees—in the woods on the mountain Kitayama.[55] They gain the friendship of animals and play exquisite koto music, which ultimately calls the father of the boy to them. Womb-like, hollow spaces are where things come to life. In *Taketori*, a bamboo cutter discovers a small person within a stalk of bamboo. In the tale of the woodcutter with a wen (summarized in Chapter 4), the old man has found shelter from a storm in a tree hollow when a hundred demons appear for a banquet. Later in the same story, a second old man also hides in the hollow because he wants to encounter the demons.[56] Entering the tree hollow is a way of summoning them. A *Konjaku* tale describes how Jikaku Daishi (Ennin, 794–864) secludes himself within the hollow of a large cedar tree and copies the *Lotus Sutra* while practicing ritual abstinence.[57] The story of the beckoning hand (discussed in Chapter 2) similarly adds to the sense that tree holes, hollows, and other voids either within the trees or formed by them are hardly empty but rather spaces where gods and demons dwell.

Along with the zelkova tree, the birds suggest early, possibly pre-Buddhist, views. They resist Buddhism, thereby affirming their identity apart from it. However, the tale does not make the relationship of the spirits, the tree, and the birds entirely clear. The spirits may first reside in the tree and later take flight in the bodies of birds. Another way to read the tale is to see the birds as the spirits with the tree as their sacred dwelling. It would then be their voices overheard by the monk. Their flight from the tree ironically leads to their suppression since the people who privilege Buddhism appropriate them as objects of worship once the tree is felled. Nakamura Teiri sees rivalry between the birds in their conversation. According to this view, one bird may be a traitor, intentionally revealing information on how to destroy the tree. The interaction of the birds then reflects the strife between the Mononobe, Soga, and Nakatomi *uji*. It was the Soga who sided with Buddhism, thereby facilitating the domination of other forms of worship.[58]

It is not surprising that powerful elements of *kami*-worship come into play in a tale about the founding of a Buddhist temple since the spread of Buddhism shaped the fate of other traditions. Sinologist Daniel Overmyer has discussed how Buddhism conquered various local traditions. He focuses on texts and China, but his descriptions also apply to Buddhist practices and institutions as well as to Japan:

> Wherever it has spread Buddhism has had to deal with local religious practices that were already in place. As they circulated, Buddhist texts implicitly accepted the religious and psychological needs behind old forms of worship, but these forms were either co-opted or replaced. The Buddhists either declared that the old gods had converted into supporters of Buddhism, or explained that they were ineffective and that sacrifices to them would produce bad karma.[59]

Rather than attack *kami*-worship directly, Buddhist scriptures characteristically co-opt the old gods into the service of their new gospel by portraying them as converts to Buddhism. They are said to be reincarnations or manifestations of the true forms, buddhas or bodhisattvas, in the process that comes to be called *honji-suijaku* in the Japanese context. However, not all gods are easily converted or rejected. Tales sometimes suggest overt hostility on the part of old gods. Resistance to Buddhism naturally stands out in a tale about the founding of a temple since the new institution cannot be established unless it is overcome. *Kami*-worship fights for its existence here, in what Nakamura describes as "a story of how native gods are defeated by Buddhism and surrender to it."[60] The Buddhists are the woodcutters, all too ready to clear the way for their own beliefs and practices with the empress and her court behind them. At the same time, many non-Buddhist elements surface in the tale. The human voices coming from the tree refer to people with non-Buddhist worldviews. One dissenting voice expresses the belief that men will not risk their lives to cut down the tree because "there is no one in this world who doesn't value life." This line harbors a negative judgment of the Buddhists who willingly die for the founding of the temple by raising the question of how human they are. The native gods are not defeated entirely since they affect and redefine Buddhism. The ability of spirits associated with the tree to kill alludes to the use of zelkova wood in bow making.[61] The tree as material for weapons further evokes the idea of conflict between men, including battles between concepts.

Kami-worship in this *engi* helps to define Buddhist power. The monk discovers that the secret of how to destroy the tree lies in what is later considered Shinto ritual: the demarcating of sacred space for the gods with a holy rope, purification, and festive activity, including the recitation of prayers. Encircling the tree with a sacred hemp yarn festoon is the first step to removing it. It imprisons the "evil spirit" in the tree as it is cut down.[62] Rather than reject the spirits as murderers, the Buddhists build a shrine for them so that a healing can take place. Festoons were ordinarily made of straw, not hemp, but hemp suggests healing since its roots and leaves were ingredients in medicine.[63] However, the gods are forever changed by Buddhism and will never recover their former status.

Hemp is used in the festival of *Nakatomi no harae*, also called *Ō-harai* or the Great Purification. The *Nakatomi no harae* recited in the tale are prayers for that ceremony. *Nakatomi* is the name of the family of priests who led the festival, a divine service held on the last day of the sixth month. They along with the Mononobe initially resisted Buddhism but their threat to Buddhism was minimal because they were not a military family. During the ceremony, "the Nakatomi chieftain was assigned to offer *nusa* (expiatory offerings made of hemp or flax) of purification and recite ritual prayers."[64] The hemp rope in the tale may allude to this practice.

The cutting of a tree was often a significant part of the festival as well: when certain offenses were committed, the Nakatomi family priest had to "cut off the bottom and ends of a sacred tree and place them in abundance as offerings to the kami."[65] The scattering of rice and the presentation of offerings called *mitegura*, which were usually of cloth (later represented by paper) and included streamers, are also consistent with Shinto ritual.

The construction of the temple begins as this part of the tale is ending. Meanwhile, the shrine is built for the birds, making the symbolic connection between them and *kami*-worship even stronger. Imagine the same tale told from the perspective of people who put *kami*-worship before Buddhism. They might have celebrated the ability of *kami*-worship to survive, albeit altered, despite Buddhist aggression. Surely, the name of the shrine would have been mentioned. The *Konjaku* compilers try to keep the Buddhist perspective dominant since to them the tale is about the founding of Gangōji. But tales have wills of their own. The first part of this tale directs attention to *kami*-worship and its struggle.

SNAKES AND THE BUDDHIST UNDERSTANDING
OF ATTACHMENT

While some snake stories focus on passion or lust (see Chapter 3), others deal also or exclusively with desires that involve the senses but not sex, such as viewing beautiful objects or enjoying fragrances. The snake in them tends to be symbolically associated with deep and often excessive attachments. The yearning for visual, olfactory, tactile, and auditory pleasures shapes thoughts and behaviors. Such tales may initially appear less grotesque than those more sexual, but bodily desires operate within them as well to undermine dominant modes of thought.[66]

In the *Konjaku* tale "How a Woman in Accordance With the Power of the *Lotus Sutra* Changes from the Body of a Snake and Is Born in a Heaven," sexual relations and the reincarnation of a materialistic person as a snake both come into play. This tale follows the Dōjōji Temple tale discussed in Chapter 3, so that when the two are taken as a pair, the focus initially appears to shift from sexual desire leading to rebirth as a snake to avarice resulting in the same outcome. It begins:

> Now it is the past; the capital is in Nara and the reign is of Emperor Shōmu. A certain woman lives in the capital's east side. The emperor summons her because her features and her form are perfectly beautiful and affectionately embraces her for a night. He then places one thousand *ryō* of gold in a round bronze box and gives it to her, probably because she is dear to him.[67] The emperor passes away not long after presenting this [gift] to the woman. Moreover, the woman also dies shortly afterwards. Her last wishes are, "Be certain to bury the one thousand *ryō* in my grave after I die." And so, in accordance with this last request, this round bronze box is buried in her grave with the gold inside it.[68]

The narrator introduces the haunted Iwabuchi Temple in Higashi-yama next. No one who enters it comes out alive before the Kibi minister (Kibi no Makibi, ca. 695–775) visits. A yin-yang diviner, he confronts the lethal spirit, who turns out to be the woman whose corpse has gold buried with it. She explains that she has been unintentionally frightening people to death. Since the minister reacts differently from them, she can tell him of her plight: she was reborn in the body of a poisonous snake guarding the gold at the grave. She asks him to exhume the gold, use half to commission a copying and dedication of the *Lotus Sutra* to release her from her suffering, and to keep half as a reward. To the initial horror of others, the minister digs up the grave and discovers both the snake and the gold. Instead of keeping a portion of the treasure, he spends all of it on the appropriate dedicatory services. Later, the spirit appears in a dream to inform the minister of its release and birth in Tuṣita Heaven.

The woman is initially defined largely in terms of a sexual experience with Emperor Shōmu. While the immediate cause of her rebirth as a snake is her attachment to the gift, she would not have had the treasure without him. However, his role in shaping her fate is never scrutinized. Nor is he judged for using the gold as a personal gift. In a tale with obvious Buddhist intent, the connection of this woman to Emperor Shōmu suggests the physically and emotionally bound side of this politically and spiritually powerful man who elsewhere declares himself "a servant of the Three Treasures."[69] The woman represents the part of him that early Japanese Buddhists would have wanted to downplay. She cannot be degraded in the usual way, however, by turning her sexual desire into an uncontrollable force, malice, or evil, without also implicating Emperor Shōmu since he summons her. Instead, she has the flaw of excessive attachment.

Emperor Shōmu may have seemed too important in Buddhist history to criticize because his reign, from 724 to 749, was a crucial time for the spread of the religion in Japan. The system of national temples was established in 741. As part of this project, government-supported temples were either constructed or created by restoring and converting already existing temples in every province. Labor and materials were also consumed to construct the Great Buddha of Nara at Konkōji, soon to become Konkōmyōji and then Tōdaiji. Gold became of concern when there appeared to be an insufficient amount for gilding the huge statue (which ended up fifty-three and half feet tall and four hundred and fifty-two tons) until it was discovered in Michinoku Province in the spring of 749.[70] The insistence of the woman on having the gold buried with her creates bad karma precisely because hoarding it prevents its use for Buddhist interests. This view of what constitutes gold well spent is reinforced when Makibi, a renowned scholar and diplomat to China who becomes Minister of the Right in 765, spends his reward to finance the dedicatory services. As a figure who serves the interests of the government most of his life, Makibi contrasts sharply with the woman, who withholds her treasure even in death.[71]

Hoarding gold is not always motivated by selfishness. Preceptor Mukū is an exemplary monk who devotes himself to reciting the *nenbutsu*. He secretly stores coins for his funeral expenses above the ceiling of his room because he worries that his disciples will suffer hardship after his death. Unfortunately, he dies before telling anyone.[72] Clearly, he differs from a certain Maniwa Temple monk in another tale, whose greedy attachment to the coins he hoards leads him to instruct his disciples to wait three years until after his death before entering his room.[73] However, both monks are born in the next life as snakes. Only their sizes mark a difference: the Maniwa Temple monk appears large and poisonous whereas Mukū the snake is small and harmless. Neither can progress spiritually until other people find the money and use it for scripture readings.

Snakes can also suggest a clinging to worldly beauty and simple pleasures. In a pair of tales—"How Monk Kōzen of Rokuhara Hears Preaching on the *Lotus Sutra* and Receives Its Benefits" and "How a Girl Who Dies and Is Reborn as a Snake Hears *The Lotus Sutra* and Obtains Release"—the reincarnations of essentially pure-hearted people as snakes reveal a Buddhist perspective on the aristocratic celebration of flowering trees.[74] Both tales also show the protective powers of a Buddhist text or practice.

In the first, monk Kōzen is the official reciter of the scriptures at Rokuhara-Mitsuji, a Tendai branch temple. Over the years, he listens to the preaching of many wise, reputable holy men who visit and preach or lecture. He is an exemplary Buddhist practitioner himself: renouncing secular life, rectifying his deeds, words, and thoughts (*sangyō*), repenting for sins caused by the six consciousnesses (*rokukon*, which includes the five senses and mind consciousness), and dying properly (without doing anything to accumulate negative karma).[75] All expect him to be born in the Pure Land or a Buddhist heaven, but he returns to this world as a three-shaku-long snake. His spirit possesses someone to explain:

> I am the official reciter of scriptures, Kōzen, who lived at this temple. Having regularly listened to explications of the *Lotus Sutra* for many years, my faith was frequently inspired and I prayed for birth in the Pure Land, never neglecting to chant the *nenbutsu*. And so, I had high expectations for the next life, but because of a small pointless thing, I have received the body

of a tiny snake. Here is the reason: during my [human] existence, I planted a mandarin orange tree outside in front of my room and it gradually matured with the passing of the years: its branches grew thick and its leaves flourished, flowers bloomed and it produced fruit. And so, I tended to this tree day and night. From the time it had two leaves until it bore fruit, I always guarded and loved it. Although doing so is not a grave sin, I received the body of small snake in accordance with the wrongdoing of attachment caused by love (*aishu*) and live beneath that tree. I request the favor of having the *Lotus Sutra* copied and services offered for my sake so that I may escape this suffering and be born in a good place."[76]

The birth of Kōzen as a snake is confirmed when the Rokuhara-Mitsuji monks find a snake coiled around the mandarin orange tree. In *Hokkegenki*, these monks see the incident as attesting to the limitless nature of sins accumulated in past lives and lament that someone could become a snake because of such a minor offense. In both versions, they fulfill the request of the spirit. The dream of a priest confirms the consequent birth of Kōzen in the Pure Land. The next morning, that man discovers the snake dead by the tree.

Although the lives of monks and girls are very different, their flaws and fates can be similar. The second tale concerns a beautiful and gentle young girl with talents in calligraphy, poetry, and music. Her loving parents raise her carefully in a picturesque setting with running streams and gorgeous trees. The girl delights in springtime flowers and brilliant autumn leaves and develops a deep appreciation of them. Her one flaw is that she grows too fond of the flowers of the red plum tree, so much that it appears to interfere with other things in her life. When a plum tree planted in front of her room blossoms, she opens her shutters in the early morning to stand alone and gaze at it. Its fragrance keeps her there until night. She does not allow grass to grow beneath it or birds to build nests in its branches. When the petals fall, she collects them and places them in the lid of a lacquered box so that she can continue to enjoy their scent. When the petals finally wilt, she mixes them into incense and continues to savor their perfume for as long as possible.

The girl dies while still infatuated with the plum tree. Because of the intensity of her feelings, she returns to this world as a tiny snake that wraps itself around the lovely tree when it blooms. The poor creature even collects the petals when they fall. Realizing that the snake is the spirit of their daughter, the parents arrange for two monks to perform eight lectures on the *Lotus Sutra* beneath the tree, expounding one fascicle in each as is customary. The snake dies during the fifth lecture, after listening to the preaching on the *Devadatta* chapter of the *Lotus Sutra*, describing how the daughter of the dragon king, the Naga Princess, attains enlightenment. The father later dreams of his daughter. At first, she is dressed in dirty and stained clothes and appears distressed. Then an eminent priest arrives and has her undress, revealing glittering golden skin. He has her dress in magnificent robes and a *kesa* (a Buddhist surplice), whereupon they float away together on a purple cloud. This imagery indicates that she attained birth in the Pure Land.

These stories undermine more than one ideology. To begin, consider the belief that the will and behavior of individuals, especially men, enable them to achieve enlightenment and the privileging of Buddhist practitioners that results. The fate of the official reciter demonstrates that even someone greatly esteemed for his devotion to Buddhism may need a different form of salvation because of a spiritual weakness. The assumption that dedicated monks and priests are likely to achieve *ōjō* is challenged when Kōzen returns as a snake because of a slight, innocuous flaw. The salvation of the girl in the second tale reinforces the move away from depicting a holy man as more likely than others to progress. Her birth in the Pure Land does not depend on anything she thinks or does but on what others do for her spirit, namely copy and dedicate the *Lotus Sutra*.

The inclusion in setsuwa collections of numerous miracle tales focusing on the power of devotional objects such as Amitābha Buddha and the *Lotus Sutra* reflected and contributed to the general trends in Buddhism during the late Heian and early Kamakura periods. The concept of concentrated devotion to a single figure or object is much older, apparent in the teachings of Tanluan (476–542), one of the first Pure Land scholars to devote himself to Amitābha, and elsewhere in Chinese Buddhism. Many tales focused on a particular object of worship appear in Chinese collections such as the *Hongzan fahua zhuan* (*Biographies of People Who Propagate and Honor the Lotus Sutra*, Tang dynasty, 618–907).[77] In Japan, single-practice first shows signs of being widespread in the late Heian period, although concentration on one object appears alongside other meditative practices in Japanese Buddhism before then.

The popularity of focusing on one devotional object is intertwined with the belief in *mappō*: a time when only the Buddhist teaching remains and there is no true practice or attainment of enlightenment. According to the Heian Japanese, the world enters the third stage in the cycle of the true Dharma, the simulated Dharma, and the degeneration of the Dharma from the year 1052. While the first two periods last one thousand years each, in most schemes, *mappō* is ten thousand years of disorder, violence, and moral decay, rendering the attainment of enlightenment impossible for even very devout people.[78] The most anyone can hope for during this time is birth in the Pure Land, where becoming a buddha is relatively easy. There is a gradual shift from an emphasis on the power of the self (*jiriki*) as exercised through strict monastic discipline to the power of a spiritual force outside the self or other (*tariki*), with the interest in *tariki* reaching a new height in the Kamakura period. A greater demand for religious practices suited to people with various occupations and lifestyles arose as Buddhism spread to the general population. The emphasis on relatively simpler forms of devotion simultaneously facilitated that expansion. In the tale of the monk who loves orange blossoms, the potential failure of relying on one's own spiritual practices for attaining a higher rebirth is brought to an extreme since even the chanting of the *nenbutsu* and a chaste lifestyle prove inadequate. Other people must supplement the behavior of the monk by copying the *Lotus Sutra* and holding dedication services to honor it and his spirit.

Since many miracle tales are not grotesque, I will clarify what in the tales about Kōzen and the girl allows us to see them in this way. It is the snake in conjunction with the focus on sensuality. Are the sensual elements in the tales also or mainly sexual? Royall Tyler has suggested that the love of the girl for plum blossoms may allude to her sexual fantasies.[79] If this is true and the plum blossoms are erotic, how do we understand the flowers of the mandarin orange tree in the other story? Should the attachment of a young girl to blossoms be interpreted as any more or less sexual than that of a man? If we assume that the attachment of the monk is also erotic, then would not his sin be graver than hers since he is pursuing enlightenment while she is simply growing up? Why, then, do their similar fates suggest no difference?

By viewing the attachment to flowering trees in either story as an indirect way of addressing sexual fantasies, we may overlook an entire range of human experience in jumping immediately from sensuality to sexuality in our interpretations. The deep attachment to flowering trees suggests a clinging to life and its beauty and an implicit mourning of its inevitable passing. The same can be said of the intimate relations of aristocrats and their constant pursuit of them since they, too, are about more than the physical. The feelings of longing and desire evoked by the flowers resemble those marking relationships.

According to the particular Buddhist perspective in the tales, the love of flowering trees exemplifies attachment, which produces negative karma. This type of admiration and devotion may be under attack because it does not serve a Buddhist purpose. Since flowers and their trees are frequently the subjects of classical poetry, attributing lower rebirths to the celebration of them must be seen not merely as a criticism of the excessive admiration of nature but also of poetry marked by the same interest while "lacking" a concern with the search for Buddhist meaning. Under attack here is *waka* from the early classical period and the values it represents. Only later, in the late twelfth and early thirteenth centuries, do many poets explore the relationship between the pursuits of poetry and enlightenment.[80] Along with the celebrated cherry blossom in classical poetry, plum blossoms, too, evoke the world of Heian aristocrats. How can anyone blame the girl for being mesmerized by these sweet flowers when even Ki no Tsurayuki (?–945) writes about constantly gazing at them and being unable to imagine "when they are alone to fade and scatter."[81] The beauty of this flower, its lovely scent, and the desire to preserve it figure prominently in seventeen consecutive *Kokinshū* poems in "Spring," section one.[82]

In the tale, an appreciation of aristocratic pleasure is embedded in the critical view of it. While the negative judgment turns a precious child into a snake, the association of a plum blossom with a girl is appropriate. This flower is an image of early spring (from the first through the third month)—a sign of things to come—blossoming often in the snow or during a latent period when change occurs mostly beneath the surface. Just as the plum blossom foreshadows the spring in full bloom and particularly the cherry blossom, so too does the beauty and charm of a girl hint at the future woman. To cling to the perfume of the first flowers is to cherish the time when everything is just beginning and full of promise. The desire of the girl to preserve the fragrance of the plum blossoms for as long as possible suggests her attachment to this moment in her development, before maturation spurs her on to a new stage and the outside world makes demands on her. In this sense, the tale has more to do with the relationship of the girl to herself than with future partners (as *fantasy* suggests). The girl dies young, just as the plum blossoms scatter before spring peaks.

The mandarin orange tree is also a sensuous image with its fragrant blossoms and its association to the melodious nightingale in some poems.[83] Its fruit and its flowers are central images in *Ise monogatari* section 60. There, the male protagonist causes a woman to experience painful feelings, perhaps shame, about her lack of constancy. The woman had left the man for someone in another province after he neglected her by spending too much time performing his palace duties. One day, while acting as imperial messenger to the Usa Hachiman Shrine, he discovers that the woman is now the wife of the local official providing him with lodging. After insisting that she pour his wine, he picks up an orange used as a relish and recites a poem about how the fragrance of the orange blossom evokes the scented sleeves of a person he once loved: her. She responds by becoming a nun.[84]

In the *Konjaku* tale as well, the attachment of the monk to the mandarin orange tree points to a lack of constancy. The monk appears to be faithful to Buddhist practice, but the beauty of the tree has swayed his heart. Although he has not abandoned Buddhism as the woman in *Ise monogatari* has the first man, he, too, is motivated by worldly pleasures. Even a slight distraction while reciting the *nenbutsu* before dying can prevent birth in the Pure Land. In one tale, a monk chanting the *nenbutsu* during his final moments begins to worry about who will get a beloved object, a vinegar bottle, after he dies and consequently returns to this world as a small snake inside it.[85] The notion that the chance at salvation can be lost in a single moment (the flip side of the belief that salvation can be achieved instantly) is evident in tales describing the sudden slips of people who have spent years or even lifetimes pursing better rebirths. Such tales demonstrate that devotion can be difficult even for the most dedicated, especially under the pressure of impending death. No wonder the monk who loves the mandarin orange tree needs a backup.

What happens to all the devout Buddhists who err in some spiritual way? The *Lotus Sutra*, copied and offered in dedicatory services for suffering spirits, is the perfect solution. Nor is the power of that sutra reserved for people who have taken vows. The story of the Naga Princess indicates that even a girl can be saved. The tale of the girl captivated by plum blossoms adds another dimension to that possibility: whereas the daughter of the dragon king is a wise, spiritually active being who offers a precious gem to the Buddha, the girl born as a snake does not even have Buddhism on her mind. With interests in calligraphy, poetry, music, and flowers, she could be the young daughter of any aristocrat.

WILD BOARS AND RACCOON DOGS:
FEARS AND VISIONS

While we expect Buddhists to struggle with sexual desire and material attachments, the impediment to spiritual development discussed in this section is somewhat surprising. How do people aiming for enlightenment or the Pure Land prevent that yearning from becoming a form of attachment? Is there such a thing as wanting to reach the next stage too much, so that zealousness becomes an obstacle in itself? As it turns out, Buddhists can long too much for spiritual growth or a sign of it. In "How the Holy Man of Mt. Atago Is Tricked by a Wild Boar," a deluded Buddhist monk tries either too hard or in the wrong way, rendering him vulnerable to an animal spirit while a sensible hunter cannot be fooled. The same reversal takes place in a nearly identical *Uji shūi* tale, "How a Hunter Shoots a Bodhisattva."[86]

In both, the holy man of Mt. Atago has been devoted to the sutras, particularly the *Lotus Sutra*, for a very long time. He never even leaves his quarters, but survives because a hunter comes periodically to supply him with food and other necessities. Yet, in *Konjaku*, the narrator tells us that, "lacking wisdom, he has never studied scripture."[87]

One day, the holy man exclaims to the hunter, "Recently, something truly hallowed has been occurring! Perhaps it is because I have been wholeheartedly revering the *Lotus Sutra* for many years, but recently Samantabhadra Bodhisattva (Fugen) has been appearing nightly. Stay here tonight and do reverence to him." A boy servant also tells the hunter that he, too, has seen the Bodhisattva. Sure enough, that very night when the hunter is watching, Samantabhadra arrives riding his white elephant.

Suspicious, the hunter reasons to himself that while one would expect a holy man to see such a thing after numerous years of dedication to the *Lotus Sutra*, it is strange that the Bodhisattva appears also to him and the servant. As the holy man prostrates himself in front of the manifestation, the hunter shoots the seemingly sacred visitor in the chest with an arrow. The spirit proves to be a fraud: the next morning they find a dead wild boar near the very site of its appearance. The commentator concludes: "And so, a person with no wisdom will be deceived in this way even if he is a holy man. Although the hunter mainly commits sins, he is able to shoot and expose the wild boar because of good judgment," and finally "Beasts of this sort deceive people in this way. However, they are killed and their deaths have no value. And so the story is told and passed down."[88]

Central to this tale is a reversal of what would normally be expected from a holy man and a hunter. Their reactions to the illusion generated by the animal spirit weakens assumptions about these types of people in the common-sense version of the Buddhist worldview. People would figure on a dedicated holy man being wiser and spiritually more advanced than a hunter. The tale may have also kept the religious, especially those not affiliated with large

Buddhist institutions, humble about their spiritual growth. Excessive confidence is a great danger for people who have practiced Buddhism for years and gained the respect of others. Like the holy man of Mt. Atago, others, too, might fail to examine what appear to be signs of success. It takes someone like the hunter, with no emotional investment in those signs, to reveal their emptiness. The discerning power of the hunter underscores the gullibility of the holy man, whose very desire for the affirmation of his spiritual progress makes him susceptible to evil spirits and delusions.

Oddly, the hunter uses violence to confirm his suspicion about the false bodhisattva. How can we explain that the dispelling of an illusion in this tale, included in a Buddhist section of *Konjaku*, entails killing? Here as in the tale of the tiny hand discussed in Chapter 2, the arrow is an instrument of truth. Tales generally suggest that the destruction of forces considered evil is acceptable and necessary. The attack of the hunter protects not only against the evil spirit but also against the misdirected devotion of the holy man.

Similarly, what do we make of the fact that the person who sees through deception violates the Buddhist precept against killing nearly daily through his livelihood? The hunter clearly has as much potential for spiritual advancement as the holy man, perhaps more. Although he is not seeking a higher rebirth, the move toward equalizing the hunter and the holy man evokes the protagonists of *akunin ōjōden* or stories of people born into the Pure Land despite a lifetime of acting against the precepts. As Jacqueline Stone discusses in *Original Enlightenment and the Transformation of Medieval Japanese Buddhism*, hunters and warriors are thought to violate Buddhist precepts because of their karma, but the accumulation of more negative karma does not necessarily prevent them from being saved. When such people focus on the *nenbutsu* or a similar devotional object, even in their last moments, they are as likely as devout, seasoned Buddhists to be born in the Pure Land or a heaven. Furthermore, the beliefs that all people have the potential for salvation or enlightenment and that negative karma is not necessarily an obstacle to a positive rebirth are the essence of original enlightenment thought (*hongaku shisō*).[89] By the time *Konjaku* was compiled, this concept had already existed in Japan for several centuries. Its introduction to Japanese Buddhism is associated with the founder of Tendai Buddhism, Saichō (767–822). However, the tales would have been preserved in the collection only at the very beginning of its extensive development in Japan and may have been in circulation a while before then.[90] At least, the idea of *hongaku shisō* had not yet been spread to the general population when the tale was first told or recorded. The narrative suggests that hunters and perhaps others viewed themselves as fundamentally different from those leading religious lives. It then undermines this widely accepted view by demonstrating that someone who dedicates his life to Buddhism does not necessarily have more knowledge or greater spiritual depth than a person who does not.

We can easily imagine how the hunter with his respect for the holy man, his clarity of thought, and his decisiveness, might even turn to Buddhism before facing death. Yet, ironically, it is he who distinguishes between Buddhist practitioners and others by viewing himself and the boy, in contrast to the holy man, as undeserving of a mystical vision. That understanding prevents him from being deceived. Even as the tale undermines the view of holy men as spiritually superior to other people, it continues to support the notion of difference by suggesting that someone without the proper training and a pious heart would not normally experience a true vision. Moreover, blind devotion is insufficient here; a monk deserving of respect also studies Buddhist texts.

The mention of Mt. Atago allows for this contradictory proposition. Located in northwestern Kyoto, the mountain was a sacred site for mountain asceticism or Shugendō. The association of a deluded monk with this location reflects the critical stance of many Buddhists affiliated with institutions toward the mountain asceticism of unaffiliated practitioners. Setsuwa often suggest that affiliated monks were on the lookout for charlatans among the mountain ascetics (*hijiri*) despite their appropriation of many elements of Shugendō. Since other tales praise men associated with mountain asceticism and portray Mt. Atago as a legitimate place for religious seclusion, the issue appears to be not mountain asceticism per se but the abuses of it.[91]

Tengu come to be associated with this mountain as they do with mountain ascetics, but probably after the compilation of *Konjaku*.[92] In perhaps the earliest example, Fujiwara no Yorinaga (1120–56) mentions a Mt. Atago tengu in his diary, *Taiki* (*Diary of the Minister of the Left*, 1136–56).[93] *Konjaku* tales about tengu in Book 20 do not refer to the mountain. However, they share with the story about the holy man and the hunter a similar concern with false Buddhist visions and the susceptibility of monks to them. The mountain will eventually belong to tengu tales, but here it acts instead as a pivot, introducing us to a related spirit: the *kusainaki*.

Although kusainaki is written with the Chinese characters for wild or field (*no*) and boar (*inoshishi*), scholars are unsure what animal it indicates: a boar, raccoon dog (*tanuki*), or something else. In the *Uji shūi* version of the Mt. Atago tale, the creature is a tanuki, not a kusainaki. That tale is the first extant setsuwa showing a tanuki in a Japanese setting; tanuki are absent from "The Tales of Japan" in *Konjaku*. Consequently, one theory holds that *kusainaki* is an older term for tanuki. However, I stick to "wild boar" because the oldest extant manuscripts of the early tenth-century dictionary *Wamyō ruiju shō* state that the kusainaki resembles a domestic pig. It has a small stomach, long legs, and dark yellowish red or brown fur, travels in groups, and is hunted.[94]

Kusainaki are dense, reckless, and unworthy of awe. While they succeed in frightening and tricking people, they are inevitably killed and exposed in animal form. The *Konjaku* commentator disdains these creatures as scoundrels who pointlessly lose their lives. Yet, close readings of tales reveal that the doltishness of these spirit beasts is instrumental in the creation of psychological and spiritual meaning.

Not all wild boars are stupid or evil. The sacred boar in the earliest literature and histories suggests a link between kusainaki and *inoshishi* (pronounced *i* in the ancient texts). In the *Kojiki*, the deity of Mt. Ibuki has the form of a white boar. Its nature is violent, causing the death of the heroic Yamato-takeru-no-mikoto, who had pacified unruly deities and people in the outlying regions for the emperor.[95] Sacred but fierce boars written with the characters for *kusainaki* appear in *Shūi ōjōden* to assist the monk Gensan, mentioned in the Chapter 5 as an abandoned baby. He wishes to create a hall for Buddhist practice at Yoshimine on the mountain Nishiyama, but the rocky cliffs are too difficult to level. One night, following an auspicious dream, several thousand wild boars appear and dig out the spot for the hall, which, according to other texts, becomes a temple, Yoshimine Temple.[96] These spirit creatures are clearly deities. The divine wild boar could have easily developed into a demonic spirit since its aggressive nature and strength are apparent even in its depiction as gods.

The creatures in tales 34, 35, and 36 of *Konjaku* Book 27 only torment people.[97] The first of these stories, "How a Man Shoots and Exposes a Wild Boar after Having a Name Called," introduces two brothers. The elder sometimes hunts using a pine torch to attract deer. When the animals stare fascinated at the light, hunters aim at the reflection in their eyes. Many shoot from their horses, placing the torch in a holder attached to the saddle so that their hands are free for the bow and arrow.[98] One night, a gruff voice calls the name of the elder brother as he rides. It comes from his right side, but he cannot shoot at it because he holds his bow with the left hand. By the time he turns around, puts the torch in its holder, and prepares to aim, the voice is silent. The creature harasses him for several nights, calling only when the hunter is in the wrong position to send an arrow in its direction.

Finally, the younger brother offers to help by taking the place of the man. He realizes that the creature is dull-witted on his first night out because it continues to call out the name of his brother. "A true demonic spirit (*onigami*) would call out my name, but it still calls out yours," he explains.[99] The next night, after hearing the voice, the younger brother dismounts, changes the direction of the saddle, and mounts backwards. The bow and torch are then opposite where they would be normally. Sure enough, the creature foolishly calls out the name of the elder brother when the younger brother is positioned to attack. The next morning, the men discover the carcass of a wild boar pinned to a tree with the arrow of the younger brother. The commentator points out that "this kind of fellow loses his life pointlessly because he tries to deceive people,"[100] just as in the Mt. Atago tale, with slightly different wording. Since the Chinese character referring to the creature, *mono* 者, can refer to humans, the warning against tricking people for amusement is clearly aimed at people. Those who cause harm without a reason are low in the order of malignant beings. In addition, the story of a wise younger brother reverses the hierarchy of elder and younger brother, which generally privileges the elder. A younger brother outdoes his older brother in the next tale as well, but the commentator there is understandably critical of him.

The second and third tales about wild boars share a concern with human corpses. While ultimately serving as a means of acknowledging and undermining forces of death, these creatures embody a fear of human remains. In both stories, the haunting spirit is conquered and proven unworthy of awe.

How a Wild Boar Who Emits Light While Visiting Corpses Is Killed

Now it is the past; there are two men who are brothers in the district of [ ] , the province of [ ]. Both are brave and sensible.

It happens that their parents die, so they place the bodies in coffins and close the covers, then put the coffins in a small, separate room. Since there is still considerable time before the funeral, the coffins remain there for a number of days, during which one person reports having faintly seen something: "Something shines around midnight in the place where those dead people are lying! It's weird," he says.

In response to this, the brothers say in unison, "Could it be that the dead turned into a spirit or creature and is shining? Or else a creature may have come to the place of the dead. If that's the case, let's somehow expose it."

The younger brother says to the elder brother, "When I make a noise, you light a torch, then be sure to bring it in very quickly." And so, together they agree on a plan. When night falls, the younger brother goes quietly beside the coffins and places their covers upside down. He lies on top of the inside cover of one, naked and with his hair freed from its topknot, his sword hidden near his body. Later, he thinks it must be midnight and quietly opens his eyes a crack. Something shines on the ceiling.

It shines twice, and then breaks through the ceiling and descends. The younger brother cannot see what it is because he does not open his eyes wide. Apparently large, it reaches the wooden floor with a thud. Meanwhile, there is a deep blue glow.

This thing grasps the top of the coffin where the younger brother lies and is about to place it aside. Seizing the opportunity, the younger brother embraces [the creature] tightly against himself and screams loudly, "I got it! Hey!" Then he thrusts his sword up to its hilt into what he thinks is the side of the creature. The glow immediately extinguishes. At that moment, the older brother lights the torch right away and brings it in. The younger brother looks, still holding the creature close to himself. He is tightly embracing a hairless wild boar, dead, having been pierced in the side with the sword. Upon seeing this, the deep shock of the younger brother is fathomless.

When we reflect on what happened, the heart of the younger brother who lay on top of a coffin seems very gruesome. It is said that "there are always demons where the dead lie," but it seems truly unreal that someone would have the pluck to lie down in that way. The younger brother was probably relieved to discover that the creature was in fact a wild boar, but, before then, he must have thought it was definitely a demon. There are always people who will light torches and come quickly. And wild boars are scoundrels who pointlessly lose their lives.

So the story is told and passed down.[101]

Here again, the wild boar is an easily conquered creature that frightens people for no apparent reason, sacrificing its own life in the process. If we see creatures as embodiments of human fears, then their challenges to people—here leading a man to lie with the dead or death—may not be as pointless as the *Konjaku* commentator imagines. If a person can remain close to corpses and the spirits attracted by them and emerge triumphant, then perhaps they are not very dangerous after all. What initially appears to be a demon might be only something foolish.

As the commentator suggests, the behavior of the younger brother is unusual. While many people would be willing to assist someone confronting a supernatural creature by lighting a torch at the right moment, few would dare seeking such an encounter themselves. Read another way, many people would rather live with their fears than confront them. They prefer holding the light that clarifies things for other people to revealing the truth for themselves. Indeed, wild boar spirits or similarly invisible creatures—imagined threats—cause people to be anxious and fearful. Perhaps many of these fears could be easily destroyed were people brave enough to face them (even cautiously, with half-closed eyes). Only then could the creatures be attacked and reduced to, say, dead animals.

The fear of corpses is also apparent in "How Someone Kills a Wild Boar in Inamino, Harima Province." The story takes its audiences beyond the room used as a morgue in the previous tale to a funeral and graveyard. A professional courier traveling from the western provinces to the capital finds himself at nightfall in a desolate field with no sign of human life and without a place to lodge. He stays in an empty hut used for guarding the crops during harvest. In the middle of the night, a crowd of mourners and priests with lit torches approach, ringing bells and chanting the *nenbutsu*. To his horror, a funeral is about to be held right beside the hut. He remains still and quiet, deciding that he will simply explain who he is and why he is there should the people discover him. That the site has not been previously prepared, marked for use as a grave in accordance with the custom, strikes him as odd. This observation raises the possibility that the funeral and its participants are not human.

The funeral ends after numerous servants build a grave mound and place a Buddhist grave marker (*sotoba*) on it. The man grows even more terrified with the crowd gone, as now he is alone beside the fresh grave. Something seems to move at first, and then finally a huge naked human form emerges from the earth, blowing and brushing at flames burning his body, and charges toward the hut. Assuming the creature is a flesh-eating demon, the man draws his sword, springs out from the hut and kills it. He runs a long way to a village, where he crouches by the gate of a house in fear until morning. After he tells his story to the villagers, a group of the boldest young men go with him to investigate, but they find neither grave nor grave marker. There are no ashes anywhere. What they do find is a huge slain boar. According to the commentator, the boar saw the man enter the hut and wanted to give him a scare. Everyone criticizes the boar as a scoundrel who dies for the sake of doing something pointless. Also included in the final remarks is a warning against staying in empty fields, similar to many warnings in *Konjaku* regarding uninhabited places. The courier himself is said to have passed the story down once he arrived in the capital.[102]

The man is afraid of being in the wrong place at the wrong time. What could be more socially stressful than arriving at an extremely solemn event where one does not belong: at a funeral where one knows neither who died nor the mourners. The horror of burial grounds and of being close to a fresh grave in the middle of the night resembles the fear of the corpse in the coffin. Finally, if night can be unsettling now, it must have been especially frightening when there was no electricity. Indeed, premodern Japanese people imagined that creatures appear generally at twilight and night.

The human form emerging from the grave represents the culmination of these fears. Naked and consumed by flames and evoking depictions of people on fire in *Scroll of Hells*, this representation suggests exposure and consuming pain: extreme vulnerability.[103] Why else would the monster from the grave have a human form? The wild boar seems to create the strange funeral. However, the ceremony can also be seen as partially generated by the imagination of the man. It would not have taken place without him and his anxieties; the boar frightens people by giving a concrete form to whatever already haunts them (to the demons of the heart). These animal spirits sacrifice themselves so that people can see the folly of their own fears; their doltishness is that of the protagonists.

The mischievous tanuki also play seemingly pointless tricks. Four stories in the "Henge" ("Metamorphoses") section of *Kokon chomonjū* show how they disrupt lives by haunting important places: the palace of a princess, an old temple, the house of a minister, and a pond used by hunters.[104] Each focuses on the confrontation with and conquering of the creature. For example, when tanuki cause rains of pebbles to mysteriously fall on people in the mansion of the Minister of the Right, the people frighten them away by preparing a feast with other tanuki. They throw the bones left after their meal against an old earthen wall, warning the creatures that they, too, will be eaten if they do not stop.[105] Of particular interest is "How the Provincial Governor of Satsuma, Nakatoshi, Catches a Transformed Creature at the Old Pond on Mt. Minase," because the creature in that tale has a purpose. Many hunters try to kill the water birds flocking in great numbers around a pond on Mt. Minase, but instead end up dead themselves. A certain Minamoto no Nakatoshi, a personal imperial guard of Retired Emperor Go-Toba (1180–1239, r. 1183–98) serving at his palace on the Minase River, defeats the lethal spirit. He and a young attendant wait by the water one night until it grows late. When the spirit appears as an unidentifiable glowing object, Nakatoshi is unable to hit it with an arrow. It approaches him only after he draws his sword, whereupon he sees in the light the grinning face of an old woman. He drops his sword and seizes the creature. It tries to drown him by pulling him into the pond, but he ultimately draws his dagger and stabs it. The light goes out, whereupon a dead tanuki lies at his feet.[106]

Linked to the animal kingdom itself, the creature lashes out against hunters to avenge the dead birds and prevent additional slayings. Although *Kokon chomonjū* does not have a Buddhist scheme, the rage at the hunters coincides with the Buddhist precept against taking life. However, the dominant perspective in the story suggests that a counterattack against an aggressor of privileged status, here a personal imperial guard of a retired emperor, is unacceptable. Set against this ideology, the face of an old woman is poignant, evoking someone who is relatively defenseless in a world of men with weapons. Why does it take this face to look squarely at the hunter? The desire of the spirit to protect the birds enables her to drown many men, but that power cannot last. What the hunter sees is the face of the vulnerable fighting for its own existence. However, he sees it as malice and death.

TENGU AND THE ART OF ILLUSION

Tengu usually appear in late Heian and early Kamakura period setsuwa as the cause of disturbances, delusions, and temptations that prevent Buddhists from birth in the Pure Land or enlightenment.[107] As potential obstacles to transcendence, they share something in common with Buddhist representations of women, but tengu in setsuwa rarely impersonate women or rely on sexual powers. They have more in common with animal spirits than *oni* since they often appear as kites, a lightly built predatory bird in the hawk family. The Chinese characters used to write tengu (*tiangou* in Chinese) literally mean "celestial dog," thereby tying this creature to both the heavens and animals. Chinese precedents of the creature suggest meteors or comets whose shape is perceived as canine.[108] In some texts, including the *Shanhai jing* (*The Classic of Mountains and Seas*, third century B.C.E. to second century C.E.), a *tiangou* resembles a raccoon dog but has a white neck.[109] The development of this animal spirit in the Japanese context results in new creatures that nonetheless retain mysterious and magical qualities.

As previously mentioned, the tengu frequently uses the spiritual longing of people against them. In a *Jikkinshō* tale, on which a noh play *Dai-e* (*The Great Service*, fifteenth century) is based, a seventy-year-old monk from Mt. Hiei longs for concrete manifestations of Buddhist truth.[110] The monk first trades his fan with boys for the release of an old kite they are about to kill. Shortly after, an odd-looking monk approaches him and thanks him for saving his life. The man, whose form as a kite and then a monk reveals his identity as a tengu, offers to use his magical powers in expression of his gratitude. Desiring nothing worldly, the Hiei monk asks the tengu to simulate the scene of Śākyamuni preaching Buddhist law on Vulture Peak (Gṛdhrakūṭa). The magical monk agrees to grant this wish, but only after the first monk promises not to worship the false image. The scene turns out to be so magnificent—with its purple lapis lazuli ground, sacred trees, bodhisattvas, disciples, gods, kings, rains of flowers, lovely fragrance, and the Buddha—that the Hiei monk loses control. Overwhelmed, he prostrates himself and chants before the fabricated Buddha. The scene suddenly vanishes and the Hiei monk finds himself alone on the mountainside, as if awakening from a dream. Later, he encounters the tengu monk again and is chastised for breaking the vow. The tengu is angry because guardians of the Buddhist law have punished him for deceiving a true believer, breaking his wing and stripping him of his powers.[111]

Why is a true believer vulnerable? The appearance of the tengu can be understood as a response to the misdirected yearning of the pious monk, which would have already been inhibiting his spiritual development. After the Hiei monk saves the kite, we are told that he ponders how he is accumulating great merit and positive karma. Despite his commitment to Buddhism, he seems a bit too focused on his achievements and the consequent reward. Baba compares the fabricated scene of the Buddha on Vulture Peak in this setsuwa to the attempt by aristocrats to create the Pure Land on earth through the construction of magnificent structures such as the famous Phoenix Hall of Byōdōin Temple at Uji and the lavish, intoxicating religious ceremonies that Heian aristocrats held within them. Among other things, the tale criticizes that style of aristocratic Buddhism and the clergy who support it. She sees within the story a challenge of art to religion, observing that the old monk is at last able to experience selfless religious exultation (bōga no hōetsu), if only momentarily, through the gift of the tengu. Art or fabricated images allow him (and other people) to leap suddenly away from mundane life and beyond the self. The problem with this kind of experience is that it is inevitably followed by disillusionment.[112] But does it have to be? It is equally possible that an experience of transcendence, however brief or false, might deepen the desire for true and permanent enlightenment. We can only imagine what the monk feels after his awakening on the isolated mountainside or when encountering the tengu a second time. Did his disappointment with "art"—the magic of the tengu—crush his spirit? Or did it deepen his religious conviction?

Another monk might have refused the gift of the tengu or been able to see the false vision more objectively. Deeply longing for any glimpse of the Buddha, the monk himself asks for a fabrication of a holy moment. Why? Many people resemble this man from Mt. Hiei. We have only fabricated images through which we can hope to rise above our mundane lives—things such as art, literature, and music (tengu magic)—and our moments of exultation are consequently short. Returning to the same, ordinary existence, we are disappointed, disillusioned, or plagued by a continual sense of yearning. This tale suggests that many people in Heian and medieval Japan had a similar experience. It speaks to the majority, who are not going to make it to the Pure Land this time around.

CONCLUSION

The behaviors and functions of various animal spirits overlap with each other and with those of *oni*. Moreover, sometimes one creature can be exchanged for another in a tale without altering its plot. Yet, as the subsections of this chapter highlight, each type of animal spirit has idiosyncrasies affecting its role as a grotesque representation.

Fox spirits in setsuwa remind people of the permeability of human realms and the fragility of privilege and power. They are likely to escape, allowing for the possibility of further upset. Despite having a trickster-like quality, they sometimes compromise their assaults by respecting tradition and authority. Even the most convincing speakers run in the opposite direction when a demon appears, but foxes resemble certain ghosts in that it is often possible to reason with them. Most truly ruthless behavior on their part stems from the desire for revenge. More commonly, mutual affection marks the bonds of people and foxes. Unlike demons who impersonate women to attack men, fox spirits move hearts and shape lives. They are dedicated lovers and wives, so men continue to feel affection for them even after discovering their vulpine identities. The happy and passionate moments men and fox spirits share almost seem to make the potentially fatal attachment worthwhile.

Whereas foxes can become emotionally close to humans, monkeys have human-like emotions. With natural similarities to humans exaggerated, they mirror men in their attachments and cruelty. In the two tales about the subjugation of evil monkey gods, the demand for a sacrificial girl suggests strife between humans: a symbolic cannibalism. That strife concerns the local traditions that interfere with efforts of the aristocratic government toward centralization politically and culturally. The secular prevails over the religious in both tales, even in the second when a monk is the protagonist. The story of a man walking through a waterfall into another life can be read as an escape fantasy of a weary holy man. Sexual and emotional bonds to the designated human sacrifice energize him along with his counterpart in the other story.

While the birds in the tale about the zelkova tree are unusual as animal spirits, they function together with other representations in a grotesque mode to demonstrate how *kami*-worship resists and shapes Buddhism despite its appropriation. Trees in Japan have grotesque aspects from ancient through at least medieval times. They are physical bodies, suggesting femaleness, with holes and spaces that produce and harbor life. Yet, they are also the sites and causes of death. Since they are associated with gods and buddhas as well as with the human body, distinctions between the spiritual and material are collapsed in their representations. The spiritual essence of the zelkova tree survives after the tree is destroyed, but it is compromised in the form of the birds who find new life as worshipped beings in the shrine built for them.

The stories about snakes were concerned with the gratification of the senses and attachment. Rebirth as a snake is caused by clinging to objects and worldly beauty. Even a monk who hoards gold to enable his disciples to pay for his funeral becomes a snake, as can other people with good intentions. In the tales about people who love trees too much, storytellers use Buddhist values to undermine the aristocratic attachment to flowers while also exhibiting an appreciation of it. One story alludes to the lack of constancy of a monk in his devotion while another to the adherence of a girl to her prepubescent self. Both setsuwa undermine the idea that pious individuals have an advantage through practice and devotion in attaining birth in the Pure Land. They foreshadow future trends in Japanese Buddhism such as the increased emphasis on the potential of everyone to achieve that goal.

The story about the hunter and holy man similarly subverts the traditional privileging of monks by giving the hunter the clearest vision and the courage to expose the fake bodhisattva through violence. It does not entirely resolve the ideological problems created by this type of subversion. The creature in that tale, kusainaki, is considered stupid and unworthy of awe. However, through seemingly pointless acts, wild boars express larger concerns about human vulnerability and mortality. The holy man is susceptible to illusions because of his confidence and nowhere is terror better expressed than in the human form emerging from the grave in flames. The face of the old woman generated by the tanuki at the pond on Mt. Minase also represents human frailty. The effort of this creature to defend water birds and its initial success demonstrate a pugnacious refusal of the weak to succumb to the strong.

The last tale demonstrates how tengu can respond to the longing of people, as did the wild boar in the tale of the hunter and the holy man. However, tengu have magical abilities. Considered evil from a Buddhist perspective, their powers can offer a temporary experience of transcending mundane life, just like art or music.

Animal spirits in setsuwa correspond to animals in nature (as even tengu are associated with kites), but their animal bodies are rarely central to the narratives. Monkeys are the exceptions, but representations of them are an effective means of commenting on human behavior precisely because they resemble us. In many stories involving animal spirits, something frightening or mysterious occurs when the animal is in human form, whether in full or in part (as with a human voice or face.) Moreover, exposing the being as an animal (usually by killing it) destroys the threat. An animal spirit is viewed as a mere animal if killed or a lesser spirit if it survives. Its temporary power usually lies not in its ability to transform per se, but in its materializing in a way bringing it closer to human. The snakes in the stories discussed above do not shift into human form, but were people before and can appear in dreams or otherwise make their need for help known. Other animal spirits respond intimately to the emotions of people, particularly to fear and various types of longing. In contrast to demons, who seem to have a second realm somewhere, animals always share the world with humans. In setsuwa, they may be more easily conquered and less respected (if not loved), but they also seem to know people better.[113]

Conclusion

The grotesque appears in numerous, diverse forms because different cultures (and the same cultures at different times) have their own understandings of what constitutes such things as authority or the center, beauty, and normalcy. Ideas about humor and fear also change and shape it accordingly. The possibility of the dissolution of the familiar world and of the self (that is, of complete estrangement) as described by Kayser, probably would not have occurred to most people before the twentieth century.[1] Similarly, if the frescos of the Domus Aurea were discovered today, would they change the way we think about art and literature? The study of the grotesque outside Western contexts also demonstrates the role of culture in determining how the mode of representation is manifested in specific creatures, objects, or events.

What distinguishes the grotesque in setsuwa from its European counterparts is its relationship to Buddhism and other Asian religions. Moreover, in contrast to a grotesque that opposes Greek and Roman ideas about the classical, the grotesque in setsuwa supplements the sense of beauty apparent in Japanese poetry and in *Genji* and other Japanese classics in which language regarding the body or bodily functions tends to be absent or indirect.

In setsuwa marked by the grotesque, bizarre events center on the bodies of humans and non-human creatures, isolating and exaggerating individual parts and processes.

The grotesque representations in setsuwa tales embody the tensions between individuals and groups competing for power as well as between the dominant and the suppressed. These tensions result from such things as conflicting ideologies, goals, lifestyles, ambitions, and dreams. The triumph of one group usually means the defeat of another in classical and medieval Japanese contexts in contrast to the equalizing effect of the carnival perceived by Bakhtin. Hierarchies are frequently suspended or partially collapsed in the tales, but they are seldom completely destroyed.

As discussed in the Introduction, the grotesque is a mode of representation centered on the body and bodily realities that exaggerates features, blurs already indistinct boundaries, marks the world as constantly transforming and unfinished, debases, often combines the absurd (or funny) and the fearful, and both sustains and supports authority. The concept of setsuwa, which is examined in Chapter 1, emerged with multiple meanings. In the past and sometimes even still, scholars have spent much energy attempting to provide a single neat definition for somewhat heterogeneous narratives. This effort made sense when the field of setsuwa studies was relatively new, but now we best avoid falling into the endless trap of the question "what is setsuwa?" where someone will always come along with another incomplete answer. Little scholarly attention was given to the stories themselves until recently, perhaps because they initially seem transparent. Setsuwa are often richer than they appear at a glance. A fruitful way of learning about them is to identify and study characteristics of groups of tales, and to look closely at the narratives, concentrating on details. Theories of the grotesque—those of Ruskin, Kayser, Harpham, and especially Bakhtin among others that are modified and used with sensitivity to the Japanese cultural and historical contexts—provide a way of grappling with the meanings of certain bizarre and extraordinary representations. At the same time, those representations show us how the grotesque can be subtle, working with a force that erodes rather than immediately destroys.

The magical body parts acting apart from bodies studied in Chapter 2 oppose and topple people. Personal ambition and larger political power struggles intersect and the agents of change prove as vulnerable as the things they change. The story of the toppling of a Chinese king would have been relevant to the social and political situation in Japan during the Heian and

Kamakura periods in its concern with the fall of existing power and the spiritual forces behind that decrowning. In the setsuwa of the beckoning hand, Takaakira exemplifies the aristocrats whose social and political potential was destroyed by the northern branch Fujiwara. However, the use of the arrow to subdue the spirit suggests the vulnerability of the Fujiwara themselves to the forces of change. The tale of the disappearing penises similarly concerns rivalry that comes up again in other tales: the capital versus the provinces, Buddhist versus non-Buddhist practice, and the competition of individual men. The story addresses tensions humorously in terms of male sexual desire and a spoof about pursuing an esoteric art.

The tale in Chapter 3 involving the radish emphasizes the power of semen and its relationship to karma as well as the invasive power of men over women. Although male procreative energy transcends the body of the individual and acts independently, the behavior and decisions of the man still shape the outcome of events. The girl is sexually mature, but the story excludes her from sex and its pleasures. Ambivalent descriptions of female bodies appear in the tale of Empress Somedono and her demon lover as well, but there the representations also reveal attitudes toward the public sphere. The tale raises questions about the political boundaries and subversive potential manifested in the bodies of elite women. The stories of the abduction by Ariwara no Narihira of Fujiwara no Takaiko touch on a similar issue, with the struggle of one man against Fujiwara dominance again coming into play. Somedono and Takaiko demonstrate how certain women can disturb the order of society by either complying with or actively pursuing agents of social and political change, thereby undermining the men of their own household and lineage. The tales also show the need of others to portray possible infractions on the part of influential women as involuntary by casting doubt on their emotional and intellectual soundness or by portraying them as victims.

In addition, the grotesque can be connected to disease. Both the portrayal of a woman sexually satisfied by a demon and the illness "demon intercourse" figure in the effort to suppress female sexual pleasure. Setsuwa rarely acknowledge a side of female sexuality independent from men or male creatures or animals; depictions of female autoeroticism and lesbianism are almost non-existent, contrasting with the frequent inclusion of male autoeroticism and homosexuality. Given that the disease suggests at one level sexual fantasy and masturbation, the threat to men of women becoming inflicted with demon intercourse may lie in its failure to affirm the centrality and dominance of the male body. In contrast, representations of female bodies as sites of confrontation between men reveal the privileging of the male body. The tale describing how Retired Emperor Uda and the ghost of Tōru compete for access to a Fujiwara woman exemplifies this tendency by alluding to the competition between members of the imperial family.

For male Buddhists, the female body could be a site of internal conflict because of the precept forbidding sex. The valuing of sexual play by aristocrats in Heian Japan was at odds with the Buddhist demand for chastity, exacerbating the struggle for many religious men. The tale of a monk dreaming of a woman while a snake satisfies him depicts sexual pleasure in a revolting way, but it also affirms it. The Dōjōji tale ambivalently challenges some aspects of the negative attitudes toward women in Buddhism by holding the man partially accountable for his fate. However, the woman driven by sexual desire remains a factor in his regressive rebirth. The first tale relies on overt sexual representations whereas the second tale alludes to sexual elements and the womb entirely through other representations, such as the snake and the bell.

As addressed in Chapter 4, terrifying elements have a place in the premodern Japanese grotesque. *Oni* stand out as the dominant monsters in setsuwa, although many are humorous and musical. They do not usually have cataclysmic effects on large numbers of people in tales, but act instead over time. In particular, consumption of humans by demons affirms the underdogs of society and decrowns politically dominant people. Figuratively speaking, one body takes another into itself, as when certain individuals and groups are absorbed into a social and political system supporting the dominance of others. Such representations are linked to certain myths and forms of *kami*-worship. The consumption of women by demons frequently directs our attention to struggles between men. Or, it can simply suggest threats: tale collections and histories alike mention incidents involving the presence of demons on or near the palace grounds. The attacks address the vulnerability of the government without directly acknowledging the role of human conflict in it.

In two versions of one tale analyzed in Chapter 4, a demon consumes a young woman on what should be her wedding night. Prefaced by an omen in the form of a popular song (*waza-uta*), the *Nihon ryōiki* tale is at one level an attempt to discredit mountain ascetics unaffiliated with government-sanctioned institutions. It also manifests the hostility of the mountain ascetics toward people associated with the government. Both versions suggest tension between local inhabitants and the provincial elite who have close cultural and political ties to the capital. Flesh-eating demons can often be associated with sacrifice understood metaphorically as the concepts of subordinating certain groups to others and of giving up or losing something for a greater good. The sexualizing of violence in this setsuwa is related to the concept of human sacrifice since the woman must die to satisfy a spirit or a power such as karma. The violence is also linked to aristocratic marriage practices that strengthened some families while weakening others. In this sense, attacks by demons in setsuwa often voice the resentment of less powerful families both in the capital and the provinces. Women from the northern branch Fujiwara were most vulnerable because their families used the strategy most effectively.

However, in the *Konjaku* rendering of the abduction by Narihira, a force larger than any aristocrat, perhaps that of the retired emperors or the rise of the warrior, triumphs. Similarly, the relative decline in the power of the aristocrats and the imperial house is apparent in the tale, treated in Chapter 5, of the Agi Bridge demon. There, the act of a demon blocking the Agi Bridge hints at the rise of the warrior class: protectors of the aristocrats who begin to claim for themselves parts of the realms they guard.

As discussed in the last part of Chapter 4, demons affirm authority figures while challenging them. Even when portrayed as coming from outside the capital or Japan, demons should not be viewed as the antithesis of social and political order because they help to define it. People who can conquer demons are superior and worthy of leadership positions, as illustrated by the tale of Sōkara in the land of *rākṣasas* and the *Ōkagami* account of how Tadahira confronts a demon. In addition, struggles with demons or sometimes only the ability to see them affirm the genealogical superiority of certain people. The power of Buddhist chants and holy objects is similarly affirmed when they are used to conquer *oni* and other spirit creatures. The merging of multiple forces is exemplified by the triangular link between the aristocrats, the Nocturnal Procession of One Hundred Demons, and the *Uṣṇīṣa vijayā dhāraṇī* in the tales about how a former wet nurse of a young man conceals that tantric formula in his robe collar.

In contrast to the links of men and demons, those of women and demons considered in Chapter 5 are not defined in terms of subjugation and domination. In *The Pillow Book*, "The Young Lady Who Loves Insects," and several poems, they are either empowering or otherwise somehow affirming of women, although not exclusively. Associations of women and demons in setsuwa, too, often have positive aspects, but overtly negative attitudes toward women in general in the tales can obscure them. Tales depicting sexually alluring women impersonated by demons or associating old women with demons (or vice versa) express ambivalence, most obviously in the fig- ure of the old woman of the mountains who plays a critical role in saving a newborn even while appearing ready to eat him.

Portraying demons as lethal female impersonators is not the same as de- picting intrinsically wicked women. The tales studied subtlety differentiate between human women and malicious spirits. The demon at Agi Bridge appears as a woman, as a hideous creature whose gender is unspecified, and as a man. This fluidity clearly indicates that it is something other than a woman. As a creature, that demon has physical features such as hair linking it to earlier, gender-less creatures as well as to women.

Demons in female form reveal the insecurities and fears of men, perhaps enabling audiences to deal indirectly with the threatening emotions of them- selves and others. The jealousy and hostility of women who suspect they are not favored by their lovers is symbolically expressed by the opening of a box containing penises and eyeballs. Other emotions treated indirectly are those of adult children dealing with aging parents. Through the demonization of the mother of the hunters, certain audiences could confront the anger and pain at having to deal with demising parents without experiencing guilt for failing to consistently respect and cherish them. At the same time, the association of old women with demons suggests a certain willfulness and independence on the part of a marginalized group in society, however, cast in an ambivalent light. The mother of the hunters lashes out in discontent perhaps caused by the devaluing of women as they age. Similarly, the tale about the old woman / demon of the mountains deals on the personal level with a societal issue particularly relevant to women: unwanted pregnancy.

The animal spirits in Chapter 6 provide insight into many aspects of human nature in Japan during the classical and medieval periods. The imagi- nations behind their creation seem influenced by strong values and a keen awareness of the precariousness of life. Foxes appear as a reminder of the non-human presence in the world and of the instability of any given social and political order. They undermine aristocratic wealth and materialism in many ways, seek revenge for cruel treatment, and establish amorous attach- ments with men that raise questions about the illusory nature of life. Mon- keys reveal the multi-faceted aspects of human nature while directing the most attention to selfishness and cruelty. The demand for human sacrifices and the eating habits of evil monkey gods hint at cannibalism in two tales.

By linking the provinces with barbaric practices, storytellers could justify the suppression of the lands outside the capital and the purging of religious practices that interfered with the government's drive to centralize. One version involving a Buddhist monk surprisingly affirms marriage and secular life.

The strained relationship of Buddhism and *kami*-worship is apparent in "Bird Spirits and a Tree." The story of the founding of Gangōji suggests that there was resistance and overt hostility toward early Japanese Buddhism through a portrait of bird spirits who murder in defense of their sacred dwelling.

However, in setsuwa, resistance to Buddhism figures less prominently than the internal struggles of people either trying to embrace aspects of Buddhist thought or whose lives are affected by it otherwise. Buddhist and aristocratic values clash.

This conflict is manifested in, for example, the representation of the snake as a grotesque embodiment of sensuality and attachment. A woman hoards gold given to her by the emperor even in death; a girl cherishes plum blossoms; a mandarin orange tree wins the heart of a monk. Snakes delineated in terms of sexual desire differ from those delineated in terms of the senses, yet the two types of yearning and attachment are intertwined. Most striking is that many people reborn as snakes seem basically good and undeserving of their initial fates. Although the tales about the attachment to flowering trees undermine the aristocratic celebration of nature in poetry, they also demonstrate an appreciation of the aesthetic sensibility of courtiers. While the young girl is born as a snake because of her attachment to plum blossoms, that flower seems symbolically appropriate for her. A monk suffers a similar fate for his love of a mandarin orange tree. In an episode of *Ise monogatari*, the blossoms and fruit of this tree refer to someone whose love is not singular. For the monk, devotion is compromised.

In stories about the interaction of holy men and animal spirits, *kusainaki* and *tanuki* direct attention to spiritual longing as an obstacle to wisdom and a higher rebirth. In the tale of the holy man of Mt. Atago, a hunter proves to be wiser than a devout Buddhist. The story alludes to the understanding that ordinary people, even those who kill animals, have the potential for birth in the Pure Land. At the same time, the view that someone who kills for a living might be in some ways spiritually superior to a holy man is not fully embraced.

Despite its status as sacred in many tales, the wild boar as a grotesque representation is rather dumb. Who else would be fooled by a man riding backwards on his horse? These animal spirits are chastised because they act recklessly and without a sense of purpose. The criticism may have been aimed at unskilled hoodlums in society, but, in two tales, their doltish behavior strangely allows people to confront fear and anxiety centered on corpses and death.

We saw also how *tengu* play upon the spiritual longing of people, as do *kusainaki* and *tanuki*, but more artistically. The illusion created by a *tengu* enables a monk to temporarily forget himself and experience a state of enhanced spirituality. In a grotesque mode, the narrative challenges the notion of illusions as damaging.

While the tales analyzed are concerned with specific people and issues, they also illustrate many types of struggles, including the following: the question of who in society has the right to what material and magical resources and for what purposes; the competition between aristocrats from different *uji* and lineages within them, especially the friction between the northern branch Fujiwara and aristocrats outside that group; the vulnerability of the Fujiwara and other dominant powers; rivalry between the provinces and the capital; male bonding and the competition between men; the use of the female body in politics and religion versus the personal and political significance of these struggles to women; in-fighting among members of the imperial family; the relationship of mountain ascetics to aristocrats and to Buddhists clearly affiliated with institutions; elderly people in society; men and their aging mothers (or wet nurses); internal struggles regarding religious truth. These represent many of the major social and political concerns marking the Nara, Heian, and early Kamakura periods.

The grotesque enables creators and audiences of tales to confront these issues indirectly, without being overwhelmed. The humor of some and the concern with the lower half of the body in the same tales or others could temporarily liberate people from their fears or self-debilitating seriousness. Creatures and events that are horrifying to one group may be welcomed by another. In addition, people whose lifestyles and lives are threatened would find it less frightening to confront political and social struggles in terms of the extraordinary and the monstrous than to look hard at the true enemies: other people and time.

Many setsuwa provide a means of challenging ideologies and leaders of the late Heian and early Kamakura periods without making the attack obvious since they often deal with issues relevant to the then present while being set in an earlier period. The grotesque allows for the undermining of people who, because of their power and influence, cannot be overtly condemned as well as of dominant ideas and ideologies. The drawback is that grotesque representations are often easily appropriated by the dominant individuals and groups for their own purposes. Most people in the Heian and Kamakura periods would not have been fully conscious of how the grotesque functions in tales and how it nurtures them spiritually and psychologically. They did not acknowledge and name it as I do here, and they would have heard many types of stories, not simply those with grotesque representations. Still, setsuwa with grotesque representations had the potential to make deep impressions and shape perceptions of the world.

Despite the absence of long, elaborate descriptions and hyperbole, the grotesque in setsuwa has more in common with the Rabelaisian grotesque and grotesque caricature than with Romantic and modern forms. Most importantly, it grounds audiences in immediate, physical realities. The stories are about being (or, often lower being) rather than a higher being. Even tales about yearning for Buddhist truth work at the personal level; they tell us what that yearning does to people. In the nineteenth century, critics began to take theories of the grotesque away from the concrete. Theorists such as Ruskin and Hugo saw the grotesque as a means to the sublime or, really, to God. Even in the twentieth century, Bakhtin imagined a utopian force in the grotesque and Harpham ultimately raises "the possibility that the grotesque may harbor the essence, or symbolize the totality, of art."[2] Setsuwa cannot carry that weight.

My study consequently has humbler conclusions. The grotesque in setsuwa will not lead us to the divine, a perfect state, or the essence of Art. It will keep us focused on the bodies and minds of particular people. When we keep the culturally and historically specific situations in setsuwa at the forefront of our analyses, we cannot help but stick to reality and history, and all the fictions that developed around them. Perhaps this study will remind people exploring the grotesque in other cultures to stay grounded: to consider the relevance of the grotesque to whatever society created it. Maybe we do not need to look for something larger than life in the representations. The grotesque in setsuwa brings us back to earth . . . I mean, to Japan when now is the past.

Notes

1. All citations are in concise form, with titles of works generally shortened, while the full Bibliography provides long titles, the publication details, and other information.

2. Translations are mine unless otherwise indicated.

3. The first time a book in Japanese or Chinese is mentioned, a note will cite the most complete or most recently published English translation. Additional translations may also be mentioned, especially when only incomplete translations of the work exist or, with *Konjaku* tales, if the translation is in a selection (so that readers would otherwise need to consult the book to know whether or not a tale is included). While I expect that most readers of this book will be scholars in Japanese literature, history, and religion or related fields, I include this information to benefit newcomers to the disciplines as well as non-specialists.

4. References to tales appear as the book number followed by the tale number, so that 14:29 is tale 29 of Book 14. These numbers follow the word "tale" (tale 14:29) so that they will not be confused with the volume and page numbers.

5. When a tale is cited, the number following the title of the collection refers to the volume number of the set (as opposed to the volume number in the series): Yamada et al., *Konjaku*, 4: 77–78, refers to pages 77–78 in volume 4 of the *Konjaku* in the edition edited by Yamada Yoshio et al. (or the NKBT edition). Although I cite the page numbers from specific editions of collections, the tales in the different series and editions are the same or nearly so, with some rare, minor exceptions. Of course, annotative portions of texts differ.

6. The *Taishō shinshū daizōkyō* is abbreviated as T. The first number after the T. is the volume number and the second is the text number. For example the *Lotus Sutra* is T. 9:262 or vol. 9, text number 262.

Introduction

1. For a complete translation of *Konjaku*, see Dkystra, *Konjaku Indian Sections* (2 vols.); *Chinese Section* (1 volume); and *Japanese Sections* (3 vols.). For partial English translations in published books, see S. W. Jones, *Ages Ago*; Ury, *Tales of Times*

244 NOTES TO INTRODUCTION

Now Past; Tyler, *Japanese Tales*, passim; Emmerich, Kelsey, and Ury, "Collection of Tales of Times Now Past." The tales translated by Kelsey and Ury are taken from Ury's book and Kelsey, "*Konjaku Monogatari-shū*: Toward an Understanding of Its Literary Qualities." Robert Brower made the first major contribution to *Konjaku* studies and translation in English with his dissertation. See Brower, "*Koňzyaku*."

2. Kayser, *Grotesque in Art and Literature*, 190n1.

3. I prefer *representation* to *image* because *image* refers to the likeness of something, suggesting a correspondence to reality and truth, whereas *representation* conveys the subjectivity of the writer and allows for the possibility of discrepancy between objects or people in the world and their appearance in texts.

4. Harpham, *On the Grotesque*, 14.

5. "In a liminal image opposing processes and assumptions coexist in a single representation." Ibid., 14.

6. Bakhtin, *Rabelais and His World*, 4.

7. *Izumi no kuni fudoki* has been translated by Michiko Aoki as *Records of Wind and Earth*.

8. See Book 1, Chapters 10, 16, and 45 respectively in Ogihara and Kōnosu, *Kojiki, jōdai kayō*, and Book 1 of Sakamoto et al., *Nihon shoki, vol. 1*. For English translations of these works, see Philippi, *Kojiki*; and Aston, *Nihongi*.

9. On Chinese texts in *Konjaku* studies, see Katayose, *Konjaku monogatari shū no kenkyū*, 329–549. See also Brower, "*Koňzyaku*," 237–45 and 248–51.

10. On *zhiguai*, see Zhao, *Classical Chinese Supernatural Fiction*; Gjertson, *Miraculous Retribution*, 2–67; Kao, *Classical Chinese Tales of the Supernatural and Fantastic*, 1–51; Campany, *Strange Writing*. Along with Campany (p. 221), Chünfang Yü (*Kuan-yin*, 155) sees miracle tales as a subgenre of zhiguai.

11. *Nihon ryōiki* has been translated by Kyoko Motomochi Nakamura as *Miraculous Stories from the Japanese Buddhist Tradition*.

12. Fourteen of the eighteen *Jingang bore jing lingyanji* tales survive in *Taiping guanji* (*Extensive Records of the Taiping Era*, 978). Gjertson, *Miraculous Retribution*, 32.

13. LaFleur, *The Karma of Words*, 33.

14. The juxtaposition of the ordinary and the extraordinary is "a key poetic device of anomaly accounts." Campany, *Strange Writing*, 26.

15. LaMarre, *Uncovering Heian Japan*, 1–10. He argues that modern scholars mistakenly sought and imagined "territorial consolidation, linguistic purification, and ethnic or racial unification" or characteristics of a nation in Nara and Heian Japan (quote from p. 2).

16. Haga, *Kōshō Konjaku monogatari shū*, 19–21.

17. See Yamada et al., *Konjaku*, 4: 427, and Wang, *Soushenji*, 231–32. See also DeWoskin and Crump, *In Search of the Supernatural*, 230–31.

18. Akutagawa, "*Konjaku monogatari kanshō*," 143 and 142, respectively.

19. The term *uji* refers to kinship groups that competed for power in premodern Japan. While the word is sometimes translated as "clan," many Japanese historians see that translation as misleading and advise against using it. John Whitney Hall

defines uji as a "consanguineous familial group or lineage. Not to be translated as 'clan'" (Hall, *Terms and Concepts*, 31). However, while many consider "lineage" to be a better translation, it is not ideal either. Among other reasons, it can cause confusion because uji are further divided into branches, which have also been called lineages, such as the northern branch Fujiwara. In this book, uji is sometimes rendered as "lineage," "lineage group," or "family," but readers should bear in mind that these translations are imperfect. On uji, see also Piggott, *Japanese Kingship*, 55 and 328. For an overview of kinship groups in Heian politics, see Hurst, "The Structure of the Heian Court."

20. Hurst, "Development of the *Insei*," 70–71. The regent's house or *sekkanke* was a sublineage of the northern branch Fujiwara. It was further divided into households.

21. Farris, *Heavenly Warriors*, 242–47 and 261. Tales about violence and robbery in *Konjaku* Book 29 also give a sense of the instability of the times.

22. For an overview of devastating events, see a chronology of Japanese history such as Tōkyō Gakugei Daigaku Nihon shi kenkyūshitsu, *Nihonshi nenpyō*, 110–20; or Reischauer, "Chronicle of Events."

23. Of the collections not yet cited, there are presently three complete translations: Kamens, *Three Jewels*; Dykstra, *Miraculous Tales*; and Mills, *Collection of Tales from Uji*. For partial translations of *Nihon ōjō gokurakuki*, *Shūi ōjōden*, and *Goshūi ōjōden*, see Kotas, "Ōjōden: Accounts of Rebirth in the Pure Land," 323–517, and Deal, "Women and Japanese Buddhism." Other partial translations are included in: Ury, "Ōe Conversations" (*Gōdanshō*); Moore, "Senjūshō"; Pandey, "Women, Sexuality, and Enlightenment"; Geddes, "Partial Translation and Study of the 'Jikkinshō,'" part 2, 319–583, and a handful of tales from the same collection in Geddes, "Selected Anecdotes to Illustrate Ten Maxims"; Dykstra, "Notable Tales Old and New"; Morrell, *Sand and Pebbles*.

24. Mori, *Konjaku monogatari shū no seisei*, 31–51.

25. Tale 27:15; Yamada et al., *Konjaku*, 4: 496–98. See Chapter 5 of this book.

26. On the meaning of "ima wa mukashi" and the use of the suffix *keri* in *Konjaku*, see Kasuga, "*Konjaku kō*."

27. Okada, *Figures of Resistance*, 40.

28. Ibid., 40–41. Okada draws from St. Augustine's view of there being "'a present of past things in memory,' and a 'present of present things' in direct perception, and 'a present of future things in expectation.'"

29. Yamada et al., *Konjaku*, 4: 503. Tale 27:20.

30. Although the *Nihon ryōiki* is later reconstituted in Japanese with *ki* rather than *keri*, *ki* should not be seen simply as a past tense. Instead, we can emphasize its possible function as a suffix "added to texts written in Chinese to indicate a 'narrated,' storytelling situation or that the stories were originally orally transmitted" (Okada, *Figures of Resistance*, 37).

31. Okada uses *re-present*, written with a hyphen, to convey a similar sense. Ibid., 39.

Chapter 1

1. Komine, *Chūsei setsuwa no sekai*, 14–22. Komine writes on the same topic elsewhere in "Setsuwa no gensetsu," 9–31; "Jitsugo to mōgo no <setsuwa> shi," 240–62, especially pp. 241–42; *Setsuwa no mori*, 282–86, in a section entitled "Zatsudan no jidai: setsuwa no hyōgen shi." See also Takahashi Tōru, "Setsuwa to monogatari," in chap. 1 of *Monogatari bungei no hyōgenshi*, 9–18, and "Tsukuri monogatari to setsuwa," 51–69.

2. Komine includes the Tang dynasty in the period when *shuohua* more generally refers to the art of oral storytelling. While contemporary Chinese storytellers assert that *shuohua* meant "professional storytelling" from antiquity, many scholars of Chinese studies believe that meaning emerged in the Song dynasty. See Lévy, "About the Chinese Storyteller's Change of Name," 35–37.

3. Komine, *Chūsei setsuwa no sekai*, 16–17; "Jitsugo to mōgo no <setsuwa> shi," 242 and elsewhere (see Note 1, above).

4. Keene, *A History of Japanese Literature*, 1: 577.

5. *Furigana* are Japanese syllabic symbols (*kana*) placed beside Chinese characters to indicate their reading. On the use of the reading of *monogatari* for *setsuwa*, see Takahashi Tōru, "Setsuwa to monogatari," in chap. 1 of *Monogatari bungei*, 11. The English translations of the works mentioned by Takahashi do not provide insight into the use of the reading of *monogatari* for *setsuwa*. Chambers, *Tales of Moonlight and Rain*; Drake, "The Eight Dog Chronicles," 887–909.

6. See Brower's chart of the breakdown of tales, fragments, and titles without stories in "*Koñzyaku*," 119–21.

7. Katayose addresses fundamental issues of *Konjaku* studies in *Konjaku monogatari shū no kenkyū*. While the research is dated in some areas, many findings remain relevant. Setsuwa scholars writing in English have also summarized the basic issues: Brower, "*Koñzyaku*," 274–351; Kelsey, "Didactics in Art," 37–71, and *Konjaku Monogatari-shū*; Kobayashi, *Human Comedy of Heian Japan*, 1–21; Ury, *Tales of Times Now Past*, 1–23; Mills, *Tales from Uji*, 100–111.

8. The text is *Hongzan fahua zhuan* (*Biographies of People Who Propagate and Honor the Lotus Sutra*), a Tang dynasty collection of miracle tales. Katayose, *Konjaku monogatari shū no kenkyū*, 1: 111. However, stories may have been added to the *Konjaku* after its initial compilation.

9. Katayose, *Konjaku monogatari shū no kenkyū*, 1: 9–14; Brower, "*Koñzyaku*," 275–313; Kelsey, "Didactics in Art," 40–43.

10. According to Katayose, *Konjaku monogatari shū no kenkyū*, 1: 18–19, the challenge to the view that Takakuni compiled the collection appears first in Fujioka Sakutarō, *Konjaku monogatari sen* (1903). He gives no additional information on this source. Katayose himself lists four aristocrats who may have been the compiler, two of whom were Tendai abbots with elite upbringings (vol. 1, pp. 153–74). Among others who also attack the theory is Konno, "Konjaku monogatari shū no sakusha," 32–41. He uses factual errors in the stories to argue against the involvement of an aristocrat.

11. Brower, "*Koňzyaku*," 324–42, and Nagano, "Konjaku monogatari shū no sakusha."

12. See Kunisaki, "Konjaku monogatari shū senja shiron," for the former theory and *Konjaku monogatari shū sakusha kō* for the latter.

13. Maeda, "Konjaku monogatari shū no 'kokka zō.'"

14. Okada, *Figures of Resistance*, 50.

15. Ikegami, "Konjaku monogatari shū," 336.

16. Komine, "I. Shiryō to shūhen," in *Konjaku no keisei to kōzō*, 44. The count for the *Hokkegenki* tales is mine. On the overlap between the four collections mentioned, see Kawaguchi, "Konjaku to Kohon setsuwa shū," 60–81; Mills, *Tales from Uji*, 65–82 and 93–111.

17. This concise description of Haga's project is from Ury, *Tales of Times Now Past*, 24.

18. Haga, *Kōshō Konjaku*, 1: 1. See also Haga, "Introduction." Haga believes the *Nihon ryōiki* is not the oldest *setsuwa shū* in Japanese because it is in *kanbun*.

19. Haga, *Kōshō Konjaku*, 1: 1, 7.

20. Imanari, "Setsuwa bungaku shiron," 283.

21. Sakai is first to promote the *Konjaku* as literature (broadly understood). Piecing together ideas from Western (particularly German) literary theory, but not working entirely from them, he argues that a complete, scientific, understanding of the history of Japanese literature is impossible if only the aesthetics of the elite are considered. See *Konjaku monogatari shū no shin kenkyū*, esp. 1–20.

22. Ibid., 123.

23. Ibid., 118–24.

24. The word *koyū* translates as both *idiosyncratic* and *indigenous*. Since Sakai uses it to mean both, I translate it as *idiosyncratic/indigenous*.

25. Sakai, *Konjaku monogatari shū no shin kenkyū*, 588. *Kojiki* and *Nihon shoki* are both part mythical.

26. LaMarre, *Uncovering Heian Japan*, 2.

27. Sakai, *Konjaku monogatari shū no shin kenkyū*, 588–89. In contrast to setsuwa, *kayō* gives rise to *Manyōshū, Ise monogatari, Kokinshū, Tosa nikki, Genji monogatari, Sagoromo monogatari*, and other literature in his view. Full and partial translations of works not previously cited include: Keene, "The Tale of the Bamboo Cutter"; Cranston, "Atemiya: A Translation from *Utsubo monogatari*"; Lammers, "The Succession (Kuniyuzuri)"; Rohlich, *A Tale of Eleventh-Century Japan*; Nippon gakujutsu shinkōkai, *1000 Poems from The Manyōshū*; Helen McCullough, *Tales of Ise* and *Kokin wakashū with Tosa nikki and Shinsen waka*; Rodd and Henkenius, *Kokinshū*; D'Etcheverry, "The Tale of Sagoromo."

28. Sakai, *Konjaku monogatari shū no shin kenkyū*, 596–98.

29. Translated in William and Helen McCullough, *Flowering Fortunes*; and Helen McCullough, *Ōkagami*.

30. Mikami and Takatsu, *Nihon bungakushi*, 345. Tomi Suzuki describes *Nihon bungakushi* as "the first full-length literary history with abundant excerpts from ancient to late Tokugawa texts" ("Gender and Genre," 4).

31. Mikami and Takatsu, *Nihon bungakushi*, 338.

32. Imanari, "Setsuwa bungaku shiron," 283–84.

33. Tyler has translated *Genji*; Morris, *The Pillow Book*.

34. Haga, *Kokubungakushi jikkō*, 108.

35. Ibid., 1.

36. Honda, *Setsuwa to wa nani ka*, 13–14.

37. Yanagita, *The Legends of Tōno*.

38. Quoted in Honda, *Setsuwa to wa nani ka*, 13–14.

39. Beckson and Ganz, *Literary Terms*, s.v. "folk tale." Brower rejects the term *folktale* precisely because of its connotations, introducing the term "short tale" instead. Brower, "*Koñzyaku*," 4n5.

40. Shirane, "Issues in Canon Formation," 16.

41. Ibid.

42. Ibid., 42.

43. Used mainly for ancient imperial edits and Shinto chants (*norito*), *senmyōgaki* combines Chinese characters with Japanese phonetics. Common expressions tend to retain their Chinese word order but are read according to Japanese syntax. Nouns, pronouns, and other declinable words (words that can stand alone as predicates) are written in relatively large Chinese characters understood in terms of their semantic values. Particles and inflections are written phonetically. Early forms of *senmyōgaki* employed *manyōgana* (a system invented before *kana* using Chinese characters mostly to represent Japanese sounds). In *Konjaku* manuscripts, *katakana* is used. Smaller-sized, the katakana symbols stand beneath the Chinese characters in double rows of about two or three symbols.

44. Shirane, "Issues in Canon Formation," 15.

45. This assessment is based on data in Tasaka, *Kyūsei chūtō kyōiku*, 17, 34, and 35–36. Shirane notes this reference and the importance of the textbook *Chūtō kokubun tokuhon* in "Curriculum and Competing Canons," 235–38, including 298n42.

46. The three tales are numbers 5, 23, and 27 in Book 24. See Ochiai, *Chūtō kokubun tokuhon*, 96–113.

47. Aston, *A History of Japanese Literature*, 119. Aston refers to *Konjaku* as *Uji dainagon monogatari*, but his description of the collection indicates that he means *Konjaku*. This collection is included in a chapter called "Some Minor Works." Shibano Rokusuke translated the book by Aston as *Nihon bungakushi* in 1908.

48. Honda, *Setsuwa to wa nani ka* is vol. 1 of the six-volume series *Setsuwa no kōza*.

49. Ury, *Tales of Times Now Past*, 10.

50. Komine, *Konjaku monogatari shū no keisei to kōzō*, 1, 19, and 43. Whenever possible, Haga in *Kōshō Konjaku* includes one or more related tales after *Konjaku* tales. Taken from other collections, these are either clear versions of the *Konjaku* tales they follow or tales with looser connections to them. He sees both types as variants of the *Konjaku* tales they gloss. Kelsey notes, "While the *setsuwa* is ulti-

mately derived from oral tradition, it has been recognized that most of the collections are based largely on written transmission" ("Didactics in Art," 29).

51. On the textual connections of *Konjaku* and other works, see Katayose, *Konjaku monogatari shū no kenkyū*, 1: 329–412 and 413–59, and all of volume 2; Komine, "I. Shiryō to shūhen," in *Konjaku monogatari shū no keisei to kōzō*, 1–77; Ikegami, "Konjaku monogatari shū no seiritsu o megutte"; Brower, "*Koñzyaku*," 237–58 and 281–310; Mills, *Tales from Uji*, 94–103 and 106–7.

52. See Nakamura Fumi, *Nihon ryōiki to shōdō*; Uchigiki shū wo yomu kai, *Uchigiki shū*; Kyoko Motomochi Nakamura, *Miraculous Stories*, 43; Kelsey, *Didactics in Art*, 25–26.

53. The itinerant monk Kūya (903–72) was an early figure who attracted a following of commoners. He taught *nenbutsu odori*, a ritual chanting of the name of Amitābha (Amida) Buddha that also involved dance (*odori*) and is the type of person who might have spread Buddhist setsuwa in his teachings.

54. Tōkyō daigaku shiryō hensanjo, *Chūyūki*, 5: 204. For a translation of one *ōjōden* in the diary entry, see Kelsey, "Didactics in Art," 15. These short hagiographies of people posthumously born in the Pure Land should be thought of as a subgenre of setsuwa because they are included in thematically diverse setsuwa collections as well as in collections of only *ōjōden*.

55. Gotō, Ikegami, and Yamane, *Chūgai shō*, 339–40. Ikeda Kikan links this entry, number 31 (8/20/1150 or Kyūan 6), to the *Konjaku* tale in "Setsuwa bungaku ni okeru Chisoku-in kanpaku no chii," 32. See also Mills, *Tales from Uji*, 98.

56. Tale 19:8; Yamada et al., *Konjaku*, 4: 77–80; Ury, *Tales of Times Now Past*, 121–24; and Tyler, *Japanese Tales*, 290–91.

57. Harpham, *On the Grotesque*, 58.

58. Ibid., 23.

59. This section on the grotesque is based on these studies and other primary and secondary sources. Since the material covered by these scholars greatly overlaps, I provide notes only for direct quotes, when one study alone gives information, or when a scholar has a unique interpretation of something. Otherwise, it can be assumed that several or more scholars (often all) mention the development I note. See Clayborough, *Grotesque in English Literature*, 1–69; Thomson, *Grotesque*, 10–19 and passim; Barasch, *Grotesque*; Remshardt, *Staging the Savage God*, 18–124 and passim; Harpham, *On the Grotesque*, 23–76; Bakhtin, *Rabelais and His World*, 30–52.

60. Vasari, *Lives of Painters, Sculptors, and Architects*, 1: 924–25. Page numbers refer to where Vasari first mentions the frescos.

61. Ibid., 2: 488–89.

62. Harpham, *On the Grotesque*, 27.

63. Ibid.

64. On the character and mythology of caves in relation to the grotesque, see especially Kuryluk, *Salome and Judas in the Cave of Sex*, 19–24.

65. Fairclough, "The Art of Poetry," 451.

66. Granger, *Vitruvius: De Architectura* II: 105.

67. Barasch, *Grotesque*, 24.

68. Vasari, *Lives of Painters, Sculptors, and Architects*, 2: 680.

69. Ibid.

70. Migne, *Patrologia Latina*, 182, coll. 915/6, cited in translation in Camille, *Images on the Edge*, 62. See also Harpham, *On the Grotesque*, 34.

71. Camille, *Images on the Edge*, 62, including a quotation of the relevant passage on 61–62.

72. Ibid., 10.

73. Ibid., 30.

74. Harpham, *On the Grotesque*, 28, in the section called "Margins and Centers," 27–44.

75. Screech, *Rabelais: "Gargantua and Pantagruel,"* 510. Clayborough gives numerous other early uses of the word in discussing its semantic development (*Grotesque in English Literature*, 1–20).

76. "Of Friendship," in Frame, *Complete Essays of Montaigne*, 135.

77. Clayborough, *Grotesque in English Literature*, 4.

78. John Dennis, *Poems of the Burlesque* (London and Westminster, 1692): sig. A 2, cited in ibid, 4. See also mention of Dennis in Barasch, *Grotesque*, 123, and Barasch, "The Meaning of the Grotesque," xxxvii.

79. Barasch, *Grotesque*, 78–81. On the engravings by Callot, including sketches, see Wright, *History of Caricature and Grotesque*, 296–311.

80. Barasch, "The Meaning of the Grotesque," xxxvii, and Boileau-Despréaux, *The Art of Poetry*, Eighteenth Century Collections Online, document #T139159, p. 5/image 11.

81. Dryden, "A Parallel of Painting and Poetry," Eighteenth Century Collections Online, #CW3306147864, p. xxxvi/image 35. See also Barasch, "Meaning," xxxix, on Dryden's view of the comic.

82. Möser, *Harlequin*, Eighteenth Century Collections Online, document # CW3316673659.

83. Bakhtin, *Rabelais and His World*, 35–36, writing on Karl Friedrich Flögel, *Geschichte des groteskekomischen* (Liegnitz u. Leipzig, 1788); rev. Friedrich W. Ebeling (Leipzig, 1888). For a summary of this book, which has no English translation, see Barasch, *Grotesque*, 149–51.

84. Barasch, *Grotesque*, 151.

85. Jackson, *Fantasy*, 96. Emphasis in original.

86. Bakhtin, *Rabelais and His World*, 38.

87. Ibid., 41, and Kayser, *Grotesque in Art and Literature*, 49–51.

88. Schlegel, *Dialogue on Poetry*, 86.

89. Ibid.

90. Kayser, *Grotesque in Art and Literature*, 51.

91. Schlegel, *Dialogue on Poetry*, 95.

92. Kayser, *Grotesque in Art and Literature*, 56. See also Casey, "Preschool of Aesthetics," in *Jean Paul: A Reader*, 241–68, especially the sections "Humoristic Totality" and "The Annihilating or Infinite Idea of Humor," 250–58. For Bakhtin on Jean Paul, *Rabelais and His World*, see 41–42.

93. Baudelaire, "On the Essence of Laughter," 157.

94. Harpham, *On the Grotesque*, 70.

95. Ibid., 71.

96. Bagehot, "Pure, Ornate, and Grotesque Art in Poetry," 267–315, especially p. 301. See also Barasch, *Grotesque*, 156–57, and Clayborough, *Grotesque in English Literature*, 43–45.

97. As a result, prejudices mar the assessment Hegel makes of (Eastern) Indian art in "The Symbolic Form of Art." He views it as grotesque and hence, to him, inadequate.

98. Hugo, "Preface to Cromwell," 366.

99. Ruskin, "Grotesque Renaissance," 136.

100. Ibid., 126.

101. Ibid.

102. Barasch, *Grotesque*, 148. See also Kayser, *Grotesque in Art and Literature*, 30. For a partial summary in English of *Unterredungen mit dem Pfarrer von ***, see Shookman, *Noble Lies*, 17–19.

103. Barasch, "The Meaning of the Grotesque," lvii.

104. Bakhtin, *Rabelais and His World*, 306. There is no English translation of *Geschichte der grotesken Satire* by Schneegans. I rely mostly on Bakhtin's interpretation of his work.

105. For excellent interpretations of the theories of Kayser, Bakhtin, Harpham, and Kuryluk, see Yates, "An Introduction to the Grotesque," in Adams and Yates, *Grotesque in Art and Literature*, 1–68.

106. Kayser, *Grotesque in Art and Literature*, 184, 187, and 188 respectively.

107. Ibid., 30.

108. Pieter Brueghel the Elder, *The Triumph of Death*. Type in the title or artist at www.museodelprado.es/en/ingles/collection/on-line-gallery/

109. Kayser, *Grotesque in Art and Literature*, 185.

110. Clayborough, *Grotesque in English Literature*, 69.

111. McElroy, *Fiction of the Modern Grotesque*, 4.

112. Russo, *The Female Grotesque*.

113. Harpham, *On the Grotesque*, xxi. See chapters 2 and 3 for the codes, which need to be inferred from the wider discussion.

114. Ibid., 76.

115. Ibid.

116. Ibid.

117. Stallybrass and White, "The Grotesque Body and the Smithfield Muse: Authorship in the Eighteenth Century," chap. in *Politics and Poetics of Transgression*, 80–124.

118. Kuryluk, *Salome and Judas in the Cave of Sex*, 3.

119. Bakhtin, *Rabelais and His World*, 46.

120. Ibid., 37.

121. Ibid., 18. *Material* here refers to the physical functions of the body and does not imply that certain things can be experienced outside the realm of representation.

122. Tonomura, "Black Hair," and "Nikutai."

123. *Tsubi* is vagina, *mara* is penis, and *in* is used for both. *Totsugu* refers to genital sex or other "activities occurring at the genitals," usually involving some form of penetration. See Tonomura, "Black Hair," 134, and "Nikutai," 307–8.

124. Bakhtin, *Rabelais and His World*, 26.

125. Ibid., 28. However, in a footnote on the same page, Bakhtin points out that, in antiquity, there were also many exceptions to the classical concept of the body.

126. Cranston, *The Izumi Shibiki Diary*, and Miner, *Diary of Izumi Shikibu* are translations of the *nikki* (diary).

127. Gatten, "Death and Salvation in Genji," 7–13.

128. In addition to *ōjōden* themselves, see Ishida, *Ōjō no shisō*, 259–64, and Kotas, "Ōjōden," 229–32.

129. Okada, *Figures of Resistance*, 58.

130. Bakhtin, *Rabelais and His World*, 6.

131. Ibid., 10.

132. Ibid., 473. See also p. 4.

133. Ivan Morris makes this point when briefly contrasting Heian festivities with those of ancient Rome in *The World of the Shining Prince*, 154.

134. See Kawaguchi, "Tonkō henbun no seikaku to waga kuni shōdō bungaku." On the *utagaki* festivals, see Ortolani, *The Japanese Theater*, 9–10.

135. Bakhtin, *Rabelais and His World*, 10.

136. Ibid.

137. Ibid, 49. According to Bakhtin, even scientific innovation depends on the carnival spirit.

138. Ibid., 10.

139. Bakhtin, "Forms of Time and of the Chronotype," 167–24.

140. Morson and Emerson, *Mikhail Bakhtin*, 436.

141. Ibid., 436–37.

142. Ibid., 93.

143. Stallybrass and White, *Politics and Poetics of Transgression*, 19.

144. Stallybrass and White remark that Terry Eagleton and other "politically thoughtful commentators wonder . . . whether the 'licensed release' of carnival is not simply a form of social control of the low by the high and therefore serves the interests of that very official culture which it apparently opposes" (*Politics and Poetics of Transgression*, 13).

145. Bakhtin, *Rabelais and His World*, 43.

146. Ibid, 25.

147. Howell, "*Setsuwa*, Knowledge, and the Culture of Reading and Writing," 7.

148. Many scholars see the attribution of tales to oral sources as a literary device. See Ikegami, "Joshō sōsetsu," 14.

149. Komine, *Konjaku monogatari shū no keisei to kōzō*, 59.

Chapter 2

1. Bakhtin, *Rabelais and His World*, 10.
2. Empty brackets indicate lacunae in the text.
3. Tale 29:29; Yamada et al., *Konjaku*, 5: 189–90.
4. Hiroko Kobayashi, *Human Comedy of Heian*, 155, comments on the difficulty of interpreting the attitude of the commentator toward the woman and the warriors.
5. Tale 25:1; Yamada et al., *Konjaku*, 4: 362–66. See also Wilson, "Way of the Bow and Arrow." For paraded heads in *Heike*, see "Kubi watashi," in Takagi et al., *Heike monogatari*, 237–41, or Helen McCullough, *Heike*, 325–27.
6. Tale 25:10; Yamada et al., *Konjaku*, 4: 388–90, and Wilson, "Way of the Bow and Arrow," 216–17. Book 25 also contains other warrior tales mentioning decapitations.
7. Tale 91 (6:9) in Miki et al., *Uji shūi*, 168–74; tale 27:9 in Yamada et al., *Konjaku*, 4: 487–88; tale 2:33 in Nakada Norio, *Nihon ryōiki*, 232–34; and tale 20:37 in Yamada et al., *Konjaku*, 4: 205–6, respectively.
8. Tale 14:29 in Yamada et al., *Konjaku*, 3: 314–18, and tale 102 (8:4) in Miki et al., *Uji shūi*, 202–8.
9. The painting is from Maeda-ke bon, scroll B. Komatsu, *Jigoku zōshi*, 72–73.
10. A *shaku* is roughly one foot, but the size was not standardized at 30.303 centimeters until 1891. In ancient China, the *chi* (*shaku*) was initially much smaller, perhaps less than half the size. See *Kadokawa Nihonshi jiten*, 2nd edition, s.v. "shaku." Therefore, whereas the space between Broad-of-Brow's eyebrows would have been hyperbolic to Japanese audiences, the Chinese creators of the tales involving Broad-of-Brow must have imagined a wide space between the eyebrows that was still physically possible, unusual but normal.
11. Tale 9:44; Yamada et al., *Konjaku*, 2: 260–62. I borrow Marian Ury's free rendering of the son's name as "Broad-of-Brow" since it is more graceful than the literal "Brows-a-*shaku*-apart." See Ury, *Tales of Times Now Past*, 67–69.
12. In using the term *version*, I do not mean to imply that there is any basic story in an original or pure form from which tales about the smith and his son are derived. *Version* in this book merely refers to a tale closely related to another through similarities or sameness in plot, characters, and diction. Often, the tales are nearly identical, except for differences in language and orthographic style. For a discussion of the problems with the concepts of versions and variants, see Smith, "Narrative Versions, Narrative Theories."
13. See Hosoya, "Kanshō Bakuya setsuwa"; Takahashi Minoru, "Mikenjaku koji"; Narita, "Mikenjaku dan no jūyō"; Kuroda, "Mikenjaku gaiden."
14. These texts are the most famous of a larger group. *Yuejueshu* and *Wuyue chunqiu* are histories. *Lieyizhuan* is a collection of strange writing (*zhiguai*) and *Xiaozizhuan*, of tales about the respect of children, usually grown sons, for parents. *Soushenji* is a collection of strange tales, *Fayuan zhulin* is a Buddhist encyclopedia, and *Taiping huanyuji* is a gazetteer of the world during the Taiping period (976–83). See *Chūgoku gakugei daijiten*, 1978 ed., s.v. "Etsuzetsusho" (*Yuejueshu*), "Goetsu shunjū" (*Wuyue chunqiu*), "Retsui den" (*Lieyizhuan*), "Kōshi den" (*Xiaozizhuan*),

"Sōshinki" (*Soushenji*), "Hōon jurin" (*Fayuan zhulin*), and "Taihei gyoran" (*Taiping yulan*).

15. The *Hōbutsu shū* manuscript containing the full tale, *Genroku kanpon*, is from the Edo period. See Kuroda, "Mikenjaku gaiden," 286. The older manuscripts of *Hōbutsu shū* have only a reference to a Moye tale. See Koizumi et al., *Hōbutsu shū*, 261. Two of these books have translations: Cogan, *The Tale of the Soga Brothers*, and Helen McCullough, *The Taiheiki*.

16. *Chūgoku gakugei daijiten*, s.v. "kōshiden."

17. Kuroda, in "Mikenjaku gaiden," quotes this line, 275. I was unable to obtain a copy of *Yōmei bunko shozō kōshiden* myself.

18. Kyōtō daigaku fuzoku toshokan, *Kōshiden*, Tale 45 (pages are unnumbered) and the accompanying commentary: Yoshikawa, "*Kōshiden* kaisetsu narabi shakubun," 21–22. In "Kanshō bakuya setsuwa," Hosoya renders this version of the tale into Japanese, 62–63.

19. Wagner, *Iron and Steel in Ancient China*, 112.

20. Zhao, *Wuyue chunqiu*, 77. The quoted words are Wagner's translation in *Iron and Steel in Ancient China*, 113.

21. Wagner, *Iron and Steel in Ancient China*, 114, and Zhao, *Wuyue chunqiu*, 78, respectively.

22. Cao, *Wudiji*, 24, cited in Wagner, *Iron and Steel in Ancient China*, 114n47. Written during the Tang dynasty, this text focuses on the geography of Suzhou and its vicinity.

23. *Scoria* is the refuse of smelted metal or ore. These definitions come from Maki, *Ijutsu to jujutsu*, 252; and various dictionaries, including Morohashi, s.v. "tetsusei."

24. Ury, *Tales of Times Now Past*, 67.

25. Yamada et al., *Konjaku*, 4: 483–84.

26. Yamashita, *Taiheiki*, 2: 294. Maki, *Ijutsu to jujutsu*, 252, also interprets *tama* to mean both ball and spirit.

27. Narita, "Mikenjaku dan no jūyō," 857.

28. Wang Mang had previously usurped the throne of the Han emperor with the help of his aunt.

29. There is no way of determining if the tones for these two words are the same since the tones of ancient Chinese are not known.

30. *Lieshizhuan* is attributed to Liu Xiang (ca. 77–6 B.C.E.). Fragments of it are preserved in other texts. See Hosoya, "Kanshō Bakuya setsuwa," 59, and Campany, *Strange Writing*, 47.

31. Hosoya, "Kanshō Bakuya setsuwa," 59–60.

32. Maki, *Ijutsu to jujutsu*, 242. Similarly, Hosoya, "Kanshō Bakuya setsuwa," 59, points out that Moye evokes Wu Zixu, described in the third chapter of *Wuyue chunqiu* as having a one *chi* (*shaku*) space between his eyebrows.

33. Li, *Shiji*, 504–9, or Watson, *Records of the Historian*, 16–29. Wagner summarizes and discusses the biography in, *Iron and Steel in Ancient China*, 103–4.

34. Maki, *Konjaku monogatari to ijutsu to jujutsu*, 242.

35. Ibid. The medical text is translated in Hsia, Veith, and Geertsma, *Yasuyori Tamba's Ishimpō*.

36. Kao, *Classical Chinese Tales*, 74n3.

37. Bakhtin, *Rabelais and His World*, 165.

38. Hosoya, "Kanshō bakuya setsuwa," 67. See also Murakami, Tokue, and Fukuda, *Soga monogatari*, 138–42, and Yamashita, *Taiheiki*, 2: 291–97.

39. In *Taketori monogatari*, a woodcutter finds Kaguyahime as a tiny little girl in a bamboo stalk. An elderly couple discovers Baby Momotarō (Peach Boy) in a giant peach according to a famous Japanese folktale.

40. Tale 27:3; Yamada et al., *Konjaku*, 4: 481–82.

41. Takaakira would have become *sesshō* or *kanpaku* depending on the age of his grandson when succeeding to the position of emperor. The former is regent to a child while the latter is regent to an adult emperor.

42. Tsuchida, "Anna no hen." See also Okada, *Figures of Resistance*, 166–70.

43. The *Heian jidai shi jiten*, s.v. "Sesonji," suggests two possibilities: (1) the estate was transferred from Minamoto no Yasumitsu to Fujiwara no Yukinari, and (2) the estate was transferred from Fujiwara no Koremasa to Fujiwara no Yoshitaka and then to Yoshitaka's son, Yukinari. Support of the second view can be found in Mori, *Konjaku*, p. 25 of the glossary/index. *Shūgaishō* (mostly a record of ancient court and military practices dating from the late Kamakura period) indicates that Prince Sadazumi was the original owner. See Mabuchi, Kunisaki, and Konno, *Konjaku*, 4: 31n12.

44. Matsumura Hiroji, *Eiga monogatari*, 1: 196–97 and 199 respectively.

45. Miki et al., *Uji shūi*, 154–55.

46. Mabuchi, Kunisaki, and Konno, *Konjaku*, 4: 31n12, and Brower, "Koñzyaku," 3: 994n3.

47. Mori, *Konjaku*, 5: 25.

48. Hasegawa et al., *Tosa nikki, Kagerō nikki*, 101. For a relatively recent translation of this book, see Arntzen, *Kagerō*.

49. According to *Ōkagami*, Takaakira marries Aimiya after her elder sister (his first wife) dies in childbirth. Tachibana, *Ōkagami*, 176.

50. Matsumura, Kimura, and Imuta, *Kagerō nikki*, 212. Most annotators of *Kagerō* indicate that Aimiya inherited the estate from her father, Fujiwara no Morosuke. See n. 5 on the same page. However, the new *Iwanami* edition states that the mansion came from her mother. See Hasegawa et al., *Tosa nikki, Kagerō nikki*, 101.

51. Kawasaki, "Minamoto no Takaakira," in *Ōchō no rakujitsu*, 61–62; Okada, *Figures of Resistance*, 167.

52. Mori, *Konjaku monogatari shū no seisei*, 237. According to the *Kōjien*, 2nd edition, s.v. "te," and *Iwanami kokugo jiten*, 6th edition, s.v. "te," *te* (translated as *hand* in the tale) can refer to the entire arm and the hand and also to the hand alone. Since it is hard to imagine a beckoning arm without the hand, I use *hand* in my translation. Of course, the small hand is probably attached to at least part of an arm. Similarly, a sense of a hand reaching out seems more appropriate when visualizing grabbing and pulling. The hand-versus-the-arm dilemma arises when we

look at another version of this discussion translated by W. Michael Kelsey. Kelsey renders a line either the same or similar to the line I quote as follows: "When a demon who did not reveal his shape interacted with the human world, he would frequently show just one part of his body. This was the arm." See Mori, "Supernatural Creatures," 158. Of course, Kelsey must have an arm with a hand intact in mind. Mori uses the modern Japanese *te* (meaning either "hand" or less commonly "arm") rather than *ude* (arm). In addition, when Mori illustrates his point with the incidents in two *Konjaku* tales and *Ōkagami*, Kelsey renders the body part, *te*, as *hand* in all three instances.

53. On the incident at the haunted Kawara mansion, see Chapter 4. I discuss the tale about the encounter of the two brothers with a demon, who turns out to be their mother, in Chapter 5.

54. Mori, *Konjaku monogatari shū no seisei*, 237, and Mori, "Supernatural Creatures," 158. The article in English appears to be a translation of the section in *Konjaku monogatari shū no seisei* entitled "Reiki to chitsujo." See Yamada et al., *Konjaku*, 4: 500 and 507–8, for the tales; and Tachibana, *Ōkagami*, 112, for the episode about Tamehira and the demon.

55. Mori, *Konjaku monogatari shū no seisei*, 228. The translation is Kelsey's in Mori, "Supernatural Creatures," 157.

56. Tachibana, *Ōkagami*, 167.

57. Yamada et al. *Konjaku*, 4: 481.

58. The Takiguchi are briefly described by Takeuchi, "Rise of Warriors," 680–81, and Friday, *Samurai, Warfare, and the State*, 32–33.

59. Mabuchi, Kunisaki, and Konno, *Konjaku*, 3: 62, in the introduction to the tale. D. E. Mills discusses the theory of the two collections sharing a common source in *Tales from Uji*, 106–7.

60. The *Uji shūi* tale has two English translations: Mills, *Tales from Uji*, 300–303, and Tyler, *Japanese Tales*, 72–75. In the introduction to the second book, Tyler states that faithful translations are not appropriate for his book and admits to "combing and brushing" tales "to rid them of small idiosyncrasies which might turn our attention from what matters" (pp. lvi–lvii). He sometimes combines elements of different tales into one story and includes only those final comments that he finds amusing and appropriate. He frequently omits names of places and people as well. It would be disastrous for a researcher to approach the tales in a similar manner since their idiosyncrasies and rough spots are often suggestive or informative. Although Tyler's decision renders the stories more appealing to a wider audience and *Japanese Tales* reads smoothly and is enjoyable, it also results in the loss of many important cultural and historical elements.

61. The place is Hikū in *Uji shūi*.

62. A palace guard of the Takiguchi unit named Michinori does not appear to be mentioned anywhere else in extant literary and historical sources.

63. A *chō* is roughly 119.3 yards.

64. The word translated as "wife," *tsuma*, means either lover or wife.

65. Four *shaku* is close to four feet.

66. Tale 20:10; Yamada et al., *Konjaku*, 4: 161–65.

67. Friday, *Samurai, Warfare, and the State*, 32–33.

68. Tonomura, "Black Hair," 144, and Tonomura, "Nikutai," 308–9.

69. Ibid.

70. Bakhtin, *Rabelais and His World*, 90–91.

71. Miki et al., *Uji shūi*, 15–17; Mills, *Tales from Uji*, 142–43.

72. Tonomura, "Black Hair," 142, and Tonomura, "Nikutai," 143, respectively.

73. Tale 3:19 in Nakada Norio, *Nihon ryōiki*, 306–9; tale 2:4 in Koizumi and Takahashi, *Sanbōe shūsei*, 146; tale 3:98 in Inoue and Ōsone, *Ōjōden, Hokkegenki*, 179–80. Translations are in Motomochi Nakamura, *Miraculous Stories*, 246–48; Kamens, *The Three Jewels*, 203–5; Dykstra, *Miraculous Tales*, 119–20, respectively.

74. Faure, *Red Thread*, 140.

75. Ibid.

76. Ōgoshi, "Bukkyō bunka paradimu," 31.

77. Mills, *Tales from Uji*, 108.

78. Kitayama, *Heian kyō*, 264–65; Borgen, *Sugawara no Michizane*, 154.

79. Yamada et al., *Konjaku*, 4: 165n71. The titles of these sutras in Japanese are *Shōbō nenjo kyō* and *Bussetsu butsumyō kyō* respectively.

80. *Tengu* as grotesque representations will be discussed in Chapter 6.

81. Wakabayashi, "Tengu Images," 17.

82. Ibid., 43. See also tale 20:9; Yamada et al., *Konjaku*, 4: 159–61.

83. Wakabayashi, "Tengu Images," 44.

Chapter 3

1. Bakhtin, *Rabelais and His World*, 21.

2. Bellard-Thomson, "Rabelais and Obscenity," 168.

3. Bakhtin, *Rabelais and His World*, 25.

4. Ibid., 240.

5. Tale 37. Inoue and Ōsone, *Nihon Ōjō gokurakuki* in *Ōjōden, Hokkegenki*, 38–39; Deal, "Women and Japanese Buddhism," 181. The compiler of *Gokurakuki* is Yoshishige no Yasutane (934?–1002).

6. Rodd, "Nichiren's Teachings to Women," 2. See also Kasahara, *Nyonin ōjō shisō no keifu*, 5–30.

7. Risshō daigaku shūgaku kenkyūjo, "Hokke daimoku sho," 400. Translated in Gosho Translation Committee, "The Daimoku of the Lotus Sutra." The sutra in Japanese is *Kegon kyō*, T. 9:278. The passages quoted from the letter in this paragraph do not appear in the extant versions of the Buddhist sutras to which Nichiren attributes them. Kasahara, *Nyonin ōjō shisō no keifu*, and Rodd, "Nichiren's Teachings to Women" (pages 8 and 3 respectively), attribute this first quote to a different text, *The Realization of Consciousness Only (Cheng wei shilun / Jōyuishikiron)*, but its extant version does not include this description of women either. See T. 31:1585.

8. Cited in Kasahara, *Nyonin ōjō shisō no keifu*, 6, and translated by Rodd, "Nichiren's Teachings to Women," 3. The sutra, *Daihatsu nehan gyō* in Japanese, is

T. 1:7. Immediately before Śākyamuni attains enlightenment, King Māra tries to prevent him from succeeding by sending his daughters to seduce him.

9. R. Keller Kimbrough, *Preachers, Poets, Women*, 234. Kimbrough translates this tale on pp. 233–34. Kotas in *Ōjōden*, pp. 258–59, similarly points out that the woman wants "to put into practice the bodhisattva idea of non-discrimination."

10. Ibid., 233–34.

11. For the first story, see tale 17:44 in Yamada et al., *Konjaku*, 3: 567–70, or Ury, *Tales of Times Now Past*, 117–20. For the second, tale 24 of *Goshūi ōjōden*, see Inoue and Ōsone, *Ōjōden, Hokkegenki*, 669.

12. Tale 3:20; Inoue and Ōsone, *Shūi ōjōden* in *Ōjōden, Hokkegenki*, 375; and Kotas, "Ōjōden," 508–9.

13. Tale 2:27, Ikegami, *Sangoku denki*, 1: 151–52. Kotas, "Ōjōden," cites the tale on p. 512.

14. On Buddhist views of women, see Faure, *The Power of Denial*.

15. Tale 26:2; Yamada et al., *Konjaku*, 4: 410–12.

16. LaFleur, *Karma of Words*, 44.

17. Tale 3:19; Nakada Norio, *Nihon ryōiki*, 306–9. I discussed the unusual anatomy of Nun Sari in Chapter 2.

18. Tale 1:1; Yamada et al., *Konjaku*, 1: 52.

19. The idea of all things having a Buddha nature and therefore the potential for enlightenment was formulated in Tiantai Buddhism in China during the eighth century and in Tendai Buddhism in Japan during the ninth. See Shimizu, "*Vegetable Nehan* of Itō Jakuchū," especially "Vegetable Buddhahood: The Doctrines of Busshō and Sōmoku Jōbutsu," 212–16.

20. Ibid., 223. Shimizu discusses radishes and turnips as images suggesting blandness and poverty in certain works of Japanese art with inscriptions alluding "to the poetics of Chinese literature." While his Japanese examples were all created after the compilation of *Konjaku*, his Chinese sources are from earlier times.

21. Fujimoto, *Shikidō ōkagami*, 17. Partial translation in Rogers, "*Shinjū* and *Shikidō ōkagami*."

22. *Kokugo daijiten*, 1982 ed., s.v. "kabura."

23. The poem in *Kojiki* can be read: "The many fences of Izumo / of the rising clouds / to keep a wife / I build a mansion with many fences / Oh the many fences." Ogihara and Kōnosu, *Kojiki, jōdai kayō*, 90. See also Brower and Miner, *Japanese Court Poetry*, 58, and Philippi, *Kojiki*, 91.

24. Maki, *Ijutsu to jujutsu*, 252–53.

25. For this version of the tale, see Cao, *Wudiji*, 24. It is also cited in Wagner, *Iron and Steel*, 114n47.

26. Tale 10:34; Yamada et al., *Konjaku*, 2: 328–32.

27. Since the titles of the tales appear in Chinese characters, their reading in Japanese allows for slight variations. The romanization of the title above follows the understanding of the annotators of the new Iwamani and new Shōgakkan editions. Instead of "nyōran seraruru koto," Yamada reads the title as "nyōran seraretaru koto." His use of the suffix "tari" (conjugated as "taru") expresses completion,

thereby making "was" rather than "is" violated more suitable. However, the more recent annotations better reflect the spirit (and grammar) of the narrative by suggesting something is about to happen or is happening. See Komine, *Konjaku monogatari shū*, 3: 15, and Mabuchi, Kunisaki, and Inagaki, *Konjaku*, 46.

28. Brower, "*Koñzyaku*," 496. Brower's title is "The Story of How the Somedono Empress Was Violated by a Goblin."

29. One *shaku* is close to a foot, so the demon stands around eight feet.

30. Tale 20:7; Yamada et al., *Konjaku*, 4: 155–58. For different translations of this tale, see Brower, "*Koñzyaku*," 496–502, and Tyler, *Japanese Tales*, 178–80.

31. Takakusu and Mochitsuki, *Shingon den*, 182.

32. Kuroita, *Fusō ryakki*, 152, Kanpyō 8, 9/22. Discussed in Komine, *Setsuwa no mori*, 44, and Faure, *Red Thread*, 169. The thirty scroll *Fusō ryakki* was compiled in the late Heian period by Kōen (d. 1169), the Tendai priest who ordained Hōnen (1133–1212), founder of Pure Land Buddhism. The scroll covers the age of the gods through the reign of Emperor Horikawa (1079–1107, r. 1086–1107), with many of its entries describing Buddhist events or otherwise connected to Buddhism. On Takaiko, see Chapter 4.

33. In response to a conference paper I gave on Empress Somedono and the demon, Susan Klein of the University of California at Irvine suggested that the historical affair involving Takaiko was projected onto Somedono because Takaiko was already the protagonist of stories involving Ariwara no Narihira (Session 111: "The Role of *Setsuwa* in Early and Medieval Japanese Textuality," Annual Meeting of the Association of Asian Studies, New York, 2003.)

34. Kawashima, "The Construction of the Feminine Margin," 288, and Kawashima, *Writing Margins*, 264.

35. Tanaka, *"Akujo" ron*, 90–91; Baba, *Oni no kenkyū*, 203–6; Iizawa, "Oni no shinsō"; Tanabe, *Oni no nyōbō*, 293–316. See also Faure, *Red Thread*, 135–36 and 167–69.

36. Minamoto, "Nihon bukkyō no seibetsu," 108–9.

37. Tanaka, *"Akujo" ron*, 117.

38. See Ibid., 95–98; Wakabayashi, "Tengu Images," 25–27; Komine, *Setsuwa no mori*, 30–33. Although the *Sōō kashō-den* is said to be from the early tenth century, this story is probably a much later addition, perhaps from as late as the mid-thirteenth century according to Wakabayashi, 26n13.

39. On the recensions of the possession of Somedono by Shinzei in the *Soga monogatari* and the *Hōbutsu shū*, see Faure, *Red Thread*, 167–68.

40. The *Nagato* text is an example of an account that does not mention Somedono. Takagi et al., *Heike monogatari*, 126. Wakabayashi quotes the episode in this text in "Tengu Images," 27.

41. Faure, *Red Thread*, 136.

42. Mototsune is also the adopted son of Somedono's father as well as the biological brother of her daughter-in-law, Takaiko, and hence the uncle of her grandson Yōzei.

43. Komine, *Setsuwa no mori*, 45.

44. Susan Klein raised the possibility that the Fujiwara were complicit in the circulation of this tale after Somedono's lineage had become defunct. According to this theory, they wanted to disassociate themselves from her. Session III: "The Role of *Setsuwa* in Early and Medieval Japanese Textuality," Annual Meeting of the Association of Asian Studies, New York, 2003. On the deposition of Yōzei, including a thorough investigation of the historical sources treating it, see Hesselink, "The Emperor Who Committed Murder."

45. Tale 15:8 (also 193); Miki et al., *Uji shūi*, 388; and Mills, *Tales from Uji*, 429–30.

46. Miki et al., *Uji shūi*, 388, and Mills, *Tales from Uji*, 430.

47. In *The Red Thread*, Faure argues that Sōō is represented as a "flawed ascetic" since the opening of the same tale tells how, unable to recite the *Lotus Sutra*, he was previously unable to enter Maitreya's Inner Palace from Tuṣita Heaven. However, past or future failures do not negate successes in the present. Despite this past flaw, he later adheres to Buddhist virtues. Similarly, although representations of Sōō in subsequent texts depict him as prey to passion, he is different in *Uji shūi*. Should we string all the tales about a particular figure together and read them as one narrative? This approach makes more sense in regard to the newest tales in a group about a given figure since audiences may have been aware of earlier stories. When we are not biased by later tales, Sōō in *Uji shūi* can be seen as someone who upholds the precepts in the process of becoming more devout.

48. Hori, "On the Concept of Hijiri," 141.

49. Ishihara, *Ishinpō*, 204–5. Translated in Hsia et al., *Yasuyori Tamba's Ishimpo*, 1: 216, with my addition of *demons* in parentheses.

50. Strickmann, *Magical Medicine*, 72.

51. On *gui*, see Kadoya, "Iwate no oni," 123, and Werner, *Myths and Legends of China*, 103.

52. A man afflicted with ghost intercourse must engage in sexual intercourse without ejaculating with up to ten women in one night. Ishihara, *Ishinpō*, 48–49, and Hsia et al., *Yasuyori Tamba's Ishimpo*, 157.

53. Teramoto, "The 'Yamai no Sōshi,'" 193.

54. Hsia et al., *Yasuyori Tamba's Ishimpo*, 2–12, and Teramoto, Appendix D, "General Description of Heian Medical Establishment" in 'Yamai no Sōshi,'" 314–28.

55. Matsunaga and Matsunaga, *Foundation of Japanese Buddhism*, 2: 88.

56. On the Priest Dōkyō and Empress Shotoku, see "Dōkyō to jotei" in Aoki, *Nara no miyako*, 466–95; Faure, *Red Thread*, 133–34; and especially Tanaka, "*Akujo*" *ron*, 17–80, who, among other things, considers how the creators of tales and scholars have seen the empress through the lenses of their own historical times.

57. A number of Buddhist temples, including Dadaiji, and one nunnery, Sairyūji, were built during the reign of Empress Shōtoku.

58. Faure, *Red Thread*, 133–34.

59. Matsunaga and Matsunaga, *Foundation of Japanese Buddhism*, 1: 126.

60. Faure attributes the scandal of Dōkyō and Shōtoku partially to the fact that a ruling empress "was condemned to celibacy, and to sterility" (*Red Thread*, 133).

61. The building is the *nurigome*.

62. Taguchi et al., *Ruijūbonkei Gōdanshō chūkai*, 97–98, and Kawaguchi and Nara, *Gōdanshō chū*, 468–73.

63. Miki et al., *Uji shūi*, 307, unnumbered note.

64. On Kawara-no-in, see Yamanaka, *Heian jinbutsu shi*, 34–42. Tale 1:27 in the *Kohon setsuwa shū* describes the garden and mentions that the mansion became a temple inhabited by a priest called Ahōgimi after remaining empty for a while after the death of Emperor Uda. This tale includes a different version of how Emperor Uda encounters the ghost of Tōru. See Miki et al., *Uji shūi*, 431–33.

65. On Emperor Uda, see Borgen, *Sugawara no Michizane*, 173–74, and Yamanaka, *Heian jinbutsu shi*, 31. On Minamoto no Tōru, see Yamanaka, *Heian jinbutsu shi*, 15–42 (chap. 2, entitled "Minamoto no Tōru"). Also, *Heian jidai shi jiten*, s.v. "Minamoto no Tōru," and Helen McCullough, "Appendices" to *Ōkagami*, 339.

66. Tachibana, *Ōkagami*, 87. According to Yamanaka, *Heian jinbutsu shi*, 26–29, scholars question whether Tōru desired to become emperor and, consequently, whether Mototsune ever made an argument against him.

67. Yamanaka, *Heian jinbutsu shi*, 32, and Helen McCullough, "Appendices" to *Ōkagami*, 341.

68. The same sources and page numbers in the preceding note, and Imaizumi et al., *Heian no shinkyō*, 426.

69. Mori, "Supernatural Creatures," 150.

70. Helen McCullough, "Appendices" to *Ōkagami*, 342.

71. Ōtsu et al., *Yamato monogatari*, in *Taketori, Ise, Yamato*, 232–33 and 259; Tahara, *Tales of Yamato*, 4 and 34.

72. Borgen, *Sugawara no Michizane*, 271.

73. Ibid., 272.

74. Yamada et al., *Konjaku*, 4: 480–81, and Miki et al., *Uji shūi*, 306–7 and 431–33 respectively.

75. Yamada et al., *Konjaku*, 3: 480–81. The *Konjaku* tale is translated by Brower, "Koñzyaku," 618–19, and McCullough in her introduction to *Ōkagami*, 50–51. The *Uji shūi* version is in Mills, *Tales from Uji*, 368–69.

76. Yamada et al., *Konjaku*, 5: 207–8. Tyler's relatively freer translation of this tale in *Japanese Tales*, 158–59, is entertaining, but omits more than one important line.

77. LaFleur, *Karma of Words*, 5.

78. Faure, *Red Thread*, 84–86.

79. Yamada et al., *Konjaku*, 5: 205–6, and Tyler, *Japanese Tales*, 159–60.

80. Strickmann, *Magical Medicine*, 258.

81. *Hokkegenki* tale, 3: 129; Inoue and Ōsone, *Ōjōden, Hokkegenki*, 217–19; and Dykstra, *Miraculous Tales*, 145–46. Tale 14:3; Yamada et al., *Konjaku*, 3: 277–80; Ury, *Tales of Times Now Past*, 93–96; and Tyler, *Japanese Tales*, 160–62. In the Dykstra translation, apparently in error, the man is born into Tōriten and the woman into Tosotsu.

82. Arthur Thornhill discusses the culpability of the monk in "The Dōjōji Tale," 4.

83. Kotas, "Ōjōden," 13.

84. Ibid., 209, and Ishida Mizumaro, *Ōjō yōshū*, 81–86.

85. Klein, "Woman as Serpent," 114.

86. Ibid.

87. Ibid., 107–8.

88. For a translation of the second play, see Keene, *Dōjōji*.

89. Freud, "Symbolism in Dreams," in *The Standard Edition of the Complete Psychological Works of Sigmund Freud*, vol. 15, lecture 10, p. 156. Similar ideas are expressed in "The Interpretation of Dreams," "A Case of Hysteria," and "A Phobia in a Five-Year-Old Boy," respectively, in vols. 4, 7, and 10 of the same collection.

Chapter 4

1. Kayser, *Grotesque in Art and Literature*, 182. Kayser discusses Bosch and the Brueghels on pp. 32–37 and refers to these artists as influences on later art and literature throughout the book. "The Millennium" in the Madrid Escorial (Ill. 7), with a detail from "Hell" (Ill. 8) and a detail of "The Garden of Lusts" (Ill. 9) are included in the book. See also Torviso and Marias, "Saint Anthony," and Francis, *Hieronimus Bosch: The Temptation of Saint Anthony*. A painting of the same title by Pieter Brueghel the Elder is in Cooke, *Painting Techniques of the Masters*, 142. See also Jan Brueghel the Elder, *The Temptation of Saint Anthony*, as reproduced in Oberhammer, plate 33, and Jan Brueghel the Elder, *The Temptation of Saint Anthony* in the Yale Art Gallery. Kayser also sees the biblical Apocalypse as a pictorial source for the European grotesque of this period.

2. Kayser, *Grotesque in Art and Literature*, 32.

3. Campbell, *The Power of Myth*, 222. The book is an edited version of a six-hour televised discussion.

4. On gates and bridges as fixed locations for the appearance of demons in setsuwa, see Mori, "Supernatural Creatures," 149–56, and Mori, *Konjaku monogatari shū no seisei*, 231–36. According to Mori in the chapter "Reiki to chitsujo," gates and bridges both mark boundaries. They link "the center with the surroundings, or order with confusion" (pp. 156 and 235 respectively, with quotes taken from the article in English). In addition, "demons live and make appearances at boundaries" which are mainly physical (pp. 155 and 234). In my view, when demons and other grotesque representations transgress boundaries, they dwell as much in the new space as in the old and help to define the realm of order. Another reason why gates were associated with demons may be that homeless people, many ill, apparently gathered under them for shelter.

5. Other translations of this poem appear in Mori, "Supernatural Creatures," 151–52, and Geddes, "Partial Translation and Study of the 'Jikkinshō,'" 491–92.

6. Entry 193 or 4:20. Kawaguchi and Nara, *Gōdan shōchū*, 658.

7. Saeki, *Kokin wakashū*, 93.

8. Rodd and Henkenius, *Kokinshū*, 35. They reverse the order of the words and put "gods" first.

9. Komachiya, *Gendai goyaku taishō Kokin wakashū*, 8. We can distinguish between spirits of the deceased in a general sense and those associated with specific people, such as the *onryō* or *goryō* of Sugawara no Michizane, since the latter are usually endowed with psychological substance. Spirits of known individuals act destructively for specific reasons; the source of their feelings can be traced because they have histories. On the ghost of Michizane, see Borgen, *Sugawara no Michizane*, 308–25.

10. *Kōjien*, s.v. "onigami."

11. Ibid., s.v. "kijin."

12. Tale 10:6; Izumi, *Jikkinshō daisan ruihon*, 182. Quoted in Kawaguchi and Nara, *Gōdan shōchū*, 660. Miyako Yoshika was an official who served as a private poet and scholar of Chinese. He administered the civil service exam to Sugawara no Michizane. See Borgen, *Sugawara no Michizane*, 103–31, passim.

13. Tale 8:3; Kojima and Asami, *Senjūshō*, 238–39.

14. Tale 24:24; Yamada et al., *Konjaku*, 4: 314–15. Also Ury, *Tales of Times Now Past*, 146–49, and Tyler, *Japanese Tales*, 87–88.

15. *Konjaku* tells us that Genjō resembles a living being who grows angry and will not resound for a player who is clumsy and lacks control.

16. Mori, "Supernatural Creatures," 152, referring to *Jikkinshō*, 10: 70, *Kokon chomonjū*, 17: 595, and the "Biwa Treasures" section of *Shichiku kuden*.

17. Ibid., 153, and Mori, *Konjaku monogatari shū no seisei*, 232.

18. Tale 1:3; Miki, et al., *Vji shui*, 9–13; Tyler, *Japanese Tales*, 239–41.

19. Benevolent demons include the Ten *Rākṣasa* Women who appear in the *Hokkegenki*, tales 1:17 and 2:59. See Inoue and Ōsone, *Ōjōden, Hokkegenki*, 74–75 and 126–127 (tales 13:41 and 13:4 in *Konjaku*). In the first tale, a priest who is a reciter of the *Lotus Sutra* sends these creatures to a second priest with daily offerings. In the second, a priest sexually attracted to the female *rākṣasas* becomes more pious when a female creature admonishes him by carrying him away from a holy cave and back to the secular world. The Ten *Rākṣasa* Women become protectors of reciters of the *Lotus Sutra* in the *Dhāranī* chapter of that sutra. See Sakamoto and Iwamoto, *Hokekyō*, 280 and tale 9:187. The tale of Shuten Dōji appears in *emakimono* (illustrated scrolls), *otogizōshi* (short stories somewhat longer than setsuwa that flourished from the Muromachi through Edo periods), and noh. See Kimbrough, "Demon Shuten Dōji."

20. Kayser, *Grotesque in Art and Literature*, 37.

21. The plank of wood is in tale 27:18; Yamada et al., *Konjaku*, 4: 501–2. In tale 19, a small demonic oil jar enters a house by jumping through the keyhole in the door. It causes the death of a young, ill woman inside. Whereas the creature is called an *oni* in tale 18, the oil jar in tale 19 is called *mononoke*. However, *oni* appears in the title of that tale and, in setsuwa, the terms are often interchangeable. Yamada et al., *Konjaku*, 4: 501–3.

22. Baba, *Oni no kenkyū*, 11–12. The introduction of the Chinese character and concepts may have occurred around the late sixth century.

23. Yanagita, "Yama no jinsei," 224–30, 233–43, and 298. In *Oni no kenkyū*, 11, Baba briefly introduces all the scholars mentioned in this section except for Ishi-bashi Gaha. I have built on what she notes about the various views of demons to provide a slightly more in-depth understanding of them and their shortcomings when applied to the Heian and Kamakura periods.

24. The transhistorical nature of Yanagita's views is evident in, for example, his controversial theory that *yamabito* are descendants of the Jōmon people and con-nected to "earthly deities" whereas people who cultivate rice are descendants of the Yayoi and connected to "heavenly deities." Morse, "Yanagita Kunio (1875–1962) and the Folklore Movement," 134–37, and Yanagita, "Yama no jinsei," 172–66.

25. Similarly, Yanagita observed that folk tales often describe mountain people as giants. Yanagita, "Yama no jinsei," 292–300.

26. Orikuchi, "Oni," 107–8, 110, and 114.

27. Kondō, "Oni no yurai," chap. 1 of *Nihon no oni*, 9–28.

28. Foucault, "Nietzsche, Genealogy, History," 142.

29. Baba, *Oni no kenkyū*, 11.

30. Baba, ibid., initially introduces the categories of oni on pages 13–14. She does not spell out the relationship of these groups to the rest of the book, but her chapters and chapter sections are in many ways elaborations of these categories. In addressing her scheme, I refer to both her initial introduction of the categories and the information she supplies about them later in the book.

31. Ibid., 11.

32. Ibid., 14 and 221.

33. Wakabayashi, "Tengu Images," 48. Mori also mentions the different place-ment of the two creatures in *Konjaku monogatari shū no seisei*, 215.

34. Tale 29:3; Yamada et al., *Konjaku*, 5: 138–42.

35. Brower, "Koñzyaku," 1029n18.

36. Book 17, section 27; Nagazumi and Shimada, *Kokon chomonjū*, 456–44.

37. Baba, *Oni no kenkyū*, 12.

38. Konishi, "Shūgyoku tokka," 324–25. The translation is by Rimer and Yama-zaki, *On the Art of Nō Drama*, 144. I changed the last word of the translation from *man* to *human* because it is closer to the original.

39. Konishi, "Shūgyoku tokka," 325.

40. Baba, *Oni no kenkyū*, 12. This reading corresponds to Zeami's explanation of *saidōfū* or "Delicacy with Strength" in his treatise "Nikyoku santai ezu" ("Illustra-tions for the Two Basic Arts and Three Role Types"). The phrase for "the Appear-ance of a Demon, the Heart of a Human" is sometimes substituted for *saidōfū*. See Konishi, "Shūgyoku tokka," 325.

41. Ikegami, "'Oni' no kanashimi," 12–18.

42. Baba, *Oni no kenkyū*, 12.

43. Bakhtin, *Rabelais and His World*, 281.

44. Ibid.

45. Toshihito became a provincial governor (*zuryō*) and general of the Head-quarters to Pacify the Ezo, established in Mutsu Province during the mid-Heian

Period. *Heian jidai shi jiten*, s.v. "Fujiwara no Toshihito," and the *Kojien*, s.v. "chin-jufu." The tale takes place when he is young.

46. Tale 26:17 in Yamada et al., *Konjaku*, 4: 458–63, and tale 1:18 in Miki et al., *Uji shūi*, 32–39. The *Konjaku* tale has been translated by Nozaki, *Kitsune*, 54–65. Translations of the *Uji shūi* tale are in Mills, *Tales from Uji*, 155–61, and Tyler, *Japanese Tales*, 118–22. The exaggerated details of the yam gruel and the *goi*'s reaction to it are also used to mock the wealthy lifestyles of the provincial aristocrats.

47. Tale 9:18; Yamada et al., *Konjaku*, 2: 209–11, from "The Tales of China" section. Its oldest extant version is in Tang dynasty collection *Mingbaoji*, tale 51; translated in Gjertson, *Miraculous Retribution*, 255–56.

48. Ōwa, *Oni to tennō*, 28–29. The most common reading for the character we now read as *oni* in the *Nihon shoki* and *Manyōshū* is *mono*. (According to Ōwa, it is not used in the *Kojiki*.) Chapter 2 of *Oni to tennō*, "Oni ga mono to yobareta no wa naze ka," 24–82, provides more information on early readings of the character *oni*.

49. Akimoto, *Izumo no kuni no fudoki*, in *Fudoki*, 236–39.

50. Michiko Aoki, *Records of Wind and Earth*, 151. I borrow several phrases from Aoki in my translation. However, an important difference in our translations is our rendering of *yamada*, literally "mountain field." Aoki's choice of "reclaimed land" does not indicate that the land is on a mountain, an important aspect of the inter-pretations of many scholars, including my own.

51. Sakamoto et al., *Nihon shoki*, 2: 350. Ōwa attributes the death of the empress to the anger of the mountain gods / demons in "Saimei tennō wa oni ni kowasareta to miru *Nihon shoki* no hensha," in *Oni to tennō*, 11–14.

52. With 75 of 116 *Nihon ryōiki* tales appearing in the "Tales of Japan" section of *Konjaku*, scholars long believed that the *Konjaku* compiler had access to *Nihon ryōiki* in a form resembling what we have today. However, as Komine points out, no complete pre-Edo period manuscript of *Nihon ryōiki* survived and the "*Nihon ryōiki* tales" in *Konjaku* most closely resemble popular editions of *Nihon ryōiki*. In other words, Edo editors of *Nihon ryōiki* may have relied on *Konjaku* in creating their text. We cannot assume that *Nihon ryōiki* versions of tales are older than those in *Konjaku* or conclude that the differences between texts are changes made by the *Konjaku* compiler. See Komine, *Konjaku monogatari shū no keisei to kōzō*, 44.

53. Tale 20:37; Yamada et al., *Konjaku*, 4, 205–6.

54. *Konjaku* tale 29:29.

55. Tale 27:17; Yamada et al., *Konjaku*, 4: 500.

56. Minamoto Tōru, Retired Emperor Uda, and the Kawara-no-in are discussed in Chapter 3.

57. Ebersole, *Ritual Poetry*, 276.

58. One *koku* (*saka*) is about 48 gallons. Tale 2:33; Nakada Norio, *Nihon ryōiki*, 232. In surviving manuscripts, the song is written in *manyōgana* whereas the rest of the text is in *kanbun*. My romanization of the Japanese is based on Nakada's render-ing of it into a form mixing *kana* and Chinese characters. However, I have made one change: whereas Nakada writes *hijiribito* (ascetic person) for "ascetic," I use *hijiri*. The *manyōgana* and *kanbun* text in Nakada is on p. 234.

59. Kimoto, *Jōdai kayō shōkai*, 144. Since few characters in *manyōgana* are used logographically, their meanings are open to debate. The *manyōgana* rendering of the song appears also in Kimoto, *Jōdai kayō shōkai*, 144. Kimoto's reading is "Nare o zo yome ni hoshi to, tare, Amuchi no komuchi no Yorozu no ko, Namu namu, sasesakau sakamochi susuri ho ma ushi ya, Yorozu no chishiki amashi ni, chishiki amashi ni." It depends upon the dropping of certain sounds: for example, *sen* becomes *se*.

60. For the full explication, see Kimoto, *Jōdai kayō shōkai*, 144–46. The translation of this line from page 145 of Kimoto's book is by Kyoko Motomochi Nakamura, *Miraculous Stories*, 205.

61. My translation is based on the interpretations of Baba and Ōwa, which agree with the reading and the notes provided in the Shōgakkan edition of *Nihon ryōiki* edited by Nakada Norio, 232. In the newer Iwanami edition, the annotator explains the song in terms of play on Buddhist words such as Śākyamuni. See Izumoji, *Nihon ryōiki*, 111–12n25–29. In contrast to earlier scholars, Izumoji does not think that the song conveys anything mysterious. Nor does he see it as an omen. In his view, the first line is the voice of the suitors saying half in jest, "I want to make you my wife." His reading is weak for several reasons: (1) it does not take the function of *waza-uta* into consideration; (2) it suggests a kind of sarcasm about relationships rare in classical and medieval times; (3) it does not account for why Buddhist words and word play are being used.

62. Baba, *Oni no kenkyū*, 61, and Matsunaga and Matsunaga, *Foundation of Japanese Buddhism*, 1: 115–16.

63. Nakada, *Nihon ryōiki*, 232n4.

64. Baba, *Oni no kenkyū*, 60. See also Ōwa, *Oni to tennō*, 87.

65. On the Kagamitsukuri, see Ōwa, "Kagamitsukuri-make jinja," 331–33, and Ikuzawa, "Kodai no Kagamitsukuri Uji." On the relationship of the Kagamitsukuri to the Mononobe, see Ōwa, "Kagamitsukuri-make jinja," 332–33, and Ikuzawa, "Kodai no Kagamitsukuri uji," 42.

66. Sakamoto et al., *Nihon shoki*, 2: 458–61 (the fifth day of the tenth month of Tenmu 12). On the status of *uji* whose chiefs were granted the title of *muraji*, see Hane, *Premodern Japan*, 16–17, and Piggott, *Japanese Kingship*, 85. In the case of the Kagamitsukuri and numerous other families, the title was granted to the entire household rather than to an individual. See Aston, *Nihongi*, 2: 361n2.

67. Yanai, Murofushi, and Ōasa, "Tamakazura," in *Genji*, 336–41.

68. Tales 20:25 to 20:40.

69. Ōwa, *Oni to tennō*, 87–88; Ōwa, "Kagamitsukuri-make jinja"; and Ōwa, "Osada-ni-masu-Amateru-mitama jinja," 6–23. Amateru-mitama jinja, Kagamitsukuri-make jinja and Kagamitsukuri-ita jinja were in Kagamitsukuri Village, where the Mononobe likely resided. The location is now Tawaramoto county of Nara.

70. Ōwa, "Kagamitsukuri-make jinja," 331–43. That same one-eyed god is listed at the present-day shrine as the dedicatee. Oddly, in *Oni to tennō*, Ōwa writes that the god was worshipped at Kagamitsukuri-ita shrine. He may have meant one or both of the other two shrines since he had previously mentioned them in this context. Whatever the case, Kagamitsukuri-ita shrine is currently associated

with Ishikoridome-no-mikoto. Connection to smithery links the gods in question. Moreover, the smith god is Ama-tsu-mara in *Kojiki* and Ama-tsu-ma-ura in *Nihon shoki*. (There is a sexual connotation to the god's name as *mara* can mean *penis*.) Ōwa notes that the various one-eyed gods in different texts merged into one figure in the shrine record.

71. Ōwa, *Oni to tennō*, 52–53. Yanagita notes that numerous gods and mysterious creatures associated with the mountains have a single eye or leg. See Yanagita, "Me hitotsu no Gorō kō," section in "Hitotsume kozō sonata," 165.

72. Ōwa, *Oni no Tennō*, 60. He refers to a myth from *Kogo shūi* (*Gleanings from Ancient Stories*, ca. 807) illustrating the practice of offering a live animal sacrifice for the sake of a good harvest. The figures involved are all gods. See Iida and Kurita, *Kogo shūi*, 48–49. The *Kogo shūi*, covering the years 729–49, is considered a polemical history. It was compiled by Inbe no Hironari in 807 to justify the role his lineage played in religious and ceremonial affairs at court. Containing the legends of the Inbe, the book was created in resistance to the Nakatomi, who, supported by the Fujiwara offshoot of the *uji*, defeated the Inbe in the early ninth century.

73. Ōwa, *Oni to tennō*, 88. He singles out the chiefs, as indicated by the last part of the family name, *miyatsuko*, a title of nobility used in ancient Japan.

74. Hane, *Premodern Japan*, 20, gives the examples of numerous male and female attendants buried alive with the body of Himiko in *Weizhi* and of how, in *Nihon shoki*, Emperor Suinin is disturbed by the live burial of the attendants of his deceased son because they are heard crying for days. According to the legend, *haniwa* or clay figures usually in the shapes of humans and animals were soon created as a substitute for living beings. See Sakamoto et al., *Nihon shoki*, 1: 272–75. In addition, because of other entries in *Nihon shoki* many scholars believe that humans were sacrificed to the gods to ensure the construction of buildings, bridgeheads, and dikes (Hane, *Premodern Japan*, 20.) There is also a legendary practice of offering women to water deities, which in turn has relevance for the study of *hashihime* (female bridge deities). See Iijima, "Hitobashira densetsu," 320–21.

75. Hurst, "The Structure of the Heian Court," 44–45.

76. Tale 27:7; Yamada et al., *Konjaku*, 4: 485–86.

77. *Iwanami kogo jiten*, 1979 ed., s.v. "mukotori." The official union of a man and woman in Heian society takes place when the couple spends three consecutive nights together and are served rice cakes on the third night in acknowledgment of their bond.

78. Mabuchi, Kunisaki, and Konno, *Konjaku*, 4: 39.

79. Sei Shōnagon uses *yamugoto nashi* in regard to Middle Counselors, Major Counselors, and Ministers of State in section 179; Watanabe, *Makura no sōshi*, 229.

80. The discussion of Narihira's genealogical line and the Kusuko incident (*Kusuko no hen*) is a combined summary of accounts in the following texts: Okada, *Figures of Resistance*, 140–41; Borgen, *Sugawara no Michizane*, 38; and Katagiri et al., "Ariwara no Narihira to *Ise monogatari*" in *Taketori, Ise, Yamato, Heichū*, 113–14.

81. See McCullough and Craig, *Flowering Fortunes*, 2: 812–13, for information on the Six Guards Headquarters and the positions in the bodyguards.

82. Mabuchi, Kunisaki, and Konno, *Konjaku*, 4: 38.

83. Tachibana, *Ōkagami*, 48.

84. Katagiri et al., *Taketori, Ise, Yamato, Heichū*, 138.

85. Kawashima, *Writing Margins*, 263.

86. Scholars differ slightly in regard to which of these sections refer to Takaiko. See Tsunoda, *Ōchō no eizō*, 111–13, and McCullough, *Tales of Ise*, 47.

87. Tsunoda, *Ōchō no eizō*, 98 and 113–22. At the same time, the depictions of the affair are viewed as fictionalized.

88. Kuroita, *Fusō ryakki*, 163–64 and 170. See also Tsunoda, "Fujiwara no Takaiko no shōgai," in *Ōchō no eizō*, 102–75. A concise account of the life and legends of Takaiko and references for further research can be found in the *Heian jidai shi jiten*, s.v. "Fujiwara no Takaiko."

89. The sketchy story of a woman involved with a high priest brings to mind the fuller and historically later account of Lady Nijō in *Towazugatari* (1307). See Misumi, *Towazugatari*, or Brazell, *Confessions of Lady Nijō*.

90. Yōzei is also discussed in Chapters 2 and 3.

91. In *The Red Thread*, p. 169, Faure briefly mentions this incident as part of the effort to discredit the imperial line, but he does not consider that Takaiko and Somedono may have had their own reasons for defying the wishes of the court. In addition, Takaiko is the first cousin of Somedono, not her daughter as he states. She becomes the consort of Emperor Seiwa, son of Somedono.

92. Baba, *Oni no kenkyū*, 67. Helen McCullough writes of an older, similar theory: "According to some Tokugawa scholars, the seduction was a political ruse devised by Narihira because, as a partisan of Prince Koretaka and the Ki family, he wished to prevent the match between Seiwa and Kōshi" (*Tales of Ise*, 46). The issues McCullough raises about the impossibility of knowing whether the affair ever took place are not problematic here. Important to the grotesque is that some people imagined Ariwara resisting, not whether the historical person actually did.

93. For the accounts in histories of a transformed being appearing on Pine Grove, see Takeda, *Kundoku Nihon sandai jitsuroku*, 1179, and Kuroita, *Fusō ryakki*, 152. One of six national histories, the fifty-scroll *Nihon sandai jitsuroku* was compiled by Fujiwara no Tokihira (871–909) and others in accordance with the imperial command of Emperor Uda. It covers the years 858–87, the reigns of Emperors Seiwa, Yōzei, and Kōkō. After an interruption, the collection was completed in 901 during the reign of Emperor Daigo (885–930, r. 897–930).

94. Baba's interpretation becomes problematic because she summarizes three versions of the event as one story. See *Oni no kenkyū*, 70.

95. Tale 17:589; Nagazumi and Shimada, *Kokon chomonjū*, 271–72.

96. Takeda, *Kundoku Nihon sandai jitsuroku*, 1179, and Kuroita, *Fusō ryakki*, 152.

97. Tale 27:8; Yamada et al., *Konjaku*, 4: 486–87.

98. The question of how confined Heian women were continues to be explored. A challenge to the notion that they rarely went outside and avoided public places can be found in Yiengpruksawan, "What's in A Name?" 426. Yiengpruksawan citing

kanbun diaries as evidence, asserts that works such as *Genji* have disproportionately shaped our view of Heian social history.

99. Yamada et al., *Konjaku*, 4: 487–88. Since most extant manuscripts of *Konjaku* are from the Edo period (1600–1868) or later, we do not know for certain whether the titles of the tales were part of the earliest versions of the collection. They may have been later additions. However, the oldest extant manuscript, the *Suzukabon*, has tale titles. Until recently, scholars believed that the *Suzukabon* was copied from another manuscript in the late Kamakura or early Muromachi period. In the mid-1990s, research employing radiocarbon dating raised the possibility that it is from the late Heian or early medieval period. *Sankei shinbun* (Osaka), 31 July 1995. A national treasure, the *Suzukabon Konjaku* can be viewed through the Kyoto University Digital Library at http://edb.kulib.kyoto-u.ac.jp/exhibit/index.html

100. The Jijūden was converted into a hall used along with its grounds for "Buddhist services in honor of Kannon, for such annual observances as the Palace Banquet (*naien*, a Chinese poetry gathering in the First Month) and the wrestling matches, as well as for amusements like football and informal dancing." McCullough and McCullough, *Flowering Fortunes*, 847–48. The tale is 27:10; Yamada et al., *Konjaku*, 4: 488–89.

101. Kuroita, *Fusō ryakki*, 202, and tale 17:590 in Nagazumi and Shimada, *Kokon chomonjū*, 456–57. Footprints are also spotted in *Kokon chomonjū* on the tenth of the eighth month of Tengyō 8 (945). See tale 17:594, p. 458.

102. Farris, *Heavenly Warriors*, 129, including note 33, touches on the relationship between the life of the elite and the exploitation of the masses.

103. Baba, *Oni no kenkyū*, 71–72.

104. On the Akō incident, see Chapter 3.

105. Instead of embracing the view of the *insei* period as marked by a new political system, I am following the lead of Kuroda Toshio, John W. Hall, G. Cameron Hurst III, and others who see "the activities of the abdicated emperors in the late Heian period . . . as an organizational attempt on the part of the imperial house to reassert its own control within the existing system." Hurst, "The Development of the *Insei*," 62–63 and the full chapter.

106. *Nihon kiryaku* consists mostly of excerpts from the six national histories and public and private diaries.

107. Kuroita, *Nihon kiryaku*, 73.

108. Entry 50 in Satake and Kubota, *Tsurezuregusa* in *Hōjōki, Tsurezuregusa*, 126–27; Keene, *Essays in Idleness*, 43–44.

109. Sakamoto et al., *Nihon shoki*, 2: 91–92. According to other theories of the identity of the *Mishihase no hito*, the characters for the Tunguses were borrowed from the Chinese classics or elsewhere and used in reference to another group of people. See n31 on p. 9 of the same book.

110. Shiryō hensanjo, *Shōyūki*, 140. These events are described in Tsunoda, *Ōchō no eizō*, 350–76.

111. Tale 11:12; Yamada et al., *Konjaku*, 3: 84. Ryūkyū is thought to be either present day Okinawa or Taiwan.

112. Mori, "Supernatural Creatures," 155.

113. Ibid.

114. Tale 5:1; Yamada et al., *Konjaku*, 1: 338–43, and tale 91 (6:9) in Miki et al., *Uji shūi*, 168–74, respectively. For a translation, see Dykstra, *Konjaku Tales*, 2: 165–71 for the *Konjaku* version, and Mills, *Tales from Uji*, 266–69 for the *Uji shūi* version.

115. According to the Mandate of Heaven, the destinies of people depend upon whether or not their words and actions are virtuous and the futures of dynasties similarly on the behavior of their rulers. See Chan, *Chinese Philosophy*, 3 and 6–8.

116. Tachibana, *Ōkagami*, 112–13, and Helen McCullough, *Ōkagami*, 106.

117. On Tadahira, see Tachibana, *Ōkagami*, 364, and *Heian shi jiten*, s.v. "Fujiwara no Tadahira."

118. *Hokkegenki* tale 2:57 in Inoue and Ōsone, *Ōjōden, Hokkegenki*, 124–25, and tale 17:42 in Yamada et al., *Konjaku*, 3: 564–65. Also, Dykstra, *Miraculous Tales*, 82–83, and Tyler, *Japanese Tales*, 207–8.

119. *Hokkegenki* tale, 3:110 in Inoue and Ōsone, *Ōjōden, Hokkegenki*, 191–94. Tale 12:28 in Yamada et al., *Konjaku*, 3: 171–73. Translations in Dykstra, *Miraculous Tales*, 128–29, for the first version, and Ury, *Tales of Times Now Past*, 87–89, and Tyler, *Japanese Tales*, 209–11, for the second. Another Japanese version is tale 2:21 of *Shūi ōjōden* in Inoue and Ōsone, *Ōjōden, Hokkegenki*, 340–41.

120. Brower, "*Koñzyaku*," 873–74n1. The note includes a summary of a Tang dynasty translation of the sutra, tale 968. In short, "a certain male inhabitant of the thirty-three-fold heaven of Indra" is doomed to be "born as an animal for seven successive reincarnations" because of inappropriate behavior with the heavenly maidens. The male being is able to avert this karma by chanting the formula once the Buddha imparts it "for the sake of all sentient beings." Several different translations of this sutra were used in both China and Japan.

121. It is also called the *Fusōshin emaki*. Komatsu Shigemi, *Hyakki yagyō emaki*, 69–90, and 126–41 for the commentary.

122. Yamada et al., *Konjaku*, 3: 336. Versions of this tale appear in numerous collections.

123. Tale 23; Nakajima, *Uchigiki shū*, 115–19.

124. Baba, *Oni no kenkyū*, 84.

125. Tale 134; Kawaguchi and Nara, *Gōdan shōchū*, 488–93. The story appears as part of a longer entry in the oldest extant text, *Suigenshō*, and separately in *Ruijūbonkei Gōdanshō*. See Kawaguchi and Nara, 493 and 1543.

126. Ibid., 492.

127. The tale is 14:42 in *Konjaku*, 213 in *Uchigiki*, and 2:51 in *Kohon*. See Yamada et al., *Konjaku*, 3: 335–37, Nakajima, *Uchigiki shū*, 115–19, and Miki et al., *Uji shūi*, 458–63, respectively. Fujiwara no Tsuneyuki became Major Captain of the Right Division of the Imperial Bodyguards in 864 and a Major Counselor in 872. Brower, "*Koñzyaku*," 875n4. Brower translates the term for *konoe* as "Inner Palace Guards" whereas I use "Imperial Bodyguards."

128. Baba, *Oni no kenkyū*, 83–84 and 91–92 respectively, for the two views.

129. Tale 24:15; Yamada et al., *Konjaku*, 4:298–99. Loosely translated in Tyler, *Japanese Tales*, 230.

130. In using the term *kami*-worship instead of Shinto, I follow the lead of Helen Hardacre. According to her, Shinto was not always an organized religion associated with an institution but a tradition probably invented in modern Japan (she argues Meiji) that brought together many disparate elements. Hardacre, *Shintō and the State*, especially the introduction and the first chapter.

Chapter 5

1. See Chapter 3 on the evils of women according to sutras.

2. Tsukahara, "Mushi mezuru himegimi," in *Tsutsumi Chūnagon*, 47. For a translation of this collection of stories, see Backus, *The Riverside Counselor's Stories*. For the tale discussed, see also Seidensticker, "The Lady Who Preferred Insects."

3. Tsukahara, "Mushi mezuru himegimi," in *Tsutsumi Chūnagon*, 50.

4. On *kaimami*, see Field, *The Splendor of Longing*, 123, 141–43, 251–56, 269–74. On women viewing men, see Sarra, "The Poetics of Voyeurism in *The Pillow Book*," in *Fictions of Femininity*, 222–64.

5. Tsukahara, "Mushi mezuru himegimi," in *Tsutsumi Chūnagon*, 48.

6. Ibid., 47.

7. *Japanese-English Buddhist Dictionary*, Daitō shuppansha, 1965 ed., s.v. "honji."

8. In the Japanese, the word used is *keshin*.

9. Nickerson, "The Meaning of Matrilocality," 445.

10. According to one theory, these stories were produced in the literary salons of Kanshi and Princesses Yūshi and Baishi (daughters of Emperor Go-Suzaku) around 1055. Some scholars have cast doubt on the assertion that women wrote all the stories. Tsukahara, *Tsutsumi Chūnagon*, 191–92, and Hirano, *Tsutsumi Chūnagon Monogatari*, ix–xiv.

11. The author's attempt to make the character pitiful may be to enhance her sexual appeal. Margaret H. Childs suggests that pity aroused love in characters in *Genji* and other works of Heian literature in "The Value of Vulnerability," 1061.

12. Tsukahara, "Mushi mezuru himegimi," in *Tsutsumi Chūnagon*, 55.

13. Watanabe, *Makura no sōshi*, 142.

14. Morris, *Pillow Book*, 1: 117.

15. Although Motoko's ladies-in-waiting are present, the empress was apparently unable or unwilling to have Sei come out into the view of her guests.

16. Komatsu, "Mino kasa o meguru fuokuroa" in *Ijinron*, 188–89 and 208–09. Komatsu argues that Orikuchi allows for a broad view of the bamboo hat and coat. Although the study focuses on the use of this outfit in modern rituals of passage such as marriages and funerals, the idea of demons crossing boundaries or of showing people places beyond their immediate existence applies also to premodern demons. On the straw raincoat and hat, see also Orikuchi, "Mino kasa no shinkō," 20–22.

17. Ōwa, "Mino kasa," 229–32.

18. Katagiri et al., *Yamato*, in *Taketori, Ise, Yamato, Heichū*, 305. *Michinoku* is also read *Mutsu*. The last line in the *Shūi shū* is *Iū wa makoto ka*. See also Yatagiri, *Shūi waka shū*, 138.

19. Baba mentions the similarity in the genealogies in reference to the brother of the girls, *Oni no kenkyū*, 21.

20. Hall, *Government and Local Power in Japan*, 122–23, and Hurst, "The Structure of the Heian Court," 50–51.

21. Lady Chikuzen became the principal wife of a grandson of retired Emperor Kazan (968–1008, r. 984–86), Prince Nobuzane, who headed the Department of Shrines, and the mother of Prince Yasusuke, who ultimately held the same position as his father. On her collection of poems and life, see Morimoto, "Azumaji no tabi," 239–54, and *Heian jidai shi jiten*, s.v. "Yasusuke ō no haha."

22. Takizawa, *Mototoshi shū zenshaku*, 98.

23. Baba, *Oni no kenkyū*, 25–26.

24. Baba erroneously states that the poem by Mototoshi has no response. Ibid.

25. Nagasawa, *Yasusuke ō no haha no shū*, 353.

26. For the second and third definitions, see *Kojien*, s.v. "minori."

27. This interpretation requires inferring a causal relationship between the first line and the second two not indicated by the grammar; there is no equivalent of "because of" in the Japanese.

28. Nanba, *Murasaki Shikibu shū zen hyōshaku*, 258.

29. Ibid., 263–68.

30. For translations/readings of this poem incorporating the standard view, see Field, *Splendor of Longing*, 63; Bowring, *Murasaki Shikibu*, 231; and Kawashima, *Writing Margins*, 270.

31. Bargen, *A Woman's Weapon*, 24.

32. Nanba, *Murasaki Shikibu shū zen hyōshaku*, 269.

33. Katagiri et al., *Ise monogatari* in *Taketori, Ise, Yamato, Heichū*, 179.

34. O'Flaherty, *Evil in Hindu Mythology*, 62. See also Knappert, *Indian Mythology*, 204. *Rākṣasīs* appropriated by Buddhists serve as defenders of the Dharma.

35. Bethe and Brazell, *Yamamba*, 207–25.

36. Ema, *Nihon yōkai henka shi*, 442, and Miyata, *Hime no minzokugaku*, 177.

37. I do not distinguish sex as a pre-discursive biological fact from gender as a cultural construction because, in the words of Judith Butler, "there is no recourse to a body that has not always already been interpreted by cultural meanings." See Butler, *Gender Trouble*, 8.

38. The line, which literally says the man almost falls off the horse, can also be interpreted figuratively to mean that he almost jumped down. See Yamada et al., *Konjaku*, 4:493n35, and Mabuchi, Kunisaki, and Konno, *Konjaku*, 4:54n3.

39. This is about six inches since one *sun* is 1.2 inches.

40. Tale 27:13; Yamada et al., *Konjaku*, 4: 491–94. Also translated in Brower, *Koñzyaku*, 625–31, and Tyler, *Japanese Tales*, 19–22.

41. Kondō and Baba emphasize the connection of the Agi Bridge story to Wata-

nabe no Tsuna and other demon-quellers (*Nihon no oni*, 62–64, and *Oni no kenkyū*, 122–30, respectively). Kawashima addresses the place of the woman waiting at the Agi Bridge in the development of Hashihime of Uji. She notes that scholars often cite the Agi Bridge demon as a prototype of the demonic Hashihime in *Yashirobon Heike* and addresses that story, which involves Tsuna (*Writing Margins*, 272–73 and 274–80, passim). Elsewhere in the same chapter, Kawashima relates key characteristics of demons in setsuwa to the figure of Hashihime as a jealous demon (255–65).

42. On the fingers of demons, including their connection to the claws of dragons and birds, see Kondō, *Nihon no oni*, 87–91.

43. Ōwa, *Oni to tennō*, 206–7. The hair of a small figure that Ōwa identifies as the earliest visual image of a demon in Japan, an early sixth-century gold and silver inlay on the pommel cap of the hilt of a round-headed sword, is loose and sticking upright. The pommel cap was found at the site of the Hagamiyama tombs in Kannonji City, Kagawa Prefecture.

44. A wealthy father has trouble getting his sons to come out of their burning house because they are distracted by pleasures within it. He succeeds in saving them by telling them that certain playthings, various carts, stand outside for them to enjoy. In other words, since the followers of Buddha were not ready for the highest truth, the Buddha was justified in giving them another, lesser, means of escaping spiritual danger. Sakamoto and Iwamoto, *Hokekyō*, 1: 160–69.

45. Ibid., 186.

46. Yamada et al., *Konjaku*, 4: 493.

47. The tale can be found in *Hokkegenki*, *Konjaku*, and other collections. See tale 3:81 in Inoue and Ōsone, *Ōjōden, Hokkegenki*, 156; and tale 12:1, in Yamada et al., *Konjaku*, 3: 130.

48. For a photo of a famous example of such a statue, see *Raijinzō*, as reproduced in Kondō, *Nihon no oni*, 27, or Miyama, *Kamakura no chōkoku, kenchiku*, plate 40. The statue is located in the Sanjūsangen-dō in Kyoto. See also wind and thunder gods in Tawaraya Sōtatsu, *Fūjin Raijin zu*, screen painting, seventeenth century, Kenninji, Kyoto.

49. Baba, *Oni no kenkyū*, 140–45. She draws from "Oni no shison," a discussion by Yanagita of an eighteenth-century demon supposedly descended from the Ōeyama demons. See Yanagita, "Oni no shison," 427–33. In *Oni to tennō*, 199–202, Ōwa discusses the link between the hair of demons, children, and women in mainly *Kojiki* and *Nihon shoki*.

50. See the *Kiritsubo* chapter of *The Tale of Genji*; Yanai, Murofushi, and Ōasa, *Genji monogatari*, 24.

51. On Heian hairstyles, see Hashimoto, "Heian jidai no kamigata," 27–35. The oldest extant *Genji monogatari emaki* is from the late Heian period. *Makura no sōshi emaki* is from the late Kamakura period.

52. Kojima et al., *Nihon shoki*, 3: 418–19.

53. Ibid., 436–37.

54. Baba, *Oni no kenkyū*, 143–44. Both Baba and Ōwa, *Oni to tennō*, 199–202, discuss these edicts in connection to the hair of demons and children.

55. Imaizumi, *Kundoku Shoku Nihongi*, 55. Itsuki no miya are the eastern and western shrines for the offerings of the new crop of rice during the Great Thanksgiving Festival Service following the enthronement of an emperor. *Kōjien*, s.v. "izuki."

56. Farris, *Population, Disease, and Land*, 43–44.

57. Tale 29:18; Yamada et al., *Konjaku*, 5: 169–70. English translations in Ury, *Tales of Times Now Past*, 183, and Tyler, *Japanese Tales*, 88.

58. This title is Tyler's translation, *Genji*, 299.

59. Hashimoto, "Heian jidai no kamigata," 32–34.

60. Kondō, *Nihon no oni*, 183. The Hashihime of the Nagara and Yodo Bridges appear to come from a later period, as in a tale about Hashihime of the Nagara Bridge in *Shintō shū* (Shinto Collection), a setsuwa collection from the Nanboku chō period (1336–92) discussed by Miyata, *Hime no minzokugaku*, 104–2.

61. Kawashima, *Writing Margins*, 233–49.

62. The creature at the bridge does not always take the form of a woman in setsuwa. In the story following the tale of Agi Bridge, a demon threatens a traveler who decides to lodge at an abandoned, dilapidated house not far from the Seta Bridge. The creature is not described because the man cannot see it in the dark. The man escapes and ends up hiding by a pillar beneath the bridge. When the demon speaks, nothing about its speech suggests a female being. It may be that the demon was supposed to assume a female form at some point since the tale is a fragment, but the story does not appear to be going in that direction. Yamada et al., *Konjaku*, 4:495.

63. See Motomochi Nakamura, *Miraculous Stories*, 107n14.

64. Mori discusses the connection of bridges and rivers to the supernatural in "Supernatural Creatures," and *Konjaku monogatari shū no seisei*, 231 and 234, respectively. He sees them, along with gates, as marking boundaries between the worlds of demons and people as well as other realms. See also Kawashima, *Writing Margins*, 228–33. The corresponding section of her dissertation has an informative title, "Bridges and Rivers: Marginality, Purity, and the Supernatural," that does not appear in the book ("The Construction of the Feminine Margin," 245–51). She observes the following about bridges: they could potentially connect heaven and earth in pre-Heian literature; they were used as sites for divination later in history; Buddhist monks often participated in their construction as a form of religious practice. In *Konjaku*, the famous holy man E no Ubasoku summoned demonic deities to construct a bridge between Mt. Kazuraki and Mt. Mitake. Tale 11:3; Yamada et al., *Konjaku*, 3: 62–63; and Ury, *Tales of Times Now Past*, 82–83.

65. Karl F. Friday discusses the client-patron relationship of warriors of Minamoto descent and the Fujiwara regents as well as warriors of Taira descent and successive retired emperors in *Hired Swords*, 1–93 and 98–112.

66. This opening differs from those of most *Konjaku* tales in that the narrator uses the suffix *ki* instead of *keri* (*ariki* instead of *arikeri*). Since *keri* is used in many other lines, *ki* seems to be functioning here primarily "to indicate a 'narrated,' storytelling situation." See Okada, *Figures of Resistance*, 37.

67. Tale 27:21; Yamada et al., *Konjaku*, 4: 505–7; Tyler, *Japanese Tales*, 18–19.

68. Tonomura discusses this tale in terms of its depiction of jealousy ("Black Hair," 139).

69. Tale 27:23; Yamada et al., *Konjaku*, 4: 507–8; Ury, *Tales of Times Now Past*, 163–65; and Tyler, *Japanese Tales*, 316–17.

70. Her room is a *tsuboya*, which some scholars understand to be a small separate building. See *Kojien*, s.v. "tsuboya." See Yamada et al., *Konjaku*, 4: 476 and 508n17; Mabuchi, Kunisaki, and Konno, *Konjaku*, 4: 86n1; Ury, *Tales of Times Now Past*, 164.

71. Baba, *Oni no kenkyū*, 133–34.

72. Yamada et al., *Konjaku*, 4: 508.

73. Tale 5:32; Yamada et al., *Konjaku*, 1: 399–402; Dykstra, *Konjaku Tales, Indian*, 2: 239–42.

74. Tale 9:45; Yamada et al., *Konjaku*, 2: 262–63; Ury, *Tales of Times Now Past*, 70.

75. *Obasute* by Zeami has been translated in Jones, "The Nō Plays." The others are in "Sarashina Journal" in Barnhill, *Basho's Journey*, 45–48, and Inoue, "Obasute."

76. Section 156 and Book 30:9, respectively. Katagiri et al., *Taketori, Ise, Yamato, Heichū*, 405–6. Translated by Tahara, *Tales of Yamato*, 109–10. Tale 30:9; Yamada et al., *Konjaku*, 5: 236–37. Translations by Brower, "*Koñzyaku*," 709–11, and Tyler, *Japanese Tales*, 215–16.

77. Kawai, *Mukashi banashi*, 49–50, and *The Japanese Psyche*, 33. *Mukashi banashi* are relatively recent folk and fairy tales.

78. Ibid., 50 and 33, respectively.

79. Bettelheim, "Transformations: The Fantasy of the Wicked Stepmother," chap. in *The Uses of Enchantment*, 66–73.

80. Bettelheim made the devastating mistake of blaming mothers of autistic children for the condition.

81. See *Konjaku* tales 1–12 in Book 9 and 23–34 in Book 19.

82. Kawashima, *Writing Margins*, 260.

83. As Rodd explains, the *Li ji* or "*The Book of Ritual* describes the three subordinations (*san jū*) as the submission of a woman to her parents while young, to her husband while in her prime, and to her sons when old." See "Nichiren's Teachings to Women," 2. On the three subordinations and five obstacles of women, see also Kasahara, *Nyonin ōjō shisō no keifu*, 10–16, and Nagata, "Butten ni okeru josei kan no hensen," 11–22.

84. Tale 48 (3:16); Miki et al., *Uji shūi*, 96–102; and Mills, *Tales from Uji*, 209–14.

85. Tale 2:3; Minobe, *Kankyo no tomo*, 129–32; Pandey, "Women, Sexuality, and Enlightenment," 339–40; Satō and Haruta, *Yashirobon Heike monogatari* 2: 542–44, with a slightly different version in Hajime, *Heike monogatari*, 3: 275–76; Tanaka Makoto, *Kanawa*, 206–10; and Keene, *Dōjōji*. The *Kankyo no tomo* tale is an early example of the transformation of a jealous woman into a demon. The motif becomes more common post-Heian. See also Kawashima, *Writing Margins*, 265–66, and Ikegami, "'Oni' no kanashimi," 12–18.

86. On p. 25 of *Rabelais and His World*, Bakhtin gives his source for the art pieces as H. Reich, *Der Mimus, ein literarentwicklungsgeschichlicher Versuch* (Berlin, 1903), pp. 507–98.

87. Bakhtin, *Rabelais and His World*, 25–26.

88. Russo, *Female Grotesques*, 219.

89. Ibid.

90. Gasbarrone, "'The Locus for the Other,'" 13.

91. Tale 27:15; Yamada et al., *Konjaku*, 4: 496–99; and Ury, *Tales of Times Now Past*, 161–63.

92. Viswanathan, "In Pursuit of the Yamamba," 245.

93. LaFleur, *Liquid Life*, 113.

94. Viswanathan raises the possibility that the mother keeps the baby because it is a boy, "In Pursuit of the Yamamba," 245.

95. Tale 1:16; Inoue and Ōsone, *Ōjōden, Hokkegenki*, 303–5; Kotas, *Ōjōden*, 460–64.

96. Tale 19:44; Yamada et al., *Konjaku*, 4: 138–39; and Brower, "*Koñzyaku*," 493–95.

97. Tale 30:6; Yamada et al., *Konjaku*, 5: 226–33. The tale is missing its ending.

98. Only occasionally do both sides appear in the same narrative. Kawai, *Mukashi banashi*, 64, and *The Japanese Psyche*, 42.

Chapter 6

1. Komatsu, *Nihon yōkai ibunroku*, 44. View another rendition of the legend of Tamamo no mae and other *otogi zōshi* (Muromachi period illustrated stories) at Kyoto University Digital Library, "Enjoying Otogi Zōshi with the Help of Synopsis and Illustrations" in English and Japanese versions at http://edb.kulib.kyoto-u.ac.jp/exhibit-e/otogi/cover/index.html. Studies on foxes in Japan include Bathgate, *Fox's Craft*; De Visser, "Fox and the Badger"; Kaneko, *Nihon kitsunetsuki shi*; Smyers, *Fox and the Jewel*; and Smits, "An Early Anthropologist?"

2. Tale 27:37 and 27:41 in Yamada et al., *Konjaku*, 4: 530–32 and 535–38 respectively. A translation of the first tale is in Nozaki, *Kitsune*, 54–65. The second is in Nozaki, 38–45; Ury, *Tales of Times Now Past*, 167–71; and Tyler, *Japanese Tales*, 300–303.

3. Gunsho ruijū kanseikai, *Kobiki*, 968–69. Translations of this work appear in Ury, "A Note on the Supernatural," and Smits, "An Early Anthropologist?" 86–89. In the essay portion of his study, Smits is concerned with "what prompted a scholar like Masafusa to devote a treatise to a witch animal like the fox?" (p. 84). I would argue that setsuwa suggest the important role of such animal spirits in the imaginations and psyches of aristocrats. Smits seems correct in concluding that Ōe's interest in foxes has something to do with the power shift away from the aristocrats and the sense they had of their privileged life nearing an end. However, I would not attribute this quality of *Kobiki* to a conscious effort on the part of Ōe "to structure and overcome the hidden anxieties of Late Heian intellectuals" (p. 86). Rather, the accounts reveal such hidden anxieties because Ōe is steeped in Heian aristocratic culture, thereby sharing certain elements of the imagination with other people of his time.

4. Yamada et al., *Konjaku*, 4: 460.

5. Miki et al., *Uji shūi*, 39.

6. Tale 27:40; Yamada et al., *Konjaku*, 4: 533–35; Nozaki, *Kitsune*, 33–35; and Tyler, *Japanese Tales*, 299–300.

7. Tale 2:40; Izumoji, *Nihon ryōiki*, 119–20; and Motomochi Nakamura, *Miraculous Stories*, 212–13.

8. The man is the slave (*yakko*) of the evil Tachibana no asomi Naramaro and his actions reflect on the character of his master. The tale indicates that the merciless response of the fox parallels the reaction of the emperor to Naramaro's attempt to usurp the throne: a sentence to death by sword.

9. Tale 52 (3:20); Miki et al., *Uji shūi*, 107–8; Mills, *Tales from Uji*, 218; and Tyler, *Japanese Tales*, 298–99.

10. Tale 27:32; Yamada et al., *Konjaku*, 4: 521–23; and Tyler, *Japanese Tales*, 294–95.

11. Tale 16:17; Yamada, *Konjaku*, 3: 456–58; Ury, *Tales of Times Now Past*, 102–5; and Tyler, *Japanese Tales*, 116–18.

12. Tale 2; Izumoji, *Nihon ryōiki*, 8; and Motomochi Nakamura, *Miraculous Stories*, 105.

13. Tale 14:5; Yamada, *Konjaku*, 3: 283–85; and Ury, *Tales of Times Now Past*, 96–98.

14. Jordan, "Trickster in Japan," 129–37. For an intriguing discussion of the fox as shapeshifter, see Bathgate, *Fox's Craft*.

15. Bakhtin, *Rabelais and His World*, 8. Claude Lévi-Strauss, Victor Turner, Mary Douglas, and Joseph Campbell are among the scholars who have written on the trickster. A survey of the seminal literature on tricksters, including a chapter on Susano-o by Robert S. Ellwood, can be found in Hynes and Doty, *Mythical Trickster Figures*. For an influential early study, see Radin, *Trickster*.

16. Bakhtin, *Rabelais and His World*, 93.

17. C. G. Jung, "On the Psychology of the Trickster Figure," 199. This essay is one of two commentaries included in this book by Paul Radin on the mythology of American Indians. Jung discusses medieval festivals on pp. 196–99.

18. Jordan, "Trickster in Japan," 137, and 137n1.

19. Hynes and Doty, "Fascinating and Perplexing Trickster Figure," in *Mythical Trickster Figures*, 2.

20. Doty and Hynes, "Historical Overview of Theoretical Issues: The Problem of the Trickster," chap. in *Mythical Trickster Figures*, 21. This description of the trickster according to Douglas coincides with her view of the "joker" in "The Social Control of Cognition," 373. The concepts of trickster and joker overlap in Douglas's work.

21. "Deceiver / trick-player" is one of many categories attributed to trickster figures by Hynes in "Mapping the Characteristics of Mythic Tricksters: A Heuristic Guide," in *Mythical Trickster Figures*, 33–45.

22. The unflattering description of the nose of Suetsumuhana is in Yanai, Murofushi, and Ōasa, *Genji monogatari*, 1: 224.

23. Tale 27:31; Yamada et al., *Konjaku*, 4: 519–52. See also Tyler, *Japanese Tales*, 122–24.

24. The fox spirit does not always have a low status. It was associated with the deity Inari, beginning from between the eleventh and thirteenth centuries according to Smyers, *The Fox and the Jewel*, 86. It also has connections to the deities Dakini and Benzaiten.

25. Tale 29:35; Yamada et al., *Konjaku*, 5: 198–200, and Tyler, *Japanese Tales*, 219–20.

26. Miyata, *Utsubo monogatari*, 125.

27. Nagazumi and Shimada, *Kokon chomonjū*, 527–28.

28. Ibid., 536.

29. Tale 19:2; Yamada et al., *Konjaku*, 4: 57–60; Brower, "*Koñzyaku*," 467–74; and Kelsey, "Didactics in Art," 304–9.

30. Tale 19:6; Yamada et al., *Konjaku*, 3: 74–75; and tale 20:713 in Nishio and Kobayashi, *Kokon chomonjū*, 401–2. The *Konjaku* version has been translated by Kelsey, "Didactics in Art," 329–31.

31. *Konjaku* tales 5:14 and 5:24, respectively; Yamada et al., *Konjaku*, 1: 367–70 and 390–91; Dykstra, *Konjaku Tales Indian section*, 2: 201–4 and 228–30.

32. *Konjaku* tales 9:18 and 9:19 involve the rebirth of daughters as sheep. Yamada et al., *Konjaku*, 2: 209–12. The tale about the hunter killing his mother in the form of the deer is 19:7; Yamada et al., *Konjaku*, 4: 75–77.

33. Research on the first tale includes Ikegami, *Konjaku monogatari shū no sekai*, 68–103; Saigō, "Ikenie kō," 170–79; Maeda, "Konjaku monogatari shū no 'kokka zō,'" 89–90.

34. The tale initially states that the gods demand a virgin, but the chosen woman and the hero become sexually involved before the day of the ritual. However, the loss of her virginity is never problematized. Tonomura suggests that the tale supports the idea of spiritual purity rather than the lack of sexual experience. Tonomura, "Hair," 140–41 and note 51, and Tonomura, "Nikutai," 305.

35. The term *koto no en aru ni yorite* can mean either "in accordance with a karmic affinity" or "on some occasion or business," so it is difficult to determine whether there is Buddhist meaning here. See Yamada et al., *Konjaku*, 3: 179n2.

36. The meaning of this line, *kataki arumono ni yukitsurete, itazurajhini suru mono wa naki ya wa aru*, is a subject of debate centered on the use of *ya wa*. If *ya wa* is taken as a rhetorical question, the line suggests that there is someone who would give up his life to fight the enemy. However, if *ya wa* is viewed simply as an emotive with no irony intended, the line would indicate the opposite—that certainly no one would act in that way. Ikegami suggests that the first interpretation is correct by focusing on the nuance of *itazuraji* (to die pointlessly). According to him, this word implies fighting to the end rather than intentionally getting into a situation where one anticipates dying pointlessly. In my view, the man is saying that there must be someone willing to confront the evil gods even if doing so means death. After all, he becomes that person. See Ikegami, *Konjaku shū no sekai*, 84–100.

37. *Sakaki* is a type of evergreen believed sacred.

38. Tale 26:7; Yamada et al., *Konjaku*, 4: 427; Brower, "*Koñzyaku*," 602–7. See Tyler, *Japanese Tales*, 107–10, for a rendering of the *Uji Shūi* tale.

39. Maeda, "Konjaku monogatari shū no 'kokka zō,'" 79–97.

40. Ibid., 88–91.

41. Ibid., 89–90.

42. Ikegami Jun'ichi connects this tale to the Nakayama Shrine in present-day Okayama Prefecture. See *Konjaku monogatari shū no sekai*, 74–84.

43. Ogihara and Kōnosu, *Kojiki, jōdai kayō*, 86–90. See also Ikegami, *Konjaku monogatari shū no sekai*, 72–73. "Kushi" can mean both comb and wondrous. "Nada" is a contraction of Inada, which was located in Izumo (Philippi, *Kojiki*, 509).

44. Wang, *Soushenji*, 231–32; DeWoskin and Crump, *In Search of the Supernatural*, 230–31.

45. Tale 26:8; Yamada et al., *Konjaku*, 4: 430–39; and Tyler, *Japanese Tales*, 274–80.

46. W. Michael Kelsey briefly mentions this tale in "Salvation of the Snake" to support his argument that the demon who devours monks at Gangōji in *Nihon ryōiki* tale 1:3 exemplifies "Shinto deities who attempted to oppose the building of the temple on their native soil" (p. 91). He argues that in a cluster of certain stories about snakes "we can find . . . first conflict between Buddhism and Shinto and then, as the relationships between the two settle down, a creative Buddhist use of those ancient Shinto deities that appeared as reptiles" (p.83). I agree with his view that the tension between Shinto and Buddhism in many tales is "a sometimes violent conflict lurking beneath the surface" (p. 83).

47. The eighth day of the fourth month of the fourteenth year of the reign of Suiko; Sakamoto et al., *Nihon shoki*, 2: 186–87; and Aston, *Nihongi*, 2: 134.

48. Although there is a lacuna where the name should be, Kuratsukuri no tori is given in other texts describing the founding of Gangōji. Yamada et al., *Konjaku*, 3: 100n1.

49. We can infer that the tree has killed the person who tried to chop it down from what follows.

50. Tale 11:22; Yamada et al., *Konjaku*, 3: 100–102. The translated portion ends on p. 101.

51. Wang, *Soushenji*, 216; and Dewoskin and Crump, *In Search of the Supernatural*, 213–14.

52. My description of the Japanese zelkova draws from *Iwanami kogo jiten*, 6th ed., s.v. "tsuki"; Maki, *Ijutsu to jujutsu*, 212; Mabuchi, Kunisaki, and Konno, *Konjaku*, 1: 155n6.

53. Xiang, "Utsuho monogatari Toshikage no maki ni okeru kankyō," 35–36.

54. Ibid., and Ogihara and Kōnosu, *Kojiki, jōdai kayō*, 91–96.

55. Miyata, *Utsuho monogatari*, 119–20.

56. Tale 3; Miki et al., *Uji shūi monogatari*, 9–13; Mills, *Tales from Uji*, 137–40; and Tyler, *Japanese Tales*, 239–41.

57. Tale 11:27 in Yamada et al., *Konjaku*, 3: 109–10.

58. Nakamura, *Nihon no dōbutsu minzoku shi*, 23.

59. Overmyer, "Buddhism in the Trenches," 197–98.

60. Nakamura, *Nihon no dōbutsu minzoku shi*, 23.

61. Maki makes a similar point, *Ijutsu to jujutsu*, 211–12.

62. Ibid., 214.

63. Ibid., 213.

64. Kitagawa, *On Understanding Japanese Religion*, 151. See also 154–55, and Mabuchi, Kunisaki, and Konnō, *Konjaku*, 1: 158n12.

65. Kitagawa, *On Understanding Japanese Religion*, 155.

66. Two informative sources for the study of early snake stories are De Visser, "The Snake in Japanese Superstition," 267–322, and Sasama, *Hebi monogatari*, especially 49–78. Although both studies lack analyses, their authors collect and categorize numerous snake stories. See also Kelsey, "Salvation of the Snake," 98–101, and Koopmans-de Bruijn, "Fabled Liasons."

67. One *ryō* is approximately 15 grams.

68. Tale 14:4; Yamada et al., *Konjaku*, 3: 280–83.

69. Aoki, *Nara no miyako*, 359. According to *Shoku Nihongi*, the term *Mihotoke no yatsuko to tsukaematsuru tennō* was included in an imperial edict read in front of the unfinished statue of the Great Buddha expressing gratitude for the discovery of gold in the Oda district of Michinoku. See Imaizumi Tadayoshi, *Kundoku shoku Nihongi*, 410. (*Hotoke* is written as "The Three Treasures.")

70. On the reign of Emperor Shōmu and the construction of the Great Buddha, see Imaizumi Atsuo, *Heian no shinkyō*, 206–427; Aoki, *Nara no miyako*, 329–65; Ueda, "Gaisetsu"; Kawasaki, "Shōmu Tennō"; and Brown, *Ancient Japan*, intro. and chap. 4 and 7–10 passim.

71. On Kibi no Makibi, see Miyata, *Kibi no Makibi*.

72. Tale 1:7 in *Hokkegenki*; Inoue and Ōsone, *Ōjōden, Hokkegenki*, 22; Dykstra, *Miraculous Tales*, 37.

73. Tale 20:24 in Yamada et al., *Konjaku*, 4: 187–88; and tale 2:38 in Nakada, *Nihon ryōiki*, 243–44; Motomochi Nakamura, *Miraculous Stories*, 211.

74. Tales 13:42 and 43 in Yamada et al., *Konjaku*, 3: 264–67; Tyler, *Japanese Tales*, 198–99. The first tale also appears in the *Hokkegenki*, 1: 37; Inoue and Ōsone, *Ōjōden, Hokkegenki*, 97–99; and Dykstra, *Miraculous Tales*, 62–63.

75. His religious practices are listed as such in the *Hokkegenki* version.

76. Yamada et al., *Konjaku*, 3: 265–66. See also Inoue and Ōsone, *Ōjōden, Hokkegenki*, 97, or Dykstra, *Miraculous Tales*, 62–63.

77. The priest Hui Xiang compiled this ten-scroll collection during the Tang dynasty. Katayose, *Konjaku monogatari shū no kenkyū*, 1: 112–14; Brower, "*Koñzyaku*," 29; and Dykstra, *Miraculous Tales*, 1.

78. Among the many sources on *mappō* and its connection to Pure Land Buddhism are Sueki, "Mappō to Jōdo," in *Nihon Bukkyō shi*, 92–118.

79. Tyler, *Japanese Tales*, 2.

80. Poets who searched for Buddhist meaning in their work include Saigyō, Shunzei, and Teika. See LaFleur, "'Floating Phrases and Fictive Utterances': The Rise

and Fall of Symbols" and "Symbol and Yūgen: Shunzei's Use of Tendai Buddhism," in *Karma of Words*, 1–25 and 80–106, respectively; Plutschow, "Is Poetry a Sin?"

81. Poem 45; Saeki, *Kokin wakashū*, 112.

82. Poems 32–48 are a sequence about plum blossoms. Saeki, *Kokin wakashū*, 110–13. The plum blossom appears in other poetry collections as well.

83. The mandarin orange tree is associated with the nightingale in *Kokinshū* poems 141 and 155; ibid., 130 and 132.

84. Ōtsu et al., *Ise monogatari*, in *Taketori, Ise, Yamato*, 143–44.

85. Tale 20:23 in Yamada et al., *Konjaku*, 4: 185–87.

86. Tale 104 (8:6) is in Miki et. al, *Uji shūi*, 213–15; Mills, *Tales from Uji*, 297–98; and Tyler, *Japanese Tales*, 174–75.

87. Tale 20:13; Yamada et al., *Konjaku*, 4: 169.

88. Ibid., 171. The summary is of pages 169–71.

89. Stone, *Original Enlightenment*, 221 and 229 respectively.

90. According to Stone, the most creative phase in the development of *hongaku shisō* is the twelfth through early fourteenth centuries.

91. Model monks who spend time on this mountain appear in *Hokkegenki* tales 1:16 and 1:21 among others; Inoue and Ōsone, *Ōjōden, Hokkegenki*, 73–74 and 79–80. (The same tales are included in *Konjaku* as well.)

92. In *Tengu no kenkyū*, Chigiri sees the Japanese tengu of *Konjaku* tale 20:2 as the tengu of Mt. Atago, but the creature is not associated with any particular mountain in that story. Mt. Atago is not even mentioned. See Chigiri, *Tengu no kenkyū*, 126; and Yamada et al., *Konjaku*, 4: 145–49.

93. Chigiri, *Tengu no kenkyū*, 126–27. According to the *Engyōbon* text of *Heike*, which is the *yomihon* line (texts for reading rather than reciting), the tengu named Tarōbō is Shinzei, the priest who backed Prince Koretaka and possessed Empress Somedono in the form of a fox, mentioned in Chapter 3 of this book. See Komine, *Setsuwa no mori*, 39.

94. Tōkyō daigaku kokugo kenkyūshitsu, *Wamyō ruiju shō*, 421. This theory draws from the *Senchū wamyō*, an annotated version of the oldest dictionary of Japanese pronunciations for Chinese characters by Edo period bibliographer Kariya Ekisai (1775–1835). Among the texts Kariya quotes to define kusainaki is the *Yakumo mishō*, a treatise on poetic opinion and practices by Emperor Juntoku (1197–1242). That book lists *kusainaki* under *tanuki*. A Chinese dictionary mentioned, the *Shuo-wen jiezi* (*Setsumon kaiji*, ca. C.E. 100), defines the type of badger called *mami* in Japanese as a "wild boar." Kariya, *Senchū wamyō ruiju shō*, 7: 65. On kusainaki, see also Chiba, *Shuryō denshō*, 108–11; Sutō, *Yama no hyōteki*, 119; Nakamura, *Nihonjin no dōbutsukan*, 130–32; *Nihon no dōbutsu minzoku shi*, 49; Mabuchi, Kunisaki, and Konno, *Konjaku*, 4: 119.

95. Ogihara and Kōnosu, *Kojiki, jōdai kayō*, 223–30. Mentioned by Nakamura, *Nihon no dōbutsu minzoku shi*, 50.

96. Tale 1:16; Inoue and Ōsone, *Ōjōden, Hokkegenki*, 303–4; and Kotas, "Ōjōden," 460–68.

97. Tales 27:34–36; Yamada et al., *Konjaku*, 4: 524–29. In *"Koñzyaku,"* Brower translated tale 34, 643–45. Tyler includes 36 in *Japanese Tales*, 296–97.

98. Yamada et al., *Konjaku*, 4: 524n3,and Mabuchi, Kunisaki, and Konno, *Konjaku*, 4: 119n18, n22. See also Brower, *"Koñzyaku,"* 1008n1, n3.

99. Yamada et al., *Konjaku*, 4: 525.

100. Ibid.

101. Ibid., 524–25.

102. Tale 27:36; Yamada et al., *Konjaku*, 4: 527–29.

103. Komatsu, *Jigoku zōshi*, 49, 62–63, and 68.

104. Tales 17:602, 603, 607, and 608; Nagazumi and Shimada, *Kokon chomonjū*, 283–87 and 296–99. Exceptions to the trickster-type tanuki can be found in *Konjaku*, "Tales of India." There, tanuki are ordinary but violent animals that appear to act instinctively. See tales 3:12 and 4:19 in Yamada et al., *Konjaku*, 1: 220–22 and 300–301.

105. Tale 17:608; Nagazumi and Shimada, *Kokon chomonjū*, 298–99.

106. Tale 17:603; Nagazumi and Shimada, *Kokon chomonjū*, 285–87; and Tyler, *Japanese Tales*, 297–98.

107. According to Mori, *Konjaku tengu* in Book 20 are associated with evil karma and the obstruction of Buddhist Law. Similarly, Wakabayashi sees them as external evil or *ma* (anti-Buddhist thoughts and practices), arousing delusions and temptations in Buddhists. See Mori, *Konjaku monogatari shū no seisei*, 215, and Wakabayashi, "Tengu Images," 35–49.

108. De Visser, "Tengu," 33.

109. Ibid., 30. *Shanhai jing* is the oldest Chinese anomaly account, with curious descriptions of "strange people and hybrid beasts." Its earliest sections may date back to the Warring States period (403–221 B.C.E.). Yuan, *Shanhai jing*, 53–54. See Campany, *Strange Writing*, 34–36 (above quote is from p. 35), and Birrell, *Classic of Mountains and Seas*.

110. Tendai Buddhism was founded by Saichō (767–822) at Mt. Hiei.

111. Tale 1:7 in Izumi, *Jikkinshō daisan ruihon*, 11–13; Geddes, "Partial Translation and Study of the 'Jikkinshō,'" 138–43; Tyler, *Japanese Tales*, 173–74.

112. Baba, *Oni no kenkyū*, 212–16.

113. Space constrains prevent me from addressing all the animal spirits in setsuwa functioning as grotesque representations. There are more tales involving those already addressed as well as dragons, turtles, hares, lions, dogs, and others.

Conclusion

1. Kayser, *Grotesque in Art and Literature*, 184–85. Kayser discusses alienation or estrangement in different types of work, including *Surrealism* (pp. 169–70).

2. Harpham, *On the Grotesque*, 191.

Bibliography

The place of publication for works in Japanese is Tokyo unless otherwise noted.

Primary Sources

Akimoto Kichirō, ed. *Fudoki*. Nihon koten bungaku taikei 2. Iwanami shoten, 1958.

Brueghel, Jan the Elder. *The Temptation of Saint Anthony*. Oil on copper. 1594. Yale Art Gallery, New Haven, CT.

———. *The Temptation of Saint Anthony*. As reproduced in Vinzenz Oberhammer, *Die Gemäldegalerie des Kunsthistorischen Museums in Wien* 1. Vienna: Schroll, 1959. Plate 33.

Brueghel, Pieter the Elder. *The Temptation of Saint Anthony*. As reproduced in Hereward Lester Cooke, *Painting Techniques of the Masters*, 142. New York: Watson Guptill Publications, 1973.

———. *The Triumph of Death*. Oil on panel. Ca. 1530–1569. Museo Nacional del Prado, Madrid. www.museodelprado.es/en/ingles/collection/on-line-gallery/

Cao Lindi, ed. *Wudiji*. Nanjing: Jiangsu guji chubanshe, 1986. Cited in Donald B. Wagner, *Iron and Steel in Ancient China*, 114n47. Leiden: E. J. Brill, 1993.

Fujimoto Kizan. *Kanpon Shikidō ōkagami*. Edited by Noma Kōshin. Kyoto: Yūzan bunko, 1961.

Fujioka Tadaharu, Nakano Kōichi, Inukai Kiyoshi, Ishii Fumio, and Fujiwara Nagako, eds. *Sarashina nikki*. In *Izumi Shikibu nikki, Murasaki Shikibu nikki, Sarashina nikki, Sanuki no suke nikki*. Nihon koten bungaku zenshū 18. Shōgakkan, 1971.

Gotō Akio, Ikegami Jun'ichi, and Yamane Taisuke, eds. *Chūgai shō*. In *Gōdanshō, Chūgai shō, Fuke go*. Shin Nihon koten bungaku taikei 32. Iwanami shoten, 1997.

Gunsho ruijū kanseikai, ed. *Kobiki*. In *Gunsho ruijū* 6: 968–69. Keizai zasshisha, 1898.

Haga Yaichi, ed. *Kōshō Konjaku monogatari shū*. 3 vols. Fuzanbō, 1913–21. Reprint, 1970. Page references are to the 1970 reprint.

Hasegawa Masaharu, Imanishi Yūichirō, Itō Hiroshi, Yoshioka Hiroshi, eds. *Tosa nikki, Kagerō nikki, Murasaki Shikibu nikki, Sarashina nikki.* Shin Nihon koten bungaku taikei 24. Iwanami shoten, 1989.

Iida Mizuho, and Kurita Hiroshi, eds. *Kogo shūi tsuketari chūshaku.* Shintō taikei: Koten hen 5. Shintō taikei hensankai, 1986.

Ikegami Jun'ichi, ed. *Sangoku denki.* Chūsei no bungaku. Miyai shoten, 1976.

Imaizumi Tadayoshi, ed. *Kundoku shoku Nihongi.* Kyoto: Rinsen shoten, 1986.

Inoue Mitsusada, and Ōsone Shōsuke, eds. *Ōjōden, Hokkegenki.* Nihon shisō taikei 7. Iwanami shoten, 1974.

Ishida Mizumaro, ed. *Ōjō yōshū.* In *Genshin.* Nihon shisō taikei 6. Iwanami shoten, 1970.

Ishihara Akira, ed. *Ishinpō: maki dai 28, Bonai.* Shibundō, 1967.

Izumi Motohiro, ed. *Jikkinshō daisan ruihon: Shōkōkan zō.* Osaka: Izumi shoin, 1984.

Izumoji Osamu, ed. *Nihon ryōiki.* Shin Nihon koten bungaku taikei 30. Iwanami shoten, 1996.

Kakimoto Tsutomu, ed. *Yamato monogatari chūshaku to kenkyū.* Musashino shoin, 1981.

Katagiri Yōichi, Fukui Teisuke, Takahashi Shōji, and Shimizu Yoshiko, eds. *Taketori monogatari, Ise monogatari, Yamato monogatari, Heichū monogatari.* Nihon koten bungaku zenshū 8. Shōgakkan, 1972.

Kawaguchi Hisao, and Nara Shōichi, eds. *Gōdan shōchū.* Benseisha, 1984.

Kobayashi Chishō, ed. *Uji shūi monogatari.* Nihon koten bungaku zenshū 28. Shōgakkan, 1973.

Koizumi Hiroshi, and Takahashi Nobuyuki, eds. *Shohon taishō Sanboe shūsei.* Kasama shoin, 1980.

Koizumi Hiroshi, Yamada Shōzen, Kojima Takayuki, and Kinoshita Motoichi, eds. *Hōbutsu shū* and *Kankyo no tomo.* In *Hōbutsu shū, Kankyo no tomo, Hirasan kojin reitaku.* Shin Nihon koten bungaku taikei 40. Iwanami shoten, 1993.

Kojima Noriyuki, Naoki Kōjirō, Nishimiya Kazutami, Kuranaka Susumu, and Mori Masamori, eds. *Nihon shoki*, vol. 3. Shinpen Nihon koten bungaku zenshū 4. Shōgakkan, 1998.

Kojima Takayuki, and Asami Kazuhiko, eds. *Senjūshō.* Ōfūsha, 1985.

Komatsu Shigemi, ed. *Hyakki yagyō emaki.* In *Nōe hōshi emaki, Fukutomi sōshi, Hyakki yagyō emaki,* 69–90 and 126–41. Nihon emaki taisei 25. Chūō kōron sha, 1979.

———. *Jigoku zōshi.* In *Gaki zōshi, Jigoku zōshi, Yamai zōshi, Kusō shi emaki,* 49–76. Nihon no emaki 7. Chūō kōron sha, 1987.

———. *Ōeyama ekotoba.* In *Tsuchigumo zōshi, Tengu zōshi, Ōeyama ekotoba,* 75–103 and 142–46. Zoku Nihon no emaki 26. Chūō kōron sha, 1993.

Komine Kazuaki, ed. *Konjaku monogatari shū*, vol. 4. Shin Nihon koten bungaku taikei 36. Iwanami shoten, 1999.

Konishi Jin'ichi, ed. "Shūgyoku tokka." In *Zeami shū.* Nihon no shisō 8. Chikuma shobō, 1970.

Kuroita Katsumi, ed. *Fusō ryakki*. Kokushi taikei 12. Nichiyō shobō, 1932.
————, ed. *Nihon kiryaku*. Kokushi taikei, vols. 10 and 11. Nichiyō shobō, 1929.
Kyōtō daigaku fuzoku toshokan, ed. *Kōshiden*. Transcribed by Kiyohara Edakata.
    Kyoto: Benridō, 1960.
Kyoto University Digital Library. *Konjaku monogatari shū*. Suzuka-ke kyūzō.
    http://edb.kulib.kyoto-u.ac.jp/exhibit/index.html
————. *Tamamo no mae*. In "Enjoying Otogi Zōshi with the Help of Synopsis
    and Illustrations," in English and Japanese versions at http://edb.kulib.kyoto-u
    .ac.jp/exhibit-e/otogi/cover/index.html
Li Quanhua, ed. *Shiji*. Changsha: Yuelu shushe, 1988.
Mabuchi Kazuo, Kunisaki Fumimaro, and Inagaki Taiichi, eds. *Konjaku mono-*
    gatari shū, vol. 3. Shinpen Nihon koten bungaku zenshū 37. Shōgakkan, 2001.
Mabuchi Kazuo, Kunisaki Fumimaro, and Konno Tōru, eds. *Konjaku monogatari*
    shū, vols. 1–4. Nihon koten bungaku zenshū 21–24. Shōgakkan, 1971–76.
Matsumura Hiroji, ed. *Eiga monogatari*. Nihon koten bungaku zensho 44. Asahi
    shinbun sha, 1956.
Matsumura Seiichi, Kimura Masanori, and Imuta Tsunehisa, eds. *Kagerō nikki*. In
    Tosa nikki, Kagerō nikki. Nihon koten bungaku zenshū 9. Shōgakkan, 1973.
Miki Sumito, Asami Kazuhiko, Nakamura Yoshio, and Kouchi Kazuaki, eds.
    Uji shūi monogatari, Kohon setsuwa shū. Shin Nihon koten bungaku taikei 42.
    Iwanami shoten, 1990.
Minobe Shigekatsu, ed. *Kankyo no tomo*. Chūsei no bungaku. Miyai, 1982.
Misumi Yōichi, ed. *Towazugatari*. In *Towazugatari, Tamakiharu*. Shin Nihon
    koten bungaku taikei 50. Iwanami shoten, 1994.
Miyama Susumu, ed. *Raijinzō*. As reproduced in *Kamakura no chōkoku, kenchiku:*
    Unkei, Kaikei. Gakushū kenkyūsha, 1978. Plate 40.
Miyata Waichirō, ed. *Utsuho monogatari*. Vol. 1. Nihon koten zenshū. Asahi shin-
    bun sha, 1951.
Mizuhara Hajime, ed. *Heike monogatari*. Shinchō Nihon koten shūsei 25.
    Shinchōsha, 1979.
Mori Masato, ed. *Konjaku monogatari shū*. Vol. 5. Shin Nihon koten bungaku
    taikei 38. Iwanami shoten, 1996.
Murakami Manabu, Tokue Gensei, and Fukuda Akira, eds. *Soga monogatari*.
    Denshō bungaku shiryō shū 4. Ōbunsha, 1974.
Nagasawa Mitsu, ed. *Yasusuke ō no haha no shū*. Nyonin waka taikei 2. Kazama
    shobō, 1965.
Nagazumi Yasuaki, and Shimada Isao, eds. *Kokon chomonjū*. Vol. 2. Nihon koten
    bungaku taikei 84. Iwanami shoten, 1966.
Nakada Norio, ed. *Nihon ryōiki*. Nihon koten bungaku zenshū 6. Shōgakkan, 1975.
Nanba Hiroshi, ed. *Murasaki Shikibu shū zen hyōshaku*. Kasama shoten, 1983.
Nishio Kōichi, and Kobayashi Yasuharu, eds. *Kokon chomonjū*. Vol.2. Shinchō
    Nihon koten shūsei 76. Shinchō shuppan, 1986.
Ōeyama ekotoba. Scroll painting. Muromachi period. Itsuō Art Museum, Osaka.

Ogihara Asao, and Kōnosu Hayao, eds. *Kojiki, jōdai kayō.* Nihon koten bungaku zenshū 1. Shōgakkan, 1973.

Risshō daigaku shūgaku kenkyūjo, ed. "Hokke daimoku sho." In *Shōwa teihon Nichiren shōnin ibun,* 1: 391–405. Minobu: Kuonji, 1965.

Saeki Umetomo, ed. *Kokin wakashū.* Nihon koten bungaku taikei 8. Iwanami shoten, 1958.

Sakakura Atsuyoshi, Ōtsu Yūichi, Tsukishima Hiroshi, Abe Toshiko, and Imai Gen'e, eds. *Taketori monogatari, Ise monogatari, Yamato monogatari.* Nihon koten bungaku taikei 9. Iwanami shoten, 1957.

Sakamoto Tarō, Ienaga Saburō, Inoue Mitsusada, and Ōno Susumu, eds. *Nihon shoki.* 2 vols. Nihon koten bungaku taikei 67–68. Iwanami shoten, 1965.

Sakamoto Yukio, and Iwamoto Yutaka, eds. *Hokekyō.* Vol. 3. Iwanami bunko 33-304-3. Iwanami shoten, 1967.

Satake Akihiro, and Kubota Jun, eds. *Hōjōki, Tsurezuregusa.* Shin Nihon koten bungaku taikei 39. Iwanami shoten, 1989.

Satō Kenzō, and Haruta Akira, eds. *Yashirobon Heike monogatari.* Vol. 2. Ōfūsha, 1973.

Shiryō hensanjo, ed. *Shōyūki.* In *Dai Nihon kokiroku,* part 10, vol. 5. Iwanami shoten, 1969.

Tachibana Kenji, ed. *Ōkagami.* Nihon koten bungaku zenshū 20. Shōgakkan, 1974.

Taguchi Kazuo, Nezu Tadashi, Gotō Akio, and Nihei Michiaki, eds. *Ruijūbonkei Gōdanshō chūkai.* Musashino shoin, 1983.

Takagi Ichinosuke, Ozawa Masao, Atsumi Kaoru, and Kindaichi Haruhiko, eds. *Heike monogatari.* Vol. 2. Nihon koten bungaku taikei 33. Iwanami shoten, 1960.

Takakusu Junjirō, and Mochitsuki Shinkō, eds. *Shingon den.* In Dai Nihon Bukkyō zensho 106. Ushio shobō, 1932.

Takakusu Junjirō, and Watanabe Kaigyoku et al., eds. *Taishō shinshū daizōkyō.* Taishō issaikyō kankōkai, 1924–34. N. 7, 9, 10, 24, 278, and 1585.

Takeda Yūkichi, ed. *Kundoku Nihon sandai jitsuroku.* Rinsen shoten, 1986.

Takeda Yūkichi, and Mizuno Kumao, eds. *Yamato monogatari shōkai.* Yukawa kōbundō, 1936.

Takizawa Sadao, ed. *Mototoshi shū zenshaku.* Shikashū zenshaku sōsho 5. Shikashū zenshaku sōsho kankō kai, 1988.

Tanaka Makoto, ed. *Kanawa.* In *Yōkyoku shū.* Nihon koten zensho 68. Asahi shinbun sha, 1953.

Tawaraya Sōtatsu. *Fūjin raijin zu.* Screen painting. Seventeenth century. Kenninji, Kyoto.

Tōkyō daigaku shiryō hensanjo. *Chūyūki.* Vol. 5. Dai Nihon kokiroku, vol. 21. Iwanami shoten, 1993.

Tsukahara Tetsuo. *Tsutsumi Chūnagon monogatari.* Shinchō Nihon koten shūsei 17. Shinchōsha, 1983.

Uchigiki shū o yomu kai, eds. *Uchigiki shū, kenkyū to honbun.* Kasama shoin, 1971.

Wang Shaoying, ed. *Soushenji.* Beijing: Zhonghua shuju, 1979.

Watanabe Minoru, ed. *Makura no sōshi*. Shin Nihon koten bungaku taikei 25. Iwanami shoten, 1991.

Yamada Yoshio, Yamada Tadao, Yamada Hideo, and Yamada Toshio, eds. *Konjaku monogatari shū*. Vols. 1–5. Nihon koten bungaku taikei, 22–2. Iwanami shoten, 1959–63.

Yamagishi Tokuhei, ed. *Genji monogatari*. Vol. 2. Nihon koten bungaku taikei 15. Iwanami shoten, 1958.

Yamashita Hiroaki, ed. *Taiheiki*. Vol. 2. Shinchō Nihon koten shūsei 38. Shinchō shuppan, 1980.

Yanai Shigeshi, Murofushi Shinsuke, and Ōasa Yūji, eds. *Genji monogatari*. Vol. 1. Shin Nihon koten bungaku taikei 19. Iwanami shoten, 1993.

Yatagiri Yōichi, ed. *Shūi waka shū: Teikabon*. Vol. 1. Koten bunko, 1964.

Yoshimoto Endō, and Kasuga Kazuo, eds. *Nihon ryōiki*. Nihon koten bungaku taikei, vol. 70. Iwanami shoten, 1967.

Yuan Ke, ed. *Shanhai jing*. Shanghai: Shanghai guji chubanshe, 1980.

Zhao Ye, ed. *Wuyue chunqiu*. Taipei: Shijie shuju, 1959.

Secondary Sources, Including Translations

Adams, James Luther, and Wilson Yates, eds. *The Grotesque in Art and Literature: Theological Reflections*. Cambridge, UK: William B. Eerdmans, 1997.

Akutagawa Ryūnosuke. "*Konjaku monogatari* kanshō." In *Nihon bungaku kōza* 6. Shinchōsha, 1927. Reprinted in *Konjaku monogatari shū*, ed. Nihon bungaku kenkyū shiryō kankōkai, 140–43. Nihon bungaku kenkyū shiryō sōsho. Yūseidō, 1970.

Aoki Kazuo. *Nara no miyako*. *Nihon no reikishi*, vol. 3. Chūō kōron sha, 1965.

Aoki, Michiko Y., trans. *Records of Wind and Earth: A Translation of Fudoki with Introduction and Commentaries*. Monograph and Occasional Paper Series, number 53. Ann Arbor, MI: Association for Asian Studies, 1997.

Arntzen, Sonja. *Kagerō: A Woman's Autobiographical Text from Tenth Century Japan*. Michigan Monographs in Japanese Studies, no. 19. Ann Arbor: University of Michigan, 1998.

Aston, W. G. *A History of Japanese Literature*. New York: D. Appleton, 1899. Reprint, 1930. Page references are to the 1930 reprint.

———. *Nihon bungakushi*. Translated by Shibano Rokusuke. Dai Nihon tosho kabushiki kaisha, 1908.

———, trans. *Nihongi: Chronicles of Japan from the Earliest Times to A.D. 697*. Rutland, VT: Charles E. Tuttle, 1972.

Baba Akiko. *Oni no kenkyū*. Sanichi shobō, 1971. Reprint, Chikuma bunko, Chikuma shobō, 1988. Citations refer to the reprint.

Backus, Robert L., trans. *The Riverside Counselor's Stories: Vernacular Fiction of Late Heian Japan*. Stanford, CA: Stanford University Press, 1985.

Bagehot, Walter. "Wordsworth, Tennyson, and Browning; or Pure, Ornate, and Grotesque Art in Poetry." In *The Works and Life of Walter Bagehot*, ed. Emilie Barrington, 4: 267–315. London: Longmans, Green, 1915.

Bakhtin, Mikhail. "Forms of Time and of the Chronotype in the Novel." In *The Dialogic Imagination*, ed. Michael Holquist, trans. Caryl Emerson and Michael Holquist. Austin: University of Texas Press, 1981.

———. *Rabelais and His World*. Translated by Hélène Iswolsky. Bloomington: Indiana University Press, 1984.

Barasch, Frances K. *The Grotesque: A Study in Meanings*. The Hague: Mouton, 1971.

———. "Introduction: The Meaning of the Grotesque." In Thomas Wright, *A History of Caricature and Grotesque in Literature and Art*. London, 1865. Reprint, New York: Fredrick Ungar, 1968. Citations refer to the reprint.

Bargen, Doris G. *A Woman's Weapon: Spirit Possession in The Tale of Genji*. Honolulu: University of Hawaii Press, 1997.

Barnhill, David Landis. *Basho's Journey: The Literary Prose of Matsuo Basho*. New York: State University of New York Press, 2005.

Bathgate, Michael. *The Fox's Craft in Japanese Religion and Culture: Shapeshifters, Transformations, and Duplicities*. Religion in History, Society, and Culture—Outstanding Dissertations 7. New York: Routledge, 2004.

Baudelaire, Charles. "On the Essence of Laughter." In *Charles Baudelaire: The Painter of Modern Life and Other Essays*, trans. Jonathan Mayne, 147–165. New York: Phaidon, 1964.

Beckson, Karl, and Arthur Ganz. *Literary Terms: A Dictionary*. New York: Noonday, 1989.

Bellard-Thomson, Carol. "Rabelais and Obscenity: A Woman's View." In *The Body and the Text: Hélène Cixous, Reading and Teaching*, ed. Helen Wilcox, Keith McWalters, Ann Thompson, and Linda R. Williams, 167–74. New York: Harvester Wheatsheaf, 1990.

Bethe, Monica, and Karen Brazell, trans. *Yamamba*. In *Traditional Japanese Theater: An Anthology of Plays*, ed. Karen Brazell, 207–25. New York: Columbia University Press, 1998.

Bettelheim, Bruno. *The Uses of Enchantment: The Meaning and Importance of Fairy Tales*. New York: Vintage Books, 1977.

Birrell, Anne, trans. *The Classic of Mountains and Seas*. New York: Penguin Putnam, 1999.

Blacker, Carmen. "Supernatural Abductions in Japanese Folklore." *Asian Folklore Studies* 26:2 (1967): 111–48.

Boileau-Despréaux, Nicolas. *The Art of Poetry, in Four Cantos*. Translated by Sir William Soames, revised by John Dryden. London: printed for E. Curll, and F. Burleigh, 1715. Eighteenth Century Collections Online, document # T139159, p. 5/ image 11, Gale Group: http://galenet.galegroup.com/servlet/ECCO.

Borgen, Robert. *Sugawara no Michizane and the Early Heian Court*. Honolulu: University of Hawaii Press, 1994.

Bowring, Richard, trans. *Murasaki Shikibu: Her Diary and Poetic Memoirs, A*

Translation and Study. Princeton Library of Asian Translations. Princeton, NJ: Princeton University Press, 1982. Reprint, first Princeton Paperback Printing, 1985. Citations refer to the reprint.

Brazell, Karen. *The Confessions of Lady Nijō*. Stanford, CA: Stanford University Press, 1976.

Brower, Robert H. "The *Konzyaku monogatarisyū*: An Historical and Critical Introduction, with Annotated Translations of Seventy-eight Tales." Ph.D. diss., University of Michigan, 1952.

Brower, Robert H., and Earl Miner. *Japanese Court Poetry*. Stanford, CA: Stanford University Press, 1961.

Brown, Delmer M., ed. *Ancient Japan*. Vol. 1 of *The Cambridge History of Japan*. Cambridge, UK: Cambridge University Press, 1993.

Butler, Judith. *Gender Trouble: Feminism and the Subversion of Identity*. New York: Routledge, 1990.

Camille, Michael. *Images on the Edge: The Margins of Medieval Art*. London: Reaktion Books, 2002. First published in 1992.

Campany, Robert Ford. *Strange Writing: Anomaly Accounts in Early Medieval China*. Albany: State University of New York Press, 1996.

Campbell, Joseph. *The Power of Myth with Bill Moyers*. Edited by Betty Sue Flowers. New York: Doubleday, 1988.

Casey, Timothy J. *Jean Paul: A Reader*. Translated by Erika Casey. Baltimore: Johns Hopkins University Press, 1992.

Clayborough, Arthur. *The Grotesque in English Literature*. Oxford: Clarendon Press, 1965. Reprinted (with corrections), 1967. Citations refer to the reprint.

Chambers, Anthony H., trans. *Tales of Moonlight and Rain: A Study and Translation*. Translations from the Asian Classics. New York: Columbia University Press, 2007.

Chang, Wing-Tsit, trans. and comp. *A Source Book in Chinese Philosophy*. Princeton, NJ: Princeton University Press, 1969.

Chiba Tokuji. *Shuryō denshō*. Mono to ningen no bunkashi 14. Hōsei daigaku shuppankyoku, 1975.

Chigiri Kōsai. *Tengu no kenkyū*. Tairiku shobō, 1975.

Childs, Margaret H. "The Value of Vulnerability: Sexual Coercion and the Nature of Love in Japanese Court Literature." *Journal of Asian Studies* 58 (November 1999): 1059–79.

Cogan, Thomas J. *The Tale of the Soga Brothers*. Tokyo: University of Tokyo Press, 1987.

Cranston, Edwin A. "Atemiya: A Translation from *Utsubo monogatari*." *Monumenta Nipponica* 24:3 (1969): 289–314.

———. *The Izumi Shibiki Diary: A Romance of the Heian Court*. Cambridge, MA: Harvard University Press, 1969.

Deal, William E. "Women and Japanese Buddhism." In *Religions of Japan in Practice*, ed. George J. Tanabe, Jr., 176–84. Princeton, NJ: Princeton University Press, 1999.

D'Etcheverry, Charo B., trans. "The Tale of Sagoromo." In *Traditional Japanese Literature: An Anthology, Beginnings to 1600*, ed. Haruo Shirane, 503–18. New York: Columbia University Press, 2007.

De Visser, Marinus Willem. "The Fox and the Badger in Japanese Folklore." *Transactions of the Asiatic Society of Japan* 36, pt. 3 (1908): 1–159.

———. "The Snake in Japanese Superstition." *Mitteilungen des Seminars für Orientalische* 14 (1911): 267–321.

———. "The Tengu." *Transactions of the Asiatic Society of Japan* 36, pt. 2 (1908): 25–100.

DeWoskin, Kenneth J., and J. I. Crump, Jr., trans. *In Search of the Supernatural: The Written Record*. Stanford, CA: Stanford University Press, 1996.

Douglas, Mary. "The Social Control of Cognition: Some Factors in Joke Perception." *Man* (1968) 3: 361–76.

Drake, Chris. *The Eight Dog Chronicles*. In *Early Modern Japanese Literature: An Anthology, 1600–1900*, ed. Haruo Shirane and James Brandon, 887–909. New York: Columbia University Press, 2002.

Dryden, John. "A Parallel of Painting and Poetry." Preface to *The Art of Painting* by C. A. Dufresnoy, containing a parallel between poetry and painting by Mr. Dryden, a new edition. London, 1769. Eighteenth Century Collections Online, #CW3306147864, p. xxxvi / image 35.

Dykstra, Yoshiko Kurata, trans. *The Konjaku Tales: From a Medieval Japanese Collection. Indian Section*. 2 vols. Intercultural Research Institute Monograph Series 17 and 18. Osaka: Kansai University of Foreign Studies Press, 1986.

———. *The Konjaku Tales: From a Medieval Japanese Collection. Chinese Section*. Intercultural Research Institute Monograph Series 23. Osaka: Kansai University of Foreign Studies Press, 1994.

———. *The Konjaku Tales: From a Medieval Japanese Collection. Japanese Section*. 3 vols. Intercultural Research Institute Monograph Series 25, 27, and 28. Osaka: Kansai University of Foreign Studies Press, 1998, 2001, and 2003.

———. *Miraculous Tales of the Lotus Sutra: The Dainihonkoku Hokekyōkenki of Priest Chingen*. Honolulu: University of Hawaii Press, 1984.

———. "Notable Tales Old and New: Tachibana Narisue's *Kokon Chomonjū*." *Monumenta Nipponica* 47:4. (Winter, 1992): 469–93.

Eagleton, Terry. *Walter Benjamin or Towards a Revolutionary Criticism*. London: Verso, 1981.

Ebersole, Gary L. *Ritual Poetry and the Politics of Death in Early Japan*. Princeton, NJ: Princeton University Press, 1989.

Ema Tsutomu. *Nihon yōkai henge shi*. In *Ema Tsutomu chosaku shū* 6. Chūō kōron sha, 1977.

Emmerich, Michael, Michael Kelsey, and Marian Ury, trans. "Collection of Tales of Times Now Past." In *Traditional Japanese Literature: An Anthology, Beginnings to 1600*, ed. Haruo Shirane, 529–60. New York: Columbia University Press, 2007.

Fairclough, H. R., trans. "The Art of Poetry." In *Horace: Satires, Epistles, and Ars Poetica*. Loeb Classical Library 194. Cambridge, MA: Harvard University Press, 1966.

Farris, William Wayne. *Heavenly Warriors: The Evolution of Japan's Military, 500–1300*. Harvard East Asian Monographs 157. Cambridge, MA: Harvard University Press, 1992.

―――. *Population, Disease, and Land In Early Japan, 645–900*. Cambridge, MA: Harvard University Press, 1995.

Faure, Bernard. *The Power of Denial: Buddhism, Purity, and Gender*. Princeton, NJ: Princeton University Press, 2003.

―――. *The Red Thread: Buddhist Approaches to Sexuality*. Princeton, NJ: Princeton University Press, 1998.

Field, Norma. *The Splendor of Longing in the Tale of Genji*. Princeton, NJ: Princeton University Press, 1987.

Foucault, Michel. "Nietzsche, Genealogy, History." In *Language, Counter-Memory, Practice: Selected Essays and Interviews*. Ithaca, NY: Cornell University Press, 1977.

Frame, Donald M., ed. *The Complete Essays of Montaigne*. Stanford, CA: Stanford University Press: 1965.

Francis, Anne F. *Hieronymus Bosch: The Temptation of Saint Anthony*. Smithtown, NY: Exposition, 1980.

Freud, Sigmund. *The Standard Edition of the Complete Psychological Works of Sigmund Freud*. Edited by James Strachey et al. Vols. 4, 7, 10, and 15. London: Hogarth Press and the Institute of Psycho-Analysis, 1974.

Friday, Karl F. *Hired Swords: The Rise of Private Warrior Power in Early Japan*. Stanford, CA: Stanford University Press, 1992.

―――. *Samurai, Warfare, and the State in Early Medieval Japan*. Warfare and History. New York: Routledge, 2004.

Fujioka Sakutarō. *Konjaku monogatari sen*. Fuzanbō, 1903. Cited in Katayose Masayoshi, *Konjaku monogatari shū no kenkyū*, 1: 18–19. Sanseidō, 1943. Reprint, Geirinsha, 1974. Page numbers refer to the reprint.

Gasbarrone, Lisa. "'The Locus for the Other': Cixous, Bakhtin, and Women's Writing." In *A Dialogue of Voices: Feminist Literary Theory and Bakhtin*, ed. Karen Hohne and Helen Wussow, 1–19. Minneapolis: University of Minnesota Press, 1994.

Gatten, Aileen. "Death and Salvation in *Genji Monogatari*." In *New Leaves: Studies and Translations of Japanese Literature in Honor of Edward Seidensticker*, ed. Aileen Gatten and Anthony Hood Chambers, 5–27. Michigan Monograph Series in Japanese Studies, no. 11. Ann Arbor: University of Michigan Center for Japanese Studies, 1993.

Geddes, John Van W. "A Partial Translation and Study of the 'Jikkinshō.'" Ph.D. diss., Washington University, 1976.

Geddes, Ward. "Selected Anecdotes to Illustrate Ten Maxims." In *Religions of Japan In Practice*, ed. George J. Tanabe, Jr., 25–37. Princeton, NJ: Princeton University Press, 1999.

Gjertson, Donald E. *Miraculous Retribution: A Study and Translation of T'ang Lin's Ming-pao chi*. Berkeley Buddhist Studies Series 8. Berkeley, CA: Centers for South and Southeast Asia Studies, 1989.

Gosho Translation Committee, ed. and trans. "The Daimoku of the Lotus Sutra." In *The Major Writings of Nichiren Daishonin*, 3: 19–20. Tokyo: Nichiren Shoshu International Center, 1986.

Granger, Frank, trans. *Vitruvius on Architecture*. Books VI–X. Loeb Classical Library 280. Cambridge, MA: Harvard University Press, 2004. First published in 1934.

Haga Yaichi. Introduction to *Kōshō Konjaku monogatari shū*. In *Ochiai Naobumi, Ueda Kazutoshi, Haga Yaichi, Fujioka Sakutarō shū*, ed. Hisamatsu Sen'ichi, 291–98. Meiji bungaku zenshū 44. Chikuma shobō, 1968.

———. *Kokubungakushi jikkō, kōchū*. Annotated by Shimazu Hisamoto. Fuzanbō, 1939.

———, ed. *Kōshō Konjaku monogatari shū*. 3 vols. Fuzanbō, 1913–21.

Hall, John Whitney. *Government and Local Power in Japan, 500–1700: A Study Based on Bizen Province*. Princeton, NJ: Princeton University Press, 1966.

———. "Terms and Concepts in Japanese Medieval History: An Inquiry into the Problems of Translation." *Journal of Japanese Studies* 19:1 (Winter 1983): 1–32.

Hane, Mikiso. *Premodern Japan: A Historical Survey*. Boulder, CO: Westview, 1991.

Hardacre, Helen. *Shintō and the State, 1868–1988*. Princeton, NJ: Princeton University Press, 1989.

Harpham, Geoffrey Galt. *On the Grotesque: Strategies of Contradiction in Art and Literature*. Princeton, NJ: Princeton University Press, 1982.

Hashimoto Sumiko, ed. "Heian jidai no kamigata." *Nihon no bijutsu* 23 (March 1968): 27–35.

Hegel, G. W. F. "The Symbolic Form of Art." In T. M. Knox, trans. *Hegel's Aesthetics: Lectures on Fine Art*, 1: 301–61. Oxford: Oxford University Press, 1975.

Hesselink, Reinier. "The Emperor Who Committed Murder." Unpublished paper read at the Center of Japanese Studies, University of California, Berkeley, January 20, 1998. Posted on "Reinier Hesselink's Nihonshi Eitaigura: A Treasure House of Japanese History" at Reinierhesselink.com.

Hirano, Umeyo, trans. *The Tsutsumi Chūnagon Monogatari: A Collection of 11th-Century Short Stories of Japan*. Tokyo: Hokuseidō, 1963.

Honda Giken. *Setsuwa to wa nani ka*. Setsuwa no kōza 1. Benseisha, 1991.

Hori, Ichirō. "On the Concept of Hijiri (Holy-Man)." Part 1. *Numan* 5–2 (April 1958): 129–232.

Hosoya Sōko. "Kanshō Bakuya setsuwa no tenkai." *Bunka* 33:3 (February 1970): 48–71.

Howell, Thomas Raymond, Jr. "*Setsuwa*, Knowledge, and the Culture of Reading and Writing in Medieval Japan." Ph.D. diss., University of Pennsylvania, 2002.

Hsia, Emil C. H., Ilza Veith, and Robert H. Geertsma, trans. *The Essentials of Medicine in Ancient China and Japan: Yasuyori Tamba's Ishimpō*. 2 vols. Leiden: E. J. Brill, 1986.

Hugo, Victor. "Preface to Cromwell." In *Prefaces and Prologues to Famous Books*, ed. Charles W. Eliot, 354–408. Harvard Classics 39. New York: P. F. Collier and Sons, 1910.

Hurst, G. Cameron III. "The Structure of the Heian Court: Some Thoughts on the Nature of 'Familial Authority' in Heian Japan" and "The Development of the *Insei*: A Problem in Japanese History and Historiography." In *Medieval Japan: Essays in Institutional History*, ed. John W. Hall and Jeffrey P. Mass, 39–59 and 60–90 respectively. New Haven, CT: Yale University Press, 1974. Reprint, Stanford, CA: Stanford University Press, 1988. Citations refer to the reprint.

Hynes, William J., and William G. Doty, eds. *Mythical Trickster Figures: Contours, Contexts, and Criticisms*. Tuscaloosa: University of Alabama Press, 1993.

Iijima Yoshiharu. "Hitobashira densetsu." In *Nihon 'shinwa, densetsu' sōran*, ed. Yoshinari Takeshi, 320–21. Shinjinbutsu ōrai sha, 1992.

Iizawa Tadasu. "Oni no shinsō." *Kokubungaku* 17:11 (September 1972): 142–53.

Ikeda Kikan. "Setsuwa bungaku ni okeru Chisoku-in kanpaku no chii." *Kokugo to kokubungaku*, 11:2 (1934). Reprint, *Nihon bungaku kenkyū shiryō sōsho, Konjaku monogatari shū*, ed. Nihon bungaku kenkyū shiryō kankō kai, 25–33. Yūseidō, 1970.

Ikegami Jun'ichi. "Joshō sōsetsu: Setsuwa bungaku o kangaeru." In *Setsuwa bungaku no sekai*, ed. Ikegami Jun'ichi and Fujimoto Tokumei. Sekai shisō sha, 1987.

———. "Kaisetsu." In *Konjaku monogatari shū*, ed. Ikegami Jun'ichi and Nihon bungaku kenkyū taisei kankōkai. Nihon bungaku kenkyū taisei. Kokusho kankōkai, 1990.

———. "Konjaku monogatari shū." In *Chūko no bungaku*, ed. Akiyama Ken and Fujihira Haruo, 335–39. *Nihon bungakushi* 2. Yūhikaku, 1976.

———. *Konjaku monogatari shū no sekai: chūsei no akebono*. Chikuma shoten, 1983.

———. "Konjaku monogatari shū no seiritsu o megutte: kisoteki mondai no kentō." In *Konjaku monogatari shū to Uji shūi monogatari: setsuwa to buntai*, ed. Komine Kazuaki, 3–20. Nihon bungaku kenkyū shiryō shinshū 6. Yūseidō, 1986.

———. "'Oni' no kanashimi: chūsei no 'ningen' rikai." *Kokugo tsūshin, tokushū: chūsei o ikiru hitobito*, no. 266 (June 1984): 12–18.

Ikuzawa Eitarō. "Kodai no Kagamitsukuri Uji ni taisuru ikkō satsu—shisō teki hōmen o chūshin ni shite." *Shintō shi kenkyū* 5:4 (June 1957): 40–47.

Imaizumi Atsuo, ed. *Heian no shinkyō*. Kyōto no reikishi, vol. 1. Gakugei shorin, 1970.

Imanari Genshō. "Setsuwa bungaku shiron." In *Konjaku monogatari shū*, ed. Ikegami Jun'ichi and Nihon bungaku kenkyū taisei kankōkai. Kokusho kankōkai, 1990.

Inoue Enryō. *Meishinkai*. Shinpen yōkai sōsho 4. Heigo shuppansha, 1926. Reprint, Kokusho kankōkai, 1983. Citations refer to the reprint.

Inoue Yasushi. "Obasute." In *The Izu Dancer and Other Stories*, trans. Leon Picon, 95–118. Rutland, VT: Charles E. Tuttle, 1974.

Ishida Mizumaro. *Ōjō no shisō*. Kyoto: Heirakuji shoten, 1968.

Jackson, Rosemary. *Fantasy: The Literature of Subversion*. New York: Methuen, 1981. Reprint, New York: Routledge, 1998. Citations refer to the reprint.

Jones, Stanleigh H., trans. *Obasute*. In "The No Plays: Obasute and Kanehira." *Monumenta Nipponica* 18:1/4 (1963): 262–72. Reprinted in Donald Keene and Royall Tyler, ed., *Twenty Plays of Noh Theater*, 115–28. New York: Columbia University Press, 1970.

Jones, S. W. *Ages Ago: Thirty-seven Tales from the Konjaku monogatari Collection*. Cambridge, MA: Harvard University Press, 1959.

Jordan, Brenda. "The Trickster in Japan: *Tanuki* and *Kitsune*." In *Japanese Ghosts and Demons: Art of the Supernatural*, ed. Stephen Addiss, 129–37. New York: George Braziller, in association with the Spencer Museum of Art, University of Kansas, 1985.

Jung, C. G. "On the Psychology of the Trickster Figure." In *The Trickster: A Study in American Indian Mythology* by Paul Radin. New York: Greenwood, 1956.

Kadoya Mitsuaki. "Iwate no oni." In *Tōhoku no oni*, ed. Ōyu Takuji, 115–61. Niwate shuppan, 1989.

Kamens, Edward. *The Three Jewels: A Study and Translation of Minamoto Tamenori's Sanbōe*. Michigan Monograph Series in Japanese Literature, no. 2. Ann Arbor: Center for Japanese Studies, University of Michigan, 1988.

Kaneko Junji. *Nihon kitsunetsuki shi shiryō shūsei*. Makino shuppan sha, 1976.

Kao, Karl S. Y. *Classical Chinese Tales of the Supernatural and Fantastic; Selections from the Third to the Tenth Century*. Hong Kong: Joint Publishing Co., 1985.

Kariya Ekisai. *Senchū wamyō ruiju shū*. Insatsu kyoku zōhan, 1883.

Kasahara Kazuo. *Nyonin ōjō shisō no keifu*. Yoshikawa kōbunkan, 1975.

Kasuga Kazuo. "*Konjaku* kō: setsuwa no jisei to buntai." *Kokugo kokubun* (July 1966); reprint, *Nihon bungaku kenkyū shiryō sōsho: Konjaku monogatari shū*, ed. Nihon bungaku kenkyū shiryō kankōkai, 8–17. Yūseidō, 1970. Citations refer to the reprint.

Katayose Masayoshi. *Konjaku monogatari shū no kenkyū*. 2 vols. Kamakura: Geirinsha, 1974. Vol. 1 was published first by Sanseidō, 1943.

Kawaguchi Hisao. "Konjaku shū to Kohon setsuwa shū ni tsuite." *Bungaku* 23:4 (April 1955). Reprint, *Nihon bungaku kenkyū shiryō sōshō: Konjaku monogatari shū*, ed. Nihon bungaku kenkyū shiryō henkō kai, 60–81. Yūseidō, 1970. Page references refer to the reprint.

———. "Tonkō henbun no seikaku to waga kuni shōdō bungaku: Setsuwa to sekkyōshi no keifu." *Kanazawa daigaku hōbungaku ronshū, Bungaku-hen* 8 (January 1960): 1–20.

Kawai Hayao. *The Japanese Psyche: Major Motifs in the Fairy Tales of Japan*. Translated by Hayao Kawai and Sachiko Reece with a forward by Gary Snyder. Woodstock, CT: Spring Publications, 1996.

———. *Mukashi banashi to Nihonjin no kokoro*. Iwanami shoten, 1982.

Kawasaki Tsuneyuki. *Ōchō no rakujitsu*. Jinbutsu Nihon no rekishi 3. Yomiuri shinbun sha, 1966.

Kawasaki Yasuyori. "Shōmu Tenno." In *Tenpyō no meian*, ed. Ueda Masaaki et al., 51–68. Jinbutsu Nihon no rekishi 2. Shōgakkan, 1975.

Kawashima, Terry. "The Construction of the Feminine Margin: An Examination of Texts from the Mid-Heian to the Early Kamakura Periods in Japan." Ph.D. diss., Harvard University, 1997.

————. *Writing Margins: The Textual Construction of Gender in Heian and Kamakura Japan*. Cambridge, MA: Harvard University Asia Center, 2001.

Kayser, Wolfgang Johannes. *The Grotesque in Art and Literature*. Translated by Ulrich Weisstein. Bloomington: Indiana University Press, 1963. Reprint, New York: McGraw Hill Book Company, 1966. Citations refer to the reprint.

Keene, Donald, trans. *Dōjōji*. In *Twenty Plays of Noh Theater*, 238–63. New York: Columbia University Press, 1970. Reprinted in *Traditional Japanese Theater: An Anthology of Plays*, ed. Karen Brazell, 193–206. New York: Columbia University Press, 1998.

————, trans. *Essays in Idleness*. New York: Columbia University Press, 1967. Reprint, Rutland, VT: Tuttle, 1981. Citations refer to the reprint.

————. *A History of Japanese Literature*. Vol. 1, *Seeds in the Heart*. New York: Henry Holt, 1993. Reprint, Columbia University Press, 1999. Citations refer to the reprint.

————, trans. *Kanawa*. In *Twenty Plays of Noh Theater*, 194–205. New York: Columbia University Press, 1970.

————, trans. "The Tale of the Bamboo Cutter." *Monumenta Nipponica* 24:4 (1956): 1–127.

Kelsey, William Michael. "Didactics in Art: The Literary Structure of the 'Konjaku Monogatari-shū.'" Ph.D. diss., Indiana University, 1976.

————. *Konjaku Monogatari-shū*. Boston: Twayne, 1982.

————. "*Konjaku Monogatari-shū*: Toward an Understanding of Its Literary Qualities." *Monumenta Nipponica* 30:2 (1975): 121–50.

————. "Salvation of the Snake, The Snake of Salvation: Buddhist-Shinto Conflict and Resolution." *Japanese Journal of Religious Studies* 8:1–2 (March–June 1981): 83–113.

Kikuchi Hisakichi. "Konjaku monogatari shū to Kohon setsuwa shū ni tsuite." *Bungaku* 30 (April 1955). Reprint, *Nihon bungaku kenkyū shiryō sōsho: Konjaku monogatari shū*, ed. Nihon bungaku kenkyū shiryō kankōkai, 60–81. Yūseidō, 1970.

Kimbrough, R. Keller, tr. "The Demon Shuten Dōji (*Shuten Dōji*)." In *Traditional Japanese Literature: An Anthology, Beginnings to 1600*, ed. Haruo Shirane, 1123–38. New York: Columbia University Press, 2007.

————. *Preachers, Poets, Women, and the Way: Izumi Shikibu and the Buddhist Literature of Medieval Japan*. Ann Arbor: Center for Japanese Studies, University of Michigan, 2008.

Kimoto Michifusa. *Jōdai kayō shōkai*. Musashino shoin, 1942.

Kitagawa, Joseph. *On Understanding Japanese Religion*. Princeton, NJ: Princeton University Press, 1987.

Kitayama Shigeo. *Heian kyō*. Nihon no rekishi 4. Chūō kōron sha, 1964.

Klein, Susan B. "Woman as Serpent: The Demonic Feminine in the Noh Play *Dōjōji*." In *Religious Reflections on the Human Body*, ed. Jane Marie Law, 100–36. Bloomington: Indiana University Press, 1995.

Knappert, Jan. *Indian Mythology: An Encyclopedia of Myth and Legend.* London: Aquarian, 1991.

Kobayashi, Hiroko. *The Human Comedy of Heian Japan: A Study of the Secular Stories in the Twelfth-Century Collection of Tales, Konjaku Monogatarishū.* East Asian Cultural Studies Series, 19. Tokyo: Centre for East Asian Cultural Studies, 1979.

Komachiya Teruhiko. *Gendai goyaku taishō Kokin wakashū.* Ōbunsha, 1982.

Komatsu Kazuhiko. *Ijinron: minzoku shakai no shinsei.* Seidosha, 1985.

————. *Nihon yōkai ibunroku.* Shōgakkan, 1995.

Komine Kazuaki. *Chūsei setsuwa no sekai o yomu.* Iwanami seminaa bukkusu 69. Iwanami shoten, 1998.

————. "Jitsugo to mōgo no <setsuwa> shi." In *Nihon bungakushi o yomu.* Vol. 2, *Kodai kōki,* 240–62. Yūseidō, 1991.

————. *Konjaku monogatari shū no keisei to kōzō.* Kasama shoin, 1985.

————. "Setsuwa no gensetsu." In *Setsuwa no gensetsu: kōshō, shoshō, baitai,* ed. Honda Giken, Ikegami Jun'ichi, Komine Kazuaki, Mori Masato, and Abe Yasurō, 9–31. Setsuwa no kōza 2. Benseisha, 1991.

————. *Setsuwa no mori: Tengu, tōzoku, ikei no dōke.* Taishūkan shoten, 1991.

Kondō Yoshihiro. *Nihon no oni: Nihon bunka tankyū no shikaku.* Ōfūsha, 1966.

Konno Tōru. "Konjaku monogatari shū no sakusha o megutte." *Kokugo to kokubungaku,* 35:2 (February 1958): 32–41.

Koopmans-de Bruijn, Ria. "Fabled Liasons: Serpentine Spouses in Japanese Folktales." In *JAPANimals: History and Culture in Japan's Animal Life,* ed. Gregory M. Pflugfelder and Brett L. Walker, 61–88. Michigan Monograph Series in Japanese Studies, no. 52. Ann Arbor: Center for Japanese Studies, University of Michigan: 2005.

Kotas, Fredric. "Ōjōden: Accounts of Rebirth in the Pure Land." Ph.D. diss., University of Washington, 1987.

Kunisaki Fumimaro. "Konjaku monogatari shū senja shiron." *Waseda shōgaku* 150 (January 1961): 57–85.

————. *Konjaku monogatari shū sakusha kō.* Musashino shoin, 1986.

Kuroda Akira. "Mikenjaku gaiden: kōshiden to no kanren." Chap. in *Chūsei setsuwa no bungakushi-teki kankyō,* 270–91. Izumi shoin kan, 1987.

Kuryluk, Ewa. *Salome and Judas in the Cave of Sex: The Grotesque: Origins, Iconography, Techniques.* Evanston, IL: Northwestern University Press, 1987.

LaFleur, William R. *The Karma of Words: Buddhism and the Literary Arts in Medieval Japan.* Berkeley: University of California Press, 1983.

————. *Liquid Life: Abortion and Buddhism in Japan.* Princeton, NJ: Princeton University Press, 1992.

LaMarre, Thomas. *Uncovering Heian Japan: An Archaeology of Sensation and Inscription.* Durham, NC: Duke University Press, 2000.

Lammers, Wayne P. "The Succession (Kuniyuzuri): A Translation from *Utsuho monogatari.*" *Monumenta Nipponica* 37:2 (1982): 139–78.

Lévy, André. "About the Chinese Storyteller's Change of Name." In *The Eternal*

Storyteller: Oral Literature in Modern China, ed. Vibeke Børdahl, 33–39. NIAS in Asian Studies 24. Surrey: Curzon, 1998.

Maeda Masayuki. "Konjaku monogatari shū no 'kokka zō.'" In *Chūsei setsuwa to sono shūhen*, ed. Kunisaki Fumimaro, 79–97. Meiji shoin, 1987.

Maki Sachiko. *Konjaku monogatari to ijutsu to jujutsu*. Tsukiji shoten, 1984.

Matsuda Toyoko. *Zusetsu Nihon no yōkai*. Kawade shobō shinsha, 1990.

Matsunaga, Alicia, and Daigan Matsunaga. *Foundation of Japanese Buddhism*. Vol. 1, *The Aristocratic Age*. Los Angeles: Buddhist Books International, 1974.

———. *Foundation of Japanese Buddhism*. Vol. 2, *The Mass Movement: Kamakura and Muromachi Periods*. Los Angeles: Buddhist Books International, 1976.

McCullough, Helen Craig, trans. *Kokin wakashū: The First Imperial Anthology of Japanese Poetry, with Tosa nikki and Shinsen waka*. Stanford, CA: Stanford University Press, 1985.

———, trans. *Ōkagami, The Great Mirror*. Princeton, NJ: Princeton University Press, 1980.

———. *The Taiheiki: A Chronicle of Medieval Japan*. New York: Columbia University Press, 1959. Reprint, Tokyo: Tuttle, 2004.

———, trans. *The Tale of Heike*. Stanford, CA: Stanford University Press, 1988.

———, trans. *Tales of Ise: Lyrical Episodes from Tenth-Century Japan*. Stanford, CA: Stanford University Press, 1968.

McCullough, William H., and Helen Craig McCullough, trans. *A Tale of Flowering Fortunes: Annals of Japanese Aristocratic Life in the Heian Period*. 2 vols. Stanford, CA: Stanford University Press, 1980.

McElroy, Bernard. *Fiction of the Modern Grotesque*. London: Palgrave Macmillian, 1989.

Mikami Sanji, and Takatsu Kuwasaburō. *Nihon bungakushi*. Vol. 1. Kinkōdō, 1890.

Mills, D. E. *A Collection of Tales from Uji: A Study and Translation of Uji Shūi Monogatari*. Cambridge, UK: Cambridge University Press, 1970.

Minamoto Junko. "Nihon Bukkyō no seisabetsu." In *Seisabetsu suru Bukkyō*, ed. Ōgoshi Aiko, Minamoto Junko, and Yamashita Akiko, 87–134. Kyoto: Hōzōkan, 1990.

Miner, Earl, trans. *The Diary of Izumi Shikibu*. In *Japanese Poetic Diaries*. Berkeley: University of California Press, 1969; reprint, 1976.

Miyata Noboru. *Hime no minzokugaku*. Seidosha, 1987.

Miyata Toshihiko. *Kibi no Makibi*. Edited by Nihon rekishi gakkai. Yoshikawa kōbun kan, 1961.

Moore, Jean. "Senjūshō: Buddhist Tales of Renunciation." *Monumenta Nipponica* 41:2 (Summer 1986): 127–74.

Mori Masato. "*Konjaku Monogatari-shū*: Supernatural Creatures and Order." Translated by W. Michael Kelsey. *Japanese Journal of Religious Studies* 9/3:3 (June–September 1982): 147–70.

———. *Konjaku monogatari shū no seisei*. Osaka: Izumi shoin, 1986.

Morimoto Motoko. "Azumaji no tabi." In *Shikashū no joryūtachi*. Kyōiku shuppan sentaa, 1985.

Morita Tei. *Heian jidai seiji shi kenkyū.* Yoshikawa kōbun kan, 1978.

Morrell, Robert E. *Sand and Pebbles: The Tales of Mujū Ichien: A Voice for Pluralism in Kamakura Buddhism.* Albany: State University of New York Press, 1985.

Morris, Ivan, trans. *As I Crossed the Bridge of Dreams: Recollections of a Woman in Eleventh-Century Japan.* London: Penguin, 1975.

————, trans. *The Pillow Book of Sei Shōnagon.* 2 vols. New York: Columbia University Press, 1967.

————. *The World of the Shining Prince: Court Life in Ancient Japan.* New York: Alfred A. Knopf, 1964.

Morse, Ronald A. "The Search for Japan's National Character: Yanagita Kunio (1875–1962) and the Folklore Movement." Ph.D. diss., Princeton University, 1975.

Morson, Gary Saul, and Caryl Emerson. *Mikhail Bakhtin, Creation of a Prosaics.* Stanford, CA: Stanford University Press, 1990.

Möser, Justus. *Harlequin: or, a defence of grotesque comic performances*, trans. Joach. Andr. Fred. Warnecke, LL.C. London, 1766. Eighteenth Century Collections Online, document #CW3316673659.

Nagano Takeshi. "Konjaku monogatari shū no sakusha ni tsuite." *Kokugo* 5:1–2 (April 1957): 20–32.

Nagata Mizu. "Butten ni okeru josei kan no hensen: sanjū, goshō, hakkyōhō no shūhen." In *Sukui to oshie,* ed. Ōsumi Kazuo and Nichiguchi Junko, 11–43. Josei to bukkyō 2. Heibonsha, 1989.

Nakajima Etsuji, ed. *Uchigiki shū.* Hakuteisha, 1961.

Nakamura Fumi. *Nihon ryōiki to shōdō.* Miyai shoten, 1995.

Nakamura, Kyoko Motomochi, trans. *Miraculous Stories from the Japanese Buddhist Tradition: The Nihon ryōiki of the Monk Kyōkai.* Cambridge, MA: Harvard University Press, 1973. Reprint, Richmond, Surrey: 1997.

Nakamura Teiri. *Nihonjin no dōbutsukan: henshintan no rekishi.* Kaimeisha, 1984.

————. *Nihon no dōbutsu minzoku shi.* Kaimeisha, 1987.

Narita Mamoru. "Mikenjaku dan no jūyō." In *Koten no henyō to shinsei,* ed. Kawaguchi Hisao, 855–64. Meiji shoin, 1984.

Nickerson, Peter. "The Meaning of Matrilocality: Kinship, Property, and Politics in Mid-Heian." *Monumenta Nipponica* 48:4 (Winter 1993): 429–68.

Nippon gakujutsu shinkōkai, ed. *1000 Poems from the Manyōshu: The Complete Nippon gakujutsu shinkōkai Translation.* Mineola, NY: Dover, 2005. First published in 1940 by Iwanami shoten.

Nozaki, Kiyoshi. *Kitsune: Japan's Fox of Mystery, Romance, and Humor.* Tokyo: Hokuseidō, 1961.

Ochiai Naobumi, ed. *Chūtō kokubun tokuhon.* Meiji shoin, 1896.

O'Flaherty, Wendy Doniger. *The Origins of Evil in Hindu Mythology.* Berkeley: University of California Press, 1980.

Ōgoshi Aiko. "Bukkyō bunka paradimu o toinaosu." In *Seisabetsu suru Bukkyō,* ed. Ōgoshi Aiko, Minamoto Junko, and Yamashita Akiko, 3–86. Hōzōkan, 1990.

Okabe Takeshi. "Tengu densetsu." In *Nihon "shinwa, densetsu" sōran,* ed. Yoshinari Takeshi, 266–67. Rekishi yomihon tokubetsu zōkan 16. Shinjinbutsu ōrai sha, 1992.

Okada, H. Richard. *Figures of Resistance: Language, Poetry and Narrating in The Tale of Genji and Other Mid-Heian Texts*. Durham, NC: Duke University Press, 1991.

Orikuchi Shinobu. "Mino kasa no shinkō." Section in "Kokubungaku no hassei." In *Orikuchi Shinobu zenshū*. Vol. 1, *Kodai kenkyū (Kokubungaku hen)*, ed. Orikuchi hakase kinen kodai kenkyūjo. Chūō kōron sha, 1995.

———. "Oni." In *Orikuchi Shinobu zenshū*, ed. Orikuchi hakase kinen kodai kenkyūjo. Vol. 5, *Nōtō hen*. Chuō kōron sha, 1971.

Ortolani, Benito. *The Japanese Theater: From Ritual to Contemporary Pluralism*. Princeton, NJ: Princeton University Press, 1995.

Overmyer, Daniel L. "Buddhism in the Trenches: Attitudes toward Popular Religion in Chinese Scriptures Found at Tun-Huang." *Harvard Journal of Asiatic Studies* 50 (June 1990): 197–222.

Ōwa Iwao. "Kagamitsukuri-make jinja—kanuchi gami 'Mara' to 'marebito.'" In *Jinja to kodai minkan saishi*, 331–51. Hakusuisha, 1989.

———. *Oni to tennō*. Hakusuisha, 1992.

———. "Osada-ni-masu-Amateru-mitama jinja: 'himatsuri' to 'hiyomi' to 'hishiri.'" In *Jinja to ōken saishi*, 331–33. Hakusuisha, 1989.

Pandey, Rajyashree. "Women, Sexuality, and Enlightenment: *Kankyo no Tomo*." *Monumenta Nipponica* 50:3 (Autumn 1995): 325–56.

Philippi, Donald L., trans. *Kojiki*. Tokyo: University Press, 1968.

Piggott, Joan R. *The Emergence of Japanese Kingship*. Stanford, CA: Stanford University Press, 1997.

Plutschow, Herbert. "Is Poetry a Sin? *Honjisuijaku* and Buddhism versus Poetry." *Oriens Extremus* 25, 2 (1978): 206–18.

Radin, Paul. *The Trickster: A Study in American Indian Mythology*. With commentaries by Karl Kerényi and C. G. Jung. New York: Greenwood, 1956.

Reischauer, Robert Karl. "A Chronicle of Events: The Late Heian Era (947–1167)." In *Early Japanese History*, A: 302–405. Gloucester: Peter Smith, 1967.

Remshardt, Ralf E. *Staging the Savage God: The Grotesque in Performance*. Carbondale: Southern Illinois University Press, 2004.

Rimer, J. Thomas, and Yamazaki Masakazu, trans. *On the Art of Nō Drama: The Major Treatises of Zeami*. Princeton, NJ: Princeton University Press, 1984.

Rodd, Laurel Rasplica. "Nichiren's Teachings to Women." Selected Papers in Asian Studies New Series, no. 5. Paper presented at the Western Conference of the Association for Asian Studies, Tucson, October 1978.

———, with Mary Catherine Henkenius, trans. *Kokinshū: Collection of Poems Ancient and Modern*. Princeton, NJ: Princeton University Press, 1984.

Rogers, Lawrence, trans. "She Loves Me, She Loves Me Not: *Shinjū* and *Shikidō Ōkagami*." *Monumenta Nipponica* 49:1 (1994): 31–60.

Rohlich, Thomas H., trans. *A Tale of Eleventh-Century Japan: Hamamatsu chūnagon monogatari*. Princeton, NJ: Princeton University Press, 1983.

Ruskin, John. "Grotesque Renaissance." In *The Stones of Venice*, vol. 3, *The Fall*. Sunnyside: George Allen, 1886; New York: Dover, 2005. Citations refer to the 2005 edition.

Russo, Mary. "Female Grotesques: Carnival and Theory." In *Feminist Studies/Critical Studies*, ed. Teresa de Lauretis, 213–29. Bloomington: Indiana University Press, 1986.

———. *The Female Grotesque: Risk, Excess, and Modernity*. New York: Routledge, 1994.

Saigō Nobutsuna. "Ikenie kō." *Gendai shisō* 10 (1973): 170–79. Reprinted as "Ikenie ni tsuite," in Saigo Nobutsuna, *Shinwa to kokka, kodai ron shū*. Heibonsha sensho 53: 147–70. Heibonsha, 1977. Citations refer to the original.

Sakai Kōhei. *Konjaku monogatari shū no shin kenkyū*. Seinodō shoten, 1925.

Sarra, Edith. *Fictions of Femininity: Literary Inventions of Gender in Japanese Court Women's Memoirs*. Stanford, CA: Stanford University Press, 1999.

Sasama Yoshihiko. *Hebi monogatari, sono shinpi to densetsu*. Daiichi shobō, 1991.

Schlegel, Friedrich. *Dialogue on Poetry and Literary Aphorisms*. Translated by Ernst Behler and Roman Struc. University Park: Pennsylvania State University Press, 1968.

Schneegans, Heinrich. *Geschichte der grotesken Satire*. Strassburg: K. J. Trübner, 1894.

Screech, M. A., trans. *Rabelais: "Gargantua and Pantagruel."* London: Penguin, 2006.

Seidensticker, Edward, trans. "The Lady Who Preferred Insects." In *Traditional Japanese Literature: An Anthology, Beginnings to 1600*, ed. Haruo Shirane, 497–503. New York: Columbia University Press, 2007.

Shimizu, Yoshiaki. "Multiple Commemorations: The *Vegetable Nehan* of Itō Jakuchū." In *Flowing Traces: Buddhism in the Literary and Visual Arts of Japan*, ed. James H. Sanford, William R. LaFleur, and Masatoshi Nagatomi, 201–33. Princeton, NJ: Princeton University Press, 1992.

Shirane Haruo. "Curriculum and Competing Canons." Chapter 9 of *Inventing the Classics, Modernity, National Identity, and Japanese Literature*, ed. Haruo Shirane and Tomi Suzuki. Stanford, CA: Stanford University Press, 2000.

———. "Issues in Canon Formation." Introduction of *Inventing the Classics, Modernity, National Identity, and Japanese Literature*, ed. Haruo Shirane and Tomi Suzuki. Stanford, CA: Stanford University Press, 2000.

———, ed. *Traditional Japanese Literature: An Anthology, Beginnings to 1600*. New York: Columbia University Press, 2007.

Shirane Haruo, and James Brandon, eds. *Early Modern Japanese Literature: An Anthology, 1600–1900*. New York: Columbia University Press, 2002.

Shookman, Ellis. *Noble Lies, Slant Truths, Necessary Angels: Aspects of Fictionality in the Novels of Christoph Martin Wieland*. Chapel Hill: University North Carolina Press, 1997.

Smith, Barbara Herrnstein. "Narrative Versions, Narrative Theories." In *On Narrative*, ed. W. J. T. Mitchell, 209–32. Chicago: University of Chicago Press, 1981.

Smits, Ivo. "An Early Anthropologist? Ōe no Masafusa's *A Record of Fox Spirits*." In *Religion in Japan: Arrows to Heaven and Earth*, ed. Peter F. Kornicki and I. J. McMullen, 78–89. Cambridge, UK: Cambridge University Press, 1996.

Smyers, Karen. *The Fox and the Jewel: Shared and Private Meanings in Contemporary Japanese Inari Worship*. Honolulu: University of Hawaii Press, 1999.

Stallybrass, Peter, and Allon White. *The Politics and Poetics of Transgression*. Ithaca, NY: Cornell University Press, 1986.

Stone, Jacqueline. *Original Enlightenment and the Transformation of Medieval Japanese Buddhism*. Honolulu: University of Hawaii Press, 1999.

Strickmann, Michel. *Magical Medicine*. Edited by Bernard Faure. Stanford, CA: Stanford University Press, 2002.

Sueki Fumihiko. *Nihon Bukkyōshi: shisōshi toshite no apurōchi*. Shinchōsha, 1992.

Sutō Isao. *Yama no hyōteki: inoshishi to sanjin no seikatsushi*. Miraisha, 1991.

Suzuki, Tomi. "Gender and Genre: Modern Literary Histories and Women's Diary Literature." Chapter 3 of *Inventing the Classics: Modernity, National Identity, and Japanese Literature*, ed. Haruo Shirane and Tomi Suzuki. Stanford, CA: Stanford University Press, 2000.

Tahara, Mildred M. *Tales of Yamato: A Tenth-Century Poem-Tale*. Honolulu: University Press of Hawaii, 1980.

Takahashi Masaaki. *Shūten dōji no tanjō—mō hitotsu no Nihon bunka*. Chūō kōronsha, 1992.

Takahashi Minoru. "Mikenjaku koji: Chūgoku no minkan denshō." In *Chūgoku no koten bungaku*, ed. Itō Sōhei, 189–201. Tōkyō daigaku shuppan kai, 1981.

Takahashi Tōru. *Monogatari bungei no hyōgenshi*. Nagoya: Nagoya daigaku shuppankai, 1987.

———. "Tsukuri monogatari to setsuwa." In *Setsuwa to sono shūen: monogatari, geinō*, ed. Honda Giken, 51–69. Setsuwa no kōza 6. Benseisha, 1993.

Takeuchi Rizō. "The Rise of the Warriors." *The Cambridge History of Japan*. Vol. 2, *Heian Japan*, ed. Donald H. Shively and William H. McCullough. Cambridge, UK: 1999.

Tanabe Seiko. *Oni no nyōbō*. Kadokawa shoten, 1977.

Tanaka Takako. *"Akujo" ron*. Kinokuniya shoten, 1992.

Tasaka Fumiho, ed. *Kyūsei chūtō kyōiku, Kokugoka kyōkasho naiyō sakuin*. Kyōkasho kenkyū sentaa, 1983.

Teramoto, John Tadao. "The 'Yamai no Sōshi': A Critical Reevaluation of Its Importance to Japanese Secular Painting of the Twelfth Century." Ph.D., diss., University of Michigan, 1994.

Thomson, Philip. *The Grotesque*. London: Methuen, 1972.

Thornhill, Arthur. "The Dōjōji Tale: Codependent Salvation in *Konjaku Monogatari*." Unpublished paper presented at the annual meeting of the Association of Asian Studies, Chicago, 1990.

Tōkyō daigaku kokugo kenkyūshitsu, ed. *Wamyō ruiju shō, Tenmon bon*. Kyūko shoin, 1987.

Tōkyō Gakugei daigaku Nihon shi kenkyūshitsu, ed. *Nihonshi nenpyō*. Tōkyō dō shuppan, 1984.

Tonomura Hitomi. "Black Hair and Red Trousers: Gendering the Flesh in Medieval Japan." *American Historical Review* 99:1 (February 1994): 129–54.

————. "Nikutai to yokubō no keiro: *Konjaku monogatari shū* ni miru onna to otoko." In *Jendaa no Nihon shi*. Vol. 1, *Shūkyō to minzoku, shintai to seiai*, ed. Wakita Haruko and S. B. Hanley, 293–330. Tōkyō daigaku shuppan, 1994.

Torviso, Isidoro Bango, and Fernando Marias. "Saint Anthony." In *Bosch: Reality, Symbol, and Fantasy*. Translated by Josephine Breggazzi, 204–12. Madrid: Silex, 1982.

Tsuchida Naoshige. "Anna no hen." In *Ōchō no kizoku*, 17–48. *Nihon no rekishi*, vol. 5. Chūō kōronsha, 1973.

Tsunoda Bun'ei. *Ōchō no eizō; Heian jidaishi no kenkyū*. Tōkyōdō, 1970.

Tyler, Royall, trans. *Japanese Tales*. New York: Pantheon, 1987.

————, trans. *The Tale of Genji*. New York: Viking, 2001.

Ueda Masaki. "Gaisetsu." In *Tenpyō no Meian*, ed. Ueda Masaki. Jinbutsu Nihon no rekishi 2. Shōgakkan, 1975.

Ury, Marian. "A Note on the Supernatural." *Journal of the Association of Teachers of Japanese* 22:2 (November 1988): 189–94.

————. "The Ōe Conversations." *Monumenta Nipponica* 48:3 (Autumn 1993): 359–80.

————, trans. *Tales of Times Now Past: Sixty-two Stories from a Medieval Japanese Collection*. Berkeley: University of California Press, 1979. Reprinted in Michigan Classics in Japanese Studies 9. Ann Arbor: Center for Japanese Studies University of Michigan, 1993. Citations refer to the 1979 edition.

Vasari, Giorgio. *Lives of Painters, Sculptors, and Architects*. Translated by Gaston du C. de Vere. Everyman's Library 129. 2 vols. New York: Alfred A. Knopf, 1996.

Viswanathan, Meera. "In Pursuit of the Yamamba: The Question of Female Resistance." In *The Woman's Hand, Gender and Theory in Japanese Women's Writing*, ed. Paul Gordon Schalow and Janet A. Walker, 239–61. Stanford, CA: Stanford University Press, 1996.

Wagner, Donald B. *Iron and Steel in Ancient China*. Leiden: E. J. Brill, 1993.

Wakabayashi, Haruko. "Tengu Images and the Buddhist Concepts of Evil in Medieval Japan." Ph.D. diss., Princeton University, 1995.

Watson, Burton, trans. *Records of the Historian: Chapters from the Shih Chi of Ssu-ma Ch'ien*. New York: Columbia University Press, 1969.

Werner, E. T. C. *Myths and Legends of China*. London: George G. Harrap, 1922. Reprint, London: Sinclair Brown, 1984. Citations refer to the reprint.

Wilson, William Ritchie. "The Way of the Bow and Arrow: The Japanese Warrior in *Konjaku Monogatari*." *Monumenta Nipponica* 28:2 (February 1973): 177–233.

Wright, Thomas. *A History of Caricature and Grotesque in Literature and Art*. With an introduction by Frances Barasch. London, 1865. Reprint, New York: Fredrick Ungar, 1968. Citations refer to the reprint.

Xiang Qing. "Utsuho monogatari, Toshikage no maki ni okeru kankyō—Nakatada oyako no Kitayama no utsuho komori wo chūshin ni." *Wakan hikaku bungaku* 6 (February 1996): 26–40.

Yamanaka Yutaka. *Heian jinbutsu shi*. Tōkyō daigaku shuppan kai, 1974.

Yanagita Kunio. "Hitotsume kozō sonata." In *Shinpen Yanagita Kunio shū* 5. Chikuma shobō, 1962.

———. *The Legends of Tōno*. Translated by Robert Morse. Tokyo: Japan Foundation, 1975.

———. "Oni no shison." In *Teihon Yanagita Kunio shū* 9. Chikuma shobō, 1962.

———. "Yama no jinsei." In *Teihon Yanagita Kunio shū* 4. Chikuma shobō, 1964; and *Shinpen Yanagita Kunio shū* 1. Chikuma shoten, 1978.

Yiengpruksawan, Mimi Hall. "What's in A Name? Fujiwara Fixation in Japanese Cultural History." *Monumenta Nipponica* 49:4 (Winter 1994): 423–53.

Yoshikawa Kōjirō. "*Kōshiden* kaisetsu narabi shakubun." Supplement to *Kōshiden*. Transcribed by Kiyohara Edakata. Edited by Kyōtō daigaku fuzoku toshokan, 1960.

Yoshinari Takeshi, ed. *Nihon "shinwa densetsu" sōran*. Rekishi yomihon tokubetsu zōkan 16. Shinjinbutsu ōrai sha, 1992.

Yü, Chün-fang. *Kuan-yin: The Chinese Transformation of Avalokiteśvara*. New York: Columbia University Press, 2001.

Zhao, Xiaohuan. *Classical Chinese Supernatural Fiction: A Morphological History*. Lewiston, NY: E. Mellen, 2005.

Index

Abo, Prince, 136
Agi Bridge, demon at, 166–72, 173–75, 178–79, 190, 238, 239, 272n41, 274n62
Akō incident, 105, 144
Akutagawa Ryūnosuke: on *Konjaku*, 7, 23
Ama-no-ma-hitotsu-no-mikoto, 133, 153, 170, 266n70
Amaterasu, 132
Anderson, Hans Christian, 37
animal spirits, 1, 11, 41, 192–233; and Buddhism, 3, 229–31, 241, 282n107; vs. demons, 90, 122–23, 192, 195, 196, 231, 233. *See also* birds; foxes; monkeys; raccoon dogs (*tanuki*); *tengu*; wild boars (*kusainaki*)
Anna no hen, 67
Anthony, St. in art, 116
Aoki, Michiko, 265n50
Aristophanes, 2
Ariwara no Narihira, 119, 164–65, 267n80; "How a Woman of Middle Captain Ariwara no Narihira is Eaten by a Demon" (*Konjaku* Tale 27:7), 96–97, 135–41, 236, 238, 268n92; and Takaiko, 95, 97, 138–40, 236, 259n33, 268n92. *See also Ise monogatari*
Aston, W. G., 25, 248n47
Augustan poetry, 41
Augustine, St., 245n28
authority: affirmation of, 1, 3, 11, 32, 41, 120, 148–49, 151–52, 153, 223, 238; subversion of, 1, 3, 8, 11, 31, 32, 37, 52, 56–65, 80, 89–90, 95, 97–99, 117, 120, 126, 140–41, 145–46, 148, 152, 153, 166, 193–94, 217, 221–22, 232, 235–36, 237, 238, 240, 241–42
avadāna, 5

Baba Akiko, 95, 266n61, 272n19, 273n54; on aristocratic Buddhism, 230; on categories

of demons, 122–23, 264n30; on demon at Agi Bridge, 272n41; on demons and resistance to central government, 144; on demons and the Fujiwara, 151; on *kyōki shinnin* (the Appearance of a Demon, the Heart of a Human), 124–25; on Lady Chikuzen, 162; *Oni no kenkyū*, 120, 121, 122–25, 264n23, 272n24, 272n41; on Ōeyama demons, 171, 273n49
Bagehot, Walter: "Wordsworth, Tennyson, and Browning; or Pure, Ornate, and Grotesque Art in Poetry," 37
Baishi, Princess, 271n10
Bakhtin, Mikhail: on the body, 42–45, 51, 81, 83, 125, 185–86, 252n125; on the carnivalesque, 36, 41, 42, 45–49, 52, 83, 196, 235; on degradation, 81; on eating, 125; "Forms of Time and of the Chronotrope in the Novel," 47; on the gothic, 35; on the grotesque, 4, 10, 14, 35, 36, 38, 39, 41, 42–49, 54, 64, 76, 83, 185–86, 196–97, 242; on humor (and folk humor), 45, 49, 76; on the isolated individual, 42; on Kayser, 40, 42; on Kerch terracotta figurines, 185–86, 275n86; on the oral and the folk, 49; on praise and abuse, 64; on Rabelais, 4, 42, 45, 47, 125, 196; on Richter, 36; on senile pregnant hags, 185–86; on tricksters, 196; on women, 83, 114, 185–86
Barasch, Frances K.: on Dennis, 33; *The Grotesque: A Study in Meanings*, 30; on Wright, 39
Bargen, Doris, 164
Bashō: *Sarashina kikō*, 181
Baudelaire, Charles: on the grotesque, 36; "On the Essence of Laughter," 36
Beardsley, Aubrey, 41

German literary theory, 24, 247n21
ghosts: and sexual activity, 81, 90, 99, 100–
101, 103–7, 237, 260n52; spirits of the dead,
81, 90, 99, 100, 118, 122, 124, 173, 263n9
Giovanni da Udine, 31, 33
Gōdanshō (The Ōe Conversations), 8, 9, 29, 90,
96; demons in, 117–18, 119, 150–51; "How
Minister of State Tōru Grabs the Waist
of the Cloistered Emperor of the Kanpyō
Era" (Tale 3:32), 103–7, 237, 261nn64,66;
Tale 3:38, 150–51; Tale 3:50, 119; Tale 4:20,
117–18
gods (*kami*): and Buddhism, 157, 207,
207–13, 232, 240, 279n46; vs. demons
(*oni*), 118, 121, 170, 237; worship of, 152–53,
207–13, 232, 237, 240, 271n130
Gokurakuki. See Nihon ōjō gokurakuki
Golden Palace (Domus Aurea): frescos in,
30–31, 234
Go-Reizei, Emperor, 162
Go-Sanjō, Emperor, 8, 107
*Goshūi ōjōden (More Gleanings of Biographies
of People Born in the Pure Land)*, 8–9; Tale
24, 84
Go-Suzaku, Emperor, 271n10
gothic novels, 35
Go-Toba, Retired Emperor, 228
*Great Nirvana Sutra (Mahā-parinirvāṇa
sūtra)*, 84
Greek literature, 2, 5
Grimm's fairytales (*Märchen*), 23, 37
grotesque, the: vs. classical art style, 31–32, 34;
definitions of, 2–4, 14; liminality of, 4, 11,
35, 41, 43, 117, 120, 125, 235, 244n5, 262n4,
271n16, 274n64; and Nero's Golden Palace
(Domus Aurea), 30–31, 33; relationship
to burlesque, 33, 34; relationship to
caricature, 38–39, 42; relationship to
culture, 234–35, 242; relationship to
gender, 42–43, 236–37; relationship to
gothic novels, 35; relationship to myth,
37, 40; relationship to reality, 36, 38–39,
42–45, 109, 152, 242; relationship to
the arabesque, 35; relationship to the
carnivalesque, 36, 41, 42, 45–49, 52, 56,
235, 252n144; relationship to the cave, 31,
41; relationship to the frightening, 3, 31,
35–36, 38, 40, 42, 48–49, 56, 76, 119–20,
226–28, 233, 234, 235; relationship to the
humorous/comic, 33–34, 36, 38–39, 40,
41, 42, 47, 48–49, 56, 76, 77, 78, 234,
235, 241; relationship to the sublime, 35,
37; relationship to the trickster, 196–97;

relationship to the unfathomable, 119–20;
theories of, 30–51
gunki monogatari (martial tales), 9, 55, 177

Hachiman, 102
Haga Yaichi: influence of, 27;
*Kokubungakushi jikkō (Ten Lectures on the
History of Japanese Literature)*, 22–23, 24,
247n18; *Kōshō Konjaku monogatari shū
(Konjaku monogatari shū and Its Literary
Parallels)*, 6, 18–19, 23, 248n50
Hall, John Whitney, 269n105; on *uji*, 244n19
*Hamamatsu chūnagon monogatari (Tale of the
Middle Counselor Hamamatsu)*, 20
Han dynasty, 5
Hane, Mikiso, 267n74
Hardacre, Helen, 271n130
Harpham, Geoffrey Galt: on Baudelaire, 36;
on Christianity, 36; on the grotesque, 3, 30,
31, 33, 40–41, 235, 242, 244n5
Hashihime (Lady at the Bridge), 169, 173,
185, 273n41, 274n60. *See also* Agi Bridge,
demon at
Hegel, Georg Wilhelm Friedrich: on the
grotesque in art, 37, 251n97
Heian jidai shi jiten, 255n43
Heian period, 4, 5, 16, 20, 21, 22, 23, 25, 89,
146, 197, 241; aristocrats in, 46, 48, 60, 100,
115, 117, 123, 136, 141, 145, 152, 155, 156–57,
161, 188, 190, 191, 193, 204–5, 218–19, 230,
236, 237, 241–42, 276n3; Buddhism in, 28,
98, 101, 102–3, 110, 112, 115, 217–18, 259n32;
capital and provinces in, 71, 78, 79–80,
204–5, 236, 237–38, 240, 241; demons in,
120, 123, 126, 152, 155, 156–65, 169, 170–71,
193; elderly parents in, 180–81, 183–84, 239,
241; hidden vs. perceived in literature of,
155, 156–65, 190; internal conflict during,
2, 8, 62, 235–36; marriage during, 134–35,
267n77; medicine during, 99–101; and
national identity, 244n15; role of ex-
emperors in, 145, 269n105; warriors in, 54,
55, 161; women in, 143, 154, 155, 156–65,
178–79, 180–81, 183–85, 188, 190, 191,
268n98, 271nn10,11
Heike monogatari, 55, 96, 169, 185, 275n85,
281n93
Heizei, Emperor, 136
henge vs. *oni*, 118, 123–24
Hida Province, 206
Hidesato-ryū Fujiwara, 174
hijiri, 3, 98. *See also* Shugendō
Hindu mythology, 123

Wu Zixu, 63, 254n32

Xiaozizhuan (Tales of Filial Children), 59, 60, 253n14

Yakushiji Temple, 131
yamabushi, 98. *See also* Shugendō
Yamato monogatari (Tales of Yamato), 106, 139, 161–62, 181
yamauba (yamanba), 165, 182, 186–89
Yanagita Kunio, 264n24; on animal spirits, 121; on demons, 121; on demons and gods with a single eye or leg, 267n71; "Oni no shison," 273n49; on *setsuwa*, 23–24; *Tōno monogatari (The Legends of Tōno)*, 23; on *yamabito* (mountain people), 121, 264nn24, 25; on *yamauba*, 189
Yashirobon Heike, 185, 273n41, 275n85
Yasusuke, Prince, 272n21
Yiengpruksawan, Mimi Hall, 268n98
Yin and *Yang*, 99, 151–52
Yodo Bridge, Lady of the, 274n60

Yōmei bunko shozō kōshiden (Tales of Filial Piety in the Yōmei collection), 59, 60, 61, 64
Yomi, land of, 5, 126, 155
Yoshida Kenkō, 146
Yoshimine Temple, 224
Young Lady Who Loves Insects, tale of, 156–59, 165, 185, 190, 238, 271n11
Yōzei, Emperor, 71, 74, 78–79, 97, 104, 138, 140, 259n42, 268n93
Yuejueshu (The Book of Yue), 58–59, 61, 253n14
Yūshi, Princess, 271n10

Zeami Motokiyo: *Obasute*, 181; on *saidōfū*, 264n40; "Shūgyoku tokka" ("Finding Gems and Gaining the Flower"), 124–25, 264n40
zelkova trees, 1, 207–13, 232, 279n52
Zenke hiki (Secret Records of the Miyoshi Family), 94, 95, 96
Zenyū of Tōkōji, Priest, 94, 101, 139
Zōchin, Precept Master, 194